SACRED RHETORIC

Sacred Rhetoric

THE CHRISTIAN GRAND STYLE IN
THE ENGLISH RENAISSANCE

by

DEBORA K. SHUGER

PRINCETON, NEW JERSEY
PRINCETON UNIVERSITY PRESS
MCMLXXXVIII

COPYRIGHT © 1988 BY PRINCETON UNIVERSITY PRESS
PUBLISHED BY PRINCETON UNIVERSITY PRESS, 41 WILLIAM STREET
PRINCETON, NEW JERSEY 08540
IN THE UNITED KINGDOM: PRINCETON UNIVERSITY
PRESS, GUILDFORD, SURREY

PE
877
.S58
1988

Library of Congress Cataloging in Publication Data will be found on the last printed page of this book. Clothbound editions of Princeton University Press books are printed on acid-free paper, and binding materials are chosen for strength and durability. Paperbacks, although satisfactory for personal collections, are not usually suitable for library rebinding. This book has been composed in Linotron Bembo

ISBN 0-691-06736-8

PRINTED IN THE UNITED STATES OF
AMERICA BY PRINCETON UNIVERSITY PRESS
PRINCETON, NEW JERSEY

In memory of my grandparents
Jessie & Edward
Dora & Meyer

CONTENTS

ACKNOWLEDGMENTS

THIS BOOK grew and matured under the watchful guidance of many godparents. Thanks are due above all to Wesley Trimpi, whose knowledge and kindness guided the germination of these ideas. I am also grateful to John Knott and Stanton Garner, who read parts of the manuscript at various stages of revision and offered valuable suggestions, and to many friends and colleagues whose advice and support helped me on countless occasions, especially Emerson Brown, Carla Cusic, John Hannay, Lorraine Helms, William Ingram, Tiina Kirss, Constantine Patrides, and Donna Wessel Walker. John O'Malley and James J. Murphy, who read this manuscript for the Press, likewise provided encouragement and thoughtful criticism. Finally, I owe a profound debt to those masters of sacred rhetoric, the Reverends E. L. Conly, John Burns, and Douglas Evett, who themselves could both teach and move.

Funds for study and travel were graciously provided by grants from the Horace H. Rackham School of Graduate Studies at the University of Michigan, the American Council of Learned Societies, and the Newberry Library. These funds allowed me to visit numerous libraries in the United States and England and thus collect the rather hard-to-find sources that comprise the substance of this study. Earlier versions of sections of Chapters One, Three, and Five have appeared in *Traditio*, *Viator*, and *Rhetorica*. Ann Munster, Dale Shuger, and Ben Victor provided careful and patient editorial assistance.

I am deeply grateful to my whole family, especially my husband, Scott Shuger, who listened, encouraged, and endured throughout.

SACRED RHETORIC

Ἔργον τὸ μέγα καὶ καλὸν τίμιον τοῦ γὰρ
τοιούτου ἡ θεωρία θαυμαστή.

ARISTOTLE, *Nicomachean Ethics* 4.2

Or if the VAULT of GOTHIC Gloom o'erarch,
In pillar'd Majesty, a mingled Crowd
. . . yet [they] feel
The lightning Flash—the vehemence of Thought—
Yet feel RELIGION's Fervors—feel their Hopes—
Their Fears all trembling, as his warning Voice
Displays her awful Sanctions in a Strain
That echoes the whole Heart—here—here alone
PASSION, the Soul of ORATORY, reigns.

RICHARD POLWHELE, "The Art of Eloquence"
(1785), ll. 354–55, 362–68.

INTRODUCTION

IN AN English version of *The City of God*, published in 1610, the translator offers a comment on Augustine's claim that Paul uses rhetorical figures: "*Augustine* makes *Paul* a Rhetorician. Well it is tolerable, *Augustine* saith it: Had one of vs said so, our eares should ring of heresie presently, heresies are so ready at some mens tongue ends." In the English Renaissance, sacred rhetoric is a polemical issue, possibly even a heresy. Under Elizabeth and James, Puritans accused High Churchmen of using rhetoric, a charge which the latter denied; after the Civil War, Anglicans directed the same accusation against Dissenters, a charge again rejected. Renaissance Englishmen rarely admitted using rhetoric, much less the grand style. Writers of English sacred rhetorics like Perkins, Baxter, Herbert, and Glanville disparage attempts at religious eloquence, preferring instead the unadorned sanctity of what was sometimes called spiritual preaching. There are no studies of a sacred grand style in the English Renaissance because, even according to its practitioners, it was not supposed to exist.

If the reticence of Englishmen is one reason for the modern neglect of the grand style, a second lies in modern scholarship itself. Contemporary studies of the characters of style or *genera dicendi* in the English Renaissance derive from G. L. Hendrickson's "The Origin and Meaning of the Ancient Characters of Style" (1905), but Hendrickson's analysis is vitiated by a characteristically modern distaste for rhetoric and has misled subsequent scholarship into the familiar but reductive dichotomies of oratory and the plain style, rhetoric and philosophy, Ciceronianism and "Atticism," *verba* and *res*, and so forth. Hendrickson argued that there were originally—and therefore really—only two characters of style.[1] These are the oratorical style, including both the middle and grand style of Ciceronian theory, and the plain style, which

[1] G. L. Hendrickson, "The Origin and Meaning of the Ancient Characters of Style," *AJP* 26(1905): 249–50, 260, 286, 289. For the dissenting view that there were originally three characters of style, see George Kennedy, "Theophrastus and Stylistic Distinctions," *Harvard Studies in Classical Philology* 62(1957): 93–104.

originated in and remained closely related to philosophical dialectic.[2] The first aims at subrational persuasion of largely ignorant
audiences through emotional and sensuous enchantment (psychagogia).[3] The plain style, on the contrary, is unadorned, brief,
and philosophical. Originating in Aristotle's dialectically based
rhetorical proof, the plain style is developed by the Stoics and Roman "Atticists" as a philosophical alternative to an alluring and
deceptive psychagogic oratory. Hendrickson concludes, "The
grand style is rhetoric itself in the original conception of it as an
instrument of emotional transport (ψυχαγωγία), the plain style is
dialectic, the middle style a *tertium quid* intermediate between
them."[4]

Hendrickson strongly influenced Morris Croll's seminal studies of Renaissance prose. Like Hendrickson, Croll assumes a twofold division of style into oratorical and philosophic, but while
Hendrickson, I think correctly, defines the former as primarily
affective, Croll tends to view oratory in terms of copia, periodicity, and schematic ornament—the style of Isocrates and the
early Cicero. Croll thus contrasts an aural, full, rhythmic "Ciceronianism" to the introspective, brief, and philosophical "Atticism."[5] The history of Renaissance prose according to Croll
traces the triumph of this skeptical, dialectical plain style over the
arid and vacuous formalism of Renaissance neo-Ciceronianism.
Except for this issue of Ciceronian imitation, Croll generally ignores the grand or oratorical style. Demosthenes, however, presents problems for Croll's analysis because he is neither schematic
and copious nor primarily philosophical. What Croll suggests is
that although Isocrates represents the true and original grand
style and although the intensity and inwardness of Demosthenes
allies him with the plain style, later critics scrambled the plan of

[2] Hendrickson, "The Origin," pp. 255, 262–65, 267.
[3] Ibid., p. 285. On the meanings of psychagogia in antiquity, see Jacqueline de
Romilly, *Magic and Rhetoric in Ancient Greece* (Cambridge, Mass., 1975), p. 15.
[4] Ibid., p. 290.
[5] Morris Croll, *"Attic" and Baroque Prose Style: Essays by Morris Croll*, ed. J. Max
Patrick and R. O. Evans, with John M. Wallace (Princeton, 1966), pp. 54–55, 59–
61, 68–69; see also John M. Steadman, *The Hill and the Labyrinth: Discourse and
Certitude in Milton and His Near Contemporaries* (Berkeley, 1984), pp. 31–33.

the genera dicendi, thrusting the Isocratic grand style into some indeterminate "middle" position and elevating Demosthenean oratory as the model for a new grand style.[6] While Croll is perfectly aware that this tripartite division dominates most post-Aristotelian rhetoric, he rejects it as a fatal obfuscation of the original twofold distinction between oratorical and philosophic styles. This rejection means that the grand style is defined with respect to periodicity and the Gorgianic schemes, not passion or subject matter.[7] The curious consequences of this position appear in both Croll and later scholarship. For Croll, "if the name of Cicero himself is eliminated from the history of the grand style, a comparatively small number of important names remains to it."[8] Silver Latin, Thucydides, and Demosthenes all belong to the plain style, even though ancient rhetoric considered the latter two preeminent models of grandeur, dignity, and force.[9] Aldo Scaglione goes further, wresting the sublime, Demosthenes, Saint Augustine's grand style, and Dionysius of Halicarnassus's austere composition into the plain style.[10] This is all very puzzling to anyone familiar with Classical rhetoric, where the notion of a grand, passionate, or elevated plain style would have seemed self-contradictory. Even Erich Auerbach's justly famous depiction of the Christian *genus humile* suffers from some of the same paradoxical results, for if, as Auerbach admits, the genus humile can be sublime and impassioned, in what sense is it *humilis*?[11]

---

[6] Croll, *"Attic" and Baroque*, pp. 73, 77–78; Robert Adolph, *The Rise of Modern Prose Style* (Cambridge, Mass., 1968), p. 14.

[7] The Gorgianic schemes are isocolon or the approximate equality of length among members of a period; parison or similarity of form among such members; and paramoion or likeness of sound among words thus similarly placed (Croll, *"Attic" and Baroque*, p. 54). Croll probably borrows his criteria for the oratorical style from Eduard Norden, who likewise considers periodicity (rhythm) and schematic word play as the two main attributes of *kunstprosa* (*Die antike Kunstprosa vom VI. Jahrhundert v. Chr. bis in die Zeit der Renaissance* [Leipzig, 1898], p. 16). See also Aldo Scaglione, *The Classical Theory of Composition from its Origins to the Present: A Historical Survey* (Chapel Hill, 1972), pp. 71, 145, 164.

[8] Croll, *"Attic" and Baroque*, p. 91.

[9] Ibid., pp. 91, 93–96, 193; Adolph, *Modern Prose Style*, pp. 30, 38, 62–65, 86.

[10] Scaglione, *The Classical Theory of Composition*, pp. 59, 61, 73, 164; Steadman, *The Hill and the Labyrinth*, p. 63.

[11] Erich Auerbach, ch. 1, *"Sermo humilis,"* in *Literary Language and Its Public in*

More recently, Richard Lanham and Stanley Fish have revived Hendrickson's Platonic dichotomies along epistemological rather than stylistic lines, opposing rhetoric, self-satisfying commonplaces, flattering deceit, and sophistry to dialectic, philosophy, disturbing truth, and intellectual honesty. Lanham, borrowing from contemporary critical theory, defends the legitimacy of such rhetoric as liberating play, but his account still leaves Christian rhetoric and much serious Classical oratory in a no man's land.[12] Fish follows the more traditional path of exalting dialectic at the expense of rhetoric,[13] but as we shall see, the very qualities he attributes to dialectic actually belong, according to both antiquity and the Renaissance, under rhetoric.

Thus the comments of Renaissance Englishmen suggest that a Christian grand style did not exist, while those of modern scholars imply that its only significance was to play the antithesis in the dialectical evolution of the plain style. The thesis of this book, on the contrary, is that the Christian grand style is one of the most far-reaching and innovative developments in Renaissance rhetoric. Its importance becomes apparent the moment we turn from the English vernacular rhetorics to their neo-Latin counterparts, which, although often published on the Continent, were widely used in England throughout the Renaissance. The preeminence granted the grand style in these texts suggests that the Hendrickson-Croll paradigm may be seriously misleading. If we go back and examine both the ancient rhetorics and the full range of Renaissance discussions of sacred discourse—rather than just the few available vernacular rhetorics—we find that beginning with the Greeks, the grand style was not described as primarily periodic, schematic, or playful but as passionate. The grand style moves

---

Late Latin Antiquity and in the Middle Ages, trans. Ralph Manheim (New York, 1965), pp. 47, 53, 56, 101. A similar paradoxical result appears in George Kennedy's *The Art of Persuasion in Greece* (Princeton, 1963), p. 15, which divides writers into philosophers and rhetoricians but puts Demosthenes, along with Dante, Vergil, and Milton, into the former category.

[12] Richard A. Lanham, *The Motives of Eloquence: Literary Rhetoric in the Renaissance* (New Haven, 1976), ch. 1.

[13] Stanley E. Fish, *Self-Consuming Artifacts: The Experience of Seventeenth-Century Literature* (Berkeley, 1972), pp. 1–3.

the emotions, whether the harsher forensic impulses of pity and fear or the numinous feelings of wonder and mystery. Its language is not necessarily periodic and copious but often brief, dense, and jaggedly asymmetrical. It is neither playful nor subrational. Rather, the grand style expresses a passionate seriousness about the most important issues of human life; it is thus the style of Plato and the Bible as well as Cicero and Demosthenes. This ancient grand style becomes the basis for the Christian grand style of the Renaissance. From the late fifteenth to the late seventeenth century, there are dozens of learned and thoughtful rhetorics advocating a passionate and lofty religious prose. These texts borrow their terminology and framework from ancient rhetoric—especially, interestingly enough, the late hellenistic rhetorics—but rarely rest content with mere imitation. Unlike most Renaissance secular rhetorics, they do not simply paraphrase their sources but remain fully aware of historical change, especially the changes introduced by Christianity. They therefore adapt the Classical tradition to reflect a Christian anthropology and to accommodate both the needs of Christian preachers and the distinctive features of biblical or patristic prose. The sacred rhetorics of the Renaissance emphasize the passion, sublimity, and grandeur of sacred discourse, grounding these qualities in the Classical grand style and in the principles of Renaissance theology and psychology. They advocate a style at once ardently expressive, deeply spiritual, and highly rhetorical—a Christian grand style that is neither a refurbished Ciceronianism nor a late descendant of medieval schematic *kunstprosa*. They thus present a paradigm of what the Renaissance desired in its call to revive antiquity—the genuine fusion of past and present, of Classical and Christian traditions—and can only be understood as a response both to their Classical heritage and to the needs and assumptions of Renaissance culture.

The grand style, then, is not a minor though real aspect of rhetorical theory. Although in Ciceronian rhetoric the genera dicendi are technically only a subtopic of *elocutio*, historically they have been the pivot for the major issues in rhetorical theory. In Roman rhetoric, the distinction between the grand and plain styles forms the core of the controversy between Cicero, Quintilian, and the "Atticists." In the Renaissance, the antithesis structures the development of rhetorical theory: on the one hand the rise of the plain style, whether scientific or neo-Classical; on the other, the defense of a passionate, figurative, and expressive grandeur as best suited to articulate the contours of spiritual existence. The genera dicendi are pivotal in a way that, let us say, *dispositio* is not because they pull broader cultural issues into the orbit of rhetorical theory. The relation of the plain style to the rise of modern science and modern individualism has frequently been remarked. The Christian grand style likewise becomes a bridge between the word and the world, connecting problems of style to the role of emotion and imagination in the mind's journey toward God, to the relation between thought and feeling, to the Christian concept of selfhood. It reflects the revival of Augustinianism in the Renaissance and with it a defense of emotion as inseparable from Christian inwardness. For Augustine spiritual existence, with its joy, desire, sorrow, and hope, is affective. In the Renaissance, this Augustinianism develops into the belief that spiritual life is primarily a matter of the heart and will, that love is more important than knowledge. Sin therefore results from defective love rather than ignorance and is healed not by suppressing emotion but by redirecting it. The importance of the grand style in the sacred rhetorics follows from this conviction that man comes to God through love and desire. The association between affective spirituality and the grand style is further strengthened by the Renaissance conviction that all thought and feeling depend on imagination. Unlike philosophy, rhetoric appeals to the imagination and is therefore able to move and transform the desires of the heart. Study of the sacred grand style thus illuminates not only the intramural tensions of rhetorical theory but also the delicate connections between ideas about language and ideas about reality.

Because Renaissance rhetoric derives from Classical, some notion of the grand style in antiquity is necessary for understanding its Renaissance offspring. Chapter One therefore treats the Classical grand style through Augustine. Since there exist numerous general histories of Classical rhetoric, I will focus primarily on the origins and development of the grand style: its gradual shift from artistic richness to power and sublimity, the separation of distinct Roman and hellenistic strands, its relation to the other genera dicendi, and finally the implications of Augustine's new understanding of the will and emotions. From the fourth century on, the concept of grandeur moves away from Isocrates' written, meticulously antithetical smoothness toward a greater appreciation of passion, spontaneity, and fierce strength. This anti-Isocratic stance persists throughout antiquity, although modified by the Theophrastean tendency to conjoin power and beauty and by the association of the grand style with the heroic qualities of epic and tragedy. The Theophrastean influence is most visible in Roman rhetoric, which tends to view the grand style as combining emotional intensity and harmonious beauty. Hellenistic rhetoric, however, places less emphasis on harmony, copia, and smoothness. Instead, the hellenistic grand style, which influenced the Renaissance more than is often suspected, remains harsher, more compact and asymmetrical than its Roman equivalent; and while Roman rhetoric deals primarily with civic (usually forensic) oratory, hellenistic grandeur includes the sublime and numinous. In addition, Classical rhetoric, especially hellenistic, does not support the modern assumption that rhetoric and philosophy are somehow ontological antagonists. Although the early Stoics transmit the Platonic hostility toward rhetoric, antiquity generally accepts the ideal union of wisdom and eloquence, listing Plato, along with Demosthenes, Thucydides, and Cicero, as an exemplar of the grand style.

By the beginning of the Christian era, the uneasy balance between power and artistic richness shifts in favor of the former. For Hermogenes, Longinus, and Augustine, the grand style no longer needs figurative or rhythmic elaboration; passion or sublimity remains the sole criterion. In the same writers, the meaning of passion begins to change. For Longinus and Augustine, emotion is not subrational but the mind's response to the divine. Augustinian voluntarism, which identified willing, feeling, and love, subsequently becomes the ground of sacred grandeur in the Renaissance. The chapter concludes with a brief glance at medieval sacred rhetoric, because what has often been identified as the Puritan plain style seems rather to be a medieval variant of the grand style, one that retains the power of the Classical *genus grande* but carries to an extreme the late antique tendency to subordinate artistry to passion.

The issues present in the Classical treatment of the grand style resurface in the Renaissance, but because most of the major sacred rhetorics are unfamiliar and often unavailable, I have chosen to present an overview of these texts before attempting to probe the specific questions they raise. Chapter Two thus offers a preliminary history of sacred rhetoric from about 1475 to 1675, concentrating on classifying basic types and movements and the lines of transmission between them. While I emphasize those works most probably used in England, the fact that Englishmen drew broadly on continental scholarship means that the basic outline of this history would apply to other European countries as well (although the relevance of vernacular rhetorics would vary from country to country).

The last three chapters address the sources, theory, and characteristics of the Christian grand style. Chapter Three deals with the legitimation of passionate discourse against the interrelated tendencies to conflate it with sophistic or oppose it to philosophy. Following Plato's attack on rhetoric as flattering sophistry, rhetorical theory has persistently confronted the metaquestion of its own justification. The grand style in particular stands open to the charge that it uses emotion to obfuscate truth: a charge not easily answered given the intellectualist bias of Classical thought. In the Renaissance, the sacred rhetorics adopt the ancient position that rhetoric differs sharply from the ostentatious and playful self-display of the sophists while being compatible with serious philosophy, but they also reject the whole intellectualist tradition and, borrowing from Augustine, erect an anthropology connecting emotion (and therefore passionate rhetoric) to man's noetic and spiritual activities. This connection between Augustinian voluntarism and the grand style entails that the tendency to treat rhetoric as the alternative to the West's philosophical logocentrism does not apply to sacred rhetoric in the Renaissance, for such a style need not rest on a skeptical or probabilist epistemology but could serve to direct the mind and heart to truth.

Both the theoretical justification and the specific features of the sacred grand style draw from a combination of Classical and Christian sources. Chapter Four focuses on the Classical contribution to sacred grandeur in the Renaissance, particularly the contribution of hellenistic rhetoric. The hellenistic influence is more important than the Roman because from the mid-sixteenth century on, sacred rhetoric reacts against the earlier attempt to Ciceronianize religious discourse. Particularly the more scholarly and comprehensive rhetorics (what I have called general rhetorics, since they deal with both secular and sacred topics) begin to develop a grand style based on Demetrius, Dionysius, Longinus, and Hermogenes. The effect of this is threefold. The general rhetorics borrow the numinous and sacral cast of hellenistic rhetoric, a sense quite different from the forensic vehemence of the Romans. The influence of these Greeks also fosters a non-Ciceronian description of the grand style. On the one hand, it shares the paratactic brevity, vividness, and density of Holy Scripture; on the other, it includes not only agonistic vehemence, but also a mystical, ceremonial epideixis, the qualities of festal preaching.

Hellenistic rhetoric, however, provides only one influence on the sacred grand style. The other major stimulus comes from within the Christian tradition. For almost all sacred rhetorics in the Renaissance, the defining characteristic of the grand style is passion, and passion in turn is created first by the union of vividness and the excellent object and second by expressivity. The connections between emotion and these stylistic features derive from the religious epistemology and concept of selfhood current in the Renaissance. Chapter Five traces these connections, examining first the pivotal role of the imagination in creating both emotion and thought, and second the notion of the self not as self-awareness but as love or the response of the soul to God's pull. The importance of the imagination leads to the demand for a vividness enabling the heart to grasp the invisible and distant reality of God. The notion of the self as the loving response of the soul to God's inner activity entails that the passionate expression of feeling communicates the presence of God; the language of passion with its figures and tropes is also the language of divine disclosure. The stylistic qualities of sacred grandeur are thus rooted in theology and religious anthropology, and the sacred rhetorics of the Renaissance interpret the relation between psyche, world, and language. For this reason, if no other, they remain significant for us.

In 1659 Johann-Henricus Ursinus, superintendent of the churches in Ratisbon, prefaced his *Ecclesiastes* with the comment:

> In the schools we honor rhetoric, but for what purpose? In our courts there is little or no need of this for handling forensic cases successfully. That political eloquence used by princes' counselors, ambassadors, and by princes or secular rulers themselves, does not endure subjection to rules and to be forced under the laws of school-teachers—and I'm not talking about the ordinary kind—not even those of professors. Even if I do not dispute that it bestows something; yet how little is that something. Finally, unless our rhetoric shapes the mind and lips of the aspiring preacher, it is learned only as an academic exercise. . . . For unless it is transferred to the purposes of common life, it remains the superfluous study of a superfluous and ivory-towered (*umbraticus*) scholar.[14]

The fall of the ancient republics demoted secular rhetoric from the senate to the schoolroom. Most of the secular rhetorics written in the Renaissance are designed for grammar schools, and although these had considerable influence on Renaissance literature, they often contain only predigested precepts and horrendous lists of figures. Only the Ciceronian controversies produced any considerable body of theoretically motivated secular rhetorics, and even these are, in part, a response to the offensive classicization of Christian preaching.[15]

Sacred rhetoric, on the contrary, is, as Ursinus notes, the only kind still supported by a living and culturally significant oratory. It is also the only large body of rhetoric designed for adults. It

[14] Johann-Henricus Ursinus, *Ecclesiastes, sive de sacris concionibus libri tres* (Frankfurt, 1659), preface. For earlier versions of this recognition that ancient political rhetoric has very little place in the modern absolutist state, see Marc Fumaroli, "Rhetoric, Politics, and Society: From Italian Ciceronianism to French Classicism," *Renaissance Eloquence: Studies in the Theory and Practice of Renaissance Rhetoric*, ed. James J. Murphy (Berkeley, 1983), p. 258.

[15] On the Ciceronian controversy, see Izora Scott, *Controversies Over the Imitation of Cicero as a Model for Style and Some Phases of their Influence on the Schools of the Renaissance*, Columbia University Contributions to Education 35 (New York, 1910), and Erasmus, *Ciceronianus; or A Dialogue on the Best Style of Speaking*, trans. Izora Scott (1908; repr. New York, 1972).

therefore offers a window on the process by which the Christian West transformed its Classical heritage and a model for how theories of language relate to the larger concerns of a society, to its religion, psychology, and politics. Augustine's conflation of the will and emotions, the theology of the Holy Spirit, theories on the role of images in cognition and motivation, the conflict between Dissenters and Restoration Anglicans all leave their mark on the sacred rhetorics. Precisely because these works deal with a controversial living tradition, they cannot rest on Classical assumptions and precepts but are forced to a self-consciousness about the implications and grounds of their own enterprise. Unlike most secular rhetorics, they therefore exhibit a theoretical concern for language, making them articulate witnesses to the sacred aesthetics of the Renaissance. Hence sacred rhetoric is not a narrowly specialized compartment of the history of Renaissance rhetoric but its most vital and reflective branch.

CHAPTER ONE

THE CHARACTERS OF STYLE FROM ANTIQUITY THROUGH THE MIDDLE AGES

The Hellenic Beginnings of the Characters of Style

THE GENERA DICENDI originate in fourth-century Athens. Although Athenian culture had made the transition from craft literacy to popular literacy in the previous century, oral discourse still dominated public life. Oratory flourished in the law courts, in public meetings, at the panhellenic gatherings, at funerals, at religious ceremonies, and at banquets. Different occasions called for different types of speeches; the style used when composing the legal defense of a private citizen would naturally differ from that appropriate at a state funeral. The multiple functions of oratory in Athenian culture gave rise to a sense of distinct styles suited to different types of speeches. Thus Aristotle divides oratory into a deliberative (political), forensic, and epideictic (ceremonial) branch and assigns each a distinctive style. But the genera dicendi reflect not only the different civic functions assigned to oratory but also competing ideals within Athenian culture. The heroic ethos of epic and Aeschylean tragedy—and of Demosthenes—Isocrates' civic humanism, Socratic dialectic, the eristics and ostentation of the sophists all possessed stylistic implications. Both the connection between style and social function and this tension among ideals helped determine the early evolution of the grand style, as well as that of the other genera dicendi. Of course, the terms "grand style" and "genera dicendi" appear only much later and are Roman not Greek, but even in this early period one sees an attempt to describe a style uniquely suited to the most important and serious subjects and to differentiate kinds of style. The association of the grand style with passionate oratory emerges out of this period, but in the fourth century that definition is still at issue; the grand style simply signifies the style appropriate to the most valuable subjects. Instead, during this period two alternative definitions of grandeur coexist. One, the Isocratic, identifies the style concerned with the most valuable subjects as the highly polished epideictic oratory of the humanist statesman; the other, which is at least implicit in Aristotle, describes it as rough (skiagraphic), passionate, and deliberative. It is agonistic or "fighting" oratory and hence the inheritor of the heroic rather than the humanist ideal. Although this passionate and agonistic definition prevailed apparently unanimously, the original competition between the Isocratic and Aristotelian conceptions of grandeur meant that the grand style would subsequently be defined in opposition to the Isocratic.

Isocrates' *Against the Sophists*, *Antidosis*, and *Pangyricus* contain the earliest extant discussions of the characters of style. Isocrates recognizes two styles: his own ornate, rhythmic, musical compositions on the great topics of panhellenic significance and an unpolished low style practiced by forensic pleaders and suited to their petty concerns.[1] Passion is not a criterion for either genus, nor is Isocrates' own style, although lofty, oratorical.[2] Isocrates was a writer, not an orator, concerned with creating a beautiful artistic prose of lasting value, not with arousing the momentary assent of the crowd. Isocrates' twofold classification influenced later theory largely through Theophrastus, who, although the student of Aristotle, apparently followed Isocrates in dividing prose into a type characterized by an ornate grandeur that fuses loftiness with sweetness, and one of inartistic factual clarity. Neither Isocrates nor Theophrastus differentiates elevation and polish into distinct genera or emphasizes passion as a stylistic criterion.[3] But even during his lifetime, Isocrates' ideal of a polished,

---

[1] Isocrates, *Panegyricus* 11, *Against the Sophists* 16–19, *Antidosis* 37, 41, 47–48. All citations from Classical texts are from the Loeb Classical Library editions unless otherwise noted.

[2] Scaglione is therefore mistaken in his claim that Isocrates exemplifies the popular oratorical style (*The Classical Theory of Composition*, p. 23). Classical rhetorics uniformly deny that the Isocratic style is suitable for oratory. See Cicero, *De opt gen* 6.17; Quintilian 10.1.79; Dionysius of Halicarnassus, "Isocrates" 2, "Demosthenes" 18.

[3] Scaglione, *The Classical Theory of Composition*, p. 23; Hendrickson, "The Origin," p. 255; Franz Quadlbauer, "Die genera dicendi bis Plinius d.J.," *Wiener Stu-*

ornate, and meticulously wrought grandeur was challenged by
another student of Gorgias—Alcidamas. Alcidamas praises the
rougher *ex tempore* oral discourse of the practical orator over the
written refinements introduced by Isocrates, because the latter
lacks passion, spontaneity, and truth.[4] Their artificiality arouses
suspicion and, unable to alter the set words to the precise demands of the moment, they fail to persuade. Alcidamas does not
refer to a grand style, but he does suggest the criteria—passion
and persuasiveness—that come to form the basis of this genus in
later rhetorical theory.

Traces of this disagreement between Isocrates and Alcidamas
remain in Aristotle's *Rhetoric*.[5] While Isocrates contrasted low forensic rhetoric with his own panhellenic oratory, which combined both epideictic and deliberative functions, Aristotle distinguishes three types of oratory: the forensic, deliberative, and
epideictic (1.3.1–1.3.6). But in Aristotle, the last two are not virtually identical but opposite. Epideictic oratory is polished, written, and aims at displaying the artistic skill of the speaker; deliberative is rougher, oral, and passionate (3.12.1–3.12.6). The
former resembles the Isocratic manner, the latter that of Alcidamas. Moreover, it is deliberative oratory, not epideictic, that
deals with the most important subjects of general welfare (1.1.10)
and that therefore appropriately uses a loftier, although less polished, style (3.12.5, 3.7.1). Here then we have the outline of a tripartite classification of styles, the first two—the deliberative and
epideictic—respectively characterized by a rough, oral intensity
and polished, written meticulousness. Thus, by the fourth cen-

dien 71(1958): 63; Stanley F. Bonner, *The Literary Treatises of Dionysius of Halicarnassus: A Study in the Development of Critical Method* (Cambridge, 1939), pp. 16–
17.

[4] LaRue Van Hook, "Alcidamas Versus Isocrates: The Spoken Word Versus the
Written Word," *Classical Weekly* 12(1919): 12, 22; Quadlbauer, "Die genera dicendi," p. 61. See also Margorie J. Milne, "A Study in Alcidamas and his Relation
to Contemporary Sophistic" (Ph.D. diss., Bryn Mawr College, 1924). The distinction between a meticulous and a passionate style closely parallels the modern
distinction between analytic/written and agonistic/oral composition. See Walter
J. Ong, s.j., *Orality and Literacy: The Technologizing of the Word* (London, 1982),
pp. 43–45.

[5] Quadlbauer, "Die genera dicendi," p. 62.

tury B.C., the agonistic, emotional rhetoric of the forum and popular assembly emerges as a possible alternative to the Isocratic
ideal.

Aristotle, however, shows no marked preference for one or the
other, nor does he arrange them in hierarchical genera. Not until
the following century does consideration of Demosthenes'
achievement lead to a complete reversal of the Isocratic paradigm.[6] In post-Aristotelian rhetoric the passionate oratory of the
practical speaker becomes the grand style; the ornate, harmoniously balanced Isocratic manner is relegated to some inferior position. Kleochares, a third-century rhetorician, thus recognizes
two characters, one embracing grandeur and power, the other
sweetness and plainness.[7] These two characters differ sharply
from the Isocratic, in which grandeur and sweetness together
formed one style, plainness and forensic power the other. Terminological changes during this period also mark a trend away
from Isocratic formulations. Beginning with Aristotle, the original term for the grand style, *hadros*, which refers to verbal fullness and copia, is gradually replaced by ethically nuanced terms
suggesting height or size, such as *megaloprepes* and *hypselos*.[8] This
verbal change suggests a shift in the criteria for the grand style,
from surface richness and verbal copia to more inward qualities
like emotional intensity or grandeur of conception.

The question of terminology for the grand style brings us back
to Aristotle and the Classical period once more. Two of the terms
Aristotle uses to describe that style which rises above the ordinary
and clear are striking. In the beginning of Book III of the *Rhetoric*
he notes that "departure from the ordinary makes it [language]
appear more dignified (σεμνοτέραν)" (3.2.2). Dignity is not only
a regular attribute of the genus grande in Demetrius, Dionysius
of Halicarnassus, and Hermogenes,[9] but it is also Aristotle's own
term for the language of tragedy in the *Poetics*.[10] Similarly, in the

---

[6] Ibid., p. 68.

[7] Ibid., pp. 66–67, 75.

[8] Ibid., pp. 65–68, 72–75, 89, 91, 97–98, 110.

[9] Johann Ernesti, *Lexicon technologiae Graecorum rhetoricae* (Leipzig, 1795),
p. 306.

[10] ἀπεσεμνύνθη, *Poetics* 1449a.

Rhetoric, Aristotle offers rules for creating loftiness of style (3.6.1), where the Greek word translated as "loftiness" is actually *ogkos* or "massiveness"—a term Aristotle associates with the bulk and richness of epic.[11] Aristotle thus borrows his own terms for tragic and epic language from the *Poetics* and applies them to those qualities of prose that lift it above the ordinary and clear. Although he does not develop the association, he at least suggests that poetry and poetic criticism may lie behind the development of the rhetorical grand style. If we move back again in time to the late fifth century, this is precisely what we find.

One of the most valuable early documents on the meaning of the genera dicendi is not concerned with rhetoric at all but is instead an analysis of Aeschylean and Euripidean tragedy—*The Frogs* (405 B.C.) of Aristophanes. The issues involved in this debate over dramatic poetry, however, are identical to those treated throughout ancient rhetoric: the contrasting philosophical and aesthetic implications of the genus grande and the Isocratic or sophistic style. Wesley Trimpi writes, "The stylistic differences between Euripides and Aeschylus correspond to Aristotle's distinctions between the style of written speeches which are ακριβής and στενός (tenuis), highly finished and narrow in scope, and the 'larger, freer, bolder tone required by the loftier and more comprehensive subjects' of deliberative oratory."[12] Even a brief analysis of the debate should prove useful for understanding the values and ideals lying behind varying stylistic allegiances.

Aristophanes criticizes Aeschylus's fondness for lengthy, highflown diction. He is "the thunder-voiced monarch" (815), "uncurbed, unfettered, uncontrolled of speech, / . . . bombastiloquent" (837ff.). But Aeschylean tragedy involves more than "plume waving words" (816); like the genus grande it possesses a fiery, passionate, and difficult style, the product of a heroic and lofty mind. The chorus thus praises Aeschylus's "fiery soul," his "noble heart," and "high loftily-towering verse" (995ff.). For

---

[11] Ibid., 1459b.
[12] Wesley Trimpi, "Horace's 'Ut Pictura Poesis': The Argument for Stylistic Decorum," *Traditio* 34(1978): 45.

Aristophanes, the basic defect of Euripides lies in his rejection of the heroic virtues of the Homeric statesman-warrior (1013ff.). The loss of the heroic ideal destroys the splendid, passionate eloquence of archaic epic and tragedy. To Euripides' remark that dramatic characters should speak like men not demigods, Aeschylus replies, "for mighty thoughts and heroic aims,/ the words themselves must appropriate be" (1056).

The qualities of Aeschylean tragedy—its verbal splendor, passion, noble themes, and soldierlike strength—closely resemble those of the grand style, suggesting that the origin of this rhetorical genus cannot be restricted to the poetic style of Isocrates or even the psychagogic vehemence of the great Attic orators. The light of heroic sublimity and noble endeavor that illuminates later descriptions of the grand style derives from the legacy of epic and tragedy. From these the purely pragmatic elements of persuasive rhetoric acquire a new moral and spiritual elevation. Not inappropriately, then, did Cicero term the *"grandis"* speaker a *"tragicus orator"* (*Brutus* 203).[13]

Aristophanes' description of Euripides evokes a surprisingly complex picture of the sophistic style, one which links this style to a variety of tendencies operating within the Greek Enlightenment. On the one hand, Euripides' poetry has much in common with the dialectical plain style. Thus the chorus notes his clarity, logical subtlety, and radical questioning (900, 975). These, of course, are the attributes of pre-Socratic sophists like Protagoras. Also, the Euripidean manner seems to have something in common with the low forensic style scorned by Isocrates. Aeschylus complains that Euripides badgered the inmates of Hell with "his twists/And turns, and pleas and counterpleas" (773–74). The association of sophistic and plain style appears again when Euripides boasts how he made ancient tragedy "slim down (ἴσχνατα)" (941) and when the chorus describes him as "dissecting, detracting, maligning / . . . and with subtle analysis paring / The lung's large labor away" (825–29). The realism of Euripidean tragedy

---

[13] See de Romilly, *Magic and Rhetoric* (pp. 3–7), on the relation between Aeschylean tragedy and the rhetorical grand style.

(961, 1056) also links it with the drive toward verisimilar accuracy characteristic of the plain style genres of satire and comedy. On the other hand, this style betrays the softness and polish characteristic of the *genus medium*. The chorus speaks of Euripides' poetry as "splinters, / And phrases smoothed down with the plane" (917–18); he wields "with artistic skill, / Clearcut phrases, and wit refined" (901). Aeschylus accuses him of introducing effeminate melodies and harlotry into his verses (849, 1043).

That the sophistic style displays both the polish of the genus medium and the dialectical subtleties native to the *genus tenue* gains particular significance from the fact that Hendrickson implied just the opposite: that while the origins of the grand style lay in the artistic prose of the sophists, the plain style evolved from philosophy, in particular Stoic extensions of Aristotelian dialectic.[14] The description of Euripides' language in *The Frogs*, however, suggests that both the plain and middle styles share a common ancestry in sophistic, the one developing its logical acumen, clarity, and realism,[15] the other its lascivious refinement. Aristophanes' implied division of style into a tragic genus grande over and against the sophistic attributes of subtlety and polish better corresponds to the distinctions felt by antiquity than does Hendrickson's division into oratory, embracing both power and refinement, versus dialectic. Alongside the psychagogic power of the practical orator, the grand style preserves the connotations of heroic strength and noble idealism that link it to the values of epic and tragedy, while the plain and middle styles often seem by contrast scholastic and *umbratilis*—the marks of the sophist's logical sharpness and verbal ostentation.[16]

[14] Hendrickson, "The Origin," pp. 259–61, 272–73.
[15] Wit may be another aspect of the sophistic legacy of the plain style. In *The Frogs* (965), Euripides claims that he was the first to introduce witticisms into tragedy. Also note that while for Cicero wit characterizes the Attic plain style, for Demetrius it is a feature of the sweet style—again suggesting the close relation between the two.
[16] *Orator* 64. *Umbratilis* refers to the shaded gardens of the Academy and, by extension, to the dimly lit schools of the declaimers—as opposed to the dust and sun of the forum.

The Triple Tradition of the Grand Style

The central traditions of the genera dicendi emerge from this early period. These systems of classification, which we may call the anti-Isocratic, the Theophrastean, and the poetic, blend and intertwine in later rhetorics, giving each of the genera considerable latitude—a latitude that has given rise to some confusion. For example, in the Theophrastean tradition, which conjoins power and ornate beauty, Cicero becomes the preeminent model for the grand style; but the anti-Isocratic, which separates the two, treats Thucydides as the exemplar of the loftiest type of discourse.

From the first century B.C. to the second century A.D., the central period of Classical rhetoric, the anti-Isocratic opposition of polish and power pervades all treatments of the genera dicendi.[17] In this tradition, passion and agonistic force replace artistic refinement as criteria for the grand style. This shift has its roots in Aristotle, who, unlike Isocrates, treats the emotional aspects of rhetoric extensively and explicitly distinguishes passionate from polished discourse, the one being rough and oral, the other highly wrought and written. The inversion of Isocratic standards appears vividly in the contrasting images of the athlete and soldier frequently associated with the characters of style. This imagery probably derives from the terms for the original Isocratic genera, the full (*hadros*) and the thin (*ischnos*), which are based on contrasting bodily types.[18] The Isocratic grand style resembles the fleshy, well-developed, and harmoniously proportioned figure of the athlete, while the low forensic style has a soldierlike tautness and lean muscularity. By the third century B.C., however, the evaluation implied by these body types has begun to shift, so that soldierly strength and power come to seem

[17] The *terminus a quo* for this period may be two centuries earlier, depending on whether we place Demetrius's *On Style* in the third century B.C. or as late as the first century A.D. The former position is defended by G.M.A. Grube in his *A Greek Critic: Demetrius on Style* (Toronto, 1961), the latter by W. Rhys Roberts in his introduction to the Loeb Demetrius.

[18] Quadlbauer, "Die genera dicendi," p. 65; Kennedy, *The Art of Persuasion*, p. 189.

"grander" than full-fleshed, conspicuous symmetry. Kleochares thus compares Isocrates' style to the body of an athlete, Demosthenes' to that of a soldier. Yet for him the latter's agonistic strength and emotional power do not seem "low," but instead constitute true elevation.[19] In subsequent centuries, the contrast between the athlete and soldier, the gymnasium and the battlefield, invariably distinguishes the balanced sweetness of Isocratic prose from the new Demosthenean grand style with its fierce and passionate grandeur. This contrast appears throughout Classical rhetoric, from the first century B.C. onward.[20] So Cicero, speaking of Demetrius of Phaleron, remarks that "his training was less for the field than for the parade-ground (*palaestra*). He entertained rather than stirred his countrymen; for he came forth into the heat and dust (*sol et pulvis*) of action, not from a soldier's tent, but from the shady retreat (*umbraculum*) of the great philosopher Theophrastus" (*Brutus* 36–37). Quintilian likewise notes, "in those portions of our speech which deal with the actual question at issue we require not the swelling thews of the athlete, but the wiry sinews of the soldier" (10.1.33). He later adds, "[Isocrates] is neat and polished and better suited to the fencing-school (*palaestra*) than to the battlefield" (10.1.79). Tacitus echoes the same antithesis: "And I maintain that the only orator is, and ever has been one who, like a soldier equipped at all points going to the battle-field, enters the forum armed with every learned accomplishment" (32.2).

The contrast between the soldier and athlete relates to the purpose as well as the style of oratory. The athlete plays a highly structured game (*ludus*); he endeavors to display his skill by defeating his opponent, but, finally, all is artificial and make-believe. The soldier fights out in the sun and dust, risking his life for what is dear to him. Thus, in Classical rhetoric, the Isocratic style resembles a game, a display of rhetorical virtuosity that flourishes only in the shady halls of declamation or the schoolroom's shel-

[19] Quadlbauer, "Die genera dicendi," p. 66.
[20] Cicero, *De oratore* 1.81, 1.157, 2.84; *Orator* 42; *De opt gen* 17; Tacitus, *Dialogus* 32.2–34.5; Quintilian 10.5.17–20, 11.3.26–27, 12.2.6–14; Seneca the Elder, *Controversiae* 3.pr.13, 9.pr.1–5; Dionysius of Halicarnassus, "Demosthenes" 32; Saint Augustine, *On Christian Doctrine*, trans. D. W. Robertson (Indianapolis, 1958), 4.42.

ter, while the oratorical grand style involves risk and commitment to the urgent issues pressing upon the state.[21]

Thus, after the first century B.C., Isocrates never serves as a model for the grand oratorical manner. Although Cicero and Dionysius acknowledge his real virtues, they carefully distinguish them from the more emotional, persuasive qualities proper to the practical orator.[22] Isocrates is smooth, symmetrical, schematic, and passionless. His balanced antitheses, better suited for reading than oral delivery, seem too artificial to persuade. The oratorical style, on the contrary, relies on the more dramatic and emotional figures of thought, on asyndetic roughness, and on stinging (*aculeatus*) brevity, rather than the aural Gorgianic schemes.[23] It is harsh, muscular, and energetic, avoiding the ostentatious symmetries of the genus medium in favor of an apparent spontaneity and passion.[24] The Isocratic and oratorical styles are hence not simply variants of a "rhetorical" (as opposed to a "philosophical") ideal but diametrically opposed to each other, and their antagonism provides the mainspring of rhetorical debate in antiquity—a debate intensified by the rise of the schools of declamation, whose florid artificiality was frequently associated with Isocratic or sophistic tendencies.[25]

[21] Richard Lanham's Derridean equations of philosophy and seriousness, oratory and play are therefore inaccurate. Philosophy, agonistic oratory, and preaching are all serious, committed activities, in contrast to the playful sophistic tradition. Thomas Walys, a fourteenth-century English Dominican, makes clear this connection between "seriousness," preaching, and the image of the soldier: "The man who undertakes the duty of preaching should not be soft and unnerved but undaunted and strong in the face of everything. For no one should even approach the enjoyment of this noble duty unless he has been prepared like a soldier to surrender his life in death." Cited in Lorraine Helms, "Popular and Scholastic Styles: The London Playhouses 1599–1609" (Ph.D. diss., Stanford University, 1986).

[22] Dionysius of Halicarnassus, "Isocrates" 1–3; Cicero, *Orator* 37–42.

[23] On *aculeos*, see Cicero, *De oratore* 2.64, 3.138; *Brutus* 38; *Orator* 62. On asyndeta, see Aristotle, *Rhetoric* 3.12.3–4; Demetrius 193–94, 269; Quintilian 9.3.50, 9.4.126. On the figures of thought, see Cicero, *Orator* 136; Quintilian 9.1.19–21, 9.3.102.

[24] Cicero, *Orator* 37, 65, 91; *Part orat* 10–11; Demetrius 27–28, 247, 250–52, 300; Quintilian 9.3.102; Dionysius of Halicarnassus, "Demosthenes" 4, 18–22.

[25] In antiquity, only the Epicurean Philodemus prefers demonstrative, Isocratic oratory over practical, civic rhetoric (*The Rhetorica of Philodemus*, ed. and trans.

This opposition appears sharply in Dionysius of Halicarnassus, who divides composition into two types, the austere and the polished, exemplified by Thucydides and Isocrates respectively. The former is asymmetrical, rough, old-fashioned, and asyndetic rather than periodic. But it also dignified (*semnos*) and lofty (*megaloprepes*)—unmistakable attributes of the grand style. Polished composition, on the contrary, is sweet, smooth, and periodic but not dignified.[26] The same anti-Isocratic tendencies manifest themselves in Cicero's transformation of the Aristotelian kinds of proof—rational, ethical, pathetic—into the *officia oratoris*.[27] Cicero replaces Aristotle's ethical proof with *delectare* or the aesthetic delight produced by Isocratic and nonoratorical prose, thus creating the familiar tripartite genera dicendi based on psychological function—to teach, to delight, and to move. As in Dionysius, polish and power separate into distinct and opposing styles, the former smooth and flowing, the latter terse and vigorous (*Orator* 65–66, 91–96).

The opposition between polish and power depends on the psychological premise repeated from Aristotle through Hermogenes that aesthetic delight inhibits emotional response by calling attention to the skill of the speaker.[28] Such delight creates a psychological detachment, a "disinterestedness," that destroys the possibility of passionate involvement in the issues at stake. In addition, the aural schemes and symmetries of Isocratic rhetoric thwart oratorical persuasion because such elaboration seems insincere and manipulative; people do not usually plead and storm in perfectly balanced periods. Quintilian thus writes: "For the majority of these figures aim at delighting the hearer. But when terror, hatred

Harry M. Hubbell, *Transactions of the Connecticut Academy of Arts and Sciences* 23[1920]).

[26] "Demosthenes" 36–40; *On Literary Composition*, ed. and trans. W. Rhys Roberts (London, 1910), pp. 211–47.

[27] Friedrich Solmsen, "The Aristotelian Tradition in Ancient Rhetoric," *AJP* 62(1941): 178–79.

[28] Aristotle, *Rhetoric* 3.2.4; *Rhetorica ad Herennium* 4.32; Dionysius of Halicarnassus, "Isocrates" 12–13, "Demosthenes" 4, 18, 44–45; Demetrius 27–28; Quintilian 9.3.102; Hermogenes, *Opera omnia*, ed. Hugo Rabe (Leipzig, 1913), p. 301. I would like to thank Cecil Wootten for letting me use his unpublished translation of Hermogenes' *On Types of Style*.

and pity are the weapons called for in the fray, who will endure the orator who expresses his anger, his sorrow or his entreaties in neat antitheses, balanced cadences and exact correspondences? Too much care for our words . . . weakens the impression of emotional sincerity . . ." (9.3.102). When, therefore, ancient (and Renaissance) rhetorics criticize periodicity, ornament, and symmetry, they should not be perceived as rejecting oratory in favor of the plain style, but as defending the power and passion of genus grande from the encroachments of sophistic overrefinement.[29]

The second strand in the development of the genera dicendi descends from Theophrastus. His rhetorical works are lost, but later references indicate that he divided discourse into a poetic-rhetorical type, which both delights and moves, and an unadorned factual style suitable for teaching[30]—a division probably based on Aristotle's distinction between ordinary and dignified language (*Poetics* 1458a–1459a).[31] In his discussion of ornamentation (*kataskeue*), the fourth virtue of style, Theophrastus again links sweetness and grandeur. They are both parts of ornamentation, not competing ideals.[32] Although the emphasis on emotional power was probably stronger in Theophrastus than Isocrates, the division of style into an elaborate, ornate, and affective manner and a spare, plain one, along with the conjunction of sweetness and grandeur, suggest Isocratic influence. For both, the lofty and the sweeter qualities of speech do not untwine into distinct genera.

Theophrastus's undeniable influence on later rhetorical theory would suggest a steady, if indirect, transmission of the twofold Isocratic categories throughout the Classical period. This, how-

[29] Croll erroneously identifies the figures of thought with the plain style, the figures of words with the oratorical style (*"Attic" and Baroque*, pp. 54, 89–91). There is *no* justification for this identification in either Classical or Renaissance rhetoric, both of which link the figures of thought with the grand style, the figures of words with the middle.

[30] Hendrickson, "The Origin," pp. 255–57; Solmsen, "The Aristotelian Tradition," p. 185; Quadlbauer, "Die genera dicendi," p. 63; Kennedy, *The Art of Persuasion*, p. 267; Scaglione, *The Classical Theory of Composition*, p. 19.

[31] Kennedy, "Theophrastus," 93–104.

[32] Quadlbauer, "Die genera dicendi," p. 63; Bonner, *Dionysius of Halicarnassus*, p. 20.

ever, is not the case. The same rhetorics that make use of Theophrastean material also display marked anti-Isocratic tendencies,
dividing polish from power, the middle from the grand style.
They reconcile these apparently incompatible classifications by
erecting a further distinction between beauty and charm. This
distinction first appears in the *Rhetorica ad Herennium*, which divides the grace and elegance of the Gorgianic figures from a
beauty compatible with dignity, gravity, and severity (4.32). The
former are appropriate only for epideictic oratory, the latter for
forensic and deliberative. The same contrast between a lofty and
austere beauty and a schematic charm reappears in Cicero, Dionysius, and Quintilian.[33] In this way, Classical rhetoric readmits
rhythm, some periodicity, and figurative richness into the grand
style, differentiating it from Aristotle's rougher deliberative oratory, without allowing it to slip back into Isocratic cultivation.
This conjunction of artistry and emotional force appears most
clearly in Quintilian, who writes: "Why then should it be
thought that polish is inevitably prejudicial to vigour, when the
truth is that nothing can attain its full strength without the assistance of art, and that art is always productive of beauty? . . . the
study of structure is of the utmost value, not merely for charming
the ear, but for stirring the soul" (9.4.7–10). Theophrastean influence preserves the unity of beauty and power in the grand style,
particularly that of Roman rhetoric,[34] but that union remains subordinate to the anti-Isocratic disjunction of power and polish that
dominates ancient rhetorical theory.

The third tradition, that stemming from poetry and poetic criticism, influences the rhetorical genera dicendi in more subtle and
indirect ways than the other two. It surfaces in Aristophanes, in
Aristotle's borrowings from the terminology of the *Poetics* to describe an oratorical language that rises above simple clarity, and
in Cicero's picture of the *tragicus orator*. In addition, the contrast
between tragedy and comedy affects the formulation of the grand
and plain styles. In the *Rhetorica ad Herennium*, the passage ex-

[33] Dionysius of Halicarnassus, "Demosthenes" 47; *On Literary Composition*, p.
121; Cicero, *De oratore* 3.98, 3.103; Quintilian 9.3.102, 9.4.7, 10.1.30.
[34] Quadlbauer, "Die genera dicendi," p. 110.

emplifying the *genus grave*, which describes the pathetic and fearful consequences of treason, resembles ancient tragedy in both style and subject, while the selection representing the plain style is an unmistakably comic narrative (4.12, 4.14). The relation between drama and the characters of style reappears in Dionysius of Halicarnassus, who observes that while Thucydides, his exemplar for the grand style, created larger-than-life characters, those of the plain stylist, Lysias, were smaller ("Demosthenes" 2)—a distinction based on Aristotle's contrast between tragedy and comedy in the *Poetics* (1448a–1449a). Furthermore, although there are few explicit references to the parallels between drama and the rhetorical genera, the Classical attitude toward comedy and tragedy actually had a pervasive effect on the characters of style. Ancient dramatic criticism and practice equate a realistic, conversational style with the everyday, domestic, and "low" subjects of comedy. Conversely, tragedy takes its plots from the heroic, mythological past and uses elevated, distinctive, and striking diction.[35] These associations spill over into rhetoric, yoking the *sermo*, the language of ordinary conversation, with smaller realistic subjects, the unusual diction of the grand style with urgent, communal, political themes. For both drama and rhetoric, conversational simplicity seems "low," more serious and excellent topics demanding a correspondingly elevated style. Thus poetic theory lies behind rhetorical decorum—the requirement that "height" of style be proportional to the excellence of subject matter.[36] The principle of decorum, however, seems to conflict with the demand for an unaffected passionate spontaneity in the grand style.[37] The tension between the anti-Isocratic tradition and the principle of decorum, between the demands for passionate sincerity and tragic elevation, underlies the widespread claim that the orator must himself be moved if he wishes to move others,

[35] D. A. Russell, ed., *"Longinus": On the Sublime* (Oxford, 1964), p. 99; John Onians, *Art and Thought in the Hellenistic Age: The Greek World View, 350–50 B.C.* (London, 1979), p. 38.

[36] Aristotle, *Rhetoric* 3.2.2; Cicero, *Orator* 71, 100; *De oratore* 1.144; Dionysius of Halicarnassus, "Lysias" 16; Demetrius 120, 190; Quintilian 12.10.63; Hermogenes, pp. 227, 243–44.

[37] Quintilian 3.8.58ff.

insofar as this claim implies that the heightened diction of the grand style is also the natural language of strong emotion.[38]

Evolution of the Grand Style

The persistence of anti-Isocratic, Theophrastean, and poetic elements throughout Classical rhetoric binds together theories of the grand style from Aristotle to Hermogenes. Within this relatively stable framework, however, conceptions of the grand style evolve from an emphasis on copia, richness, and ornament to one on passion and sublimity. Earlier rhetoricians tend to define the grand style in terms of artistic elaboration of language and rhythm, later rhetoricians in terms of its psychological origins and effects as well as its subject matter.[39] Dionysius's contrast between Isocrates, representative of the earliest grand style, and Demosthenes suggests this shift: "[Demosthenes has] expressed the subject-matter in a nobler and more dignified way than Isocrates. . . . He has deployed more force and more powerful emphasis, and avoided the frigid and juvenile figures which adorn the other's style to excess. But above all, the whole of it, in its energy, vehemence and feeling, is wholly and entirely superior to the style of Isocrates" ("Dem" 21). Here emotional intensity replaces lavish ornament as the primary criterion of oratorical excellence. The same evolution appears in Roman rhetoric. The *Rhetorica ad Herennium* and *De oratore* both see fullness, rich ornament, and artistic composition as basic to the grand style of popular oratory.[40] In *De oratore* the only mention of the genera dicendi distinguishes them along Isocratic lines into a full rounded manner and a plain strong one (3.199); neither power nor passion is mentioned as a criterion. But while the mature Cicero and Quintilian still insist upon the copia and artistry of the grand style, they lay far more weight on its emotional intensity and agonistic strength. The officia oratoris, which in *De oratore* do not differentiate between styles, become the criteria for the genera dicendi, linking the

---

[38] Aristotle, *Rhetoric* 3.7.3–4; Cicero, *De oratore* 2.189; *Orator* 132; Quintilian 6.2.26; Longinus 18.2, 20.2; Hermogenes, pp. 353–59.

[39] Quadlbauer, "Die genera dicendi," pp. 110–11.

[40] Ibid., p. 89; see also *Rhetorica ad Herennium* 4.11.

grand style firmly to passion and power. In his later works, Cicero also recognizes the possibility of a rough and austere grand style, alongside his preferred artistic one (*Orator* 20), and begins to describe this genus in a Longinian vocabulary of height and sublimity.[41] Quintilian likewise stresses the overwhelming emotional force of the grand style, although without banishing rhythm and artistic richness. It resembles "some great torrent that rolls down rocks and 'disdains a bridge' and carves out its own banks for itself, [and] will sweep the judge from his feet, struggle as he may, and force him to go whither he bears him" (12.10.61). Such grandeur does not require the aural concinnities of the Isocratic period but uses vivid and dramatic figures of thought like apostrophe, prosopopoeia, and hypotyposis—the same figures that characterize the Renaissance grand style. While Quintilian only explicitly discusses the genera dicendi at the end of Book xii, throughout the *Institutes* he defends against both Lysian and Senecan epigones an eloquence that flows from the orator's own passion and possesses force, sublimity, and grandeur.[42]

This shift from ornament to passion and sublimity conferred a new importance on the inner life of the speaker. For Longinus, the two major elements of sublimity—greatness of thought and intensity of feeling—reflect and spring from the soul of the speaker. Sublimity is the echo of a great soul. While Longinus does not neglect trope, figure, and rhythm, these become correspondingly less significant. Elsewhere as well, the emphasis on passion psychologizes the grand style. Both Roman and hellenistic rhetoric, as we have noted, insist that a speaker can move others only if he is himself truly moved, that passionate oratory flows unforced from the ardent heart. Without minimizing the

---

[41] Cicero, *De opt gen* 12; Russell, *On the Sublime*, p. xxxi; Quadlbauer, "Die genera dicendi," p. 89. Quintilian also suggests two possible forms of the grand style in his contrast between Demosthenes and Cicero. The former is more compact, terse, and studied, the latter fuller, more lengthy, natural, and passionate. Whereas Demosthenes fights "*acumine*," Cicero conquers by his "*pondere*" (10.1.106ff.). Thus here we find both a briefer and a more copious form of the grand style.

[42] Quintilian 2.5.8–12; 8.3.1–3; 8.3.88; 10.1.27, 76; 12.10.23–26.

importance of artistic language, these rhetorics thus anchor the
grand style in the speaker's intellectual and emotional capacities.

By the Christian era, the distinction between *ornatus* and the
grand style is clearly marked. Both Longinus and Augustine observe that grandeur can exist without any of the verbal and rhythmic techniques ordinarily associated with linguistic elevation.[43]
For Augustine, "the grand style differs from the moderate style
not so much in that it is adorned with verbal ornaments but in
that it is forceful with emotions of the spirit. Although it uses almost all of the ornaments, it does not seek them if it does not need
them. . . . It is enough for the matter being discussed that the appropriateness of the words be determined by the ardor of the
heart rather than by careful choice." In addition, Hermogenes'
semnotes or solemnity, the first subcategory of the Idea of Grandeur, is severely simple, employing only the same brief direct
structure that also characterizes the Idea of Simplicity (pp. 246–
51). Figures, tropes, periodicity, rhythm, and copia are not valued for their own sake but only insofar as they create and support
the desired effect. The triple decorum of ornate language, lofty
subject matter, and affectivity still defines the grand style, but
gradually the accent has moved from the first criterion to the latter two. Thus the history of the genera dicendi in antiquity reverses rather than confirms Isocrates' position.

Passion, Philosophy, and Plainness

Before tracing the further history of the grand style, a little about
the plain style must also be said, if only because the reductive polarization of prose into vacuous eloquence and philosophic plainness has led to the virtually complete neglect of the grand style in
favor of the plain.[44] The plain style exists in two main forms

[43] Longinus 9.9; Saint Augustine, *On Christian Doctrine*, 4.42, 4.44.

[44] There is no modern scholarship on the grand style. Important works study-
ing the plain style include Croll's *"Attic" and Baroque*; Adolph's *The Rise of Modern
Prose Style*; George Williamson's *The Senecan Amble: Prose Form from Bacon to Col-
lier* (Chicago, 1951); Wesley Trimpi's *Ben Jonson's Poems: A Study of the Plain Style*
(Stanford, 1962); Perry Miller's *The New England Mind: The Seventeenth Century*
(New York, 1939); and the numerous articles of R. F. Jones.

throughout antiquity, deriving from its double origin in dialectic and in forensic oratory. A third origin in comedy remains closely associated with the forensic plain style; both involve realistic narration and character portrayal. Before Saint Augustine, the dialectical heritage of the plain style or genus tenue is less important for the rhetorical tradition than the forensic. The former appears primarily in discussions of the officia oratoris, where the plain style is linked to the functions of teaching and proof (*Orator* 69). The forensic plain style is more central. In the first century B.C. it becomes the basis for the stylistic ideals of the neo-Atticists, Cicero's chief competitors, who claimed Lysias as their champion. The major Classical rhetoricians—Cicero, Dionysius, Quintilian, and Longinus—generally agree in their descriptions of this "Attic" plain style. Positively considered, it is clear, urbane, natural, often witty and graceful, and persuasive.[45] Yet it is suitable only for small, unimportant subjects; it seems commonplace and ordinary, often losing effective strength by seeking meticulous correctness.[46]

Neither variant of the plain style possesses emotional power.[47] The Latin rhetorical tradition confines *movere* to the grand style, and similar assertions appear in the Greek. The notion of a passionate plain style is, as we shall see, a medieval Christian development that culminates in the ideal of powerful plainness found in sixteenth-century Protestant rhetorics. In antiquity, however,

[45] Cicero, *De oratore* 3.42–43; *Orator* 20, 76–87; *Brutus* 274–76; Dionysius of Halicarnassus, "Lysias" 2–10; Demetrius 208; George Kennedy, *The Art of Rhetoric in the Roman World, 300 B.C.–A.D. 300* (Princeton, 1972), p. 71.

[46] Cicero, *De opt gen* 4.12; *Brutus* 283–85; Quintilian 8.pr.27; Hermogenes, pp. 227–28, 241. The term "Attic" possesses several quite different meanings in antiquity. Depending on the context, "Attic" may mean: (1) The characteristic qualities of the masterpieces of Athenian literature, especially oratory. (2) A simpler, more succinct and conversational style, best exemplified in the speeches of Lysias. This is the Attic style that Cicero describes at length in *Orator* 75–90. (3) The mannered extreme of (2), deliberately cultivating an archaic roughness or an overanxious and deadening concern for correctness. (4) While (2) and (3) represent movements in Roman oratory, the fourth type of Atticism is primarily Greek and refers to the demand for linguistic purity based on the idiom of Classical Athens. The "Attic" plain style concerns senses (2) and (3) alone.

[47] Cicero, *Brutus* 274–76, 283–85; Dionysius of Halicarnassus, "Lysias" 13; Demetrius 194; Quintilian 12.10.43.

passionate rhetoric belongs within the genus grande. This fact has sometimes been obscured by the existence of two variants of the grand style in Greek rhetoric, the first characterized by massiveness, the second by concentrated intensity. Critics like Scaglione and Kennedy have tried to place the latter type under the plain style, but this seems unwarranted. Hermogenes, for example, distinguishes between solemnity and amplitude, a distinction corresponding to that between sublimity and amplification in Longinus and between force and grandeur in Demetrius; yet he places both the austere brevity of the first as well as the intricate copia of the latter within the Idea of Grandeur. Conversely, the neo-Atticism of Cicero's day—the style of Calidius and Calvus—abjures emotional appeals. It is precisely for this reason that Cicero finds it deficient.[48]

In modern scholarship, the question of the plain style has become intertwined in the relationship between philosophy and eloquence. Hendrickson and Croll argue that the plain style, in both antiquity and the Renaissance, "is properly characterized by its origin in *philosophy*."[49] Concerned more with objective and psychological truth than popular persuasion, such a style rejects the psychagogic ornaments of rhetoric, preferring instead a lucid brevity that is able to articulate the precise contours of its subject and the movements of the inquiring mind.

With respect to Classical rhetoric, there are in fact two issues involved here: the relation between philosophy and rhetoric, and that between philosophy and the plain style. The first really pertains to epistemology, to the question of whether rhetoric is inherently meretricious, rather than to style, although touching on the latter insofar as it concerns the legitimacy of emotional and aesthetic persuasion. Even the liberal rhetorical tradition of Cicero, Tacitus, and Quintilian, which insisted on the philosophical grounding of genuine eloquence, admitted that if men were wholly rational, eloquence would be superfluous. On the other hand, Classical rhetorics emphatically deny the claim that the grand style serves up self-congratulatory commonplaces de-

---

[48] Cicero, *Brutus* 274–76, 283–85.
[49] Croll, *"Attic" and Baroque*, pp. 60–61; Williamson, *Senecan Amble*, p. 12.

signed to reinforce popular assumptions, while the plain style encourages questioning and radical inquiry. For Dionysius, the Thucydidean grand style "has power to shock the mind, the [plain] style of Lysias to gratify it" ("Dem" 2). According to Cicero, the grand style likewise "implants new ideas and uproots the old" (*Orator* 97). We will discuss this problem in more detail when we turn to Saint Augustine and the origins of Christian rhetoric. For our present purposes, we need to focus on the second issue—whether the plain style is the native and proper language of philosophic discourse.

Classical rhetoric offers no univocal answer to this question. Some philosophical schools, especially the Epicurean and Stoic, displayed an overt hostility toward eloquence,[50] advocating instead a lucid, brief, unadorned style. Plato is the key figure in the opposition between oratorical and philosophic styles. In the *Gorgias, Protagoras,* and *Sophist*, he depicts philosophic discourse as a series of brief, dialectical exchanges in a conversational manner, contrasting this with the copious, artistic, unbroken speech of oratory and sophistic.[51] Yet there remains a curious passage in the *Theatetus* that suggests further dimensions to this dialectical style. The speaker in the courts, Plato argues, is a slave to the judges, the clock, and to circumstances; he must be brief, to the point, and wary. There is no time for detached reflection, since in the law courts matters of vital personal concern, even one's life, are at stake. Oratory is, therefore, the language of emotional engagement, not intellectual detachment. The philosopher, on the other hand, is free. He possesses the leisure to ramble digressively from one point to the next as he chooses (172CE) and can range at will among various arguments (173B). If such a man, Plato continues, enters the forum, he seems absurd, since he is accustomed to an abstracted leisure. The word Plato uses for "leisure" is particularly interesting; leisure is *schole*, which also means "school" (172D). Thus the philosophical style is, in Cicero's sense, scholastic; it deliberately retreats from civic life in order to wander lei-

---

[50] Theodore Burgess, *Epideictic Literature* (Chicago, 1902), p. 222; Diogenes Laertius 7.59; Philodemus, pp. 302, 314, 335, 340; Cicero, *De oratore* 3.66; *De finibus* 4.3.5.

[51] *Gorgias* 448DE, *Sophist* 230A–231B; *Protagoras* 337E–338A.

surely among ideas, removed from the urgency of personal or political concerns.[52] One can easily see how the philosophic style could become vulnerable to a rambling, umbratical digressiveness, how naturally it approaches a smooth, relaxed, and graceful middle style—like the style of Cicero's own philosophic dialogues.[53]

If we turn from Plato's somewhat ambiguous comments on philosophic language to the rhetorical tradition's own observations on the Platonic dialogues, the connection between philosophy and the plain style almost vanishes. Only Demetrius emphasizes the dialogues' Socratic simplicity or seems to equate them with the plain style at all. For Cicero, Plato is the "prince of sweetness and dignity"; for Quintilian he possesses a divine Homeric eloquence soaring above ordinary prose. Hermogenes makes Plato the exemplar of epideictic dignity and splendor—both parts of Grandeur. Dionysius even criticizes him for being too flowery and poetic.[54] Moreover, among philosophers, Plato seems exceptional only with regard to his excellence. Classical rhetoric regularly admires the eloquence of philosophy, especially that of the Academics and Peripatetics.[55] Nor is this peculiar; throughout antiquity, philosophical prose borrowed lavishly from the schools of the rhetors and poets.[56] As a result, no ancient rhetorician thought to equate the philosophical and plain styles. The Stoic plain style really forms the exception, and by the second century B.C. even the Stoics had mitigated their opposition to eloquence.[57]

---

[52] On *scholasticus* as leisurely and removed from the struggles of the forum and assembly, see Tacitus 14; Quintilian 11.1.82; Gellius 15.1.1.

[53] Cicero, *De officiis* 1.3; Solmsen, "Greek Ideas about Leisure," *Wingspread Lectures in the Humanities* 1(1966): 25–38.

[54] Cicero, *De oratore* 1.49; *Orator* 62; *Brutus* 121; Dionysius of Halicarnassus, "Demosthenes" 5–7; Demetrius 37, 51; Quintilian 10.1.81; Tacitus 31.9; Hermogenes, p. 386; George L. Kustas, *Studies in Byzantine Rhetoric*, Analecta Vlatadon (Thessalonica, 1973), p. 40; Norden, *Die antike Kunstprosa*, p. 399.

[55] Cicero, *De oratore* 1.49, 3.141; *Orator* 62; Quintilian 10.1. 81–84.

[56] Burgess, *Epideictic Literature*, pp. 214ff.; Norden, *Die antike Kunstprosa*, p. 1; Onians, *Art and Thought*, p. 94; Hans von Arnim, *Leben und Werke des Dio von Prusa* (Berlin, 1898), pp. 42, 68, 80–84, 89, 97, 113.

[57] Onians, *Art and Thought*, p. 94; Quadlbauer, "Die genera dicendi," p. 72.

Like the passionate plain style, the philosophical has its roots in the Middle Ages, this time in the contrast between scholastic and poeto-rhetorical discourse. Only after Abelard does philosophy divorce itself from poetry and eloquence and assume an exclusively dialectical coloration[58]—a division reflected in the distinction, which persists through the Renaissance, between the unadorned, logically subtle university sermon and the elaborate, moving popular one. It seemed natural for a fifteenth-century humanist raised on Aristotle, Aquinas, and Scotus to contrast philosophical plainness to rhetorical eloquence, but this was not the case in ancient rhetoric. Antiquity distinguishes philosophy from oratory not on the basis of plainness but of power. For all its beauty and grandeur, philosophic eloquence lacks the sinewy strength and combative force of the practical orator.[59] Roman rhetoric, which equates forensic power and the grand style, thus tends to lump philosophy, along with all forms of written eloquence, in the middle style. Even Seneca, who generally espouses the ideals of the Stoic plain style, compares philosophical prose to the gentle, honey-sweet rhetoric of Nestor—a traditional image for the genus medium.[60] Since, however, hellenistic rhetoric does not separate written and oral discourse, it unhesitatingly places at least some philosophy within the loftiest categories of style.

Romans and Greeks

This difference between Roman rhetoric and what we may loosely call hellenistic—that is, Greek rhetoric from the third century B.C. to the second century A.D.—concerning the place of philosophy within the genera dicendi points to a crucial split in the rhetorical tradition. As Solmsen has shown, Aristotelian rhetoric survives only in Rome, the later Greek tradition splitting off into two branches: the Hermagorean and the stylistic.[61] The former, with its elaborate theories of forensic argumentation, does

[58] Ernst Robert Curtius, *European Literature and the Latin Middle Ages*, trans. Willard Trask (Princeton, 1973), pp. 213, 480–82.

[59] Cicero, *Orator* 62; *Brutus* 121; *De oratore* 1.81.

[60] *Moral Epistles* 40.2–8.

[61] Solmsen, "The Aristotelian Tradition," pp. 49, 178.

not concern us here, as it has little or nothing to do with the characters of style. The stylistic rhetorics, those by Demetrius, Dionysius, Longinus, and Hermogenes, however, constitute a vital and largely forgotten background for Renaissance rhetoric.[62] Hellenistic rhetorics differ sharply from Roman in their treatment of the grand style, and the increasing influence of the former on the Renaissance shapes its understanding of this genus.

The difference between these two traditions stems from historical considerations. Rome, at least until Quintilian's time, possessed a living practical rhetoric. In Greece, however, the Macedonian and Roman conquests eroded the possibility for significant public debate in either the court or the senate. Even though most hellenistic rhetorics claim to address the problems of popular oratory,[63] they are all affected by what Kennedy calls *"letteraturizzazione,"* or the use of rhetorical analysis for treating literary rather than oral discourse.[64] The distinction between oratory and other forms of artistic prose seems less important in these rhetorics than it does in Cicero and Quintilian.[65]

These divergent orientations have important repercussions. Although in *De oratore* Crassus argues that oratory deals with all subjects, Cicero's rhetorical works focus on popular civic oratory. He excludes philosophy and history from principal consideration. Thus he rather brusquely dismisses Thucydides on the grounds that he is a dreadful model for public speakers (*Brutus* 287; *Orator* 30). As a result, the effects of the grand style are usually limited to the forensic emotions of anger and pity.[66] In general, the emotions proper to oratory strike one as rather primitive, self-interested, and harsh: hatred, vengeance, ill-will, personal triumph (*Part orat* 96), although Cicero also mentions oratory's calming and pacific effects. Nonforensic emotions, like

---

[62] The only exceptions are John Monfasani's *George of Trebizond: A Biography and a Study of His Rhetoric and Logic* (Leiden, 1976), and Annabel Patterson's *Hermogenes and the Renaissance: Seven Ideas of Style* (Princeton, 1970).

[63] Bonner, *Dionysius of Halicarnassus*, pp. 11, 72, 83, Longinus 1.1.

[64] George Kennedy, *Classical Rhetoric and its Christian and Secular Tradition from Ancient to Modern Times* (Chapel Hill, 1980), p. 5.

[65] Bonner, *Dionsyius of Halicarnassus*, pp. 2, 13, 40.

[66] Cicero, *De oratore* 1.53, 1.220, 2.196; *De inventione* 1.98–109.

wonder and surprise, are listed along with the Gorgianic schemes under the sweeter middle style (*Part orat* 21, 32). This forensic interpretation of emotion reappears in Quintilian and even as late as Augustine, for whom the grand style is primarily suited for ardent reproof of deliberate sin. For both, the grand style may bring forth tears and excite anger or pity but not feelings like sublimity, joy, or awe.[67]

Finally, Roman rhetoric tends not to disjoin passion and full, rich, artistic development in the grand style.[68] While stressing that ostentatious ornament dissipates power and passion, it also insists that beauty and art do not destroy vigor; that the grand style is copious, rhythmic, and ornate as well as passionate; that the weapons of agonistic oratory should not be defaced by mold and rust, but, in Quintilian's words, "shine with a splendour that shall strike terror to the heart of the foe, like the flashing steel that dazzles heart and eye at once."[69] Cicero thus prefers the more polished, periodic, and rhythmic forms of the genus grande to the rougher, archaic ones—a judgment partly based on the ear's demand for harmony, and partly on the fact that these acoustic devices also subserve emotional power. Hence Cicero argues that the peroration, the most intensely affective part of a speech, should be periodic throughout (*Orator* 211). Copia also remains essential for the Roman grand style because the ear comprehends more slowly than the eye and because in spoken discourse the passions are moved by the accumulated weight of torrential oratory, whereas the lightening-like sublime moment passes unnoticed in the steady flow of words.

Roman rhetoric describes the grand style as oral, copious, and civic; it is largely forensic, often periodic, and highly embellished. In the hellenistic treatises, however, the distinction between oral and written eloquence fades and with it the practical, political orientation of Roman rhetoric. Although the continued

[67] Quintilian 12.10.62; Augustine, *On Christian Doctrine* 4.53.

[68] For the influence of Theophrastus on this conjunction of ornament and power, see Bonner, *Dionysius of Halicarnassus*, p. 20.

[69] Quintilian 10.1.30. See also *Rhetorica ad Herennium* 4.11, 4.18; Cicero, *Orator* 20, 97; Quintilian 2.12.1, 9.4.3–10; Quadlbauer, "Die genera dicendi," pp. 77, 84, 104–105.

preeminence of Demosthenes indicates that political oratory remains the underlying ideal, the hellenistic rhetorics also treat history, philosophy, theology, and poetry. This widening of rhetoric to include all artistic discourse leads to a new conception of the grand style, apparent in the choice of exemplary models. For Demetrius and Dionysius, Thucydides becomes the representative of grandeur. Hermogenes makes Plato the model for solemnity and splendor. Longinus cites passages from Genesis, Homer, and Plato to exemplify sublimity.

This shift in models points to further changes. While Roman rhetoric focuses on the forensic responses of anger and pity, the Greeks allow a broader range of emotions within the grand style. Particularly interesting is the inclusion of quasi-religious affect. Demetrius, Dionysius, and Hermogenes all describe the audience's response to the grand style in analogies drawn from the numinous terror created by the initiation rites of the Mysteries and the ecstasy of the Corybantic dancers.[70] For example, in discussing grandeur, Demetrius writes, "Any darkly-hinting expression is more terror-striking, and its import is variously conjectured by different hearers. . . . Hence the Mysteries are revealed in an allegorical form in order to inspire such shuddering and awe as are associated with darkness and night. Allegory also is not unlike darkness and night." Longinian sublimity likewise possesses strong sacral overtones. It lifts the hearers "near the mighty mind of God" (36.1) and intimates "the object of our creation" (35.3). Sublimity springs from "an unconquerable passion for whatever is great and more divine than ourselves" (35.2). Such joyous transport is essentially a contemplative rather than a practical emotion; to use Aristotle's terms, we respond as spectators, not judges (1.3.1–2). This spiritualization of the grand style culminates in Hermogenes, who had a crucial influence on both Byzantine and Renaissance sacred prose. Solemnity, the first subdivision of Grandeur (*megethos*), treats God and the divine attributes. Using gnomic sayings, prophetic assertion, and allegory, it seems oracular and mystical (pp. 243–74). As we shall see, this version

[70] Demetrius 100–101, Dionysius of Halicarnassus, "Demosthenes" 22; Hermogenes, pp. 246–47.

of the grand style strongly appealed to Renaissance Christians, for whom it provided a theoretical basis for the parabolic, prophetic darkness of Holy Scripture and its fusion of verbal simplicity with intense elevation.

The hellenistic grand style also incorporates distinctly epideictic emotions. For Hermogenes, splendor and solemnity flourish in epideictic oratory (pp. 386–88). Whereas Cicero associates wonder with the genus medium, in hellenistic rhetoric it becomes a crucial aspect of the grand style. Chapters thirty-five and thirty-six of *On the Sublime* constantly refer to man's wonder in beholding the great and unusual phenomena of nature and literature; it is man's reaction to the sublime in all its manifestations. "What is useful and indeed necessary is cheap enough; it is always the unusual which wins our wonder" (35.5). Likewise, discussing grandeur, Demetrius writes, "But everything ordinary is trivial, and so fails to win admiration" (60; cf. also 77). This linking of wonder (or admiration) with solemnity and sublimity reinforces the religious subcurrents of the hellenistic grand style, pushing it closer to epideixis and contemplative passion.

Unlike the more unitary Roman grand style, its hellenistic equivalent tends to divide into two distinct subtypes, one characterized by elevation, the other by force. This is most obvious in Demetrius, who posits grandeur and forcefulness as two separate characters, respectively exemplified by Thucydides and Demosthenes. Although Demetrius distinguishes the two only with some difficulty, it would seem that grandeur remains closer to the epideictic, contemplative pole of the grand style, forcefulness to the practical and political. A similar distinction appears in Hermogenes, where two of the subdivisions of the Idea of Grandeur—asperity and vehemence—belong to forensic oratory, while two others—solemnity and splendor—appear principally in epideictic. Dionysius and Longinus also distinguish the lofty, dignified grandeur of Isocrates from the passion and power of practical oratory.[71] This split seems to reflect the double origins of the grand style: on the one hand, the anti-Isocratic tradition

[71] Dionysius of Halicarnassus, "Isocrates" 3; Longinus 8.2; Bonner, *Dionysius of Halicarnassus*, p. 49; Quadlbauer, "Die genera dicendi," p. 96.

opposing forensic power to Isocrates' beauty and refinement; on the other, the early dramatic criticism, which distinguishes the solemn and lofty tragic style from comic realism. Thus Demetrius states that force is the opposite of polish, but grandeur of plainness (36, 258).

The forcible style more closely resembles the Roman *genus grande* than does the elevated, but crucial stylistic differences separate both hellenistic types from their Latin counterpart—differences that play a major role in the development of Renaissance rhetoric. Basically, hellenistic rhetoric eliminates copia, balance, and smoothness in the grand style, and weakens the demands for *ornatus* and clarity. Instead, it is harsh and rough, avoiding smoothness of sound, parallelism, and balanced antithesis.[72] It tends to be a brief, highly compressed style,[73] either employing short phrases that avoid periodicity altogether or using only brief, curtailed periods.[74] Rather than copia, the hellenistic grand style emphasizes a dense compactness, compressing numerous ideas into a single period.[75] It is therefore pregnant and suggestive rather than clear, often complicating syntax by long parentheses, grammatical inversion, disordered syntax, and absence of transitions.[76] These complications, in turn, defeat symmetry; instead, one finds frequent changes in construction, lack of grammatical agreement, hyberbaton, and unexpected combinations of clauses.[77] The roughness, brevity, and asymmetry of this grand style imitates the natural disorder of passionate discourse. It seems spontaneous and sincere, unlike the premeditated harmo-

[72] Demetrius 48, 241, 246, 255; Dionysius of Halicarnassus, "Demetrius" 20; Hermogenes, pp. 259–60, 359.

[73] Grandeur, Demetrius's first character of style, however, uses long members and rounded composition (44–45).

[74] Demetrius 241, 252; Dionysius of Halicarnassus, "Demosthenes" 39; Hermogenes, pp. 250–51.

[75] Demetrius 103, 241–43; Dionysius of Halicarnassus, "Thucydides" 24; Hermogenes, p. 294.

[76] Demetrius 53; Dionysius of Halicarnassus, "Demosthenes" 39; "Thucydides" 24; Hermogenes, pp. 282, 357.

[77] Demetrius 53; Dionysius of Halicarnassus, "Demosthenes" 39; "Thucydides" 24; *On Literary Composition*, pp. 213, 233; Longinus 22.1.

nies of Isocrates.[78] In addition, some forms of the hellenistic grand style are quite simple, using direct word order and little or no figural elaboration. Hermogenes' solemnity and the sublime both reside principally in qualities of thought and emotion rather than in any devices of elocutio. Solemnity is utterly plain, while sublimity often uses, but does not need, the supports of figure, trope, and composition. In the Latin tradition, it is not until Saint Augustine that we find so decisive a distinction between passionate grandeur and ornatus.

The differences between the Roman and hellenistic grand styles have significant ramifications for the interpretation of Renaissance rhetoric. Post-Classical Greek rhetorics adumbrate a version of the genus grande that is neither copious nor oral nor civic, but instead accentuates passionate numinosity, wonder, intellectual density, roughness, and asymmetry. They tend to replace persuasion with transport as the effect of the grand style: transport being more closely connected with religion, poetry, and epideixis than with the immediate judgments urged in practial oratory. If the hellenistic grand style differs sharply from the Ciceronian, it also unmistakably resembles the characteristics Croll and others have noted in baroque prose. Croll associated these characteristics with the plain style, but now an interesting alternative emerges. The widespread popularity of hellenistic rhetoric, especially after 1600, suggests the possibility that it may be an important influence on at least some aspects of seventeenth-century prose, that the baroque "plain style"—which even Croll admitted is not really plain at all—may derive from the hellenistic grand style. Before turning to the Renaissance, however, the last and greatest revision of ancient culture remains to be considered with respect to its influence on the rhetorical tradition.

Augustine and the Transformation of
Classical Rhetoric

The decisive influence on Renaissance rhetoric was neither hellenism nor Ciceronianism but Christianity. Not surprisingly, Au-

gustine is the principal figure in the adaptation of Classical rhetoric to Christian purposes, not only in his explicit discussions of
rhetoric but also through the implications of his psychology. Augustine's only extensive discussion of sacred rhetoric appears in
the fourth book of *De doctrina Christiana*, probably composed in
427.[79] The book is a defense of Christian rhetoric, a reply to the
influential current of patristic opinion that denied Christian
themes needed Classical eloquence. The defense, however, is
carefully hedged. Augustine has little interest in the rules of rhetoric, arguing that one becomes eloquent not by studying rhetorics but by hearing and reading eloquent models. Furthermore,
human eloquence alone cannot persuade. The Christian speaker
must pray that "God may place a good speech in his mouth"
(4.63), for he becomes eloquent "more through the piety of his
prayers than through the skill of his oratory" (4.32). Yet Augustine insists that the necessity of grace does not imply that art and
learning are futile. The analogy he uses to exemplify their com-
patibility is instructively odd: "Medicines for the body which are
administered to men by men do not help them unless health is
conferred by God, who can cure without them; yet they are
nevertheless applied even though they are useless without His
aid. And if they are applied courteously, they are considered to be
among works of mercy or kindness" (4.33).[80] Modern people
tend to think of causation as efficient and mechanical (i.e., lever

---

[79] Stanley Fish explores the relation between grace and art in his discussion of
Saint Augustine in *Self-Consuming Artifacts*, pp. 21–43. On Saint Augustine, see
Auerbach, *Literary Language*; J. J. Murphy, *Rhetoric in the Middle Ages: A History
of Rhetorical Theory from St. Augustine to the Renaissance* (Berkeley, 1974), pp. 43–
64; Henri Marrou, *Saint Augustin et la fin de la culture antique* (Paris, 1938); Peter
Brown, *Augustine of Hippo: A Biography* (Berkeley, 1967), pp. 259–69.

[80] One finds a curious and rather late parallel to this notion of double causality
in Lancelot Andrewes: "Because the means work nothing of themselves, neither
can bread nourish without the staff of bread, which Christ calleth the word of
God; and unless that be added to the bread we shall decay. . . . And this is called
by philosophers, infusion into nature (*A Pattern of Catechistical Doctrine, The Works
of Lancelot Andrewes*, 11 vols. [Oxford, 1854], 6: 35–36). Augustine's and Andrewes's God is very different from Locke's watchmaker. Yet despite the fact that
God alone can make the bread nourish—and presumably could nourish without
the bread—the Bishop of Winchester is not reported to have given up eating.

A hits gear B, etc.); understood in this sense, if grace causes eloquence then rhetoric is unnecessary, just as if antibiotics cause
health then prayer is superfluous. But the ancient theory of causality allowed for different *types* of causation (e.g., Aristotle's material, formal, efficient, and final causes), which were not exclusive but copresent and which could be noncorporeal as well as
mechanistic.[81] This is why, in a different context, Augustine
could affirm both predestination and free will. Yet by the Renaissance, this pluralistic causality had begun to yield to a mechanistic
monism. In theology this leads to polarization of Molinarist free
will versus Calvinist (and Jansenist) determinism, and in sacred
rhetoric to the rejection of art and, among the more radical sec-
tarians, learning, in the name of grace.[82]

Along with his endeavor to show the value of eloquence, Augustine sketches the major types of Christian rhetoric. This classification is especially pertinent, since it derives from Cicero's
genera dicendi. In most Roman rhetorics, the genera dicendi are
only one topic among many (e.g., invention, status-theory, figures); in Augustine they become the central rhetorical categories.
Although he borrows the Ciceronian genera (low, middle, high)
and officia (to teach, delight, and move), Augustine's treatment
differs significantly from his predecessor's. The plain style drops
all traces of conversational urbanity, becoming more strictly dialectical and analytic. The middle style loses the aura of sophistic
aestheticism; instead, it delights the hearer and by praising God
and the saints draws its audience to love what is truly good. Augustine's grand style likewise sheds the full artistic elaboration of
its Ciceronian counterpart. It differs from other genera not in
amount of verbal ornament but by being more "forceful with
emotions of the spirit" (4.42). Its passion arouses tears rather than
applause (4.53). Yet while Augustine makes passion the essential

[81] See Owen Barfield, *Saving the Appearances: A Study in Idolatry* (New York,
n.d.).

[82] Similarly, the Classical balance between *ingenium* and *ars* becomes polarized
into the dichotomy of originality or imitation. Although this fragmentation
reached its peak in the late eighteenth century (the age of mechanism, par excellence), the strain can be felt as early as Politian's comment that he would rather
express himself than Cicero.

characteristic of the grand style, he generally follows Cicero in re-
stricting that passion to the forensic modes of invective and reproof. The grand style directs itself against those who know the
truth yet do not obey it; it attacks the obstinate and stubborn. (In
fact, there are difficulties in Augustine's description of the grand
style, which we will discuss shortly.)

In addition, Augustine departs sharply from Cicero in his
treatment of decorum. He begins by quoting the passage from
the *Orator*: " 'He therefore will be eloquent who can speak of small
things in a subdued manner, of moderate things in a temperate
manner, and of grand things in a grand manner' " (4.34). But he
goes on to deny that the Christian genera dicendi derive from the
ostensible importance of their subjects: "[For] among our orators
. . . everything we say . . . must be referred, not to the temporal
welfare of man, but to his eternal welfare and to the avoidance of
eternal punishment, so that everything we say is of great importance, even to the extent that pecuniary matters, whether they
concern loss or gain, or large or small amounts of money, should
not be considered 'small' when they are discussed by the Christian teacher" (4.35). For Augustine, therefore, style apparently
depends on function, not subject. The same subject will require
the plain style if one is trying to teach, or the grand style, if attempting to move. But, as Augustine's examples make clear, this
alteration does not totally deny the link between subject and
style. Two farthings or a glass of water can be treated in the grand
style precisely because they are matters of the highest importance. Augustine must redefine the relation between subject and
style because he accepts the principle that the grand style deals
with things of greatest value. He thus retains the triple decorum
of style, subject, and effect, while radically altering the concept
of value. But the result of this change was to open the way for a
Christian grand style—a grand style not restricted to the kings
and warriors of neo-Classical decorum, but one that could embrace fishermen, carpenters, and old women.

Augustine's most important contribution to the Christian
grand style, however, lies in his analysis of the emotions. Ancient
thought tends to set reason and emotion in opposition, with the
result that passionate oratory appears inherently deceptive, a de-

vice for bypassing and negating rational argument. This distrust of *pathos* lies behind Plato's suspicion of both rhetoric and poetry.[83] In Aristotle the situation is more ambiguous. While he lifts pathos to the status of proof, alongside *ethos* and argument, Aristotle repeatedly condemns its use in forensic oratory as subverting justice and truth. Ideally, practical oratory should rely on reasoning and evidence alone; all other forms of persuasion are merely concessions to the audience's corruption.[84] The problem of justifying passionate oratory arises again in Roman rhetoric, although in a more muted form. Both Cicero and Quintilian defend an ideal unity of wisdom and eloquence[85] but cannot escape the old bifurcation of reason and emotion. In *De oratore* Antonius repeatedly claims that oratory substitutes emotional persuasion for reasoned conviction and that it plays upon the opinions and desires of an ignorant populace—claims that Crassus does not directly answer.[86] Quintilian's discussion of emotion in the sixth book of the *Institutes* begins in a revealing manner:

> But the peculiar task of the orator arises when the minds of the judges require force to move them, and their thoughts have actually to be led away from the contemplation of the truth. . . . For as soon as they begin to be angry, to feel favourably disposed, to hate or pity, they begin to take a personal interest in the case, and just as lovers are incapable of forming a reasoned judgment on the beauty of the object of their affections, because passion forestalls the sense of sight, so the judge, when overcome by his emotions, abandons all attempt to enquire into the truth of the arguments, is swept along by the tide of passion, and yields himself unquestioning to the torrent. (6.2.5–6)

In other words, the purpose of passionate oratory is to deceive. This function allows the grand style a very doubtful legitimacy, as philosophers in all eras have been quick to point out,[87] but it is

[83] Onians, *Art and Thought*, p. 54; de Romilly, *Magic and Rhetoric*, p. 25.

[84] Aristotle, *Rhetoric* 1.1.4–6, 3.1.5–6, 3.7.4–5; see also W. W. Fortenbaugh, *Aristotle on Emotion* (New York, 1975), pp. 9, 17; Solmsen, "The Aristotelian Tradition," p. 39.

[85] Cicero, *De oratore* 3.54–57; *Orator* 15; Quintilian 2.16.8–10.

[86] Cicero, *De oratore* 1.221, 2.30–32, 2.159, 2.178, 2.201, 2.214; *Part orat* 19.

[87] See Brian Vickers, "Territorial Disputes: Philosophy versus Rhetoric," *Rhet-*

the inevitable result of ancient psychology, which viewed the emotions as at best subrational and at worst diseases. Stoic psychology, in particular, deeply mistrusted the emotions, and its pervasive influence on post-Classical antiquity made any justification of the grand style, except on the grounds of audience imbecility, unlikely.

Augustine offers two solutions to this dilemma. The first and simpler appears in his description of the grand style in *De doctrina Christiana*. According to Augustine, "grand eloquence . . . [moves] the minds of listeners, not that they may know what is to be done, but that they may do what they already know should be done" (4.27). Argument and *pathos* are therefore wholly distinct, the former concerned with persuading the judgment that something is true, the latter—operating subsequent to this rational conviction—directed toward arousing the will to follow judgment. By distinguishing reason from volition, argument from pathos, Augustine resolves the epistemological status of the grand style. It does not circumvent rationality but enables it, stirring the will to desire what the mind already approves.

Outside a rhetorical context, Augustine offers another, more fundamental analysis of the role of the emotions. In the central books of *De civitate Dei*, he jettisons the Classical intellectualist tradition with its hierarchical faculty psychology in favor of a more unified picture of mental activity, one in which feeling, willing, and loving become closely interrelated. The emotions, he writes, "are all essentially acts of the will," for as the will is attracted or repelled by different objects, "so it changes and turns into feelings of various kinds" (14.6). Volition, subjectively experienced, is emotion, and Augustine uses the term "love" to denote this affective and volitional orientation of the self toward the desired object (14.7). Affectivity, instead of being an irrational perturbation, thus moves into the center of spiritual experience.[88]

oric Revalued, ed. B. Vickers, *Medieval and Renaissance Texts and Studies* 19 (Binghamton, N.Y., 1982), pp. 247–66.

[88] William Bouwsma, "The Two Faces of Humanism: Stoicism and Augustinianism in Renaissance Thought," *Itinerarium Italicum: The Profile of the Italian Renaissance in the Mirror of its European Transformations*, ed. Heiko A. Oberman with Thomas Brady, Jr. (Leiden, 1975), pp. 10–11.

The emotions springing from a rightly directed will—love of God and neighbor, the desire for eternal life, penitential sorrow—are inseparable from holiness (9.5, 14.9). The angels and the blessed, even Christ himself, feel joy, sorrow, love, and compassion.[89] Affectivity thus suffuses Christian existence. Rather than undermining rational judgment, it wings the mind's search for God and truth.[90] As Augustine writes in the *Confessions*, "my weight is my love; wherever I am carried, it is my love that carries me there. By your gift we are set on fire and are carried upward; we are red hot and we go" (13.9).[91]

Athough Augustine himself never connects the psychology of

---

[89] *De civitate Dei* 9.5, 10.7, 14.9. See also Tertullian, *De anima*, ed. J. H. Waszink (Amsterdam, 1947): 16.4–5. Tertullian writes, "Ecce enim tota haec trinitas [i.e., the Platonic tripartite soul] et in domino: et rationale, quo docet, quo disserit, quo salutis vias sternit, et indignativum, quo invehitur in scribas et Pharisaeos, et concupiscentivum, quo pascha cum discipulis suis edere concupiscit."

[90] *Confessions* 1.1.

[91] Medieval scholastic psychology is closer than Saint Augustine to the Classical position. While Saint Thomas criticizes Stoic apathy and maintains that the moral virtues cannot exist without passion (*ST* 1a.2ae.59,2–5), he locates the emotions in the sensitive soul, firmly separating them from the will or intellective appetite (*ST* 1a.2ae.22,3). Angels and purely spiritual substances feel no emotions, nor does Saint Thomas ever discuss emotion when analyzing the theological virtues, although it is central to his treatment of moral virtue. The emotions are aroused only by specific, sensible goods, while the will embraces good as such. He thus avoids Augustine's spiritualization of affect. In the Renaissance, Roman Catholic rhetorics tend to fuse Thomistic and Augustinian psychologies with perplexing results. Thus one will find a definition of emotion as the irascible and concupiscent motions of the sensitive soul, but the first emotion individually considered turns out to be the love of God (e.g., Nicholas Caussin, *De eloquentia sacra et humana, libri XVI* [la Fleche, 1617? repr. Paris, 1630], pp. 460, 484).

Augustinian psychology, however, persists in the traditions of monastic spirituality. William of Saint Thierry, friend and contemporary of Saint Bernard, thus writes that by love "the Creator is sensed by the creature. . . ." Reason and love "help each other, and reason teaches love and love illumines reason, when reason moves along into the affect of love and love agrees to be confined within the limits of reason" (cited in E. Rozanne Elder, "William of St. Thierry: Rational and Affective Spirituality," *The Spirituality of Western Christendom* [Kalamazoo, 1976], pp. 97, 90. See also H. M. Gardiner et al., *Feeling and Emotion: A History of Theories* [New York, 1937], pp. 100–104). For the continuation of Augustinian psychology in the later Middle Ages, see Steven Ozment, *The Age of Reform: 1250–1550* (New Haven, 1980), pp. 74–80.

De civitate Dei with rhetorical issues, the implications of his treatment of the emotions underlie numerous later discussions of Christian eloquence. Because volition and affect are inseparable, passionate oratory, oratory that moves the emotions and loves of the soul, becomes a powerful instrument of redemption. The grand style dominates Renaissance sacred rhetorics because it alone can transform the will and heart, turning them toward love of God and neighbor. But precisely because affective experience possesses such spiritual import, the claim that rhetoric can determine and compel emotional response seems rather dangerous. Christian holiness is a gift of grace not a product of artistic manipulation. Augustine, and subsequent Christian rhetoricians, therefore insist that true passion and eloquence flow from the interior motions of the Holy Spirit stirring the speaker's heart and inflaming his words. Rhetoric as artistic technique becomes correspondingly superfluous. Here we have the beginnings of the paradoxical "passionate plain style" prevalent in the Middle Ages and more conservative Renaissance homiletics. Neither Augustine nor the more liberal Renaissance rhetorics, however, wholly reject the deliberate devices of trope, figure, rhythm, and amplification but instead attempt to establish a perennially uneasy balance between art and grace. Augustine thus argues that while the grand style often "uses almost all of the ornaments, it does not seek them if it does not need them. . . . It is enough for the matter being discussed that the appropriateness of the words be determined by the ardor of the heart rather than by careful choice."[92] As in Longinus and Hermogenes, the genus grave may exist in a wholly unornamented form—although it often does not. Significantly, for all three, it is still the grand style, because elevation of thought and intensity of feeling, not artistic elaboration, define this genus.

Finally, the specific emotions discussed in *De civitate Dei* differ from those generally treated in Latin rhetoric. Instead of anger and pity, Augustine mentions love, joy, hope, sorrow, and desire (14.7, 14.9). In addition, like the hellenistic rhetors, he extends the scope of the grand style to include sacred and contemplative

[92] *On Christian Doctrine* 4.42; cf. 4.32–33.

emotion. The passages from Holy Scripture cited in *De doctrina* express Paul's exultant joy in the certitude of faith, heroic charity, ardent apprehension of the paradoxes of the Gospel, and triumphant expectation (4.42–43). But there is a problem here. Following his Latin sources, in *De doctrina* Augustine several times seems to restrict the grand style to ethical exhortation and reproof of sinners (4.6, 4.29, 4.38). Preachers use the grand style to stir the will to *act* upon reason's dictates and to denounce sin. The patristic examples of the grand style seem strongly forensic; they are invectives against cosmetics (4.49–50). *De doctrina*, in fact, seems strangely inconsistent in its depiction of the grand style. On the one hand, its passion embraces the whole range of Christian spirituality, on the other, it resembles the forensic *genus grande* in its emphasis on praxis and reproof. This tension, which resembles the hellenistic division of the grand style into elevation and force, persists into the Renaissance, producing, at times, such notable incoherencies as that in Lodovico Carbo's *Divinus orator* (1595), which first describes the grand style as harsh, vehement, tragic, and copious and then quotes the opening of the Gospel according to John as an illustration.[93] Other Christian rhetorics, apparently recognizing this problem, divide the grand style into ethical and supernatural subtypes, the former characterized by gravity, the latter by majestic sublimity.[94]

The legacy of Augustinian rhetoric for the sacred grand style is both critical and problematic. He defended the legitimacy of sacred eloquence, created a decorum based on a Christian sense of value, and established a psychological foundation for the grand style. Yet Augustine's own description of the grand style often

[93] Ludovico Carbo, *Divinus orator, vel de rhetorica divina libri septem* (Venice, 1595), pp. 345, 349.

[94] For example, Alain de Lille, *Compendium on the Art of Preaching*, in *Readings in Medieval Rhetoric*, ed. Joseph Miller, Michael Prosser, and Thomas Benson (Bloomington, 1973), p. 230; Caussin, *De eloquentia*, pp. 964–69; Iacobus Lodovicus Strebaeus, *De verborum electione et collocatione oratoria . . . libri duo* (Basel, 1539), pp. 90–91. For the development of a celebratory Christian epideictic preaching during the Renaissance, see John O'Malley, *Praise and Blame in Renaissance Rome: Rhetoric, Doctrine, and Reform in the Sacred Orators of the Papal Court, c. 1450–1521*, Duke Monographs in Medieval and Renaissance Studies 3 (Durham, N.C., 1979).

seems narrowly forensic and accusatory, while the balances he sought between art and grace, style and subject proved fragile. In later rhetorics, art and grace thus tend to split into antitheses and the genera dicendi often disappear altogether, leaving only their officia, without either stylistic or thematic correlates, as the sole criteria of decorum. Sacred rhetoric in the Renaissance rests on Augustine's understanding of the role of affective experience, but it also wrestles with the problems of broadening the grand style to include all that Augustine meant by such experience and of re-uniting Classical artistry and Christian grace.

The Christian Grand Style in the Middle Ages

In the eight centuries separating Isocrates and Augustine, the grand style evolves from a polished, elaborate written style, characterized by balance, acoustic symmetries, and poetic stateliness, to one more passionate, forceful, and harsh. Although the break with Isocratic ideals probably occurs in and soon after Isocrates' own lifetime, the major rhetorics of the late Republic and early Empire push the grand style even further in the direction of power and elevation. While Roman rhetorics continue the practical, agonistic tradition of popular oratory, the Greeks extend the grand style in the direction of sublimity, contemplative wonder, and quasi-religious transport. The Greek grand style, no longer exclusively oral, includes the asymmetric difficulty of Thucydides and Platonic solemnity. Despite these crucial differences, an underlying decorum of effect, subject, and language connects all the different versions of the grand style after Isocrates. It remains that style which uses the artistic resources of language to evoke the intensity of feeling commensurate with the most valuable subjects. If language, emotional effect, and subject matter fail to achieve this decorous interrelation, the result is either bombast or frigidity. Therefore, all ancient rhetorics vigorously oppose the sophistic notion that the purpose of artistic language is to give aesthetic pleasure or display the speaker's skill.[95] Instead, the or-

---

[95] This is a major difference between ancient rhetoric and poetics. To give aesthetic delight is always at least part of poetry's function. Poetry sugarcoats the pill; rhetoric forces it down your throat and holds your mouth shut.

naments of language, such as trope, figure, periodicity, and rhythm, acquire value as they create the desired emotional response. From the first century A.D. on, however, this triple decorum yields somewhat to an overriding preoccupation with effect. Longinus, Hermogenes, and Augustine thus allow the possibility of a simple yet intensely moving grand style. Augustine, in addition, severs the bond between subject and style. Because eternal life may hang on even a glass of water, all Christian subjects are of incalculable importance. Only the effect, therefore, whether to move, encourage, or teach, determines the appropriate style. This relaxation of decorum points, in turn, to the Christian rhetorics of the Middle Ages and from there to some of the central issues faced by the Renaissance.

Little Classical rhetoric survives into the Middle Ages outside of various late antique encyclopedias and compendiums. The great exception is Saint Augustine, whose *De doctrina* strongly influences the early medieval *ars praedicandi*, although not the secular rhetorics.[96] This medieval Augustinian tradition persists in the Renaissance's ecclesiastical rhetorics. While precise lines of transmission are hard to trace, partly because our picture of medieval rhetoric remains incomplete, partly because Renaissance authors tend to suppress medieval sources, these Augustinian treatises provide a background for several distinctive features in Renaissance conceptions of sacred discourse and the grand style.

The medieval preaching rhetorics sharply differ from the Classical tradition in that they contain almost no technical discussion of style or elocutio. Instead, they emphasize the ethical behavior required in the preacher, his preparation, and the purposes of preaching. What stylistic comments there are tend to be very general and closely related to questions of morality and function. If we examine these works for traces of the ancient characters of style, the results are rather surprising. The officium of the grand style often becomes the aim of all popular preaching; all sermons, except perhaps those addressed to a learned clerical audience, should be passionate and powerful, able to convert, inflame, and

[96] Franz Quadlbauer, *Die antike Theorie der genera dicendi im Lateinischen Mittelalter* (Vienna, 1962), pp. 19–20, 130–36, 159, 165.

uplift.[97] Yet the same medieval rhetorics generally insist that popular sermons should be simple, rough, and artless, not searching for verbal eloquence but desiring only the spiritual good of their hearers.[98] Here we have for the first time a passionate plain style in which emotional effect does not depend upon the resources of artistic language. Instead, effect resides squarely in psychological and theological operations. The passion of the sermon arises from the speaker's own ardor and from the activity of the Holy Spirit arousing his heart and giving efficacy to his words.[99] Guibert of Nogent (twelfth century) thus writes, "Let a prayer always precede the sermon, so that the soul may burn fervently with divine love; then let it proclaim what it has learned from God so as to inflame the hearts of all hearers with the same interior fire

[97] Humbert of Romans, o.p. (thirteenth century), *Treatise on Preaching*, ed. Walter M. Conlon, o.p.; trans. The Dominican Students, Province of St. Joseph (Westminster, Md., 1951), pp. 26, 82; *Aquinas-tract* in Harry Caplan, *Of Eloquence: Studies in Ancient and Medieval Rhetoric*, ed. Anne King and Helen North (Ithaca, 1970), p. 53; Guibert de Nogent (twelfth century) and Wibaldus of Stavelot (twelfth century) in *Readings in Medieval Rhetoric*, pp. 168, 213; Notker Labeo (eleventh century) and Roger Bacon (thirteenth century) in Quadlbauer, *Die antike Theorie*, pp. 56, 130–32. (Popular preaching must be distinguished from the thematic university sermon. The latter is logically intricate and designed only for a learned clerical audience.) Alastair Mannis notes that beginning in the twelfth century commentaries on the Bible likewise view it as appealing to the emotions and will (*Medieval Theory of Authorship: Scholastic Literary Attitudes in the Later Middle Ages* [London, 1984], pp. 49–50, 139). Despite—or perhaps because of—the abstruse subtlety of nominalism, late medieval scholasticism began to emphasize the affective aspects of theology, the Bible, and preaching.

[98] Guibert de Nogent, pp. 163–64, 177; Wibaldus of Stavelot, p. 212; Alain de Lille, p. 231 (all exerpted in *Readings in Medieval Rhetoric*); Humbert of Romans, *Treatise*, pp. 42–43; Thomas Walys (fourteenth century) cited in Helms, "Popular and Scholastic Styles"; Caplan, *Of Eloquence*, pp. 41, 81, 119; J. J. Murphy, *Rhetoric in the Middle Ages*, p. 282. Not all medieval rhetorics require a plain style. Wibaldus of Stavelot praises the eloquence of Saint Bernard (*Readings in Medieval Rhetoric*, p. 213) as does Robert of Basevorn (fourteenth century) (translated in J. J. Murphy's *Three Medieval Rhetorical Arts* [Berkeley, 1971], p. 131). Most medieval rhetorics, however, do not relate style and affect, and thus, despite their desire for forceful preaching, omit questions of elocutio.

[99] Humbert of Romans, *Treatise*, pp. 17, 30, 36; Guibert de Nogent, *Readings in Medieval Rhetoric*, p. 164; Notker Labeo, cited in Quadlbauer, *Die antike Theorie*, pp. 56–57.

which consumes it."[100] The principle that in order to move others, the speaker first must be moved himself appears, as we have seen, in Classical rhetoric, but in the Middle Ages it assumes a new importance as the only source of emotion and one linking the effects of language with the activity of God.[101] This stress on the speaker's own inspired passion reinforces the medieval tendency to deemphasize the role of eloquence; it becomes an ostentatious and self-congratulatory distraction from the impassionating Word.[102]

This brief summary of the fate of the grand style in medieval preaching manuals suggests their influence on the Renaissance. The notion that the speaker must feel the emotions he desires to evoke dominates the Christian rhetorics of this later period, appearing prominently even among such austere theorists as the Puritan, William Perkins, and the Restoration bishop and scientist, Gilbert Burnet. In addition, Renaissance ecclesiastical rhetorics borrow the medieval tendency to include almost all preaching within the officium of the grand style, with the result that the genera dicendi often disappear from these rhetorics. If all sermons should move as well as teach, the genera no longer provide a useful classificatory system. In the Renaissance this emphasis on passionate preaching develops in two directions. One, following medieval precedent, continues the tradition of the passionate plain style. Most vernacular rhetorics in England, for example, demand a powerful preaching stripped of all the refinements and sophistications of eloquence, its passion arising from the inherent forcefulness of the divine word and the preacher's ardor.[103] But a second, more liberal, Renaissance trend fuses the ideal of passion-

---

[100] Guibert de Nogent, *Readings in Medieval Rhetoric*, p. 168.

[101] Ibid., pp. 168, 175; Humbert of Romans, *Treatise*, p. 17; Margaret Jennings, C.S.J., "The *Ars componendi sermones* of Ranulph Hidgen," *Medieval Eloquence: Studies in the Theory and Practice of Medieval Rhetoric*, ed. J. J. Murphy (Berkeley, 1978), p. 115.

[102] Humbert of Romans, *Treatise*, pp. 32, 35; Caplan, *Of Eloquence*, p. 41; Guibert de Nogent, *Readings in Medieval Rhetoric*, p. 164.

[103] Although this distrust of artistic language appears most prominently in the strongly Protestant English rhetorics, it is not unknown among Roman Catholic writers. See Saint Francis de Sales, *On the Preacher and Preaching* [1604], trans. John K. Ryan (Chicago, 1964), pp. 32, 64.

ate preaching with the Classical requirements for the grand style, restoring the ancient principle of decorum. These rhetorics, which include most of the scholarly ecclesiastical treatises, thus devote considerable attention to the figures of thought, amplification, hypotyposis, and all the other aspects of elocutio, yet without abandoning the expressive and theological orientation of medieval Augustinianism. The next three chapters will explore the development of this attempt to pull together the Greek, Roman, and medieval strands of rhetorical theory to create a Christian grand style in which art and grace, eloquence and inspiration could cooperate.

CHAPTER TWO

THE HISTORY OF SACRED RHETORIC
IN THE RENAISSANCE

H AVING WORKED our way through antiquity and the Middle Ages, we are ready to explore the development of the grand style in Renaissance England. But immediately this project runs up against two problems. First, it is not at all obvious what texts belong to such an investigation. Most modern studies of English rhetorical history have restricted themselves to English vernacular rhetorics.[1] Yet this seems a misleadingly narrow approach. During the Renaissance, serious scholarship was usually in Latin. Furthermore, because the English presses lagged behind continental ones, Englishmen frequently used imported texts. The publication dates for Roman rhetoric immediately reveal the relative inferiority of the English presses. For example, before 1660 there are twenty-seven Parisian editions of Quintilian's *Institutes*, eleven Genevan ones, and only one English. During the same period, Cicero's mature rhetorical works are printed thirty-four times in Venice but in England only four times.[2] Unquestionably, Englishmen supplemented their libraries with foreign books, but scanty data obstruct efforts to ascertain which ones or to determine popularity with any precision. Second, before narrowing in on specific issues, the reader needs to have some broader perspective on the history of sacred rhetoric in the Renaissance. Yet there exists no reasonably comprehensive modern account of this subject, no reliable periodization or characteriza-

---

[1] For example see Williamson, *The Senecan Amble*; Adolph, *The Rise of Modern Prose Style*; Wilbur Samuel Howell, *Logic and Rhetoric in England, 1500–1700* (Princeton, 1956); and Don Paul Abbott, "The Renaissance," in *The Present State of Scholarship in Historical and Contemporary Rhetoric*, ed. Winifred B. Horner (Columbia, Mo., 1983).

[2] Unless otherwise noted all statistics come from J. J. Murphy's *Renaissance Rhetoric: A Short-Title Catalogue* (New York, 1981).

tion of trends (except Ramism).[3] The major figures—men like
Flacius, Caussin, Keckermann, Vossius—remain virtually unknown. Therefore, it seems advisable at this point to sketch some
overview of the uncharted wilds of sacred rhetoric and to determine, as best the evidence will allow, which among the dozens of
pastoral guides, preaching manuals, biblical handbooks, and
comprehensive rhetorics written between 1450 and 1700 are relevant to the English Renaissance.

While a summary of these tens of thousands of pages would be
unnecessary and unmanageable, we can describe a more pertinent
taxonomy of sacred rhetoric by focusing on the development of
the Christian grand style and related issues, such as the psychology of emotion and the reception of hellenistic rhetoric. The resulting outline breaks down into six slightly overlapping periods.
Before Erasmus's seminal *Ecclesiastes* (1535), there are several unrelated but historically important attempts both to introduce hellenistic rhetoric to the West and to adapt Classical rhetoric to
Christian purposes. This early period culminates in *Ecclesiastes*,
the first full-scale (330 folio columns in the 1704 edition) Christian rhetoric. After Erasmus, the sixteenth-century sacred rhetorics divide into two separate traditions, the Protestant, which
owes much to Melanchthon's scattered speculations on preaching
as well as to medieval homiletics, and the Tridentine, which continues Erasmus's liberal Christian humanism. Beginning with Johann Sturm's endless volumes in the last quarter of the sixteenth
century, a fourth strand emerges in the form of scholarly general
rhetorics treating both secular and sacred oratory and supported
by a vast, frequently hellenistic erudition. These general rhetorics
flourished into the first quarter of the seventeenth century and

[3] For works dealing with these neo-Latin rhetorics, see John W. O'Malley, s.j.,
Praise and Blame, and his "Content and Rhetorical Forms in Sixteenth-Century
Treatises on Preaching," *Renaissance Eloquence*; Peter Bayley, *French Pulpit Oratory, 1598–1650* (Cambridge, 1980); Marc Fumaroli, *L'Age de l'éloquence: Rhetorique et "res literaria" de la Renaissance au seuil de l'époque classique* (Geneva, 1980);
John Monfasani, *George of Trebizond*, and his "The Byzantine Rhetorical Tradition and the Renaissance," *Renaissance Eloquence*; Heinrich Franz Plett, *Der Affecktrhetorische Wirkungsbegriff in der Rhetorisch-Poetischen Theorie der Englischen Renaissance* (Bonn, 1970); William P. Sandford, "English Rhetoric Reverts to
Classicism, 1600–1650," *The Quarterly Journal of Speech* 15 (1929): 503–25.

were widely used in England. Also in the early seventeenth century, a new, more liberal Protestant rhetoric appears, one incorporating the Tridentines' sacred classicism and a sophisticated understanding of scriptural rhetoric. After the middle of the seventeenth century, the neo-Latin tradition of the Christian grand style gradually dies out. Some of its achievements begin to appear in the vernacular, but most late seventeenth-century English rhetoric moves in the direction of the plain style and away from the Augustinian psychology of the emotions that sustained sacred rhetoric for a millennium. Yet the premises of this tradition persisted, so that even in the mid-eighteenth century we find Pope writing, "the high style that is affected in so much blank verse would not have been borne even in Milton, had not his subject turned so much on strange out-of-the-world things as it does."[4] While Pope's scarcely veiled dislike for the "high style" places him outside the traditions of Renaissance rhetoric, he remains cognizant of its central assumption—that Christian supernaturalism requires the passionate elevation of the grand style.

All periodization is a kind of fiction. The fact that the early Italian Renaissance predates Chaucer or that Pope and Bach are contemporaries is inexcusable to the categorical mind. Renaissance rhetoric likewise fails to fall neatly into a linear sequence. The six stages just sketched are offered only as rough generalizations, useful for ordering the vast amount of available material. Writing a history of Classical rhetoric is a comparatively easy task because we have so few facts to complicate our theories: eleven major Classical rhetoricians covering eight centuries. The history of Renaissance rhetoric, however, lacks a clear shape precisely because it must take into account the heterogeneous multiplicity of extant texts. Even though the Christian grand style flourished for only two centuries, the bibliography of primary sources for this study includes over seventy-five different authors. In literary studies, canon formation has simplified and shaped tradition. For example, in early seventeenth-century poetry we isolate the styles

---

[4] Quoted in Joseph Spence's *Observations, and Characters, of Books and Men*, ed. James M. Osborn, 2 vols. (Oxford, 1966), 1: 173. I would like to thank Donna Landry for providing me with this quotation.

of Jonson, Donne, and their successors to form the conventional distinction between neo-Classicists and Metaphysicals. But the early seventeenth century also housed the Fletchers, Greville, Carew, Drayton, and Crashaw, whose existence, if considered, would blur any convenient schematization. The study of sacred rhetoric differs from that of poetry because it has not yet achieved a canonical simplification. Although I have attempted to emphasize texts that on historical or intrinsic grounds seem most valuable, I have also tried not to be prematurely selective. The results may be somewhat confusing.

Furthermore, this overview does not pretend to capture the actual causal links determining historical development. As Fumaroli has shown, the development of French rhetoric is closely tied to political rivalries and power struggles.[5] But books, we know, have a way of establishing a more or less ideal order among themselves. When French rhetorics migrated to England, they did not take their cultural contexts with them. Since we are dealing not only with French but also with English, German, Italian, and Dutch rhetorics *in England*, their original contexts and with them the immediate circumstances of their composition become irrelevant. These six periods, therefore, sometimes represent if not an ideal then an internal order—one based on similarities between groups of texts—sometimes mere chronological convenience (as in the first and last periods). Yet I think it is unlikely that a more coherent ordering could be found without silently suppressing whatever did not fit the preordained pattern. The advantage of rather loose periodization is that it is not embarrassed by exceptions.

The Seminal Period (c. 1450–1535)

This earliest period presents us with several texts that lay the foundation for the sacred rhetorics of the following centuries by introducing hellenistic rhetoric to Europe, beginning the Christianization of Classical theory, and suggesting new understandings of crucial concepts like passion and delight. The first of

[5] See *L'Age de l'éloquence* and "Rhetoric, Politics, and Society."

these, George of Trebizond's *Rhetoricorum libri V* was first published in 1433/1434 and, after going through at least seven Renaissance editions, continued to be cited into the late eighteenth
century.[6] This is a secular not a sacred rhetoric, but of crucial importance for the latter because, for the first time, Trebizond
makes available in Latin a detailed account of Hermogenes' *On
Ideas*, which will have a major influence on subsequent sacred
rhetorics.[7] The potential link between Hermogenic and Christian
rhetoric briefly surfaces in one of Trebizond's few references to
religion. In speaking of solemnity (which he translates as *digni-
tas*), Trebizond remarks, "Our, that is, Christian books are full
[of this]."[8] Trebizond thus locates sacred discourse not under
simplicity or verity but under solemn grandeur. As we shall see,
Hermogenes' solemnity later becomes a principal element in the
Christian grand style. While Trebizond does not explore this
connection, he does note the philosophic grandeur characteristic
of solemnity, which he, like Hermogenes, associates with epideictic oratory, Plato, and poetry.[9] Again following Hermogenes, Trebizond breaks with Ciceronian theory by dropping forensic oratory from the grand style.[10] His division of oratory into
the forensic and quiet modes is therefore not parallel to the distinction between the grand style and the middle style, as it is in
Cicero. Instead, epideictic oratory, which includes philosophic
and theological discourse, moves to the center of the Idea of
Grandeur. Finally, Trebizond again departs from Ciceronian
rhetoric by divorcing grandeur from emotion. There is no equivalent to *movere* in Hermogenic theory, which does not consider
style in terms of its effect on the audience. When Trebizond treats
emotion, he thinks of it in terms of expressivity not of effect. The
oration should "expose (*denudere*) the character and emotions" of

[6] Monfasani, *George of Trebizond*, p. 261. Johann Ernesti's *Lexicon technologiae
latinorum rhetoricae* (Leipzig, 1797) also cites Trebizond as an authority. See, for
example, pp. 125, 379.

[7] For the influence of Hermogenes, see Monfasani's *George of Trebizond* and
"The Byzantine Rhetorical Tradition," and Patterson's *Hermogenes*.

[8] *Georgii Trapezuntii rhetoricorum libri V* (Paris, 1538), p. 532.

[9] Ibid., pp. 532–33, 622–23.

[10] Ibid., pp. 618–19.

the speaker.[11] This emphasis on expressivity will reinforce the Renaissance tendency to locate the grand style in the inner ardor of the speaker as well as in the artistic resources of language, a tendency often associated with the sublime.[12]

Two other fifteenth-century works also contribute to a new, non-Ciceronian interpretation of epideixis and emotion. The epistolary rhetoric, *De ratione scribendi libri tres*, of the Italian humanist, Aurelio Brandolini (written before 1497/1498 but not published until 1549), represents an early adaptation of Classical rhetorical theory for Christian purposes. These changes are particularly visible in his sections on epideictic or demonstrative oratory, because Brandolini believes that most sacred oratory belongs to this branch of rhetoric.[13] He first denies that *delectare* constitutes a separate end or officium, since delectare is actually a part of movere: "For what else is *delectare* than to arouse the mind to happiness, to pleasure, to desire, to hope, and other emotions?"[14] Demonstrative oratory, traditionally associated with delectare, becomes for Brandolini the characteristic form of Christian preaching. It stirs men to the "wonder and contemplation" of the central mysteries of faith, serves for the praise of God and his saints, awakening "admiration and veneration" for truths surpassing human reason.[15] Although Brandolini was probably more influenced by contemporary practice than hellenistic theory,[16] his emphasis on contemplation and wonder corresponds to Greek versions of the grand style. His scattered comments on preaching also display an emerging awareness of the gulf separating ancient from sacred rhetoric and of the need to create a distinctively Christian aesthetic based on its unique subject matter and the distinctive qualities of religious emotion.

[11] Ibid., p. 579.
[12] Fumaroli, *L'Age de l'éloquence*, pp. 61, 67–68.
[13] Aurelio Brandolini, *De ratione scribendi libri tres* (London, 1573), p. 105; O'Malley, *Praise and Blame*, pp. 39–49, 70–71.
[14] Brandolini, *De ratione scribendi*, p. 11.
[15] Ibid., pp. 94–95.
[16] Yet it seems likely that Brandolini had read Trebizond's rhetoric, and surely he knew the works of the great Byzantine preachers, which reflect hellenistic theory. On this latter point, see Kustas, *Studies in Byzantine Rhetoric*.

Both Trebizond and Brandolini were reprinted in the next century, but the most influential fifteenth-century treatise dealing with rhetoric was unquestionably Rudolph Agricola's (1443–1485) *De inventione dialectica libri tres*, which went through thirty-seven editions between 1480 and 1589. Agricola is usually considered merely as a precursor of Ramist logic, but he also makes several valuable observations on delight and emotion.[17] Like Brandolini, he widens the scope of delectare, although in a different direction. For Agricola, delight (*delectatio*) has both a sensory and an intellectual aspect. The senses delight in lovely objects like music, feasts, and spring, but the mind also delights in apprehending whatever is great, wonderful, and unexpected—such things as heroic deeds and lofty virtue.[18] This latter kind of delight resembles the wonder of the Longinian sublime. Both emphasize our joyous response to whatever is great and divine. Whereas in Roman rhetoric, delectatio refers to the aesthetic pleasure produced by the elaborate music of sophistic eloquence, in Agricola it becomes primarily cognitive and emotional. In later rhetorics this interpretation of delectatio is absorbed into the Christian grand style, broadening its emotional range to include awe, joy, and intellectual passion.

Agricola makes another set of distinctions that affect the future of rhetorical theory. He first divorces dialectic from rhetoric by associating the former with teaching (*docere*), the latter with moving and delighting (movere and delectare).[19] Here we clearly have a dialectical plain style. Having sheared rhetoric of its teaching function, Agricola goes on to lop off delectare as too subjective to permit methodical analysis.[20] Thus rhetoric is left with movere, the officium of the grand style. Instead, however, of opposing di-

---

[17] On Agricola as a proto-Ramist and his place in the history of logic, see Walter J. Ong, s.j., *Ramus, Method, and the Decay of Dialogue* (Cambridge, Mass., 1958), pp. 92–126; Marc Cogan, "Rodolphus Agricola and the Semantic Revolutions of the History of Invention," *Rhetorica* 2(1984): 163–94.

[18] Rudolph Agricola, *De inventione dialectica* (Cologne, 1523; repr. Frankfurt, 1967), pp. 394–95. (Note: the 1523 date must be wrong, for the notes by Alardus Amstelredamus refer repeatedly to Erasmus's *Ecclesiastes*, which was not published until 1535.)

[19] Ibid., p. 192.

[20] Ibid., p. 204.

alectic to rhetoric, teaching to moving, Agricola insists on their fundamental similarity. Both use the same *loci* of invention, the same lines of argument, although for different ends.[21] In fact, Agricola regularly considers emotional power as an aspect of invention rather than of elocutio or style. This is very un-Ramist but also very important for subsequent sacred rhetorics, which, like Agricola's, often conjoin teaching and moving. Instead of a strict bifurcation of rhetoric and dialectic, they describe a style that simultaneously moves and instructs. The genera dicendi disappear in many Renaissance rhetorics as delectare approaches movere and movere, docere—a collapse already perceptible in Augustine's *De doctrina Christiana*. Despite this disappearance, the result of fusing the characters of style is to move all sacred discourse in the direction of the grand style, because it is precisely by adding amplification, figures of thought, tropes, and the other attributes of the genus grande that instruction rises to passion.

Although not primarily concerned with Christian rhetoric, Trebizond, Brandolini, and Agricola all explore concepts of fundamental importance to the history of sacred oratory. The first humanistic sacred rhetoric, Johann Reuchlin's (1455–1522) *Liber congestorum de arte praedicandi* (1504), on the other hand, possesses much less intrinsic value. The treatise is twenty-odd pages long and contains a curious mix of Classical and scholastic elements. For example, Reuchlin defines the preacher as a "vir religiosus, dicendi peritus," but the three species of sermons are the tropological, allegorical, and anagogical.[22] Curiously, Reuchlin omits elocutio and dispositio from his list of the parts of preaching, treating organization under invention and dropping stylistic questions altogether, except for some brief advice on the necessity of hiding art.[23] The main purpose of the work seems to lie in its recommendation of a simplified oratorical structure instead of the intricate subdivisions of medieval university sermons.

The first decades of the sixteenth century are suprisingly barren of works dealing with sacred oratory. The only exception,

[21] Ibid., pp. 199–201.

[22] Joannis Reuchlin, *Liber congestorum de arte praedicandi*, reprinted in *De arte concionandi* (London, 1570), pp. 3–4.

[23] Ibid., p. 4.

Melanchthon's *Elementorum rhetorices libri duo* (1519), will be discussed with Melanchthon's other rhetorics in the next section. But in 1535 Erasmus published his last major work, *Ecclesiastes sive concionator evangelicus*, which went through twelve editions in the next twenty years.[24] *Ecclesiastes* is the first full-scale rhetoric since antiquity and the very first comprehensive preaching rhetoric. It still displays considerable medieval influences: a large proportion of the book concerns the moral life of the preacher; the very brief section on the genera dicendi follows the post-Classical habit of distinguishing the genera according to the excellence of the subject matter rather than according to elocutio; the Bible is treated as *humilis* yet concealing lofty mysteries beneath its unprepossessing language.[25] But Erasmus does not simply repeat and enlarge medieval precepts. *Ecclesiastes* offers a serious exploration of the theological foundations of Christian rhetoric, based on Augustinian theory but worked out in far more detail than in *De doctrina Christiana*.[26] Significantly, most of this theological groundwork pertains to the defense of passionate preaching. Erasmus probes the interrelation between the Holy Spirit, the preacher's own ardent expressivity, and affective discourse.[27] He distinguishes the forensic emotions of pity and fear from Christian joy, hope, sorrow, and love, like Augustine insisting upon the affective nature of spiritual experience.[28] From Augustine he also borrows a sense of close connection between love and knowledge to explain why the preacher needs to move as well as teach.[29] Erasmus departs from earlier tradition by connecting this psychological and religious analysis of the sources and functions of passionate preaching with an extensive treatment of elocutio that covers the various stylistic means for moving the emotions and

[24] See Ferdnand ven der Haeghen, *Bibliotheca Erasmiana: Repertoire des Oeuvres D'Erasme*, 1re série (Ghent, 1893); Robert Kleinhaus, *Erasmus' Doctrine of Preaching: A Study of the 'Ecclesiastes, sive De Ratione Concionandi'* (Ann Arbor, 1969), pp. 28–34.

[25] Desiderius Erasmus, *Ecclesiastes sive concionator evangelicus, Opera omnia*, 10 vols. (1705; repr. London, 1962), 5: 837f–838a, 1011d–f.

[26] Fumaroli, *L'Age de l'éloquence*, pp. 70, 135.

[27] *Ecclesiastes*, 5: 772e–774e, 790a, 835d, 982a–b.

[28] Ibid., 5: 799b, 951b–c, 976f–977c.

[29] Ibid., 5: 952b, 977a–c.

surveys the history of Christian rhetoric. These sections are distinctly unmedieval. Erasmus thoroughly dislikes the schematic
preaching of the Latin Fathers as well as the histrionics of late medieval popular sermons.[30] He relates with horror the story of how
a certain preacher used to raise aloft a crucifix filled with a liquid
red dye, which, at the most pathetic moments of the sermon,
gushed out from the hands and feet. As an alternative to verbal
play and theatrical vulgarity, Erasmus emphasizes the figures of
thought, vivid depiction of biblical scenes, dramatization, and
imagery.[31] These characteristics remain the essential features of
the Christian grand style through the seventeenth century. What
Erasmus has done, in fact, is to make the Christian grand style
possible. Even though medieval rhetorics praise affective preaching, it seems awkward to think of them as recommending the
grand style because they usually do not treat style at all except to
disparage it. Erasmus reconnects the theological and artistic aspects of sacred eloquence, like the Classical rhetoricians balancing
the awareness that one can move others only if moved oneself
with the recognition that certain figural tactics produce more or
less predictable emotional results. This integration of theology,
psychology, and language forms the core of the liberal tradition
in Renaissance sacred rhetoric, running from Erasmus through
the Tridentines to the seventeenth century general and Protestant
rhetorics.

Protestant Rhetoric in the Sixteenth Century

The Protestant rhetorics of the sixteenth century form a more
closely knit school linked by allusion and citation. Nicholas
Hemmingsen's *Pastor* (1562), for example, relies heavily on Melanchthon's sacred rhetorics, while William Perkins's *Art of
Prophesying* (1607, but Latin version printed in 1592) lists Hemmingsen, Andreas Hyperius, Matthias Flacius Illyricus, and Erasmus among its sources.[32] The connection between these works,

[30] Ibid., 5: 680d, 857c, 979e, 986e–987c, 1000c–e.
[31] Ibid., 983c–999e.
[32] William Perkins, "A Treatise Concerning the Only True Manner and Meth-

however, goes deeper than cross-referencing. They are Protestant not merely because they were written by Protestants but because they attempt to use reformed theology with its antithesis of law and grace, its emphasis on faith and the Holy Spirit, and its anti-sacramentalism as a basis for rhetorical theory. Yet despite their Protestantism, they remain closely allied to the medieval ars prae-dicandi. With the exception of Hyperius and Flacius, these rhet-orics belong to the tradition of the passionate plain style with its tendency to stress emotional power while repudiating those artis-tic devices designed to elevate and impassionate language.[33]

The development of Melanchthon's homiletic theory suggests the theological origins of Protestant rhetoric. Melanchthon, the first of the Protestant rhetoricians, begins not as a reformer but a humanist and, in fact, his views on secular eloquence remained humanistic long after his sacred rhetorics had diverged in a new direction.[34] The early *Elementorum rhetorices* may be the first gen-eral rhetoric of the Renaissance, since it strays repeatedly into re-ligious topics, although mainly dealing with secular rhetoric as a literary hermeneutic. In this work, Melanchthon introduces the fourth *genus causarum*, the *genus didaskalikon* or teaching oratory, which becomes a standard feature in subsequent Protestant and Catholic homiletics.[35] This genus, which like the demonstrative aims at cognition rather than praxis, develops out of the theolog-ical changes accompanying the Reformation and the subsequent

---

ode of Preaching," *The Workes of that Famous and Worthie Minister of Christ . . . M. William Perkins*, 3 vols. (Cambridge, 1609), 2: 762.

[33] Barbara Kiefer Lewalski writes in her *Protestant Poetics and the Seventeenth-Century Religious Lyric* (Princeton, 1979), "Perkins expects that such plain preach-ing, concerned to display God's Word unadorned, would achieve the most pow-erfully moving effect upon the hearers because of the power resident in the Word itself. The preacher becomes the vehicle for that power precisely *as* he avoids any display of rhetoric" (p. 225).

[34] Thus Melanchthon's famous defense of eloquence and humanistic letters in reply to Pico's censure dates from the very end of his life. For the text of this de-bate, see Quirinus Breen, "Three Renaissance Humanists on the Relation of Phi-losophy and Rhetoric," *Christianity and Humanism: Studies in the History of Ideas*, ed. Nelson Peter Ross (Grand Rapids, Mich., 1968).

[35] Philip Melanchthon, *Elementorum rhetorices libri duo, Corpus Reformatorum*, 28 vols., ed. Carolus Gotttlieb Bretschneider (Brunswick and Halle, 1834–1860), 13: 421.

need to re-teach people the rudiments of religion. Despite its name, the genus didaskalikon does not seem to be fixed in the plain style, for Melanchthon is aware that amplification and ornament are necessary because naked argument will not convince most people.[36] Like earlier Renaissance rhetorics, Melanchthon's work acknowledges the demise of judicial oratory and spiritualizes epideictic as suited for arousing contemplative wonder.[37]

After the discussion of the four genera causarum, the *Elementorum* progresses in two somewhat different directions. On the one hand, Melanchthon defends a liberal Ciceronianism against the flowery sententiousness of Pliny and Politian.[38] On the other, we see him beginning to struggle with the role of emotion in Christian rhetoric. He begins like Agricola by equating teaching with dialectic, moving with rhetoric. But these are uneasy alliances, since, as Melanchthon immediately admits, the orator must also teach,[39] and also since Melanchthon has reservations about the value of moving the emotions. At one point he thus compares emotional appeal to flattery.[40] Yet he accepts the necessity of pathos, particularly in adorning ethical commonplaces.[41] Moving the emotions is thus linked to moral action and deliberative oratory rather than to spiritual insight—a position Melanchthon rejects in his later writings. The germ for these later developments, however, also appears in the *Elementorum* where Melanchthon divides the will into two species, *impulsio* and *ratiocinatio*. The latter is simply the Aristotelian "willing the end," but impulsio is emotion.[42] Affect is thus part of the will, not the sensitive appetite. Here we see for the first time the influence of Augustine's psychology in *The City of God* flowing into rhetorical theory, displacing Classical (and Thomist) intellectualism.

---

[36] Ibid., 13: 421. For a discussion of the tortuous diffusion of the *genus didaskalikon* into Roman Catholic rhetoric, see John O'Malley, "Content and Rhetorical Forms," *Renaissance Eloquence*, pp. 245–46.

[37] Melanchthon, *Elementorum* 13: 423, 429.

[38] Ibid., 13: 503.

[39] Ibid., 13: 420.

[40] Ibid., 13: 436.

[41] Ibid., 13: 454.

[42] Ibid., 13: 434.

Melanchthon's sacred rhetorics develop a Protestant interpretation of Augustinian psychology. These rhetorics, written between 1529 and 1552, are brief, often fragmentary, attempts to create a homiletic theory based on reformed theology. Most were not intended for publication, although *De modo et arte concionandi* (*c.* 1537–1539) achieved considerable popularity and was reprinted throughout the century. They all share certain features fateful for much later Protestant rhetoric. They never mention the genera dicendi and rarely discuss language. Instead, Melanchthon warns against solicitude for eloquence and figural ornament; these distract from the sincerity of the preacher and the power of the Spirit.[43] In addition, he rejects demonstrative oratory out of hand, including sacred panegyric popular among papal preachers.[44] Ethical or hortatory preaching also becomes suspect. The minister must preach Christ not moral philosophy.[45]

Yet as the influence of Classical rhetoric wanes, the necessity for emotion comes to dominate Melanchthon's homiletic theory. *De officiis concionatoris* (1529) spiritualizes the Classical commonplace that the preacher must be moved to move others. Effective and powerful preaching springs from the personal experience of the Word and Spirit.[46] In *De modo et arte*, Melanchthon begins by dividing sermons into two categories, those that teach dogma and those that arouse the emotions either to faith and fear or to good works.[47] But immediately after treating dogmatic sermons, he adds that *all* preaching should arouse the emotions, for the end of preaching is "renovation and spiritual life" attained by "insert-

---

[43] Philip Melanchthon, "Quomodo concionator novitus concionem suam informare debeat," *Supplementa Melanchthoniana*, 5 vols., ed. Paul Drews and Ferdinand Cohrs (1929; repr. Frankfurt, 1968), 5,2: 25. The best single study of Melanchthon's sacred rhetoric is Uwe Schnell's *Die homiletische Theorie Philipp Melanchthons*, Arbeiten zur Geschichte und Theologie des Luthertums 20 (Berlin, 1968).

[44] Melanchthon, "De officiis concionatoris," *Supplementa* 5,2: 6. On panegyric preaching in Rome, see O'Malley, *Praise and Blame*.

[45] Melanchthon, "De officiis concionatoris," *Supplementa* 5,2: 6; Schnell, *Philipp Melanchthons*, p. 68.

[46] "De officiis concionatoris," *Supplementa* 5,2: 8, 13; Schnell, *Philipp Melanchthons*, pp. 69–70.

[47] "De modo et arte concionandi" (*c.* 1537–1539), *Supplementa* 5,2: 33.

ing better emotions into the soul."[48] The division between sermons that teach and those that move thus evaporates. All sermons must do both.[49] The emotions Melanchthon specifies have
a particular significance. In *De modo et arte* he writes, "in every
sermon of whatever kind, the speech (*oratio*) should aim at [arous-
ing] a certain emotion, namely fear of God or faith, or a related
emotion, such as patience or love."[50] Two points emerge here.
First, for Melanchthon, faith is an emotion. It is a firm trust (*fiducia*) in the mercy and promises of Christ, a movement not only
of the intellect but also of the heart and will.[51] Passionate preaching elicits this affective spirituality. Melanchthon does not differentiate dogmatic preaching from ethical as docere from movere
because both types are suffused with emotion. Movere thus relin-
quishes its exclusive connection with praxis, broadening to include the spiritual movements of the heart in its inward relation
to God. Second, Melanchthon's emphasis on fear and faith suggests the theological basis of his homiletic theory. Preaching of
the law awakens terror, a terror only consoled by faith in the
promises of Christ. The Protestant antithesis of law and gospel
thus structures affective preaching, a connection even more explicit in Melanchthon's late commentary on Timothy (1550/
1551), which categorizes sermons as teaching, warning, and con-
soling, the last two corresponding to the threats of the law and the
promises of Christ.[52] We have here, then, a wholly non-Classical
revision of rhetorical theory, one which endeavors to erect Christian preaching on the foundations of Reformation theology and
psychology.

The other Protestant rhetorics of the sixteenth century tend to
follow Melanchthon in dropping the genera dicendi and elocutio,
instead focusing on invention or the division of sermons into several "types" with the arguments appropriate for each and on the

---

[48] Ibid., 5,2: 51; Schnell, *Philipp Melanchthons*, p. 87.

[49] Schnell, *Philipp Melanchthons*, p. 95.

[50] "De modo et arte concionandi," *Supplementa* 5,2: 51.

[51] Schnell, *Philipp Melanchthons*, pp. 89–90. On the contrast between Melanchthon's Augustinianism and the neo-Stoicism of the Renaissance, see William
Bouwsma, "The Two Faces of Humanism."

[52] Schnell, *Philipp Melanchthons*, pp. 102–108.

emotional aims of preaching. Both in this century and the next, most Protestant rhetorics are of Lutheran origin. The subject never seemed to hold much attraction for Calvinists, which may be one reason why so few Englishmen contributed to this field. Several of the "Lutheran" rhetorics, however, were printed in England. Niel Hemmingsen's *Pastor* was translated as *The Preacher* in 1574, Andreas Hyperius's *De formandis concionibus sacris* as *The Practis of Preaching* in 1577. Brief treatises by Johannes Hepinus and Viet Dietrich appear in the original Latin in a 1570 collection of sacred rhetorics published in London.[53] Before Perkins's *The Art of Prophesying*, however, the only sacred rhetoric by an Englishman is the Ramist *Officium concionatoris*, published at Cambridge in 1567 and twice again during the Interregnum. Unfortunately, this is a dreary exercise in dichotomization and of little value.

These sixteenth-century rhetorics divide into more liberal or more conservative types. The former point toward the great neo-Latin Protestant rhetorics of the seventeenth century, the latter resemble more closely the vernacular English tradition. Yet both absorb elements of the grand style. While the more conservative rhetorics, such as Perkins's *The Art of Prophesying*, dismiss or ignore rhetorical eloquence in favor of a plain and spiritual preaching, they, like the medieval ars praedicandi, preserve two aspects of the Classical grand style: passion and expressivity.[54] As we have seen, the passionate plain style emerges when the Holy Spirit replaces language as the "prime mover" of the emotions.

[53] The collection, which also contains Reuchlin's little treatise, is called *De arte concionandi* and is first printed in Basel in 1540. O'Malley, "Content and Rhetorical Forms," gives Viet Dietrich as the author of the third treatise in the volume, which the 1570 edition lists only as Anonymous (p. 241).

[54] By expressivity, I mean that language is viewed as a mirror of the heart. It is invariably connected with the assertion that the speaker must himself be moved before moving others. See Fumaroli, *L'Age de l'éloquence*, on the development of the Classical plain style during the Renaissance. Basically Fumaroli argues that the elegant and restrained Classical plain style becomes the basis of Bembo's Ciceronianism and thence passes into French neo-Classicism. Thus Renaissance Ciceronianism is, at least in part, an aspect of the plain style tradition (pp. 87–89). The Classical plain style is quite different both with respect to origins and intentions from the passionate Christian genus humile.

This is precisely what happens in Perkins; the "demonstration (or shewing) of the spirit . . . makes the ministerie to be lively and powerfull."[55] The language, on the contrary, need only be plain and clear. But power remains the central requirement.[56] The danger with such a theory is that language and Spirit will become so unrelated that the preacher would fade into a passive medium for a divine "force." To prevent this, Perkins makes the same maneuver we have seen since the Middle Ages and one that will reappear through Bishop Burnet in the late seventeenth century. In words adapted from Cicero, Perkins observes that "wood, that is capable of fire, doth not burne, vnles fire be put to it: & he must first be godly affected himselfe who would stirre vp godly affections in other men."[57] The Holy Spirit does not simply pass through the speaker like light through glass but first transforms and arouses him, and his own inspired passion then enables him to stir others. In antiquity and in the liberal sacred rhetorics of the Renaissance, the demand for expressivity supplements the investigation into the ways language creates the passion of the grand style. In Perkins, this latter study disappears, highlighting the spiritual and psychological sources of passionate oratory at the expense of the artistic—a distrust of artistry congenial to the antisacramental, anticeremonial temper of the stricter English Calvinists.[58]

----

[55] Perkins, *Workes*, 2: 759. Because the Puritans considered preaching as the usual and ordinary means of salvation, the role of eloquence became theologically problematic. If the preacher's language could convert the heart, what need was there for grace? While most Catholics and liberal Protestants argued that grace operates through nature and therefore true eloquence, i.e., eloquence sustained by the Holy Ghost, could be an instrument of grace, stricter Protestants tended to mistrust eloquence as a man-made intrusion into the work of the Spirit. See Samuel Hieron, "The Dignitie of Preaching" (London, 1615), pp. 3–17; Robert South, "The Scribe Instructed," *Sermons Preached upon Several Occasions*, 4 vols. (Philadelphia, 1845), 2: 76–77.

[56] See Perry Miller, *The New England Mind*, for what remains the clearest statement of the Puritan's passionate plain style (pp. 300–304).

[57] Perkins, *Workes*, 2: 760.

[58] Milton, for example, writes, "Believe it, wondrous doctors [i.e., the Anglican clergy], all corporeal resemblances of inward holiness and beauty are now past; he that will clothe the gospel now, intimates plainly that the gospel is naked, uncomely." In *Complete Poetry and Major Prose*, ed. Merritt Hughes (New York, 1957), pp. 673–74; quoted in Steadman, *The Hill and the Labyrinth*, p. 79. See also

Perkins offers the purest example of the Protestant version of the passionate plain style. Other Protestant rhetorics are less austere. Hemmingsen, Hepinus, Pangratius, and the *Officium concionatoris* recommend the use of the figures of thought, although otherwise having little to say about style except to praise clarity and plainness.[59] At the same time, however, a fresh view of sacred rhetoric begins to unfold in the Protestant ranks, a view best represented by Hyperius's *Practis of Preaching* (1553; trans. 1577) and by the extraordinary study of biblical style found in Matthias Flacius Illyricus's *Clavis Scripturae Sacrae*, a work reprinted at least twelve times between 1562 and 1719.[60] Interestingly, Perkins knew the works of Flacius and Hyperius, who lived in England from 1537 to 1541.[61] His decision to dismiss rhetoric from Christian preaching is a rejection not only of Catholic or proto-Laudian practice but of a growing movement among Protestant theorists as well.

Hyperius shares with Perkins and most sacred rhetoricians an emphasis on emotional power, on the Spirit, and on expressivity. Like too many sixteenth-century Protestant rhetoricians, he spends considerable effort in dividing sermons into various kinds based on theological or pastoral function. But the *Practis of Preaching* also belongs to the tradition of Augustine's *De doctrina* and Erasmus's *Ecclesiastes* in its willingness to plunder and transform the full range of Classical rhetoric, including the genera dicendi and the figures of elocutio.[62] Hyperius, however, does not discuss

Richard Hooker, *The Laws of Ecclesiastical Polity, Works*, 3 vols., ed. John Keeble (1888; repr. New York, 1970), 5.15.1–3.

[59] Niel Hemmingsen, *The Preacher or Method of Preaching*, trans. John Horsfall (London, 1574), p. 55; Joannis Hepinus, *De sacris concionibus compendiaria formula*, in *De arte concionandi*, p. 69; M. Andrea Pangratius, *Methodus concionandi* (1571) (Wittenburg, 1594), p. 23.

[60] The 1562 date is given by Basil Hall in his article "Biblical Scholarship: Editions and Commentaries" in *The Cambridge History of the Bible*, 3 vols., ed. S. L. Greenslade (Cambridge, 1963), 3: 87. The *National Union Catalogue* and *The British Museum General Catalogue of Printed Books* list editions from 1567 to 1719.

[61] Ruth Bozell, "English Preachers of the Seventeenth Century on the Art of Preaching" (Ph.D. diss., Cornell University, 1939), pp. 9–11.

[62] Andreas Hyperius, *The Practis of Preaching*, trans. John Ludham (London, 1577), pp. 9, 37, 49, 153.

these, simply remarking that the orator and preacher have all such matters in common. Yet the reintroduction of Classical eloquence immediately shifts the Protestant demand for powerful, affective preaching in the direction of the grand style. Thus for Hyperius, the ability to move the emotions is the most important aspect of preaching.[63] While affirming that God sometimes empowers even rude and inartistic sermons, he stresses the affective power of all the figurative and tropical resources of language and the crucial role of the imagination, "when a man with most attentive cogitation apprehendeth, and depaynteth to himselfe the formes and simylitudes of the thinges whereof he entreateth."[64] As in Erasmus, the relation between imaginative vividness and passion assumes a key position. This emphasis, borrowed from the sixth book of Quintilian's *Institutes*, develops into one of the central principles of the Christian grand style—a topic to be treated in Chapter Five.

Despite Hyperius's praise of passionate Christian eloquence, his view of the emotions seems to conflict with the demands of affective spirituality. Unlike Melanchthon and his followers, Hyperius does not treat the theological virtues as emotions but as places of invention. Instead, like Aristotle and Saint Thomas, he discusses emotion in a purely ethical context, the implication being that passionate preaching would be largely moralistic.[65] The correspondence Melanchthon had sought between the theology of law and gospel and rhetorical affect falls away. It may be that Melanchthon's concept of faith as emotion was too radical for the sixteenth and seventeenth centuries; in any case it vanishes even from Lutheran rhetorics after about 1560.[66] The new Christian psychology of the emotions emerging in the Tridentine rhetorics and spreading from there into seventeenth-century Protestant ones is more purely Augustinian. It excludes faith from the

[63] Ibid., p. 41.

[64] Ibid., pp. 37, 44, 49.

[65] Ibid., pp. 11ff., 42.

[66] This conception, however, appears clearly in the *De arte concionandi* published in Basel in 1540 and again in London in 1570. For example, Viet Dietrich writes in his *Ratio breuis sacrarum concionum tractandarum*, "Fides igitur est affectus, qui certo assentitur promissionibus dei, & comminationibus" (p. 24).

category of emotion, instead organizing itself around *caritas*, the love of God and neighbor, as chief among what Hooker calls the "supernatural passions."[67]

Matthias Flacius Illyricus's *Clavis Scripturae Sacrae* (1562), unlike the other works we have discussed, is not a preaching rhetoric but an exhaustive treatment of biblical language in its philological, grammatical, and rhetorical aspects. It belongs to this study because from Erasmus to Rapin, biblical and homiletic discourse remained closely interrelated; the Bible is the source and standard for all sacred eloquence. The *Clavis*, however, is a far more original and sophisticated study of religious language than any other sixteenth-century Protestant rhetoric. Flacius does not hesitate to analyze the Bible as a literary text and explore how its distinctive effects arise from particular verbal configurations. He begins his chapter on the style of Holy Scripture by remarking, "With the exception of the historical books, the language of the Bible seems . . . in general great, sublime, and elevated, although the plain and middle styles also not infrequently appear."[68] This sacred grand style nevertheless differs widely from the secular, because it both "attempts to teach accurately and concerning the most weighty and difficult matters" and "desires to seize and move the heart. . . . Scriptural *conciones* teach and exhort and denounce and accuse and terrify and then console their listeners; they move, form, and reform their hearts . . . until finally Christ is formed in them."[69] The Christian grand style thus unites teaching and moving, unlike the Classical grand style, which tends toward "the ostentation of the speaker, flattery of the audience, and emotional persuasion of a largely uneducated crowd."

Flacius's analysis of the biblical grand style rests on Hermogenes and Demetrius. This preference for hellenistic sources corresponds to his strongly anti-Ciceronian viewpoint. He repeatedly compares biblical style to the compact brevity and jagged harshness of Thucydides and Sallust, contrasting this mode to the

---

[67] Hooker, *Ecclesiastical Polity*, 1.11.4.

[68] Matthias Flacius Illyricus, *Clavis Scripturae Sacrae, seu de sermone sacrarum literarum, in duas partes divisae* (Leipzig, 1695), 2: 459.

[69] Ibid., 2: 460.

luxurious and tiring prolixity of Cicero.[70] The Bible combines a paucity of *verba* with an abundance of *res*,[71] yet the result is anything but the lucid, denotative precision that this opposition of res and verba suggests to post-Baconian ears. Following his Greek models, Flacius perceives dense brevity as powerful, lofty, and darkly evocative. The "violent compression" of scriptural figures, tropes, ideas, and allusions creates a difficult, multileveled suggestiveness and coiled force. Rather than explaining things in orderly abstractions, the Scriptures use intertwined tropes, parables, maxims, and types to compact the greatest number of ideas into the fewest words. Flacius's concept of brevity is thus far closer to Auerbach's hebraic style with its dark, mysterious background punctuated by starkly vivid highlights, than anything resembling Lysian or scientific directness—although it does have some interesting connections with Stoic brevity that may explain why, by the seventeenth century, Lipsius himself was classified in the grand style. For Flacius, the brevity of the Bible is not descriptive but hieroglyphic, to use Northrop Frye's terms; that is, it does not "stick to the facts" but invites the reader to make an intuitive leap from the literal to moral and spiritual meaning.

Besides brevity, the two preeminent features of biblical style are *efficacia* and *evidentia*, or power and vividness.[72] For Flacius, efficacia arises from the excellent object as it calls forth a passionate response, from the expressive figures of thought, and from typological or parabolic signs,[73] while evidentia creates emotional power by using sensory, concrete imagery, dramatic dialogue, personification, and hypotyposis to produce a quasi-visual insight into spiritual and invisible truth. In its evidentia, the Bible resembles a "comedy . . . staged in the theater of the whole world" and it resembles the Sacraments, which likewise signify inner and spiritual truths by physical signs.[74]

---

[70] Ibid., 2: 4, 462–63, 494, 498, 500.

[71] Ibid., 2: 499.

[72] Later Renaissance rhetorics often use the terms *energia* and *enargia* to denote the same pair of concepts.

[73] Flacius, *Clavis*, 2: 475–82.

[74] Ibid., 2: 488.

In many ways, the *Clavis* reaffirms the emphases of most Renaissance sacred rhetorics—power, vividness, drama, and expressivity. Yet Flacius himself seems to have originated crucial aspects
of the later rhetorical tradition. The seventeenth-century connection between the hellenistic grand style and sacred prose, its taste
for pregnant and harsh brevity, for rich evocative figures, and for
metaphoric density grow out of Flacius's hebraic style.[75] Significantly for our purposes, he identifies these qualities with the
grand style—with Hermogenic grandeur and the grand and forcible characters of Demetrius. Thus the *Clavis* redefines the aesthetic grounds of prose style to create a non-Ciceronian conception of grandeur. This radicalism appears sharply in his contrast
between Roman and biblical style personified as two opposing fe-
male figures:

Latin sentences proceed like young women adorned by their garments;
but Hebrew like women not only adorned (*ornatae*) but weighed down
(*oneratae*), so that ornaments cling to every part of her body: on her head,
back, hands, lap, belt. . . . Thus from the excessive abundance of matter
to be explained and the simultaneous desire for brevity, individual
thoughts and speeches are loaded down, oppressed, and obscured; thus
the whole fabric of the discourse swells and seems pregnant with densely
packed ideas.[76]

The image of an overdecorated garment goes back to Cicero and
Quintilian,[77] where it describes the flashy ostentation of declamatory rhetoric. Flacius inverts the evaluation implied in the original contrast. It is hard for readers used to Classical ideals even to
realize at first that the young woman glittering from head to toe
is a positive image for the Bible's suggestive complexity and
evocative darkness. The *Clavis* offers an aesthetic of *written* prose,
which is thus more extreme than that found in the preaching rhet-

[75] The similarities between Flacius's biblical style and Croll's description of
anti-Ciceronian or baroque prose are obvious. Significantly, Flacius's work appears over a decade before the major writings of Muret and Lipsius. See Croll,
"Attic" and Baroque, pp. 11–21.

[76] Flacius, *Clavis*, 2: 423–24.

[77] *De oratore* 3.100–102; Quintilian 8.5.28; see also Sir Philip Sidney, *An Apologie for Poetrie, Elizabethan Critical Essays*, 2 vols., ed. G. Gregory Smith (London,
1904), 1: 202.

orics; but it provided the basis for the later development of the Christian grand style, especially among Protestants, along hellenistic and hebraic lines.

The Tridentine Rhetorics (1575–1620)

The Roman Catholic rhetorics of the sixteenth century follow upon the heels of the revival of preaching and missionary activity encouraged by the Council of Trent.[78] They constitute the first clearly defined "movement" among the sacred rhetorics of the Renaissance, often borrowing whole passages from each other and sharing the same fundamental outlook. In addition, they represent the first fully-developed Christian rhetorics since Erasmus's *Ecclesiastes*. While the Protestant rhetorics of the same period generally run from 10 to 40 pages (Hyperius, however, is longer), the Tridentine ones extend from 150 to 500 pages. They are rhetorics in the Classical sense. Unlike Erasmus and his medieval precursors, they devote very little time to the moral life of the preacher. Rather, they treat the subject matter, structure, and style of sacred discourse. A summary of the finest of them, Luis de Granada's *Ecclesiastica rhetorica* (1576) will give some idea of their shape and content. The first book deals with general questions about the origins and functions of sacred rhetoric and the character of the preacher. Book two treats invention; book three amplification, the emotions, and the figures that arouse emotion. Book four discusses different kinds of sermons—hortatory, panegyric, homiletic, didactic—and dispositio. Book five is on elocutio, including the four virtues of style, tropes and figures, and the genera dicendi. Book six briefly covers pronunciation and gesture and then concludes with some final observations on when and how to preach. The Classical origins of this organization are obvious, but it is also significant that de Granada breaks up the fivefold ancient pattern (invention, disposition, elocutio, delivery, and memory) by adding a book on amplification and emo-

---

[78] For other discussions of the Tridentine rhetorics, see Bayley, *French Pulpit Oratory*; Fumaroli, *L'Age de l'éloquence*, pp. 136–55, 179–202; O'Malley, "Content and Rhetorical Forms"; Joseph Connors, S.V.D., "Homiletic Theory in the Late Sixteenth Century," *The American Ecclesiastical Review* 138(1958): 316–32.

tion, while dropping compositio and memory. These changes indicate a movement away from the Ciceronian emphasis on aural rhythm and periodicity toward a greater stress on emotional expressiveness—a movement found throughout Renaissance rhetoric.[79]

According to J. J. Murphy's chronology, the two earliest Tridentine rhetorics are Diego Valades's *Rhetorica christiana* (four editions between 1574 and 1587) and Augustino Valiero's *De rhetorica ecclesiastica* (four editions between 1574 and 1578). Two years later, Luis de Granada published his *Ecclesiastica rhetorica* (eleven editions between 1576 and 1698) and Diego de Estella, his *De ratione concionandi* (twelve editions between 1576 and 1635).[80] Dozens of Roman Catholic rhetorics followed during subsequent decades. Most of these seem rather derivative, but two are worth mention: the Hermogenic *Divinus orator* (1595) of Ludovico Carbo and the missionary rhetoric by Pablo Jose de Arriaga, *Rhetoris Christiani partes septem* (1619), itself a summary of Carlo Reggio's *Orator Christianus* (four editions between 1612 and 1673).

The Tridentine rhetorics differ from most contemporary Protestant texts in their willingness to accept the legitimacy of deliberate eloquence. This acceptance opened the door to the heritage of Roman rhetoric (only Carbo uses hellenistic sources) including the genera dicendi, figural ornament, and amplification.[81] Nevertheless, a similar impulse motivates the Protestant and Tridentine rhetorics. Both attempt to reground Classical rhetoric in Christian theology and psychology; both see the Holy Spirit as the source of sacred expressivity and stress the affective goals of preaching.[82] But in the Tridentine rhetorics, movere resumes its

[79] See Plett, *Der affecktrhetorische Wirkungsbegriff*, pp. 9, 40–42, 90, 118, 133–34.

[80] Diego de Estella, *De modo concionandi liber et explanatio in psalm. CXXXVI. Super flumina Babylonis*, in *Ecclesiasticae rhetoricae* (Verona, 1732), shows less influence of Classical rhetoric than the other Tridentines; however, his attempt to base homiletic theory on the characteristics of Chrysostom's preaching resembles Hermogenes' use of Demosthenes as the paradigm from which to derive the various "Ideas" of style.

[81] The Tridentine rhetorics do, however, use Aristotle and various late Latin treatises, e.g., those of Rutilius Lupus, Iulius Rufinianus, Fortunatianus, and Cassiodorus.

[82] Pablo Jose de Arriaga, *Rhetoris Christiani partes septem* (Lyons, 1619), pp. 7,

Classical connection with the grand style. Instead of being a pe-
ripheral concern, discussions of style, amplification, and other
forms of affective persuasion grow increasingly important. The
figures traditionally associated with the grand style become the
basis for all Christian preaching and are carefully redefined to illuminate their spiritual functions. Thus, for example, hypotyposis (vivid portrayal) is described in terms of man's need to vis-
ualize the spiritual in order to be moved by it; the rhetorical figure
rests on the same psychological assumptions as the *compositio loci*
of Ignatian meditation.[83] The plain style is firmly rejected. De
Granada writes, "the orator does not only teach with arguments
but ought to delight by the beauty of his speech and the variety of
his matter and to shake fiercely the emotions of his listeners."[84]
Although the Spirit creates the impassioned heart and tongue, his
influence articulates itself in lofty, ardent language.

The Tridentine rhetorics also begin to develop a psychology of
the emotions as a basis and justification for this sort of preaching.
They argue that sin usually results not from ignorance of good
but from evil desires. The preacher's primary duty, therefore, is
not to teach but to instill sacred and virtuous emotions. They explicitly distinguish between the forensic emotions proper to Classical oratory and the holy passions stirred by the preacher. These
sacred emotions turn out to be the theological virtues, especially
love and hope. The preacher awakens love of God, longing for
beatitude, hope for forgiveness, and contempt of worldly vani-

---

103, 301–303; Carbo, *Divinus orator*, pp. 4–5, 13, 19, 188–89, 297ff.; Luis de Granada, *Ecclesiasticae rhetoricae, sive, de ratione concionandi, libri sex* (Cologne, 1582),
pp. 11, 41, 168–74, 308, 328; Didacus Valades, *Rhetorica Christiana ad concionandi,
et orandi usum accommodata* (Perugia, 1579), pp. 82–84; Agostino Valiero, *De ecclesiastica rhetorica libri tres*, in *Ecclesiasticae rhetoricae* (Verona, 1732), pp. 95–96, 109,
114–16. Valades stands slightly outside the mainstream of the rhetorical tradition,
since he was the Mexican-born son of an Indian and a Spaniard, and his work with
its splendid woodcuts is designed for missionaries to the Indians. Yet it was published in Italy and may have had some European circulation; it seems to have influenced de Granada.

[83] Fumaroli, *L'Age de l'éloquence*, pp. 139–40; Arriaga, *Rhetoris Christiani*, p. 81;
Carbo, *Divinus orator*, pp. 206–207.

[84] De Granada, *Ecclesiasticae rhetoricae*, p. 41.

ties.[85] Only Carbo, however, attempts a detailed analysis of the emotions, and immediately runs into self-contradictions, since his Thomistic division of the will and sensitive appetite, the latter alone properly concerned with affect, fails to explain how or why love of God is or can be an emotion, since the sensible appetite seeks only physical goods.[86] More consistent discussion of the emotions does not appear until the seventeenth century. Most of the Tridentine rhetorics simply borrow without comment the outlook of Augustinian psychology with its strongly affective tendencies and consequent unwillingness to divorce the will and emotions or to subordinate love to understanding.

The Tridentine rhetorics represent the rhetorical fulfillment of devout humanism. They are worlds apart from the pedantic classicism Erasmus satirizes in the *Ciceronianus*. Uninterested in gluing on superficial decorations to sophisticate Christian material, they pursue a more deep-seated relationship between theology and language relevant to the demands of popular preaching. Their sacramental orientation, which perceives sensible signs as reflections of invisible realities, separates them from most of their Protestant contemporaries, for whom artistic language masked rather than revealed the power of the Spirit. For this reason, they accept the essential principle of Classical decorum, that the level of style should correspond to the excellence of subject matter,

---

[85] De Arriaga, *Rhetoris Christiani*, pp. 80, 363; Carbo, *Divinus orator*, pp. 45–48, 204–27; de Estella, *De modo concionandi*, p. 8; de Granada, *Ecclesiasticae rhetoricae*, pp. 29–30, 160–1; Valades, *Rhetorica Christiana*, pp. 159–60, 238–39; Valiero, *De ecclesiastica rhetorica*, pp. 45–48.

[86] Carbo, *Divinus orator*, pp. 201–204. This sort of inconsistency does not appear to be unusual. Renaissance psychologies vacillate alarmingly between what Bouwsma terms the Stoic and Augustinian poles of interpretation. For example, in *The Passions of the Minde in Generall* (London, 1630), Thomas Wright begins by remarking that passions are "a sensual motion of our appetitiue faculty . . . [which] trouble wonderfully the soule, corrupting the iudgement & seducing the will, inducing (for the most part) to vice" (p. 8). Twenty or so pages later we find him claiming that passions also exist in the reasonable soul, "for to GOD the Scriptures ascribe loue, hate, ire, zeale, who cannot be subject to any sensitive operations" (pp. 30–31). And by the time we have gotten halfway through the treatise, we discover that the first emotion Wright discusses is the love of God (pp. 193ff.). Stoic, Thomist, and Augustinian categories mingle throughout the work without any acknowledgment of their fundamental incommensurability.

that—as Herbert suggests only to reject—"Beautie and beauteous
words should go together" ("Forerunners" l. 30).

The General Rhetorics (1575–1625)

With the exception of the works by Flacius Illyricus and Ludovico
Carbo, sixteenth-century sacred rhetorics do not borrow from
hellenistic sources. Nor do the hellenistic rhetorics appear particularly influential for the secular rhetorics before the last quarter of
the sixteenth century,[87] despite the fact all were available by 1554.
But beginning around 1575 and climaxing in the first decades of
the seventeenth century, interest in hellenistic rhetoric surges. Its
influence appears most clearly in a relatively new kind of treatise,
which I have called the "general rhetoric." Most rhetorics before
1575 are either sacred or secular. The general rhetorics, on the
contrary, cover both. Some, such as those by Sturm and Vossius,
are primarily secular, while those by Caussin, Keckermann, and
Alsted treat each kind extensively. In addition, the general rhetorics tend to be massive scholarly compendiums, often running
close to a thousand pages and fraught not only with hellenistic
materials, but obscure Byzantine commentaries, neo-Platonic
theorizing, and a vast command of Classical literature. For example, Nicholas Caussin lists under his Greek sources for *De
eloquentia sacra et humana* (1617) not only Aristotle, Demetrius,
Dionysius, Hermogenes, and Longinus, but also Menander,
Apsinus, Sopater, Cyrus, and Licymnius, along with the major
figures of Second Sophistic and dozens of philosophers, historians, orators, and Church Fathers. With this erudition comes an
impressive level of philological sophistication. Gerhard Vossius's
Commentariorum rhetoricorum (1605), for instance, contains an argument for the third century B.C. Alexandrian authorship of *De-*

---

[87] Longinus is mentioned but not discussed in a few sixteenth-century works.
See William Thorne, *Ducente deo. Willelmi Thorni Tullius seu Rhetor in tria stromata
divisus* (Oxford, 1592); Antonio Lullius [Lulle], *De oratione libri vii, quibus non modo
Hermogenes ipse totus, verum etiam quisquid fere a reliquis Graecis ac Latinis de arte dicendi traditum est, suis locis aptissime explicatur* (Basel, 1558). For more on the use of
hellenistic rhetoric before 1600, see Monfasani's article, "The Byzantine Rhetorical Tradition."

metrius's *On Style* essentially identical to that offered by G.M.A. Grube in his 1961 commentary on the same text.

The authors of the general rhetorics include both Protestants and Catholics. Not surprisingly, most of them were men of scholarly breadth and international reputation. Caussin, the Jesuit confessor to Louis XIII of France, also writes on hieroglyphics, tragedy, ethics, politics, and Greek poetry, while the enormously popular Protestant scholar, Bartholomew Keckermann, has books on logic, theology, ethics, geography, metaphysics, and mathematics. Another widely read Protestant author, Johann-Heinrich Alsted, writes on mathematics, music, theology, logic, philosophy, chronology, and mnemonics. Unlike the Tridentine, the general rhetorics do not form a single group, although Keckermann and Alsted use Sturm and Vossius extensively. I will therefore consider each author separately, beginning with Sturm's *De universa ratione elocutionis rhetoricae* of 1575.

According to Murphy's bibliography, Sturm wrote over twenty-one separate rhetorics between 1538 and his death in 1589, a number perhaps justifying Bacon's complaint about his "infinite and curious pains upon Cicero the Orator and Hermogenes the Rhetorician."[88] *De universa* comprises about eight hundred pages of disorganized and repetitive lecture notes on Hermogenes,[89] combining a pedantic absorption in the minutia of Greek terminology with occasional moments of brilliance. Because of its Hermogenic focus, *De universa* concentrates on questions of style and the *genera dicendi*. Sturm begins by laying out the criteria for the latter. The plain, middle, and grand styles differ according to emotional power and subject matter:

It is emotional power that divides the lofty (*gravis*) oration from the low (*humilis*). . . . [Style is also] discriminated according to . . . the appropriateness or proportion of things: if the subject is low and meagre, the style is also low. . . . If, however, it concerns great matters . . . it is necessary to use the grand style. . . . These three [genera] are not only dis-

---

[88] Francis Bacon, *A Selection of His Works*, ed. Sidney Warhaft (New York, 1965), p. 223.

[89] In *De universa ratione elocutionis rhetoricae, libri IV* (Strassburg, 1576), Sturm also cites Aristides, Aristotle, Cicero, Demetrius, Quintilian, and Theophrastus.

tinguished according to verbal ornament, but also on the basis of emotional power . . . and with respect to the appropriateness of things and persons.[90]

Power, ornament, and subject together make up the triple decorum of the genera dicendi.[91] The rest of *De universa* goes on to analyze Hermogenes' Ideas. Significantly, Christian references appear only in discussions of solemnity (*semnotes*). For Sturm, God and Christ form two main topics of solemnity. He uses Christ's pastoral imagery (e.g., "ego sum pastor bonus") to illustrate how allegory drawn from small matters can add dignity and authority. Paul's "O altitudo" exemplifies the mystic spirituality of *semnotes*, as does the sacred allegory of Canticles.[92] Christ's powerfully authoritative manner is also solemn.[93] The identification of sacred and solemn discourse takes on additional interest because solemnity blends into epideixis, an association Sturm emphasizes by treating splendor immediately afterward.[94] Solemnity and splendor both concern praise and blame. In the chapter on *laudatio*, Sturm thus speaks of the splendor and solemnity of the "*Platonicum laudandi genus*" and of Gregory Nazianzen's sermon on the Trinity.[95] Sturm's scattered meditations point to a new Christian grand style, one emphasizing the celebratory, mystical, and allegorical, rather than exhortation or reproof. Like Flacius thirteen years earlier, Sturm opens up a new way of viewing biblical rhetoric, not as inartistic and humilis but as a special

[90] Ibid., pp. 4–5.

[91] Unlike most Renaissance rhetoricians, Sturm recognizes that Hermogenes' Ideas are not subdivisions of the Ciceronian genera, that they are not "styles" but variable elements of a single style (*ibid.*, p. 7).

[92] Ibid., pp. 574–75.

[93] Ibid., p. 606.

[94] In Hermogenes, the order of the subdivisions of the Idea of Grandeur is: solemnity, asperity, vehemence, splendor, vigor, and abundance. See Appendix.

[95] Sturm, *De universa*, pp. 762–63. O'Malley has shown how important epideixis is in Renaissance preaching. His identification of the epideictic with the *genus demonstrativum* is, however, too narrow. In works influenced by Hermogenes (which include most Renaissance rhetorics), epideictic elements often appear in discussions of the grand style, especially under categories like *splendor, maiestas*, and *illustratio*. What O'Malley calls the epideictic emotions—love, gratitude, joy—are fundamental to the Christian grand style throughout the Renaissance.

form of the grand style, one closer to Plato and Thucydides than Cicero.

The next important general rhetoric after *De universa* is Gerhard Vossius's *Commentariorum rhetoricorum*. Vossius was a Dutch Protestant whose scholarly eminence moved Fulke Greville to offer him a university lectureship at Cambridge.[96] Murphy gives 1606 as the date of initial publication, but the work was probably available earlier, since Keckermann used it in the *Systema rhetoricae* of 1606. Vossius's thousand-page tome covers all the topics of Classical rhetoric, shifting rather eclectically from one authority to another. Although Vossius concentrates on summarizing and discussing Classical theory, he often illustrates his observations with biblical or patristic material. The differences between sacred and secular rhetoric do not concern him. His choice of an authority for the genera dicendi is, however, significant for the history of the Christian grand style. Although he prefers Cicero's tripartite division of the genera, his primary source is Demetrius. As in Flacius and Sturm, hellenistic theory supplants Latin. The section on the grand style begins with the famous Longinian quotation on the sublimity of Genesis, thus establishing a long-enduring link between biblical style and the sublime. Vossius then continues, tying the citation from Longinus into the context of Hermogenes' Idea of Solemnity. The grand style treats God and divine themes, impressive natural phenomena, and moral or political virtue.[97] As we shall see throughout the seventeenth century, the combined influence of Longinus and Hermogenes shifts the grand style away from forensic concerns toward sacred subjects. Vossius then returns to Demetrius, again emphasizing the sacral overtones of the grand style. He cites Demetrius on the similarity between the awed fear excited by the Mysteries and the emotions proper to the grand style.[98] As in Trebizond and Sturm, explicitly religious references cluster around the treatment of the grand style, a marked departure from Roman theory. Vossius's

[96] Ronald A. Rebholz, *The Life of Fulke Greville, First Lord Brooke* (Oxford, 1971), p. 293.

[97] Gerardus Vossius, *Commentariorum rhetoricorum, sive oratorium institutionum libri sex* (c. 1606; repr. Kronberg, 1974), 2: 446.

[98] Ibid., 2: 451.

description of compositio also separates his hellenized grand style from its Roman counterpart; he stresses its aural harshness, brevity, and asyndetic roughness, although cautioning against affectation.[99]

Vossius's chapters on the grand style influence Bartholomew Keckermann's treatment of the same subject in the *Systema rhetoricae*. The *Systema* is a much more interesting work than Vossius's rather dry treatise. Keckermann synthesizes a wide array of ancient and contemporary rhetorics, including hellenistic texts, the Tridentines, Sturm, Vossius, and Agricola, but these multifarious sources never dominate or confuse Keckermann's carefully organized and reasonably succinct (about three hundred pages) exposition. Much more than Sturm or Vossius, Keckermann addresses the nature of sacred rhetoric, a change resulting from a new orientation. While the works of the former two are basically commentaries on Classical texts, Keckermann focuses upon contemporary oratory. He recommends sermons on the Gunpowder Plot, discusses Lipsius, Ramus, Erasmus, Bude, and addresses himself to the practical value of rhetoric in seventeenth-century society, in which preaching held a far more prominent place than Latin orations.

Like the Tridentines, Keckermann makes rhetoric practically coextensive with passionate oratory and thus with the grand style.[100] To teach belongs to dialectic; rhetoric endeavors to move the will and emotions. Yet Keckermann insists on the close relation between teaching and moving. Emotion springs from reason and resolves itself into understanding—an Augustinian position shared by both Agricola and Erasmus.[101] Keckermann presents, for the first time, a detailed list of the various emotions, some of which are explicitly religious, such as veneration, hope, and penitence. Delight and wonder are also emotions, and, following Agricola, Keckermann views delight as an intellectual passion

[99] Ibid., 2: 440–43.
[100] Bartholomew Keckermann, *Systema rhetoricae in quo artis praecepta plene et methodice traduntur* (1606), in *Opera omnia quae extant*, 2 vols. (Geneva, 1614), 2: 1391–93, 1610.
[101] Ibid., 2: 1394, 1612.

aroused by whatever seems wonderful, rare, and great.[102] Like most Renaissance rhetoricians, he also recognizes the emotional power of sensory vividness and the figures of thought.[103]

Keckermann's analysis of the grand style rests on Vossius and Sturm (whom he admits is almost impenetrably verbose).[104] Here again the grand style appears in close conjunction with sacred themes. Like Vossius, Keckermann cites Longinus's "golden book" on Genesis, Hermogenes on solemnity, and Demetrius on the Mysteries. But he relies most heavily on a free reinterpretation of Hermogenes, identifying the grand style with Hermogenes' Idea of Grandeur. Reshuffling Hermogenes' six subcategories of grandeur, Keckermann posits five variants of the grand style. These are power, solemnity, splendor, vigor, and abundance. The first three, which Keckermann (mistakenly) considers as separate styles rather than possible qualities of a single style, are the most important. What Keckermann has done is to create three grand styles. The first is characterized by agonistic strength and passionate expressivity, the second by a sublime, mystical authority, the third by luminous, festal richness.[105] This is not an academic exercise in distinctions. As Flacius had realized, the conventional Ciceronian picture of the grand style was not applicable to sacred discourse. The same intuition seems to lie behind the eagerness with which Renaissance rhetoricians borrowed the scattered religious allusions from hellenistic treatises to depict the grand style. But in the long run, Demetrius is no more satisfactory than Cicero as a guide to the diversities of style—Classical, biblical, and modern—confronting the Renaissance. Keckermann thus drops the unitary concept of the genera and by misinterpreting Hermogenes creates a threefold grand style able to embrace Cicero's passionate vehemence, the dark sublimity of Isaiah, and Byzantine epideixis. The fact that Keckermann was

---

[102] Ibid., 2: 1614–44.

[103] Ibid., 2: 1427, 1482–91.

[104] Keckermann's discussion of the grand style runs from 2: 1669 to 2: 1676.

[105] Ibid., 2: 1670*–1671*. The pagination in this section is erratic, the column numbers running as follows: 1663–64, 1669–72, 1669–. I will put an asterisk (*) after the column number when speaking of the second 1669–72.

widely used in both England and New England[106] has important implications for our understanding of the stylistic intentions behind seventeenth-century prose and poetry.

Somewhat less erudite and original than Keckermann's, the rhetorical works of his fellow German, Johann-Heinrich Alsted, summarize the main themes of early seventeenth-century rhetoric. Alsted's general rhetorics include the *Orator, sex libris informatus* (1612) and the relevant sections of his *Encyclopedia*. The organization of the *Encyclopedia* presents interesting evidence for the gradual reunification of Ramist and Ciceronian theory;[107] the sixth book treats grammar, the seventh rhetoric, by which Alsted means schemes and tropes, the eighth logic, and the ninth oratory, including invention and disposition. This seems to reflect pedagogical practice. Young boys would learn the Ramist tropes and figures quite early, only handling the more complex Ciceronian parts of an oration after they had mastered some logic.[108] In both the *Encyclopedia* and the *Orator*, Alsted subdivides oratory into three types: "*scholastica*" (or literary analysis of prose models), political, and ecclesiastical.[109] Some aspects of rhetoric, like the genera dicendi, tropes and schemes, and varieties of proof, are common to all three branches, others peculiar to a single area. Alsted considers the grand style both under invention as one of the Aristotelian kinds of proof and under elocutio. As part of invention, the grand style pertains to inventing powerful arguments suitable to "serious, excellent, and difficult topics."[110] Among such arguments, Alsted stresses the same four prominent in Keckermann, one of his principal sources, and the Tridentines:

[106] Miller, *The New England Mind*, p. 510; Sandford, "English Rhetoric," p. 508.

[107] Howell, *Logic and Rhetoric*, pp. 282–317.

[108] Likewise, Charles Butler confines his *Rhetoricae libri duo* (Oxford, 1597) to figures and tropes, while his *Oratoriae libri duo* (Oxford, 1629) also treats invention, disposition, and the genera. On the place of elocutio in Renaissance pedagogy, see Brian Vickers, "Rhetorical and Anti-Rhetorical Tropes: On Writing the History of *elocutio*," *Comparative Criticism: A Yearbook* 3(1981): 105–32.

[109] Johann-Heinrich Alsted, *Orator, sex libris informatus* (Herborn, 1616), p. 84; *Encyclopedia* (Herborn, 1630), p. 405.

[110] *Orator*, p. 64.

the passion of the speaker, vividness and hypotyposis, dramatic prosopopoeia, and the figures of thought—a list forming the core of Renaissance thinking on passionate oratory.[111]

The last and greatest of the general rhetorics was *De eloquentia sacra et humana* by the French Jesuit, Nicholas Caussin. *De eloquentia* was probably first published in 1617,[112] and it appeared in ten more editions in the next forty years. Stylistically it is unlike any other Renaissance rhetoric. For the most part these are straightforward academic texts, but Caussin writes like Longinus gone baroque. The book runs over a thousand pages in a prose that veers from dizzying passion to playful parody and from clear compact analysis to lavish poetic rhapsodies. It begins with the division of all oratory into the divine, the heroic, and the human. The first is the inspired eloquence of the Scriptures, the second the sacred oratory of the Church Fathers with its "heroic" mixture of the divine and human, the last is secular oratory.[113] The first thirteen books of *De eloquentia* deal primarily with this latter type and with features common to all three kinds of discourse. They include a fine history of Classical prose, a long defense of Cicero's power and grandeur against partisans of Isocratic virtuosity, and a detailed study of the emotions based on a mixture of Aristotle, Saint Thomas, Dionysius the Areopagite, and Ficino. Once again we see a clear spiritualization of affect. Caussin includes a long section from Ficino on the love of God; hope and joy are also sacred emotions, and Caussin emphasizes the role of the Holy Spirit in arousing passionate response. The section on the genera dicendi, comprising most of book two, relies on Hermogenes and Longinus. From the latter he borrows sections on the imagination, on the greatness of soul, and on sublimity. Following the trend we have seen for these late hellenistic treatises to push the grand style toward the sacred, Caussin exemplifies this

[111] *Encyclopedia*, pp. 473–74. Needless to say, these are not "arguments" in the modern sense. By *argumenta* Alsted means simply persuasive techniques.

[112] Murphy's short-title catalogue of Renaissance rhetoric gives 1619 as the original date of publication, but the *National Union Catalogue* lists a 1617 edition.

[113] Caussin, *De eloquentia*, pp. 2–3.

genus, even in book two, with the ancient spirituality of Plato and Cicero.[114]

Books fourteen through sixteen are devoted to sacred eloquence. Book fourteen argues against those hyper-Classicists who regard the Bible as low—full of carpenters, mangers, and whores—and therefore unworthy of great oratory. To this Caussin replies that sacred themes are lofty, majestic, and preeminently capable of being treated in the most excellent style. Book fifteen then moves to a vigorous attack on florid, artificial preaching equal to any English Puritan's. Christian oratory should be sublime, agonistic, and passionate, not ostentatious and ornamented with psuedo-Classical frippery. Caussin next discusses types of preaching, isolating three basic kinds: the "university" sermon, which may be either scholastic or based on humanistic philology;[115] the *gravis* sermon, characterized by an austere, powerful vehemence; and the majestic sermon with its contemplative, mystical splendor. The last two types, quite similar to those mentioned by Keckermann, seem to derive from Hermogenes' division of the Idea of Grandeur into two groupings, one involving vehemence, asperity, and vigor, the other solemnity and splendor. The *gravis* preacher "teaches acutely, fights fiercely, and triumphs powerfully." He is concise, harsh, and severe but uses powerful figures of thought, hammering hearts with a lightning-like intensity. Majestic preaching is fuller and celebratory, arousing the mind to a contemplative wonder at the mysteries of God. Whereas Athenasius best exemplifies the gravis preacher, Gregory Nazianzen and Dionysius the Areopagite represent the majestic.[116] Thus for Caussin these two homiletic types fall under the hellenistic grand style. Epideictic splendor becomes part of this grand style, sharply dividing it from the Roman genus. Despite the fact that Caussin is an ardent Ciceronian, his chapters on Christian eloquence are grounded in Byzantine practice—along with the Bible, the main literary source of sacred aesthetics in the

[114] Ibid., pp. 134–35.
[115] Ibid., p. 986.
[116] Ibid., pp. 966–69.

Renaissance. *De eloquentia* ends with a lengthy tribute to Chrysostom as the model for Christian eloquence and sanctity.

Protestant Rhetoric in the Seventeenth Century

Before the Restoration, seventeenth-century Protestant rhetorics generally adopt the liberal position first mapped out by Hyperius and Flacius. It is the great era of the German ecclesiastical rhetorics, beginning with Keckermann's *Rhetoricae ecclesiasticae* of 1600 and continuing through the midcentury in the works of Alsted, Glassius, Chemnitz, Ursinus, Hulseman, and Sohnius. In England, however, the picture is more complicated. The influence of the German rhetorics appears early in the century, contributing to a new appreciation for sacred eloquence in Richard Bernard's *The Faithful Shepherd* (1607) and in *Sacred Eloquence* (1659) by the Calvinist Bishop of Worcester, John Prideaux. Yet the heritage of the passionate plain style dominates English sacred rhetoric both among dissenters like Richard Baxter and latitudinarians like John Wilkins.

Despite the increased number of English sacred rhetorics during this period, the continental ones remain of primary importance, and this for two reasons: most English rhetorics are inferior to their European counterparts, and the continental neo-Latin sacred rhetorics seem to have been widely used in England. Even the more conservative English rhetorics admit a familiarity with the liberal Protestant tradition. Wilkins's *Ecclesiastes* exemplifies both these features. The work itself is not especially interesting. At least half is simply a bibliographic listing of scholarship on theology, ethics, and homiletics, while the rest restates the plain style doctrine-and-use method derived from Perkins. Yet despite Wilkins's preference for plain, unrhetorical preaching, he recommends all the liberal Protestant rhetorics—Keckermann, Alsted, Flacius, Glassius—and even lifts passages from Erasmus's work of the same title.

The continental Latin rhetorics thus remain a central witness to the aesthetics of Christian discourse in the English Renaissance. They reject earlier Protestant evasions of rhetoric, often prefacing their texts with a defense of conscious artistry and deliberate eloquence. Thus the introduction to Salomon Glassius's *Philologia sacra* (1623), a massive revision of Flacius that went through nine seventeenth-century editions and was still being reprinted in 1795, argues at length that Holy Scripture is neither humilis and therefore below rhetorical consideration nor so divine as to be above it. Rather, its eloquence differs only in degree not kind from that of secular authors and so can be rhetorically analyzed as the greatest triumph of artistic prose.[117] In his sacred rhetoric, *Theologia prophetica* (1622), Alsted points out that even if the apostles derived their eloquence directly from the Spirit, modern preachers cannot rely on such extraordinary assistance but must employ the ordinary means of rhetorical art.[118] In the section titled "*De elocutione ecclesiastica*," he develops the implications of this position, restoring the ancient bond between language, subject matter, and emotional effect, the absence of which separates medieval and "puritan" rhetoric from both the Classical and more liberal Christian traditions. Without elocutio, Alsted writes, "the sermon is cold, . . . incapable of teaching, moving, and persuading the people. . . . Let it be adorned with tropes and figures proportioned to the majesty of sacred themes. . . . Let it be powerful and strong, that is, let it be composed partly of emphatic, weighty epithets and antitheses, partly of passionate figures."[119] The excellence of the subject demands a proportionately elevated language, which then creates the suitable emotional response. This sense of decorum coupled with the pervasive Augustinian psychology and its emphasis on spiritualized emotion locates Alsted and other seventeenth-century Protestant rhetorics in the mainstream of the Christian grand style.

To a great extent, these rhetorics consciously continue the traditions of the Christian grand style laid down in the Tridentine and general rhetorics. Keckermann cites Erasmus, de Granada,

---

[117] Salomon Glassius, *Philologia sacra qua totius SS. Veteris et Novi Testamenti Scripturae tum stylus et literatura, tum sensus et genuinae interpretationis ratio et doctrina libris quinque expenditur ac traditur* (Leipzig, 1705), pp. 17–25.

[118] Johann-Heinrich Alsted, *Theologia prophetica, exhibens rhetoricam et politiam ecclesiasticam. acc. theologia acroamatica* (Hanover, 1622), p. 8.

[119] Ibid., pp. 79–80.

de Estella, and Valiero as well as Cicero, Quintilian, Augustine, Agricola, and Aristotle.[120] Christian Chemnitz's *Brevis instructio futuri ministri ecclesiae* (1658) uses Hyperius, Vossius, and Caussin.[121] From these Catholic and scholarly sources, the Protestant rhetorics derive an appreciation for Classical decorum with its interrelation of language, subject, and effect; a focus on passionate oratory, the emotions, and the verbal resources capable of stirring the heart; and an aesthetic of vividness, drama, and expressivity. Keckermann, the earliest and most influential of the seventeenth-century Protestant rhetoricians, thus includes a discussion of sacred emotions that lays particular weight on the "supernatural passions" of wonder, joy, and love rather than those more directed toward moral praxis. He notes furthermore that sin usually springs from the "infected will" not from ignorance; since the will is "moved more by sense than intellect," the preacher must strive to move the emotions not by rational argument but by amplification and hypotyposis.[122] The necessity of passionate eloquence rests upon the consequences of the Fall and the premises of Renaissance psychology with its intertwining of emotion and the visual image. The preacher, according to Keckermann, should therefore dramatize biblical scenes "as in a theater," "introduce God and Christ speaking and commanding," and place the subject before our eyes "surrounded with various striking details and circumstances, as if we were painting with living colors, so that the listener, carried outside himself, seems to behold the event as if placed in its midst."[123] Along with prosopopoeia, dialogue, and hypotyposis, Keckermann recommends the expressive and dramatic figures of speech: the preacher should speak to Christ and, turning to his congregation, plead with them, question them, pouring out all the desires of his soul, sometimes halting abruptly as if transgressing the boundaries of human

---

[120] Bartholomew Keckermann, *Rhetoricae ecclesiasticae sive artis formandi et habendi conciones sacras, libri duo* (Hanover, 1616), pp. 10, 17–19, 28, 49, 52, 110.

[121] Christian Chemnitz, *Brevis instructio futuri ministri ecclesiae in Academia Jenensi antehac publice praelecta* (Jena, 1660), pp. 6, 134–38.

[122] Keckermann, *Rhetoricae ecclesiasticae*, pp. 27, 44.

[123] Ibid., pp. 19, 26, 29.

speech.[124] For Keckermannn, Christian preaching is wholly assimilated into the grand style. The genera dicendi therefore drop away. While he insists that sermons must teach as well as move, the latter function dominates all discussion of elocutio.

The *Philologia sacra* (1623) of Salomon Glassius is one of the last major pieces of neo-Latin rhetorical scholarship. Like the *Clavis Scripturae Sacrae*, which it follows closely, it remained popular well into the eighteenth century. Glassius's discussion of biblical style summarizes the corresponding sections in Flacius with one important change. Apparently for polemical reasons, Glassius drops his predecessor's insistence on the darkness and difficulty of the Bible. Judging from Glassius's own comments, it seems that Flacius's work played into the hands of the Papacy; if the Scriptures were that difficult, then how could they be entrusted to private individuals? To counter the Roman claim for interpretive hegemony, Glassius emphasizes the clarity and accessibility of scriptural style; yet it remains a clarity shot through with majesty and grandeur.[125] In other respects, Glassius repeats the main points of the *Clavis*. Holy Scripture possesses power, vividness, and brevity. As in Flacius, these categories tend to run together since all basically point to the metaphoric, concrete texture of biblical discourse with its ability to use sensible images to suggest the supernatural. Power and vividness thus imply each other, for the force of biblical rhetoric lies in the persistent vertical implications of type, allegory, vision, trope, and the various dramatic figures of thought that lend sensuous immediacy to inner, spiritual events.[126] Brevity is closely related to both power and vividness, because it is through metaphor and "emphasis" that the Bible achieves the Thucydidean density which is the source of its power and which "according to Demetrius, . . . is most suitable for the grandeur of its conceptions, commands, mysteries, and other sacred matters."[127]

The biblical rhetorics of Flacius and Glassius suggest the flexibility of rhetorical concepts during the Renaissance. Both men at-

[124] Ibid., p. 39.
[125] Glassius, *Philologia sacra* (1705), pp. 17–20, 279–80.
[126] Ibid., pp. 282–92.
[127] Ibid., p. 298; cf. pp. 293–99.

tempt to analyze a text fundamentally different from any Classical work with categories developed for Classical forensic argument. Most biblical rhetorics, from Bede onward, achieve only a surface rapprochement of text and theory—usually by listing biblical passages that exemplify Classical figures. In Flacius and Glassius, however, a critical selectivity isolates those aspects of ancient elocutio particularly applicable to the Scriptures and, more important, tries to show how these terms illuminate the way biblical rhetoric actually functions. Their procedure is both inductive and synthetic rather than mechanical. In addition, unlike most Calvinist expositors, who examine biblical figures in order to find the "real" or discursive meaning, following the Ramist habit of viewing figurative language as ornamented dogma,[128] they study the distinctive rhetoric of Holy Scripture as it creates a nondiscursive apprehension of spiritual reality.

Between 1600 and 1660, England produces several works, most of them brief and in the vernacular, which at least touch on the problems of sacred rhetoric.[129] These rhetorics, unlike the neo-Latin ones written on the Continent, mostly belong to the non-Classical tradition that opposes passionate sincerity to deliberate eloquence and therefore condemns elocutio not in the name of dialectical precision but of powerful expression. Yet considerable diversity in nuance and emphasis remains. At one extreme, Samuel Hieron, a popular Puritan lecturer in the first decades of the seventeenth century, approves only a rigidly plain teaching style, designed more to instruct than to move. Hieron writes, "as the substance of [the Gospel], is crossing to man's reason, so for the fashion of it, according to the world, it is cleane out of fashion, only beautifull in this, because it is not beautified with that, without which the nice & giddy world thinketh euery thing to be deformed. . . . It is a good aduice of *Ierome*, to auoid a pompous kinde of speaking in theologicall discourses: for a man . . . that handleth holy matters, a lowe and (as it were) a foote oration is

[128] Miller, *The New England Mind*, pp. 324–28, 354–55.

[129] The only neo-Latin sacred rhetoric printed in England during this period seems to have been Matthew Sutcliffe's twelve-page *De concionum ad populum formulis* in *De recta studij theologici ratione, liber unus* (London, 1602).

necessary."[130] Hieron's combination of paranomasia, polyptoton, and patristic citation renders his austerity somewhat suspect—a gap between theory and practice often noted by students of Puritan rhetoric.[131] The connection Hieron implies between the suprarational otherness of Christianity and a low, rough plain style is less characteristic of the seventeenth century than the traditional association of affective spirituality and passionate plainness. Sutcliffe's *De recta studij theologici ratione, liber unus* (1602), Herbert's *The Country Parson* (1652), Baxter's *Gildas Salvianus* (1656), and the scattered remarks of Samuel Ward agree that the principal end of preaching is an ardent and vehement psychagogia, achieved primarily through the preacher's own expressivity. If they advocate plainness, they usually understand this to mean clarity, not conversational ease or dialectical acuity. In Ward and Herbert, the proximity between this passionate plain style and the Classical grand style becomes apparent. It must always be remembered that this Christian "plain" style from the very beginning defined itself not in contrast to the "grand" style of the great Classical orators but to the frigid overornamentation of Second Sophistic and late Latin writers like Sidonius Apollonaris. Samuel Ward, Puritan master of Sidney Sussex at Cambridge, points to historical origins of this double meaning of plainness in his sermon "A Coale from the Altar."[132] He begins wittily enough to

[130] Samuel Hieron, "The Preacher's Plea," *All the Sermons of Samuel Hieron* (London, 1614), pp. 534–35.

[131] Bozell, "English Preachers," p. 249; Miller, *The New England Mind*, pp. 351–52; Dorothy Parkander, "Rhetorical Theory and Practice: The Sermons of the English Puritans from 1570–1644" (Ph.D. diss., University of Chicago, 1962), p. 73; William Haller, *The Rise of Puritanism or, the Way to the New Jerusalem as Set Forth in Pulpit and Press from Thomas Cartwright to John Lilburne and John Milton, 1570–1643* (New York, 1939), pp. 129, 132.

[132] The whole "plain style" question in Puritan rhetoric is something of a red herring. For men like Perkins and Baxter, a plain style usually means one that avoids ostentatious learning, untranslated swatches of Latin and Greek, and erudite punning. Plain in this sense has little to do with the genera dicendi. Rather, it concerns the first two Theophrastean "virtues of style": purity and clarity. These, according to Classical theory, are always essential for good oratory. The argument about "plainness" in English sacred rhetoric, then, does not primarily relate to the relative merits of the genus tenue and the genus grande. It is perhaps a criticism of Andrewes's "witty" style, perhaps a useful warning for young, univer-

condemn witty and ornate preaching: "It is a veine of vaine preaching, turning sound preaching into a sound of preaching, tickling mens eares like a tinckling Symball . . . spoyling the plaine song, with descant and division. . . ." Ward then goes on to distinguish this verbal play from Christian eloquence, pausing in a parenthesis to praise the great Classical orators. "What is this but to shew our owne levity and want of true Art; indeed affecting such a dauncing, piperly and effeminate eloquence (as *Tully*, *Demosthenes*, or any Masculine Oratour would scorne) in stead of that divine powerfull delivery, which beccommeth him that speakes the Oracles of God."[133] For Ward, preaching "in the evidence and demonstration . . . of the Spirit and grace" entails the rejection of the same puerile affectations Caussin had criticized but not the rejection of the masculine grandeur of a Cicero or Demosthenes. Ward then describes true preaching in sentences that echo Classical passages on the genus grave: "If we euer meane to doe any good, wee must exhort and reprove with all vehemencie and authority; lifting up our voice as a Trumpet, as the sonnes of thunder; piercing their eares, witnessing, striving, and contending . . . to manifest our affections."[134] The second half of the sentence, however, suggests the thin but firm line separating Ward from ancient rhetoric: "which all the Art in the world will not teach us to doe: onely zeale at the heart will naturally produce it, without straining or affecting." Neither Ward nor Herbert rejects artistic language, yet both so subordinate it to holiness and zeal that the question of the relation between affect and elocutio drops away, although Herbert, in fact, notes several techniques, including storytelling, apostrophe, and dramatic figures, to make the sermon "show very Holy."[135]

---

sity-trained priests on their way to rural parishes, perhaps a polemical flourish designed to intimate that only the reforming clergy really cared about the people. Except for Bernard, English discussions of preaching simply avoid questions of language, style, and genera as too academic for the vernacular and too rarified given the urgent pastoral and theological issues of the day.

[133] Samuel Ward, *A Collection of Such Sermons and Treatises as Have Been Written and Published by Samuel Ward* (London, 1636), p. 294.

[134] Ibid., pp. 294–95.

[135] George Herbert, *A Priest to the Temple, or, The Country Parson, His Character,*

Also during this period, some English rhetorics begin to rejoin sacred discourse and elocutio. This is partly due to the influence of Ramism. Barton's *The Art of Rhetorick, Consisely and Compleatly Handled, Exemplified Out of Holy Writ* (1634), John Clarke's *Holy Oyle* (1630), and John Smith's *The Mysterie of Rhetorique Unvail'd* (1657) are lists of tropes and schemes with biblical illustrations, innocent of any theoretical considerations of sacred rhetoric. Yet they implicitly admit that the terminology of rhetorical elocutio can be an instrument for analyzing biblical style.[136] Another, more valuable influence on English homiletic comes from the continental Protestant rhetorics just discussed. These borrowings appear in two of the very few full-length ars praedicandi written in seventeenth-century England[137]—Richard Bernard's *The Faithful Shepherd* (1607) and John Prideaux's *Sacred Eloquence* (1659). The significance of this influence is immediately apparent in the contrast between Perkins's statement that the style which "best beseemeth the majesty of God" is "plaine, easie, and familiar"[138] and Bernard's observation that

the words must be apt and significant to expresse the matter whereof [the preacher] speaketh. . . . Varietie of things craue variety of words, and a differing manner of speech. . . . he that can paint out vice in the deformitie to make it hatefull, and set out vertue in her beauty, to make her be desired; hee that can vtter the threatenings of the law with terror, and the sweete promises of God, to mooue to ioy and thankfulnesse, he speaketh as he ought to speake. . . . There is a godly eloquence approued by Scripture and vsed in it, which is to be laboured for.[139]

---

and Rule of Holy Life in *The Country Parson, The Temple*, ed. John N. Wall, Jr., The Classics of Western Spirituality (New York, 1981), pp. 62–64.

[136] In fact, few English Puritans would deny that rhetoric is useful for analyzing biblical style. The eucharistic controversy often centered on the question of whether *hoc est corpus meum* was or was not a trope. But note Perry Miller's point that Puritans often used a Ramist rhetorical analysis as a means of *stripping* the figurative language off the plain, naked meaning of Scripture (*The New England Mind*, pp. 342–43).

[137] These continental rhetorics also influenced the secular school rhetorics written in England. See below on Farnaby and Butler.

[138] Cited in Parkander, "Rhetorical Theory," p. 22.

[139] Richard Bernard, *The Faithful Shepherd* (London, 1621), pp. 31–33.

The origins of this appreciation of eloquence and decorum are not hard to locate. Bernard several times mentions Hyperius and Alsted, two of the leading figures in continental sacred rhetoric. Throughout Bernard's treatise, their influence stands behind the correlation of language, subject, and affect. Following Alsted, Bernard observes that the enumeration of "points" often found in doctrine-and-use sermons should be disguised since obvious logical division interrupts emotional response.[140] Here again, passion is not only a matter of argument or sincerity but of language. Likewise Bernard borrows from Alsted the conviction that moving others involves the "figures of Rhetorick," especially the dramatic figures of thought listed by Keckermann and Alsted: exclamatio, interrogatio, compellatio, obsecratio, optatio, sermoncinatio, prosopopoeia, and apostrophe.[141]

After Bernard, the presence of these continental rhetorics becomes harder to trace. John Wilkins, the latitudinarian bishop and leading member of the Royal Society, recommends Alsted, Keckermann, Glassius, Flacius, Hemmingsen, and Erasmus in the bibliographical chapters of his *Ecclesiastes* (1646), but Wilkins's own views are far less sympathetic to eloquence and passionate grandeur than those of the authors he mentions. Prideaux's *Sacred Eloquence*, on the other hand, shows a considerable debt to these continental rhetorics, although he himself never names any contemporary sources. Like the works of Flacius and Glassius, *Sacred Eloquence* examines the distinctive features of biblical rhetoric; like many continental rhetorics, it contains a study of spiritual emotions, including the theological virtues. More important, Prideaux's sense of the drama, grandeur, and rhetorical exuberance of Holy Scripture, a sense seldom found in the English tradition, parallels the treatment of biblical eloquence in both Catholic and continental Protestant rhetorics. Thus, in words that must have sounded strange in the last years of the Interregnum, Prideaux describes how the Bible brings a character "in upon the stage speaking as if he were present" and "sometimes,

---

[140] Ibid., pp. 349–50.
[141] Ibid., pp. 299–304.

instead of personating one, divers are represented on the thea-
tre."[142] Elsewhere Prideaux speaks of the "weight and majesty" of
scriptural tropes, its "sublime Hyperboles" and allegories "as
sparkling Diamonds in a Ring."[143] In discussing the emotions
evoked by Scripture, Prideaux dwells on the passionate relationship between God and man. He writes of David's "extatic" love
of God, his sacred "*de arte amandi*," the "holy frolick . . . of the
Apostle to the Philippians."[144] With Prideaux, then, the sense of
Holy Scripture as lofty, eloquent, and deeply moving, familiar
from continental works at least since Flacius's *Clavis Scripturae
Sacrae* (1562), comes into the English tradition.[145]

Although Prideaux did have followers, primarily among the
dissenters, the future of English rhetoric lies in a different direction. In 1646 John Wilkins published his *Ecclesiastes*, summing up
and polishing the native passionate plain style with admixtures of
Senecanism and rationalism, and transmitting this ideal of a
warm, simple, logical preaching to Restoration Anglicanism.[146]
In most respects, Wilkins's work differs little from the more conservative rhetorics of the Protestant tradition. He praises a strict
doctrine-and-use format, stresses the necessity of moving the
emotions while simultaneously rejecting any more eloquence
than that required for clarity, and argues that the emotional

[142] John Prideaux, *Sacred Eloquence: Or, the Art of Rhetorick, As it is layd down in
Scripture* (London, 1659), pp. 68, 70.

[143] Ibid., pp. 3, 6, 22.

[144] Ibid., pp. 77–79, 94.

[145] See also the preface to John Clarke's *Holy Oyle for the Lampes of the Sanctuarie:
or Scripture-phrases Alphabetically Disposed* (London, 1630). Clarke writes, "For
who is it that findeth not an ἐνέργεια, a *maiestie*, power, *heate*, life . . . in the *Holy
Scriptures*, aboue all the . . . exquisite perfections of other writings? *Whose* super-
superlatiue expressions, favouring of *extasie* and rapture, neither *Demosthenes*, nor
Sophocles with their strongest *lines*, high-swolne sentences, lofty and passionate
streines, can possibly paralell" ([a]3ᵛ–[a]3ʳ). The remainder of Clarke's work,
however, does not live up to the promise of the preface, being yet another list of
tropes and figures. As John Knott observes in *The Sword of the Spirit: Puritan Responses to the Bible* (Chicago, 1980), Puritans tended to see the spiritual power of
God's Word operating almost independent of language. The Holy Spirit acts
through but not in the words of the text (pp. 4–5).

[146] On Wilkins, see Williamson, *The Senecan Amble*, pp. 250–55; Barbara Shapiro, *John Wilkins, 1614–1672: An Intellectual Biography* (Berkeley, 1969).

power of preaching stems from the preacher's experimental acquaintance with "all those sacred Truths, that we are to deliver
unto others," an acquaintence that must be "infused from
above."[147] Wilkins differs from earlier theorists like Perkins only
in the greater importance he grants to art and in his tendency to
moralize the ends of preaching. Unlike Herbert, Wilkins does not
speak of sermons as arousing zeal and fervency, but as leading to
"profit and edification."[148] The affections should be "ingaged
unto . . . truth or duty," not (explicitly) to love of God and longing for heavenly beatitude.[149]

   Wilkins's ideas about preaching become popular Anglican
dogma after the Restoration, reiterated and developed in most
late seventeenth-century rhetorics. Already in Wilkins, the discontinuities and contradictions more evident in post-Restoration
theory begin to surface. As Wilkins moves toward a rational, lucid, and argumentative plain style, the possibility of genuine passion seems to diminish. Lectures and conversation, no matter
how sincere, rarely produce either joy or tears. When Wilkins
claims that the preacher moves his congregation by offering "motives" and "effectual arguments"[150] in a wholesome plain style,
one wonders whether by "moving" Wilkins does not rather mean
"persuading" or "convincing." Earlier Renaissance rhetoricians
like Agricola and de Granada accepted the Aristotelian viewpoint
that the "places" of teaching and moving are the same, but had
gone on to insist that argument only moves when amplified and
energized by eloquence.[151] Wilkins inherits a strongly affective
rhetorical vocabulary from his predecessors, but in his hands this
terminology begins to shift towards Aristotle's position (especially in the first two books of the *Rhetoric*) that oratory should
persuade through probable argument not psychagogic eloquence—or the Holy Spirit. As we shall see, the irreconcilability

---

[147] John Wilkins, *Ecclesiastes; or a Discourse concerning the gift of preaching* (London, 1646). p. 3.

[148] Ibid., p. 4.

[149] Ibid., p. 14.

[150] Ibid., pp. 19–20.

[151] De Granada, *Ecclesiasticae rhetoricae*, pp. 110–11, 168ff., 328; Agricola, pp.
199–201.

of a logical plain style and the tradition of affective spirituality leaves its mark on most English rhetorics influenced by Wilkins.

Continuity and Change (1660–1700)

After the Restoration, neo-Latin scholarship declines, although several earlier works, particularly the biblical rhetorics, continue to be reprinted. Yet the main lines of the rhetorical tradition persist in the vernaculars. In England and the Continent, sacred rhetorics continue to emphasize passionate preaching either with or without the support of artistic eloquence. The popularity of the passionate plain style has been well documented by Jones, Williamson, and Adolph.[152] This tradition enters Anglican homiletics with Wilkins, but in the latter part of the century, it mutates into a more rationalistic form. Thus Restoration preachers frequently assert that the only true way to move men is by giving them solid reasons, not by such puerile tricks as eloquence or delivery.[153] The distrust of enthusiasm and a growing scientific rationalism combine to displace Augustinian psychology with an intellectualism suspicious of anything not founded on "understanding, and the knowledg of our duties, and our interest."[154] Yet the earlier version of the passionate plain style reappears in Bishop Burnet, whose *A Discourse of the Pastoral Care* (1692) stresses ardent expressivity not solid reasons. In a passage close to Melanchthon's *De officiis concionatoris*, Burnet writes, "[The preacher] must have felt in himself those things which he intends to explain and recommend to others . . . that so he may haue a

[152] Williamson, *The Senecan Amble*, pp. 265–74; Adolph, *The Rise of Modern Prose Style*, pp. 78–130, 191–94; Richard Foster Jones, "The Attack on Pulpit Eloquence in the Restoration: An Episode in the Development of the Neo-Classical Standard for Prose," *The Seventeenth Century: Studies in the History of English Thought and Literature from Bacon to Pope* (Stanford, 1951), pp. 111–42.

[153] Jones, "The Attack," pp. 114, 117–18, 128–30; Joseph Glanville, *An Essay Concerning Preaching* (London, 1678), pp. 55–56; Adolph, *The Rise of Modern Prose Style*, pp. 123–28. This distrust of eloquence and emotion seems to grow even more pronounced in the next century; see Peter Peckard, "A Sermon Preached at Huntingdon, January 7, 1770" (London, 1770), pp. v, 4–6.

[154] Glanville, *An Essay*, p. 55; Jones, "The Attack," p. 117; John Locke, *Essay concerning Human Understanding* 3.9.2, 3.10.34.

liuely Heat in himself, when he speaks of them; and that he may speak in so sensible a manner, that it may be almost felt that he speaks from his Heart."[155] While Glanville permits the use of figures only as a concession to "the most vulgar and illiterate," Burnet eschews such condescension, allowing the preacher to employ eloquence "in giuing sometimes such tender Touches, as may soften; and deeper Gashes, such as may awaken his Hearers."[156] Yet both, like their predecessors, demand that sermons be plain as well as affective.[157]

What is less well known is that versions of the Christian grand style likewise persist until the end of the century. Although not published until 1717, François Fénelon's *Dialogues on Eloquence* was probably composed in 1679.[158] The *Dialogues* are a lucid and elegant restatement of the central themes of devout humanism. The ancient contrast between the grand and middle styles, exemplified by Demosthenes and Isocrates respectively, structures the work. Fénelon develops this contrast into a critique of contemporary preaching, fiercely criticizing all merely charming or witty eloquence on behalf of the passionate grandeur revealed in Holy Scripture and the Greek Fathers.[159] The preacher who attempts to please his congregation is forced to flattery, while the true preacher resembles a physician, unafraid to threaten, arouse, and challenge his listeners in order to cure them.[160] Yet Fénelon's insistence on "the aesthetic of the good physician" never results in the rejection of rhetoric. Instead, he defends eloquence because "the manner of saying things makes visible the manner in which one feels them, and it is this which strikes the listeners the more."[161] The goal of sacred eloquence is to move, to express emotion and thereby inspire it, awakening the love of demon-

[155] Gilbert Burnet, *A Discourse of the Pastoral Care* (London, 1692), p. 118.
[156] Glanville, *An Essay*, pp. 55–56; Burnet, *Pastoral Care*, pp. 111–12.
[157] Glanville, *An Essay*, p. 25; Burnet, *Pastoral Care*, p. 111.
[158] See Wilbur Samuel Howell's introduction to his translation of *Fénelon's Dialogues on Eloquence* (Princeton, 1951).
[159] Fénelon, *Dialogues*, pp. 57–60, 63, 95, 131, 147.
[160] Ibid., pp. 62, 76, 81–82.
[161] Ibid., p. 97.

strated truth.[162] To achieve this it uses "bold and striking figures," vivid hypotyposis, sublimity, vehemence, majesty, and grandeur.[163] Like most French rhetorics of the seventeenth century, the *Dialogues* eliminates much of the traditional rhetorical terminology. In addition, its ideals are more "Classical" and overtly critical of Silver Latin mannerisms than those found in earlier sacred rhetorics. Yet it preserves the main outline of the Christian grand style throughout.

In England, too, the grand style traditions of sacred oratory remain into the late seventeenth century. While Robert South has usually been viewed as a proponent of the plain style,[164] his sermon on pastoral duties, *The Scribe Instructed* (1660), defends the grandeur of Holy Scripture and the value of passionate eloquence. "In God's word," South writes, "we have not only a body of religion, but also a system of the best rhetoric: and as the highest things require the highest expressions, so we shall find nothing in scripture so sublime in itself, but it is reached and sometimes overtopped by the sublimity of the expression."[165] South continues, praising the ardent expressivity of the Bible, its ability to represent "all the ways, effects, and ecstacies" of love, despair, and sorrow.[166] He vehemently opposes florid and schematic embellishment, but this dislike appears throughout sacred rhetoric, stemming ultimately from the Classical antithesis of the grand and middle styles. Conspicuous ornament should be elim-

---

[162] Ibid., pp. 68, 83, 89.

[163] Ibid., pp. 63, 92–97, 101–103, 109, 118, 131–33, 151.

[164] Williamson, *The Senecan Amble*, pp. 266–68; Jones, "The Attack," pp. 114–15; Norman Mattis, "Robert South," *Quarterly Journal of Speech* 59(1929): 537–60. When engaged in controversy, however, South does not mince hyperboles. Thus one can find passages defending brevity and the plain style, when such a defense suits his purpose. For example, in the sermon against the long extempore prayers of the nonconformists, South makes the extraordinary observation: "In fine, brevity and succinctness of speech is that which, in philosophy or speculation, we call *maxim* . . . and lastly, in matters of wit, and the finenesses of imagination, *epigram*. All of them, severally and in their kinds, the greatest and the noblest things that the mind of man can show the force and dexterity of its faculties in" (*Sermons*, I: 259). I suspect, however, that if pressed, South would admit Homer and Vergil are greater authors than Martial.

[165] South, *Sermons*, 2: 74.

[166] Ibid., 2: 75.

inated because it undercuts affective response: "For is it possible that a man in his senses should be merry and jocose with eternal life and eternal death, if he really designed to strike the awful impression of either into the consciences of men?"[167] The alternative for South, however, is not plain style but austere grand style. In a striking metaphor he claims, "it is indeed no way decent for a grave matron to be attired in the gaudy, flaunting dress of youth; but it is not at all uncomely for such a one to be clothed in the richest and most costly silk, if black or grave."[168]

Other late seventeenth-century figures also bisect the heritage of the Christian grand style. While James Arderne's *Directions Concerning the Matter and Stile of Sermons* (1671) shows the influence of Restoration antienthusiasm, it still affirms the preeminence of emotional appeal and advocates the same figures of thought found in the neo-Latin sacred rhetorics of the earlier half of the century. Arderne thus argues that "the design [of a sermon] is to inflame and kindle the affections. . . . here you must give yourself that liberty and boldness of speech, which resembles *ex tempore* talk upon the warmth of a sudden thought."[169] He contrasts the spontaneity of passionate discourse to the self-indulgent artifice of the Gorgianic schemes, but praises affective figures.[170] Although more restrained and moralistic than most neo-Latin rhetorics, Arderne's *Directions* reproduces the primary features of the Christian grand style within the bounds of Restoration sobriety.

Rene Rapin's *Reflections on Eloquence in General* (1671), which was translated from the French at least twice during the seventeenth century, similarly advocates a restrained version of the grand style. The work is full of eloquent contradictions, as Rapin shifts back and forth from praising lofty, impassioned preaching to excoriating all language that is not clear, unaffected, and natural. He demands a sacred eloquence based on the majestic sublimity of the prophets yet devoid of figurative boldness. Even

---

[167] Ibid., 2: 81.

[168] Ibid., 2: 82.

[169] James Arderne, *Directions concerning the Matter and Stile of Sermons* (London, 1671), pp. 49–50.

[170] Ibid., pp, 86–87, 90–91.

more than Wilkins and Glanville, Rapin lurches awkwardly from
one rhetorical ideal to its opposite. His ambivalence seems to
spring from the Renaissance tendency, already visible in Ramism, to divorce thinking and speaking. (Significantly, none of
the major Latin sacred rhetorics is Ramist.) Once language becomes decoration, it is hard to avoid the conclusion that sermons
which depend on such garnishing for their effect are trivial and
deceptive. Hence Rapin writes, "that kind of eloquence which is
so scrupulous in the ranging of Words, and so nice in all that outward Varnish which sets a Gloss on the Expression, is scarce ever
known to succeed. . . . And the most Natural Language, such as
flows from a bare Desire of being understood, is certainly the
truest and the best."[171] While Rapin is a professed Classicist, the
habit of isolating thought from expression lurks beneath his contempt for the merely verbal. Yet he cannot dissociate himself
from a love of grandeur and magnificence nor from the traditional formulations of the Christian grand style. He is thus also
capable of writing, "a Great Subject will ever furnish out great
Thoughts; and Great Thoughts are naturally fruitful in Great
Expressions, and a Majestick Phrase."[172] Here "naturally" connotes the Classical *to prepon*, whereas "Natural" in the first quotation has quasi-primitivist implications. Rapin's confusion over
the precise meaning of "natural" points to the theoretical discontinuities prevalent in late seventeenth-century criticism.[173]

As Jones notes, after 1660 the defense of eloquence suddenly
appears among the dissenters as a reaction against the rationalism
implicit in the more latitudinarian strains of Restoration Anglicanism.[174] Hence Robert Ferguson's *The Interest of Reason in Religion* (1675) defends scriptural metaphor against the Anglican
critics who claimed that the principal difference "between sober
Christians of the Church of England, and the modern Sectaries,

[171] Rene Rapin, *Reflections on Eloquence in General; and particularly on that of the
Barr and Pulpit, The Whole Critical Works of Monsieur Rapin*, 2 vols. (London, 1706),
2: 26–27.

[172] Ibid., 2: 20.

[173] For the early history of the ambiguities concerning the meanings of "nature"
and "natural," see Plato, *Laws* 10.888e–892d.

[174] Jones, "The Attack," p. 132.

[was] that while those express the precepts & duties of the Gospel in plain and intelligible Terms, these trifle them away by childish Metaphors and Allegories."[175] To this, Ferguson responds that tropes are necessary to make the supernatural intelligible and affective since "the deep things of God do so far over-match our Reasons and Understandings, that in order to their being expressed to our Capacities, they are forced to be cloathed with as much external sensibility as may be."[176] God transcends both language and thought; we can only speak about him by analogies and similitudes, which both touch us more deeply and adumbrate the secret correspondence between the material and invisible worlds.[177] While *The Interest of Reason in Religion* deals only with tropes, Ferguson recommends Flacius and Glassius for a fuller discussion of sacred rhetoric. He also mentions a more recent biblical rhetoric, *An Introduction to the Holy Scripture* (1669) by the nonconformist Henry Lukin, with a preface by John Owen. This work borrows extensively from Glassius and Alsted and thus belongs at least in part to the tradition of the Christian grand style. Like his sources, Lukin endeavors to confute those who consider the Bible "flat and low." He begins by affirming the decorum of biblical style: "For Rhetorick the whole Scripture abounds with Tropes and Figures; and although there is nothing Pedantick in it, there is such a mixture of loftiness and gravity as becomes the Author."[178] The rest of the work is largely a summary of Glassius. Lukin comments on the Scripture's use of dramatic prosopopoeia, on its compact brevity, and on the emotional power of analogy. Nevertheless, he seems less interested than Glassius or the other Latin sacred rhetorics in analyzing the eloquence of the Bible. Instead Lukin focuses on the dogmatic implications of figurative language, apparently concerned that a misunderstanding of such expressions would lead to doctrinal error. In this respect,

---

[175] Robert Ferguson, *The Interest of Reason in Religion; with the Import & Use of Scripture Metaphors* (London, 1675), p. 278.

[176] Ibid., p. 322.

[177] Ibid., pp. 317–18, 322–23.

[178] Henry Lukin, *An Introduction to the Holy Scripture, Containing the several Tropes, Figures, Properties of Speech used therein,* preface by John Owen (London, 1669), pp. 9, 11.

he resembles Perkins and the other Calvinist exegetes more than the great sacred rhetoricians.

The Christian grand style thus endures in England after 1660 among both conformists and dissenters but considerably diluted on both sides. Significantly, the only English work addressed to an educated audience, South's university sermon, *The Scribe Instructed*, is also the only unambiguous statement of the Christian grand style. The rest seem designed for a popular audience and for this reason perhaps more reluctant to probe rhetorical issues. Their footnotes to Flacius, Glassius, and Alsted suggest that Latin remains the language of theoretical discourse, at least on this subject. Yet one great and sophisticated rhetoric does appear in English during the latter portion of the seventeenth century. This is Bernard Lamy's *The Art of Speaking*, written in French in 1675 and translated the next year.[179] *The Art of Speaking* is a general rhetoric, treating poetry as well as secular and sacred prose. It has usually been regarded as a modernist work because Lamy rejects topical invention;[180] nevertheless, especially in his treatment of sacred rhetoric, Lamy offers a lucid and deeply traditional account of the essential principles constituting the grand style. Along with Fénelon's *Dialogues on Eloquence*, it is the only rhetoric available in English that approaches both the outlook and complexity of the neo-Latin texts.

Throughout most of *The Art of Speaking*, Lamy is rather critical of the grand style, preferring instead a mixture of elliptical brevity and unaffected naturalness. Yet when he turns to sacred discourse, he abruptly shifts direction: "Those who profess Divinity, and would instruct others, must as much as in them lies imitate their great master Christ Jesus, who convinc'd the understanding, wrought upon the will, and inflam'd the heart of his

[179] In the 1676 edition, the work is misascribed to the "Messieurs du Port Royal." It went through at least three English and five French editions between 1575 and 1708. For further information on the author and his rhetorical theory, see Howell, *Logic and Rhetoric*, pp. 379ff.; François Gerbal, *Bernard Lamy (1640–1715): Etude Biographique et Bibliographique*, Le Mouvement des Idees au xviie Siecle (Paris, 1964); Douglas Ehninger, "Bernard Lamy's *L'art de Parler*: A Critical Analysis," *The Quarterly Journal of Speech* 32(1946): 429–34.

[180] Howell, *Logic and Rhetoric*, p. 379.

Disciples whilst he taught them."[181] The union of moving and teaching depicted here has its roots in Augustinian psychology and is characteristic of the Christian grand style since Erasmus.[182] Lamy goes on to claim, "the Holy Scripture is majestick: The Writings of the Fathers are full of love and zeal for those truths that they teach. When the heart is on fire, the words that come from it must of necessity be ardent."[183] The passion and grandeur of sacred discourse flows from the fiery heart—a view shared by all Renaissance rhetorics. Earlier, Lamy explains how this principle fits into the decorum of language, subject, and effect: "Noble Expressions that Render a style Magnificent . . . represent things great. . . . When things are great, and cannot be considered without great Emotion, it is necessary that the Style which describes them be sprightly, full of motion, and inriched with Figures, and Tropes, and Metaphors."[184] The excellent object awakens a passionate response, which translates itself into figurative language, for "the Passions have a peculiar Language, and are expressed only by what we call Figures."[185] This concept of decorum blends naturally into a sacramental theory of language. Immediately preceding the passage beginning "those who profess Divinity," Lamy observes, "it is a kind of Irreligion to be present at Divine Service, without some outward expression of love, respect, and veneration; we cannot communicate in an irreverent posture without sin."[186] The visible signs of piety, whether corporeal or linguistic, properly accompany inner devotion.

The Art of Speaking also includes several subordinate discussions touching on the grand style and problems of sacred dis-

---

[181] Lamy, The Art of Speaking, 2.51. The pagination of this edition is highly original. It runs 1–148, 105–49, 134–35, 152–53, 138–39, 156–57, 142–43, 160–61, 146–47, 164–89, 200–206, 197–212, 1–164. I have prefixed all those page numbers up to page 212 with a "1" and the sequence running from 1–164 with a "2."

[182] On the interrelation of love and knowledge in the Middle Ages, see Marcia Colish, The Mirror of Language: A Study in the Medieval Theory of Knowledge (New Haven, 1968), pp. 52–53, 76–77, 185–87.

[183] Lamy, The Art of Speaking, 2.52.

[184] Ibid., 2.22–23.

[185] Ibid., 1.92.

[186] Ibid., 2.51.

course. Like the neo-Latin rhetorics, it discriminates passionate
from ornamental figures and emphasizes the mimetic and expressive capacities of figurative language.[187] It discusses with unusual
acuity the familiar association between vividness and emotional
power and adds an apparently original section on the relation between acoustic devices (cadence, rhythm, phoneme) and affective
response. While Lamy shares the characteristic Renaissance contempt for the *schemata verborum*, he begins to reevaluate the positive role of sound and rhythm by dropping the rhetorical categories in favor of protolinguistic methods.[188] Finally, Lamy
combines Augustinian epistemology, particularly the notion of
the "interior truth" resident in all men, which language evokes
but cannot teach,[189] with the Longinian sublime to create a theory
of how words signify supernatural truth. *The Art of Speaking* thus
makes available in English for the first time the thoughtfulness
and range of Renaissance rhetoric at the moment when it was
passing into obsolescence.

The Christian Grand Style

In summary, we can say that two traditions of sacred rhetoric exist throughout the Renaissance. Although both rest on Augustinian psychology and perceive the indwelling Spirit as the source
of the ardent heart and passionate speech, they diverge over the
issue of decorum. The conservative tradition of the passionate
plain style either ignores or rejects the artifices of elocutio because
it denies the basic axioms of Classical decorum: that height of
style should be proportional to the excellence of subject matter
and that height of style creates, in part, the intensity of emotional
response.[190] From the early Middle Ages through the seventeenth

[187] Ibid., 1.95–96, 125.
[188] On the propriety of using terms like "linguistic" to refer to seventeenth-century discussions of language, see Murray Cohen, *Sensible Words: Linguistic Practice
in England, 1640–1785* (Baltimore, 1977), p. xviii.
[189] James J. Murphy, *Rhetoric in the Middle Ages*, p. 288; Colish, *The Mirror of
Language*, pp. 54–58.
[190] On the rejection of decorum in Herbert, see Richard Streier, *Love Known:
Theology and Experience in George Herbert's Poetry* (Chicago 1983), pp. 54–58, 183.

century, the passionate plain style retains the affective orientation of the grand style but drops the Classical assumption that a heightened eloquence is necessary for divine matters or for producing emotion. The power of preaching moves invisibly like a spiritual laser from the Spirit to the preacher's heart to his words. Passionate language mirrors the inward ardor of the speaker. Art and eloquence are only hindrances, clogging up the transfer of divine energy with sensual distractions.

This first tradition is well known, largely because it dominates English vernacular rhetoric. The second tradition is Latin and continental. For these reasons, its importance for the English Renaissance has never been discussed, despite the fact that numerous references indicate the pervasive presence of continental scholarship in England. This second tradition, that of the Christian grand style, originates with Augustine's *De doctrina* and its synthesis of Ciceronian rhetoric and biblical Christianity. It reemerges with the publication of Erasmus's *Ecclesiastes* in 1535 and persists, enriched by influxes of humanistic learning, through the late seventeenth-century vernacular rhetorics of South, Lamy, and Fénelon. Like the passionate plain style, the Christian grand style stresses the ardent, spiritual expressivity and experiential grounding of sacred discourse, but it also explores how language embodies and conveys the impassionating divine word from the heart of the preacher to the heart of his audience. That exploration, in turn, presupposes the decorum of language, subject, and affect. Sacred oratory must use a style fitted to the divine majesty and able to move the emotions. This lofty moving style rests upon the Classical grand style with its tropical richness and figures of thought, although the Christian version pays less attention than the Classical to periodicity, rhythm, and other aural dimensions of language. Instead, rhetorics in the Christian grand style lay particular weight on visual, dramatic, and expressive techniques, especially hypotyposis, prosopopoeia, apostrophe, dialogue, and the other powerful figures of thought.

Within the traditions of the Christian grand style three types of

---

See also Hooker's famous comparison of Puritan and Anglican concepts of ecclesiastical architecture (*Ecclesiastical Polity*, 5.15.1–5).

rhetoric emerge: ecclesiastical, general, and biblical. The ecclesiastical rhetorics, including both the Tridentines and liberal Protestants, rely mainly on Roman and patristic sources. The best of them, such as those by de Granada and Keckermann, include discussions of the emotions, of the relationship between language and effect, and of the differences between secular and sacred discourse. All share an emphasis on vividness and passionate figural expression. The general rhetorics are less easy to fit under a single description. They treat both Christian and secular oratory, drawing on an impressive panoply of Greek, Latin, and Byzantine sources. The hellenistic treatises of Longinus, Demetrius, and Hermogenes dominate their description of the grand style, drawing it toward the sacred, solemn, and mysterious. On the one hand, it absorbs elements of epideictic splendor and celebratory richness; on the other, it moves toward a darkly numinous allusiveness and austere force. The general rhetorics also develop a neo-Longinian concept of the imagination and a comprehensive, if eclectic, analysis of emotion, both of which reinforce the psychological foundations of the Christian grand style with its emphasis on the indissoluble connection between passionate eloquence and interiority (Longinus's "great soul") and on the affective nature of spiritual experience. Finally, the two major biblical rhetorics of the Renaissance, Flacius's *Clavis Scripturae Sacrae* and Glassius's *Philologia sacra*, along with their late seventeenth-century English offshoots, make the critical connection between the grand style and the language of the Bible. Both are characterized by grandeur, power, vividness, and density. The Bible provides a stylistic norm at once linked to the Classical grand style in its passionate elevation and yet manifestly un-Classical—if by "Classical" we mean Ciceronian—in its thick abundance of interlaced figures and its use of language less to persuade than to signify supernatural reality.

The Continental Rhetorics in England

The proprieties of Christian preaching make tracing the presence of rhetorical sources in specific sermons a fruitless task. Thus Donne's sermons often mention rhetoric, but only to disparage it.[191] Even so rambunctiously rhetorical a preacher as Nashe will declare in the beginning of *Christ's Teares over Ierusalem*: "Farre be from me any ambitious hope of the vaine merite of Arte; may that liuing vehemence I vse in lament onely proceed from a heauen-bred hatred of vncleannesse and corruption. Mine owne wit I cleane disinherite: thy fiery Clouen-tongued inspiration be my Muse. . . . Newe mynt my minde to the likenes of thy lowlines: file away the superfluous affectation of my prophane puft vp phrase, that I may be thy pure simple Orator."[192] The sermon suggests that this prayer was not answered. What matters to us is that Nashe felt obliged at least to feign inspiration. The decorum of Renaissance preaching forbids the preacher from mentioning his debt to rhetoric. And the same decorum applies to all other forms of sacred discourse—poems, meditations, allegories, tracts, and so forth. We must look to less direct sources to find evidence for the availability of continental sacred rhetorics in England.[193]

Such evidence falls into four categories: translations and editions, academic curriculums and statutes, library holdings, and allusions in English rhetorics. We have already mentioned most of the translations of continental rhetorics published in England—Hemmingsen and Hyperius translated in the mid-sixteenth century, Lamy in the late seventeenth. The only English edition of neo-Latin sacred rhetorics is a little volume printed in

---

[191] For example, see *The Sermons of John Donne*, 10 vols., ed. Evelyn M. Simpson and George R. Potter (Berkeley, 1953–1962) 2: 282, 4: 87, 91, 152.

[192] Thomas Nashe, *Christs Teares over Ierusalem* (1593), *The Works of Thomas Nashe*, 5 vols., ed. Ronald McKerrow (London, 1904–1910), 2: 15–16.

[193] From antiquity on, writers claim that they are writing in an unrhetorical, plain, brief style—even when the work in which the remark occurs decisively refutes the claim. In Curtius's words, the plain style is as much a *topos* as a reality. See Cicero, *Pro Archia*, "Quae de causa pro mea consuetudine breviter simpliciterque dixi . . ." (32); St. Gregory Nazianzen, "Oration XVI: On His Father's Silence," *A Select Library of Nicene and Post-Nicene Fathers of the Christian Church*, second series, ed. Philip Schaff and Henry Wace (Grand Rapids, Mich., 1978), "The first wisdom is to despise that wisdom which consists of language and figures of speech, and spurious and unnecessary embellishments" (7: 247). On the *topos* of brevity in the Middle Ages, see Ernst Robert Curtius, *European Literature*, pp. 487–95.

1570 containing short works by Reuchlin, Melanchthon, Hepinus, and Dietrich. The academic curriculums and statutes yield
some more interesting new evidence. Baldwin cites a 1535 Royal
Injunction for Cambridge mandating the use of Agricola, Melanchthon, and Trebizond and an Oxford statute of 1555 that includes Trebizond.[194] The seventeenth century also offers scattered evidence for the popularity of the continental rhetorics.
"Directions for a Student in the Universitie," probably written by
Richard Holdsworth, the Master of Emmanuel College from
1637 to 1643, provides the best contemporary account of education at Cambridge in the first half of the seventeenth century. For
the afternoons of the Lenten term of the third undergraduate
year, Holdsworth recommends Caussin's *De eloquentia sacra et humana* or, if that is not available, Vossius's *Commentariorum rhetoricorum.*[195] Joseph Mead (1586–1638), tutor at Christ's Church,
Cambridge, regularly assigned Keckermann's *Systema rhetoricae*
to his undergraduates.[196] Karl Wallace and Perry Miller both note
that Keckermann's *Rhetoricae ecclesiasticae* was extremely popular
in England and New England during the seventeenth century. Finally, *A New Discovery of the Art of Teaching Schoole* (1660) by
Charles Hoole also recommends Vossius, Sturm, and Caussin.[197]
Even though the evidence is far from complete, it seems that several sacred rhetorics, especially those by Trebizond, Erasmus,
Melanchthon, Caussin, Keckermann, and Vossius, were used in
the English universities during the sixteenth and seventeenth centuries.

[194] T. W. Baldwin, *William Shakspere's Small Latine & Lesse Greeke*, 2 vols. (Urbana, 1944), 1: 107, 2: 34. Baldwin's massive research repeatedly points to the
widespread popularity of Hermogenes throughout the Renaissance; cf. 1: 102,
106–107, 2: 28, 30, 39, 66.
[195] Eugene E. White, "Master Holdsworth and 'A Knowledge Very Useful and
Necessary,' " *Quarterly Journal of Speech* 53(1967): 1, 9.
[196] Harris Fletcher, *The Intellectual Development of John Milton*, 2 vols. (Urbana,
1956–1961), 2: 209–10.
[197] Foster Watson, *The English Grammar Schools to 1660: Their Curriculum and
Practice* (Cambridge, 1908), p. 443; Gerald Mohrmann, "Oratorical Delivery and
Other Problems in Current Scholarship on English Renaissance Rhetoric," *Renaissance Eloquence*, p. 62; Karl Wallace, *Francis Bacon on Communication and Rhetoric*
(Chapel Hill, 1943), p. 200; Miller, *The New England Mind*, p. 510.

Examination of personal and institutional libraries corrobo-
rates this evidence. The catalogs of Renaissance libraries, with the
exception of the Bodleian, remain in manuscript and are not easily available, but those studied reveal the steady presence of major
continental rhetorics in England. We may look first at personal
holdings, one type of which consists of the libraries of three seventeenth-century Archbishops of Canterbury—Bancroft (1544–
1610), Abbot (1562–1633), and Sheldon (1598–1677). Both Bancroft and Sheldon possessed Flacius's *Clavis*, the *Opera* of Erasmus and Melanchthon, de Granada's *Ecclesiastica rhetorica*,[198] and
Agricola's *De inventione*. Abbot and Sheldon also list Caussin's
De eloquentia. In addition, Abbot has Glassius's *Philologia sacra*
and Vossius's *Commentariorum rhetoricorum*, while Sheldon includes Keckermann's *"Rhetorica"*—probably the *Systema rhetoricae*.[199] These are all large scholarly collections. When we turn to
smaller private holdings, the list changes substantially, partly because most individuals could not afford massive editions like the
nine folio volumes of Erasmus's 1540 *Opera*, but also because extant records of private libraries mostly belong to the period between 1550 and 1600, before the publication of the works of
Keckermann, Alsted, Glassius, Caussin, and Vossius. The best
collection of these records can be found in a typescript recording
wills and inventories of libraries of students and faculty who died
in Oxford during the sixteenth and seventeenth centuries. Based
on the profession of most of its subjects, this untitled typescript,
stored in a cardboard carton in the Bodleian Archives, may be
called the Dead Don Box. A few facts are important for interpreting this material. First, the inventories are much more detailed than the wills, which often itemize only a few books as special gifts. Second, as mentioned, the preponderance of these
inventories date from the sixteenth century. From a total of 186

[198] This is listed in Bancroft as *De modo concionandi*. Sheldon lists the *Opera* of de
Granada from the three-volume 1628 edition.
[199] *Catalogus librorum summa cura proprijsque sumptis Gorgius [Abbot] nuper Can-
tuariensis Archiepiscopus Bibliotecae Lambethanae comparavit* (n.d.). The catalogs of
Bancroft and Sheldon are untitled; the former is dated as 1612, the latter, in Sheldon's own hand, has no date. These manuscripts can be found in the archives of
Lambeth Palace, London.

items that mention at least 3 books, 142 are sixteenth century, 101 from 1550–1600. Most of the remaining 44 seventeenth-century items are wills rather than inventories. Thus the absence of major seventeenth-century texts should not be taken as implying a lack of interest or availability. Third, it is often impossible to determine precisely what text is being referred to. Many entries either list only the author (e.g., "Ihonnes Sturmius") or fail to specify title (e.g., "Melanthonis Rethorica"). Allowing therefore for some ambiguity, we can get a rough picture of the rhetorics available in the private library of an Oxford scholar in the late sixteenth century. The two most popular works are Erasmus's *De copia verborum et rerum* and Agricola's *De inventione*, both of which appear in dozens of lists. Other rhetorics are more sparsely represented. The Dead Don Box mentions eleven copies of Brandolini's *De ratione scribendi* and eight of Trebizond's *Rhetorica*, numbers indicative of the lasting popularity of fifteenth-century materials. Also listed are seven copies of a rhetoric by Melanchthon, in all probability the *Elementorum rhetorices*; five each of Erasmus's *Ecclesiastes*[200] and Hyperius's *Practis of Preaching* (in Latin); four items attributed to Sturm, although only one entry specifies the *De universa ratione elocutionis rhetoricae*. There are in addition three references to Hemmingsen's *Pastor* and to unnamed works of de Granada; two to Flacius's *Clavis* and one to a rhetoric by Vossius. These figures suggest that although most individuals possessed only the relatively elementary works of Erasmus and Agricola, other continental rhetorics had some currency, while none of the lists mentions any English rhetoric.[201]

The absence of seventeenth-century inventories makes the Dead Don Box a less than satisfactory witness to the diffusion of sacred rhetoric. For a more adequate index we must turn to the

[200] The Cambridge equivalent to Oxford's Dead Don Box suggests a substantially greater diffusion of *Ecclesiastes* in Cambridge, listing twenty-nine copies between 1538 and 1593. I would like to thank E. S. Leedham-Green, Assistant Keeper of the Archives of Cambridge University, for providing me with these statistics.

[201] There were, however, four English editions of Erasmus's *De copia* and one of Brandolini before 1650. By "English rhetoric" I mean one first published in England (including English translations of continental rhetorics).

early catalogs of college libraries and the Bodleian. These catalogs generally date from the seventeenth century and therefore
would have access to most of the texts we are considering. Not
every college made a catalog. I have examined eight manuscripts,
all from Oxford, six of which are seventeenth century, one early
eighteenth, one early nineteenth.[202] It should be noted that these
libraries were far from being equal in size or quality. By the late
seventeenth century, Christ Church and Queen's both had extensive holdings, but Oriel and New College libraries possessed
only a fraction of this, the latter containing neither Augustine nor
Luther, for example. It is apparent that, with the exception of the
Tridentine rhetorics, all the major sacred and general treatises
were part of college libraries in Renaissance Oxford (see Table 1,
p. 116). Nearly every college possesses a copy of Erasmus's *Ecclesiastes*, Flacius's *Clavis*, Glassius's *Philologia sacra*, Caussin's *De eloquentia*, Keckermann's *Systema* or complete works, and Vossius's
Commentariorum rhetoricorum, either as part of the collected works
or separately. On the other hand, works popular among individual collectors, like those by Brandolini or Trebizond, appear infrequently if at all in the college catalogs.

The 1620 and 1674 catalogs of the Bodleian Library fill out this
picture. By 1620 the Bodleian contained copies of general or sacred rhetorics by Agricola, Alsted, Brandolini, Caussin, Erasmus, de Estella, Flacius, de Granada, Keckermann, Sturm, Trebizond, Valiero, and Vossius. The 1674 catalog adds the names of
Glassius, Lukin, and Alsted's *Theologica prophetica*. In other
words, almost every work discussed in this chapter, with the exception of some of the Tridentine rhetorics, was available in England during the seventeenth century.[203]

[202] Only one of these catalogs has been published; this is Henry Wilkinson, *Catalogus librorum in bibliotheca Aulae Magdalenae* (Oxford, 1661). The rest remain in
manuscript in their respective colleges. Of these, I have consulted *Catalogus librorum omnium in bibliotheca Aedis Christi* (1693); *Catalogus omnium librorum qui in hac
bibliotheca Reginensi* [rest is illegible] (1663 with additions up to the early eighteenth
century in a different hand); *Catalogus librorum Colegij Corporis Christi* (c. 1630
with additions to the 1670s); untitled catalog of University College dating from
1805; *Catalogus impressorum librorum in biblioteca Balliolensi* (1709); an untitled Oriel
catalog of 1684; and an untitled catalog of New College dating from 1650.

[203] Thomas James, *Catalogus universalis librorum in bibliotheca Bodleiana* (Oxford,

TABLE I
Sacred Rhetorics in the Oxford College Libraries

	Christ Church	Queen's	Corpus Christi	University	Balliol	Oriel	Magdalene	New College
ALSTED								
– *Encyclopedia*	X				X			
– *Theol. Proph.*	X							
CAUSSIN	X	X			X		X	
ERASMUS								
– *Ecclesiastes*				X	X			
– *Opera*	X	X	X			X		
DE ESTELLA*			X		X	X	X	
FLACIUS	X	X	X	X	X	X		
GLASSIUS	X	X	X		X	X	X	
HEMMINGSEN			X					
HYPERIUS		X						
KECKERMAN								
– *Opera*		X	X				X	X
– *Systema*	X			X				
MELANCHTHON								
– *Opera*	X		X		X			
STURM			X					
TREBIZOND			X			X		
VOSSIUS								
– *Commentariorum*	X		X	X	X	X		X

★ "De Estella" here means his *In sacrosanctum Evangelium secumdum Lucam ennarationes*. In the 1592–93 edition this contains the *De modo concionandi*. I have been unable to discover whether the two works were printed together in later editions of the commentary on Luke.

The English rhetorics themselves provide another guide to the popularity of continental works in England. In the seventeenth century several curious English rhetorics are printed. These works are usually short, often designed for schoolmasters, and in themselves very unremarkable. But they contain extensive scholia and bibliographies, pointing the reader (whether student or teacher) to the major works on any given topic. We have already looked at John Wilkins's *Ecclesiastes* with its citation of Alsted,

1620); Thomas Hyde, *Catalogus impressorum librorum bibliothecae Bodleianae in Academia Oxoniensi* (Oxford, 1674).

Keckermann, Erasmus, Hemmingsen, Flacius, and Glassius. Two other "bibliographical" rhetorics contain similar information. The *Index rhetoricus scholis et institutioni tenerioris aetatis accomodatus* by Thomas Farnaby was, as the title indicates, a grammar-school text. It was, in fact, a best seller, going through nineteen printings between 1625 and 1696. The text is clear, brief, and Ciceronian rather than Ramist. The extensive scholia suggest that it was designed for the teacher as much as for the student. In these notes and the prefatory bibliography, Farnaby lists, among others, the works of Keckermann, Alsted, Vossius, Caussin, Sturm, and Trebizond. A similar work, the *Cheiragogia, Manuductio ad artem rhetoricam* (four editons between 1619 and 1650) by Thomas Vicars mentions Keckermann, Alsted, Vossius, Hyperius, and Melanchthon. These references again suggest that the rhetorics we have examined were standard, well-known scholarly works, regularly used in the universities and authoritative sources for grammar-school texts.

Like Sir Thomas Browne, we must be willing to speak of "influences" in a "loose and flexible sense." This is not a *Quellenforschung* but an attempt to discern relevant categories and values by which to analyze the sacred prose and poetry of the English Renaissance. Although outside the Bodleian Catalogues the Tridentine rhetorics are rarely mentioned, the other sacred and general rhetorics seem to have enjoyed considerable currency in Renaissance England. Yet it may not be possible to specify what sort of currency or trace particular indebtedness. What we can say is that these continental rhetorics constitute the most complete body of theory and precept on Christian aesthetics extant during the Renaissance. We know they were available in England. Whatever their direct influence, they remain an important guide to contemporary theories of religious discourse.

CHAPTER THREE

RHETORIC, SOPHISTIC, AND PHILOSOPHY: THE LEGITIMATION OF PASSIONATE DISCOURSE

H AVING SURVEYED the development and decline of sacred rhetoric, we can now circle back to examine some of the central issues in more detail. The remainder of the book will take up three main problems. First, how can rhetoric, and particularly the grand style, be a Christian discipline? That is, given the persistent Platonic-Patristic complaint that rhetoric operates in the realm of opinion, flattery, and appearance, is not sacred rhetoric a conceptual oxymoron?[1] Second, can Classical rhetoric provide a useful basis for sacred? In the eyes of more perceptive contemporaries, the attempt to mold Christian discourse to Ciceronian precepts produced only comic anachronisms. Could another, more successful method be found to assimilate these two traditions? Third, do the specific features of the Christian grand style grow out of Renaissance Christianity or are they merely imported from an alien tradition? If rhetoric is either a self-enclosed system of precepts or inescapably tied to the assumptions and circumstances of the ancient world, then Renaissance sacred rhetoric is either an empty formalism or obsolete. Does sacred rhetoric avoid these deformities and achieve a genuine integration with its culture? All these questions imply that the Renaissance grand style can only be understood in relation to the Classical tradition outlined in Chapter One and in relation to its placement in the larger intellectual landscape of Renaissance thought. The following chapters will thus not only describe the Christian grand style but also attempt to map its intersection with the horizontal

---

[1] This problem still pervades modern studies of Renaissance rhetoric. For example see Lanham, *The Motives of Rhetoric*; Fish, *Self-Consuming Artifacts*, pp. 1–20; Samuel Ijsseling, *Rhetoric and Philosophy in Conflict: An Historical Survey*, trans. Paul Dunphy (The Hague, 1976); Jonathan V. Crewe, *Unredeemed Rhetoric: Thomas Nashe and the Scandal of Authorship* (Baltimore, 1982), pp. 4–12.

axis of rhetorical theory and the vertical axis of contemporary thought.

From Plato on, rhetoric has often been awarded a dubious legitimacy. In the Renaissance, as in antiquity, the problem of legitimacy resolves itself into two related questions: Is rhetoric merely a polite name for sophistry? And, are rhetoric and philosophy *essentially* antithetical? The relation of rhetoric to sophistic and philosophy becomes especially problematic in treatments of the grand style, because insofar as the grand style is passionate, it seems particularly vulnerable to charges of demagoguery, irrationality, and theatricalism.[2] Antiquity, as we have seen, did attempt to hold philosophy and rhetoric together while distinguishing the latter from sophistic—attempts which the Renaissance borrows—but it provided no theoretical grounds for the legitimacy of *passionate* rhetoric—indeed, the Stoic cast of Roman psychology pointed in the opposite direction. In the Renaissance, however, the legitimacy of the grand style rests on an Augustinian psychology of the emotions and their relation to noetic and spiritual activity. This psychology provides the basis for the Christian grand style by reconnecting the emotions with the search for truth and the desire for God. At the same time, however, the Renaissance borrows and adapts the solutions of ancient rhetoric: the ideal of eloquent wisdom and the distinction between play and commitment. Both Classical and Christian

---

[2] This may be one reason why modern rhetorical criticism has focused on the plain style, with its alleged connections to philosophy and serious pursuits, to the exclusion of the grand style and traditional rhetoric. See Williamson, *The Senecan Amble*; Adolph, *The Rise of Modern Prose Style*; Trimpi, *Ben Jonson*; R. F. Jones, "Science and English Prose Style in the Third Quarter of the Seventeenth Century," "The Attack on Pulpit Eloquence," and "Science and Language in England of the Mid-Seventeenth Century," collected in *The Seventeenth Century: Studies in the History of English Thought and Literature from Bacon to Pope* (Stanford, 1951). For a summary of the Croll/Jones debate, see Steadman, *The Hill and the Labyrinth*, pp. 26–35, and Adolph, *The Rise of Modern Prose Style*, pp. 5–26. Only a few modern works treat the grand style and traditional rhetoric with any sympathy or comprehensiveness; these include Rosemund Tuve, *Elizabethan and Metaphysical Imagery: Renaissance Poetic and Twentieth-Century Critics* (Chicago, 1947); Fumaroli, *L'Age de l'éloquence*; Plett, *Der affecktrhetorische Wirkungsbegriff*; and the numerous works of Brian Vickers, especially *Classical Rhetoric in English Poetry* (London, 1970), and "Rhetorical and Anti-Rhetorical Tropes."

sources are essential for understanding why, in the Renaissance, the grand style was neither trivialized into sophistic nor disenfranchised by philosophy but could become the basis for Christian discourse.

The Battlefield and the Gymnasium

The Renaissance tends to make emotional power, Cicero's *movere*, the aim of all rhetorical discourse.[3] Passion thus displaces persuasion, which in the Aristotelian tradition subsumed the subordinate ends of logos, ethos, and pathos. Likewise, for Cicero, *movere* is only one of the *officia oratoris*. But in the Renaissance we find Melanchthon, for example, writing: "the end of dialectic is to teach, of rhetoric however to move (*permovere*) and incite souls, and to lead them to a certain emotion."[4] In the next century, Alsted's *Orator* restates the same point, "Teaching is not the principal job (*officium*) of the orator; this he does by means of logic. However, he moves and bends [the soul] by rhetoric. The orator therefore mainly looks to the heart, so that he may stir up in it different emotions."[5] In several rhetorics, the connection between this emphasis on emotion and the grand style becomes explicit. The great Spanish preacher and theologian, Luis de Granada, argues, "because the grand style has the sublimity and power to move souls (which indeed is the special and distinctive duty [officium] of a preacher), in every sermon he should choose one or even several topics capable of being treated in this genus."[6] The Protestant, Bartholomew Keckermann, likewise affirms that "the distinctive excellence of the orator" lies in the grand

[3] Plett, *Der affecktrhetorische Wirkungsbegriff*; Vickers, *Classical Rhetoric*, pp. 83–121, "Figures of Rhetoric / Figures of Sound," *Rhetorica* 2 (1984): 7.

[4] *Elementorum*, p. 420.

[5] *Orator*, p. 85. See also Erasmus, *Ecclesiastes* 5: 861e; Hyperius, *The Practise*, p. 41; Valades, *Rhetorica Christiana*, p. 160; de Estella, *De modo concionandi*, p. 8; Carbo, *Divinus orator*, p. 162; Keckermann, *Rhetoricae* (1614), p. 15; Fénelon, *Dialogues*, p. 83; Cyprianus Soarez, *De arte rhetorica, libri tres, ex Aristotle, Cicerone, et Quinctiliano praecipue deprompti* (Verona, 1589), pp. 1, 87; Gerardus Vossius, *Rhetorices contractae, sive partitionum oratoriarum libri quinque* (Oxford, 1631), p. 117.

[6] De Granada, *Ecclesiasticae rhetoricae*, p. 328; see also de Arriaga, *Rhetoris Christiani*, pp. 362–63.

style.[7] Even though most vernacular English rhetorics somewhat inconsistently (from a Classical point of view) reject the grand style while still emphasizing passion, and, in fact, many sacred rhetorics prefer to speak in terms of the officia rather than their respective genera, the preeminence of passionate speech throughout all these works pulls them, however obliquely, into the orbit of the grand style.[8]

The emphasis on passion in Renaissance rhetoric heightens the separation of rhetoric and sophistic already manifest in antiquity and intensified by the traditional Christian revulsion at self-display and vain eloquence. Some Puritans push this opposition to the virtual rejection of all eloquence and art, but most other Renaissance scholars preserve the Classical distinction between rhetoric and sophistry, forbidding only the latter. While sophistry can have several meanings,[9] the most widespread one connects it with the genus medium or *floridum* and therefore with aesthetic pleasure (delectatio), playfulness, and the desire for praise.[10] The sophist uses a highly wrought style to impress audiences with his own artistic virtuosity. Ludovico Carbo thus contrasts rhetoric and so-

[7] Keckermann, *Systema*, p. 1670.

[8] Why those rhetorics which so clearly use the terminology of the grand style to describe preaching decline to give it its traditional name is not altogether clear, although a hint appears in a minor German rhetoric by one Georgius Sohnius. Sohnius speaks of the grand style as that used *"in cancellariis,"* by which he apparently means the ornate, flowery manner of official documents, those late offspring of the medieval ars dictaminis. In other words, as late as the seventeenth century, the term "grand style" may have retained undesirable medieval accretions of meaning that at times discouraged its use (*Tractatus de interpretatione ecclesiastica*, in Keckermann's *Rhetoricae* [1616], p. 161). On the ars dictaminis, see Murphy, *Rhetoric in the Middle Ages*, pp. 193–268; Jerrold E. Seigel, *Rhetoric and Philosophy in Renaissance Humanism: The Union of Eloquence and Wisdom, Petrarch to Valla* (Princeton, 1968), pp. 206–25. For the grand style in the Middle Ages, see Quadlbauer, *Die antike Theorie*, pp. 17, 22.

[9] Sophistic can mean not only false rhetoric but also false logic, or eristics, as in Plato's dialogue, *The Sophist*. Humanist writers often use the term in this sense to derogate scholastic philosophy (Charles Trinkaus, *The Scope of Renaissance Humanism* [Ann Arbor, 1983], p. 171). Von Arnim treats sophistic as coextensive with all practical or therapeutic (as opposed to scientific) philosophy (*Dio von Prusa*, pp. 80, 84–87, 97–98, 113). In this broad and not necessarily pejorative sense, almost all humanist thought is sophistic.

[10] Sturm, *De universa*, p. 665.

phistic: "*Elegantia* designates a harmonious and ornate style of speaking, designed to delight, as was once popular among the sophists. . . . In *elegantia* is a certain power of delighting, in eloquence the power of persuasion. The former shines and sparkles, occupying the senses with trifles; the latter burns and flames in order to move souls."[11] The opposite of sophistic rhetoric in most Renaissance discussions is not an unadorned, dialectical style but the conjunction of power and luminosity. Although Christ did not use "sophistic elegance and a vain rouge of words and delicate harmony" nevertheless his words were not "confused nor ill-framed nor uncouth" but "sinewy and splendid . . . [and] suited for teaching and moving, which are the two principle gifts of an orator."[12]

As in antiquity, the bifurcation of rhetoric and sophistic in the Renaissance rests on the premise that visible art inhibits emotional response. As soon as the audience notices how *well* something is said, it assumes a position of critical detachment. The delight in language for its own sake thus produces a playful, distanced appreciation at odds with the commitment and unselfconscious absorption of strong emotion. The first excites applause, the latter tears.[13] Bernard Lamy summarizes the prevalent view: "The Study and Art that appear in a compt and polite Discourse, are not the Character of a Mind lively touch'd with the things of which he speaks; but rather of a Man unconcern'd and merry. . . . The Flowers and Ornaments of Rhetorick are not proper for grave and majestick Subjects."[14] The opposition be-

---

[11] Carbo, *Divinus orator*, p. 23.

[12] Ibid., p. 18.

[13] Dionysius of Halicarnassus, "Demosthenes," 40; Quintilian 12.10.62; Saint Augustine, *On Christian Doctrine*, 4.53; Valades, *Rhetorica Christiana*, p. 85. The Renaissance identification of aesthetic pleasure with play probably derives from Saint Thomas, for whom aesthetic creation and response can both be forms of sheer play, activities performed for no other end but the joy of performance. Thomas accepts the legitimacy of such play provided it is neither immoral nor excessive, as a necessary part "in the total rhythm of human life" (Edgar De Bruyne, *The Esthetics of the Middle Ages*, trans. Eileen B. Hennessy [New York, 1969], pp. 169–70).

[14] Lamy, *The Art of Speaking*, 1.145, 2.40; see also Erasmus, *Ecclesiastes*, 5: 849b, 922d; de Granada, *Ecclesiasticae rhetoricae*, p. 306–307; Keckermann, *Rhetoricae*

tween commitment and play determines the historical polarities of ancient oratory. For Caussin, during the great age of the Attic orators, eloquence "ruled all things," making war and administering armies, navies, law, justice. Orators were "councillors of princes and rulers of the people," while "other *literati* and philosophers lay hidden between the walls of the school." The decline of rhetoric began when certain teachers of *"umbratilis* eloquence" opened their own schools and "started to affect the delicacies of artificial oratory and a certain siren-like luxury of discourse," unsuited to the demands of political life. This ornamental "scholastic" eloquence flourished under the Empire because its rulers "preferred to maintain clever men among these games of eloquence (*eloquentiae ludi*) than to open the obstructed way to public speeches and popular tumult."[15] The ornamental play of the sophists supplants political oratory and the rhetoric of civic engagement. The antagonism between absolute monarchy and oratorical power resurfaces, as Caussin is well aware, in the monarchies of the late Renaissance. Popular deliberative oratory yields to ethics and the rhetoric of the courtier. Yet the modern world provides an arena for public oratory unknown to the ancients "in sacred orations . . . which need luminous wisdom and language alive with charity, not verbal cleverness (*verborum argutiae*)."[16] Sacred rhetoric inherits the tradition of ancient deliberative oratory with its seriousness and engagement in the central concerns of human life, while luxuriant verbal ornament remains a sort of amusement, excluded by its artificiality from participating in either civic or spiritual contests.

The association of aesthetic pleasure and detachment contrasts

---

(1616), p. 110; Alsted, *Theologica*, p. 8; Caussin, *De eloquentia*, pp. 5, 9, 141, 554, 576, 941; Glassius, *Philologia sacra* (1705), p. 18; Butler, *Oratoriae*, b3r; South, *Sermons*, 2: 81; Arderne, *Directions*, pp. 56, 90–91; Fénelon, *Dialogues*, pp. 57–61, 63, 87, 109; Strebaeus, *De verborum electione*, p. 292; Frederico Borromeo, *De sacris nostrorum temporum oratoribus libri quinque* (Milan, 1632), p. 81. A major difference between contemporary and traditional poetics lies in the former's preference for conspicuous artifice over emotional power. See Donald Davie, "The Rhetoric of Emotion," *The Poet in the Imaginary Museum: Essays of Two Decades* (Manchester, 1977), pp. 242–48.

[15] Caussin, *De eloquentia*, pp. 8–9.

[16] Ibid., p. 759.

with the terminology of violence commonly associated with the grand style. Words like *impellere, trahere, concitare, pugnare, permovere* suggest the loss of reflective distance and rational individuation inherent in the experience of passionate rehtoric. These polarities of detachment and violence, play and engagement, reappear in the Romantic dialectic of irony and the sublime, since both irony and conspicuous art suggest an absence of "sincerity" or unreserved commitment to one's ostensible subject.[17] What Northrop Frye says about irony could easily be extended to cover sophistic: "When we try to isolate the ironic as such, we find that it seems to be simply the attitude of the poet as such, a dispassionate construction of a literary form, with all assertive elements, implied or expressed, eliminated."[18] But there is a crucial difference between Renaissance aestheticism and Romantic irony. In the Renaissance, the relation between free play and seriousness is not dialectical but simply antagonistic. Aesthetic playfulness does not resolve into a higher seriousness and passion but destroys them. The shift from dichotomy to dialectic is symptomatic of the difference between the two periods. At least in theory, sophistic remains only the *Doppelgänger* of Renaissance rhetoric, its disturbing and distorted, if persistent, shadow.

As in antiquity, the rejection of aesthetic playfulness in the Renaissance appears under the paired images of Isocrates and Demosthenes,[19] the gymnasium and the forum,[20] and especially the game and the battle (see Chapter One). Criticizing the logical sophists of his own day, Erasmus writes,

[Such teachers] train [their students] more for the gymnasium (*palaestra*) than for battle. . . . When they come to serious matters (*seria*) they seem inept rather than instructed: wherefore scarcely any others are more unprepared for real fighting than those whose whole lives have been spent teaching and learning the art of sword fighting. In their games (*ludus*) they know how to slice with a sword the arrow hurled at them before it

[17] Ibid., p. 554.

[18] Northrop Frye, *Anatomy of Criticism* (Princeton, 1957), pp. 40–41.

[19] Strebaeus, *De verborum electione*, pp. 303, 323; Caussin, *De eloquentia*, p. 90; Fénelon, *Dialogues*, p. 63.

[20] Carbo, *Divinus orator*, p. 251; Caussin, *De eloquentia*, p. 576.

reaches its goal. But in war the archer does not warn his victim in advance nor abide by the rules of the swordsman's game.[21]

This military imagery can be easily misunderstood. In the narrower sense, the comparison between the soldier and the orator highlights the vehemence of forensic oratory. More broadly understood, however, it picks out the urgency and involvement of all true rhetoric. In this latter sense, rhetoric is not primarily a form of aggression but of commitment to the real issues of human existence. As the warrior risks his life and freedom on the battlefield, so the true orator stakes his existence on proclaiming and defending the truths of salvation. Those whose sermons are "so garnished with quibbles and trifles," South complains, act "as if they played with truth and immortality. . . . For is it possible that a man in his senses should be merry and jocose with eternal life and eternal death?"[22] Oratory resembles a battle because both are serious and therefore impatient of virtuoso flourishes and the other self-pleasing refinements of art.[23]

In the Renaissance, the sense of oratory as warfare undergoes specifically Christian transformations. The contrast between play and commitment, between the shade of the declamatory schools and the sun of the forum, between games and battles, familiar from the ancients, reappears in sacred guise in Caussin's attack on florid psuedo-Classical preaching:

The Hebrew women are not as the Egyptian; whereas the latter bore children on ivory couches among vain luxuries; the former lightened their womb in the sun and dust (*sol, & pulvis*), even among their burdens. . . . But we by whom the heat of the day and its weight must be borne, we who must preach the cross, the cross, who must arouse, prick, thunder against all sinners sunk in perfidy by their crimes, what have we in common with these luxuries. . . . Who could fight against sins if tied and bound by the laws of rhythmic speech? What energy and vehemence will he have who plays with circular periods? . . . He does

---

[21] Erasmus, *Ecclesiastes*, 5: 849f. See also 830c, 834e, 870f, 986e.

[22] South, *Sermons*, 2: 81.

[23] On the comparison between oratory and warfare see Strebaeus, *De verborum electione*, p. 323; Caussin, *De eloquentia*, pp. 70, 360; Lamy, *The Art of Speaking*, 1.99, 145.

not come to fight, he comes to show off. Do you expect him to contend? He plans to dance.[24]

The preacher assumes the role of the Classical orator with his passionate, skiagraphic style and moral responsibility. Christian urgency opposes rhythmic periods and the refinements of eloquence—but it does so in the name of passion and the grand style.

This battle against sin furthermore belongs to a larger confrontation—the interior struggle of good and evil. Christian existence is an *agon*. Valiero thus defends passionate rhetoric as a weapon in this psychomachia: "because our internal enemies, who treacherously attack us . . . are most strong and fierce, we must move [men's] souls and arouse them to this inevitable battle, lest careless and asleep they be conquered."[25] The imagery of warfare connects rhetoric to the inner struggles of moral life, not to the speaker's own aggressive intentions on his audience. The true orator, unlike the sophist, does not seek power and applause, but subordinates himself to spiritual and ethical aims. Didacus Valades thus explains that the "true end" of the sacred orator is "by persuasion to increase the kingdom of God, to gain souls for Christ. . . . to awaken souls redeemed by Christ's precious blood to eternal life and beatitude. . . . The Christian orator therefore does not seek glory for himself or for his own but the glory of Christ Jesus."[26]

The antithesis of sophistry and rhetoric emerges on the stylistic level in the distinction between the schemes of words and the figures of thought. In " 'Attic Prose' in the Seventeenth Century," Croll states, "the oratorical style was distinguished by the use of the *schemata verborum* . . . which are chiefly similarities or repetitions of sound used as purely sensuous devices to give pleasure or aid the attention. The essay style is characterized by the absence of these figures . . . and, on the other hand, by the use of metaphor, aphorism, antithesis, paradox and the other figures which . . . are known as the *figurae sententiae*, the figures of wit or

[24] Caussin, *De eloquentia*, p. 945.
[25] Valiero, *De ecclesiastica rhetorica*, p. 45.
[26] Valades, *Rhetorica Christiana*, p. 9.

thought."[27] Since the period is a form of balanced, aural composition, Croll also associates it with the schemes of words and the
oratorical style. This influential classification, however, utterly
inverts those found throughout Renaissance rhetoric, which link
the figures of thought with the power and passion of the grand
style, disparaging the schemes of words, and to a lesser extent the
symmetrical period, as merely sensuous and distracting ornament. Keckermann notes, "Isocrates is inferior to Demosthenes
because the former did not sufficiently esteem the figures of
thought but placed too much importance on schemes; wherefore
in Isocrates one finds much sweetness but little power or passion."[28] The popular school text, *Rhetoricae libri duo*, by Charles
Butler makes the same point; speaking of the figures of thought,
he observes, "there is no other kind of language more powerful in
moving souls. . . . As these [figures], along with tropes and
schemes produce delight and instruction, so they alone also will
have greatest efficacy in moving and conquering—the chief matter in oratory."[29] The distinction between figures and schemes
rests on the Renaissance's sense of the superiority of the eye to the
ear. Vision is more intimately connected with both thought and
emotion than hearing, which responds mainly to aesthetic surfaces.[30] Agricola thus remarks, "the present view of an object especially penetrates the mind, nor can anything else move the
emotions more powerfully. For those things (as Horace says)
transmitted through the ears stimulate the soul more slowly."[31]
Since all forms of visualization (e.g., hypotyposis, prosopographia, icon) and dramatization (e.g., apostrophe, interrogatio,
personification) fall under the figures of thought, these are more
passionate and therefore more properly oratorical than the

[27] Croll, *"Attic" and Baroque*, p. 54.

[28] Keckermann, *Systema*, p. 1482.

[29] Butler, *Rhetoricae*, bk. 1, chap. 24. Also Erasmus, *Ecclesiastes*, 5: 857c, 983c–
d, 1000c–d; Keckermann, *Rhetoricae* (1614), p. 38; Alsted, *Encyclopedia*, p. 389;
Arderne, *Directions*, pp. 86–87; Lamy, *The Art of Speaking*, 1.157; John Smith, *The
Mysterie of Rhetorique Unvail'd* (London, 1657), p. 7.

[30] Erasmus, *Ecclesiastes*, 5: 983c–d; Carbo, *Divinus orator*, p. 13; Vickers, "Figures," p. 12.

[31] Agricola, *De inventione*, p. 388.

schemes which merely "entice the ears."[32] As in antiquity, the emphasis on emotional power also works against the demand for periodicity, despite the immense authority of Cicero's own largely periodic style. While most rhetorics recommend periods for epideictic oratory, history, and exordia, they are considered unsuitable when either passion or force is sought.[33] The Isocratic period, with its predictable antithetic balance supported by aural schemes, is especially inappropriate in such cases. The tendency in modern scholarship to regard Isocrates as the paradigm for the oratorical style thus disregards the fact that most ancient and Renaissance rhetorics saw these two styles as opposite.

This confusion of aural ornamentation with the grand style may reach back into the Middle Ages with its elaborate rhyme-prose and conflation of grandeur with sweetness, or it may stem from the early humanists' exaggerated imitation of Ciceronian *concinnitas*.[34] In any case, by the early sixteenth century, two alternative interpretations of the *summum dicendi genus* have become sufficiently distinct to elicit contemporary comment. One version approximates Croll's schematic and periodic oratorical style, the other the harsher and more passionate elevation that becomes the core of the grand style for the next century and a half. The discrimination between these two versions appears in Jacobus Ludovicus Strabaeus's *De verborum electione et collocatione oratoria* of 1538

The highest type of oration is one thing to the prince of Roman eloquence, another to men scantily and illiberally educated. The latter falsely believe whatever seems conspicuous by the weight of its sentiments, delightful with its flowers of words, variegated by striking figures, and apt with gentle composition and beautifully flowing rhythms possesses grandeur and sublimity. . . . Therefore [they think] Isocrates, the sweetest of orators, grander than Pericles and Demosthenes, who aroused Greece with the lightening-bolts of his oratory. . . . If anyone

---

[32] Carbo, *Divinus orator*, p. 13.
[33] Cicero himself recognizes this (*Orator* 208–11). Both Caussin (*De eloquentia*, pp. 371, 945) and Vossius (*Commentariorum*, 2: 68–69) argue that the periodic style is not passionate.
[34] Michael Baxandall, *Giotto and the Orators: Humanist Observers of Painting in Italy and the Discovery of Pictorial Composition* (Oxford, 1971), p. 29.

believes these things absurd, let him believe with the greatest orator
[Cicero] that a battle is more difficult than a wrestling match (*palae-
strum*), serious matters than games. . . . The lofty and challenging style is
. . . grand, full . . . ardent. . . . It thunders, lightens . . . fights with
harsh words and terrible figures. It allows frequent hiatus, harsh joining
of syllables, few circular periods yet resounding ones, many more *incisa*
and *membra*, vehement rather than sweet rhythms. . . . [35]

Strebaeus puts together most of the qualities we have been examining: delight versus power, periodicity versus briefer and
harsher composition, Isocrates versus Demosthenes, battles versus games. Although he recognizes that both styles claim to be
the "summum genus," he clearly believes the Isocratic inferior to
the agonistic grand style of Cicero and Demosthenes. Both in the
ancient world and the Renaissance, two antithetic types of elevation thus emerge, one closely linked to sophistic and what is often
called the florid or middle style, one associated with civic and sacred oratory. To mistake the former type for the oratorical style
reverses the traditional relation between them. Playfulness, conspicuous artifice, elaborate periodic or schematic balance characterize neither the grand style nor rhetoric broadly considered.
Particularly in the Renaissance, these remain essentially serious
and affective, emphasizing expressivity, drama, and vividness far
above aural harmonies or sound play.

Conversion and Flattery

To the ancient contrast between play and commitment, Renaissance Christianity adds the opposition of flattery to conversion.
Like the former, this polarity turns on the difference between
sophistry and rhetoric (or alternatively false and true rhetoric).
The sophist flatters and entertains his audience; the true orator
converts and challenges. While the former "acts only to please
and to make beautiful pictures," the latter tries "to burn, to cut to
the quick, and . . . to effect cures by the bitterness of remedies
and the severity of the regimen."[36] As this imagery suggests, for

---

[35] Strebaeus, *De verborum electione*, p. 303.
[36] Fénelon, *Dialogues*, p. 81. For the overly Platonic identification of flattery and

the Renaissance, the orator/preacher is the "good physician"; since the orators' "chief end is to preserve the truth, they are enforced to employ all their cunning to beat down such Passions as are contrary thereunto; and in discharging themselves of their duty, they play the part of the Physitian."[37] In addition, sacred rhetoric always describes the aim of preaching as radical conversion. According to Erasmus, the preacher "first tears out of his listeners' souls the roots of evil thoughts and the wicked seeds of impious doctrine from whence sprout bitter fruits; and he demolishes the building erected on a bad foundation; he scatters the tares that have sprouted and ruins the badly begun edifice. In place of what has been torn down and destroyed he plants good seedlings and erects a building that will not yield to the tempest."[38] The preacher does not tell the congregation what it already believes; in Flacius's words, the evangel does not "flatter its hearers with the empty allurements of girls or even of whores . . . [but is like] a two-edged sword, penetrating bone and marrow, and so also like a hammer, breaking stones and the adamantine hearts of men."[39]

The sacred rhetorics frequently remark on the difference between pagan or secular eloquence, which must please and gratify its hearers, and the authority of the preacher who ascends to the pulpit like "a judge, teacher, father, and ambassador of God."[40] The subversive otherworldliness of Christian oratory attacks the

---

conversion with rhetoric and dialectic respectively, see Fish, *Self-Consuming Artifacts*, pp. 1–2.

[37] Jean François Senault, *The Use of Passions*, trans. Henry, Earl of Monmouth (London, 1671), p. 171. For other references to the orator as physician, see Fénelon, *Dialogues*, p. 82; Alsted, *Orator*, p. 162.

[38] Erasmus, *Ecclesiastes*, 5: 789e–f.

[39] Flacius, *Clavis*, 2: 461. Similarly, according to Donne, "the way of Rhetorique in working upon weake men, is first to trouble the understanding, to displace, and to discompose, and disorder the judgement, to smother and bury in it, or to empty it of former apprehensions and opinions, and to shake that beliefe, with which it had possessed it self before, and then when it is thus melted, to powre it into new molds, when it is thus mollified, to stamp and imprint new formes, new images, new opinions in it" (*Sermons*, 2: 282).

[40] Carbo, *Divinus orator*, pp. 203, 13; see also Caussin, *De eloquentia*, p. 146; Hyperius, *The Practise*, p. 43; de Granada, *Ecclesiasticae rhetoricae*, p. 95.

common-sense evaluation of the world and its pleasures, invert-
ing the popular estimate of value. It "urges things contrary to human sense, and bitter and distasteful to the depraved and mis-
guided nature of men: as the contempt of wealth, scorn of
honors, flight from pleasure, hatred of parents, love of enemies."[41] It is easier, Fredrico Borromeo observes, "to fill a judge
with fear, anger, and suspicion than to lead souls to desire pov-
erty, for we fight against men's ingrained habits of thought and
perception (*sensus ipsi*)."[42] Men naturally desire what is visible and
at hand over immaterial and distant goods. They are therefore, as
the rhetorics point out, naturally adverse to religion, since it in-
terferes with their pursuit of sensible pleasures.[43] Rhetoric, however, can restore the true order of love by creating vivid and powerful images of spiritual truth, by dramatizing, picturing, and
amplifying what would otherwise be too remote for our weakened minds to grasp or wills to desire.[44]

The essential ingredient in conversion is not the stilling of "rational consciousness" or discursive thought[45] but the transfor-

[41] Carbo, *Divinus orator*, p. 32.

[42] Borromeo, *De sacris oratoribus*, pp. 5–6.

[43] Flacius, *Clavis*, 2: 1–2, 419–20; Fénelon, *Dialogues*, p. 94; Lamy, *The Art of
Speaking*, 1.139–40; Keckermann, *Rhetoricae* (1616), p. 9.

[44] Wilkins, *Ecclesiastes*, p. 18; Lamy, *The Art of Speaking*, 1.138–39; Carbo, *Divinus orator*, pp. 187–200; Hyperius, *The Practise*, pp. 1–2, 44; Valiero, *De ecclesiastica rhetorica*, pp. 95–96; Sturm, *De universa*, p. 172; Keckermann, *Systema*, p.
1612, *Rhetoricae* (1616), pp. 53ff., 84–85; Trinkaus, *Scope*, pp. 440–41, and *In Our
Image and Likeness: Humanity and Divinity in Italian Humanist Thought*, 2 vols.
(Chicago, 1970), 1: 12, 62, 119, 144; Fumaroli, *L'Age de l'éloquence*, pp. 108, 200.

[45] Fish, *Self-Consuming Artifacts*, pp. 3–4. Fish's intuition that Renaissance texts
habitually subvert the rational structure they had created suggests in fact a crucial
feature of Christian discourse. Colish notes that Augustine's *De Trinitate* and
Thomas's doctrine of analogy work in precisely the same way as the seventeenth-
century works Fish analyzes. Concerning Saint Thomas, she writes, "He begins
by building up the analogy, underlining the similarities between God and man.
Then, he breaks down the analogy, illustrating the immense gap between God
and man" (*Mirror*, p. 221). But the fact that *ultimately* the rational structures of
language cannot contain God does not entail that the point of the attempt is to
demonstrate its futility. Sacred discourse is neither literal nor self-consuming, but
analogical and metaphoric, since "our knowledge of God in this life . . . is partial
and shadowy. It is the knowledge of faith, *per speculum in aenigmate*, and it is acquired and expressed through speech. Augustine's use of the term 'aenigma' in

mation of the emotions. Rhetoric rather than dialectic is associated with conversion precisely because it reaches not only the intellect but the heart. Because both moral and spiritual life are much less a question of theoretical knowledge than rightly ordered will and emotions, the preacher or orator must concentrate his endeavors on transforming the "loves of the soul." Keckermann writes, "The principal function of an orator lies more in moving the emotions than in teaching the minds of his hearers because men sin more from corrupt emotions than ignorance of the truth. . . . Our age has much knowledge but too little conscience; thus he [the orator] must first attempt to move (permovere) men's consciences."[46] Flacius likewise comments, "emotion or the movements of the heart govern practical knowledge and choice . . . [and] Holy Scripture deals not with speculative but practical knowledge, which God wishes to be, above all else, living, ardent, and active."[47] Whereas Classical rhetoric envisions speech in the context of judgment and therefore subordinates emotional appeal to judicial and political reasoning, sacred rhetoric presupposes an audience at least nominally Christian and therefore already intellectually convinced. As Renaissance rhetorics frequently declare, people do not sin from ignorance of what is good but rather from the perversion of appetite; they thus need less to be persuaded than moved, for wrong emotions are corrected not by eradicating all feeling but by awakening virtuous emotions.[48]

The link between emotion and conversion belongs to the Augustinian tradition. Both Aristotle and Aquinas consider emotion

---

this connection is quite important. . . . While literal signification is a suitable way to express fairly straightforward realities, metaphorical signification is far better suited to express realities that are themselves intrinsically obscure and difficult to understand. An aenigma, like any other figure of speech, and like speech itself, is designed to communicate information. Its built-in difficulties thus enhance, rather than reduce, its expressive power. In attempting to convey the infinite incomprehensibility of God, then, an aenigma is a most suitable *vox significans rem*" (p. 79).

[46] Keckermann, *Systema*, p. 1392.

[47] Flacius, *Clavis*, 1: 179.

[48] De Granada, *Ecclesiasticae rhetoricae*, pp. 82, 87; Carbo, *Divinus orator*, p. 205; Keckermann, *Rhetoricae* (1616), pp. 44–45.

in relation to *moral* virtue, but both also exclude it from man's highest activities. Thus Aristotle does not discuss the joy of contemplation in affective terms nor does Aquinas carry the analysis of emotion over from the moral to the theological virtues. For Aquinas, faith, hope, and charity pertain to the will or intellective appetite, not to the emotions. Augustine, however, as we have seen, treats the will or love as the source of emotion and all emotions as species of love. Although he does not relate this psychology to problems of rhetoric, it is easy to see that if language is able to move the heart and change the loves of the soul, then it becomes a potential means of salvation. "At one speech of a fisherman," Erasmus writes, "nearly three thousand men were transformed into new creatures."[49]

To a large extent, Renaissance psychological theory rests on this Augustinian analysis of the soul,[50] although modified by Thomist and neo-Platonic elements. In addition, the Renaissance appropriates this Augustinian psychology for rhetorical theory, restoring the connection between the emotions and rhetoric fundamental to Aristotle but thereafter largely abandoned. This is particularly true for the sacred rhetorics, since Renaissance Augustinianism belongs to the history of the religious renewal, both Catholic and Protestant, that took place in the sixteenth and seventeenth centuries.

Following Augustine, Renaissance psychology mitigates the distinction between the will and the sensitive appetite. Particularly among Protestant writers like Melanchthon and Keckermann, emotion is no longer restricted to the particular goods of sense but embraces the love of God, repentance, longing for beatitude—all the acts of what Saint Thomas had called the intellective appetite.[51] Catholic thinkers tended to be more conservative, attempting to articulate connections between volition and emotion rather than abolishing the distinction between the two: Li-

[49] Erasmus, *Ecclesiastes*, 5: 828e.

[50] For the Stoic and rationalist psychology of the Renaissance—the primary alternative to Augustinianism—see Bouwsma, "Two Faces"; Jones, "The Attack"; Gardiner et al., *Feeling and Emotion*.

[51] Anthony Levi, s.j., *French Moralists: The Theory of the Passions, 1585 to 1649* (Oxford, 1964), pp. 23–33, 117–18.

bertus Fromondus, a professor at Louvain, thus posits a certain re-
ciprocal "sympathy" between emotion and volition; the acts of
the will transform themselves into emotion but are not identical
to it.[52] Similarly, the Spanish Jesuit, Francisco Suarez, argues that
certain acts of the will are very much like emotions, yet he preserves the Thomist identification of emotion with sensible appetite.[53] Lutheran, Reformed, and English thinkers, however, defended the Augustinian identification of will and emotion. In his
Systema physicum, Bartholomew Keckermann (who wrote extremely popular textbooks on just about everything) includes human emotions in the will.[54] Likewise Melanchthon writes, "I
shall not listen to the Sophists [i.e., scholastics] if they deny that
the human affections—love, hate, joy, sadness, envy, ambition,
and the like—pertain to the will (*voluntas*). . . . For what is will
(*voluntas*) if it is not the fount of the affections? And why do we
not use the word 'heart' instead of 'will' (*voluntas*). . . . For since
God judges hearts, the heart must be the highest and most powerful part of man."[55] Melanchthon's substitution of "heart" for
"will" represents a commitment with theological as well as rhetorical implications, since if volition is emotion, then it is not a
matter of free choice. One cannot choose one's feelings. As Melanchthon immediately notes, the Protestant denial of free will
follows from the identification of will and affect. The heart cannot be moved by reasons (even Astrophil knows this) but only by

[52] Libertus Fromondus, *Philosophiae Christianae de anima libri quator* (Louvain,
1649), pp. 730–35.

[53] Francisco Suarez, s.j., "De actibus, qui vocantur passiones," *Opera omnia*, 23
vols. (Paris, 1856–1878), 4: 456–57.

[54] Keckermann, *Systema physicum septem libris adornatum, Opera*, 1: 1560, 1625.
Keckermann distinguishes between animal emotions which pertain only to the
present and human emotion which concerns past, present, and future objects. The
latter he classes as a special feature of the will ("Voluntas specialiter spectata est
affectus quidam homini proprius"). These human emotions include not only love,
happiness, and hope but also theoretical desire ("cupiditas magis theoretica")—
the longing to know the truth.

[55] Philip Melanchthon, *Loci communes theologici*, in *Melanchthon and Bucer*, ed.
Wilhelm Pauck; trans. Lowell J. Satre, The Library of Christian Classics 19 (Philadelphia, 1969), pp. 27–29. See also Melanchthon's *Liber de anima*, in *Opera quae
supersunt omnia*, 13: 58, 122–41, 167–69.

grace—and eloquence. This position is turned upside down by the seventeenth-century English psychologist, William Fenner, who identifies willing and feeling but by placing the emotions in the will rather than vice versa: "As the affections are motions, so they are motions of the will. I know Aristotle . . . place[s] the affections in the sensitive part of the Soul and not in the will. . . . But this cannot be so. . . . How could the Apostle command us to set our affections on God . . . if the affections were in the sensitive and unreasonable part?"[56] Fenner simply assumes that the love of God is an emotion as well as a virtue, from which he draws the obvious conclusion that it must be a "voluntary" emotion or else our spiritual life would be completely outside our control, as hunger and thirst are outside our control.[57] Another English psychologist of the same period, Edward Reynolds, also locates emotion in the highest activity of the soul. He divides the emotions into three categories: the spiritual, rational, and sensitive. All three are properly emotions, the first including mystical ecstacy, the second the love of God and virtue (i.e., motions of the heart/will following reason); only the last overlaps with what Aristotle and Aquinas would have called emotion.

This psychology pervades Renaissance rhetoric. The general and ecclesiastical rhetorics, especially the more scholarly ones, contain detailed lists of emotions as part of their emphasis on movere and passionate discourse. Almost always, the list begins with the love of God and includes hope and sometimes even faith, the two remaining theological virtues, along with spiritual joy, contrition, and desire for God, as well as "secular" emotions like shame and anger.[58] Only the nature of their object differentiates secular from sacred, evil from good emotion. "For the sake of example," Carbo writes, "if desire (concupiscendi vis) is directed to-

[56] William Fenner, A Treatise of the Affections; or The Souls Pulse (London, 1650), p. 4.

[57] Fenner has lost the Aristotelian distinction between physiological appetite and the irrational part of the soul that is nevertheless subject to reason.

[58] Caussin, De eloquentia, pp. 459–512; Keckermann, Systema, pp. 1615–31; Rhetoricae (1616), p. 43; Carbo, Divinus orator, pp. 211–27; de Granada, Ecclesiasticae rhetoricae, pp. 83–87, 161–66; Dietrich, Ratio brevis, p. 29; Melanchthon, Elementorum 13: 425–27, 434.

wards the heavens, it brings forth praiseworthy emotions which
move us towards perfect virtues: as weariness of this life, fear of
future punishment, desire of eternal beatitude, love of God, contempt of self, and others of this sort."[59]

Caussin's *De eloquentia sacra et humana* provides one of the most
detailed and complex treatments of emotion in Renaissance rhetoric. The sections on love are characteristic of his method.[60]
Caussin begins with the Augustinian position that love moder-
ates and moves all the other emotions, and then switches to a brief
analysis of the different words for love (*amor*) in Greek and Hebrew. A long section follows in which Caussin summarizes the
meaning of love in the neo-Platonic tradition, which he considers
superior to the Aristotelian, drawing heavily on Dionysius the
Areopagite and Ficino. Again, citing Dionysius and Augustine,
he distinguishes five kinds of love—divine, angelic, intellectual,
animal, and natural. The first "is in God and is itself God. . . . By
this He embraces created things, the drops of His infinite majesty,
in His more than maternal womb; and as if daily creating all
things new, He sustains, caresses, and fructifies them in the lap of
His providence."[61] As in Reynolds, intellectual or rational love is
the desire for true good in accordance with reason, while sensitive
love is the carnal *voluptas* common to men and animals. These five
kinds of love are Platonic in origin. What is new here is that they
are all classed as emotions (affectus) and thus belong to rhetorical
theory. Caussin proceeds to give Aquinas's distinction between

[59] Carbo, *Divinus orator*, p. 204. Some seventeenth-century writers carried this
rehabilitation of emotion to its logical conclusion and argued for the existence of
emotion in the Godhead. This is Milton's position in *A Treatise on Christian Doctrine* (trans. Charles R. Sumner, 2 vols. [Boston, 1825], 1: 22–23) and is set forth
in detail in Glassius's *Philologia sacra* (1653): "Notandum hic affectuum humano-
rum discrimen. Quidam in Deo tribuuntur, ut vere in ipso sint, sed non ea ratione
imperfecta, & per modum accidentis, ut in homine; verum ratione longe puriori
& eminentiori, adeoque per modum ipsius essentiae seu substantiae. . . . Verum
quidem est, quia in Deum non cadit accidens, commiserationem in ipso non esse
talem affectum, sicut in nobis est. Sed quia misericordia ejus non distinguitur ab
essentia ejus, est quiddam multo ardentius in Deo, quam nos cogitare possumus
&c." (p. 1129).
[60] Caussin, *De eloquentia*, pp. 484–95.
[61] Ibid., p. 487.

love-as-friendship and love-as-desire, the first of which he relates to Seneca's Stoic description of friendship. Subsequent sections deal with the allegory of Eros and Anteros, the causes of love according to the Platonic tradition and the same topic according to Aristotle. The analysis of love finally concludes with several examples, both patristic and Classical, of "the emotion of love (*affectus amoris*)." As always, Caussin's work is more eclectic and erudite than most rhetorics, but they all share his premise that spiritual life is affective and therefore that passionate eloquence can convert the soul and transform its listener into a "new creature." In the final chapters of *De eloquentia*, Caussin can advocate the grand style for preaching and other forms of sacred discourse because the whole view of the emotions has changed and broadened to include the upper reaches of distinctively human experience.

This distance between ancient and Renaissance views of emotion can be measured by looking at a revision of the Platonic tripartite soul found in Johann-Heinrich Alsted's *Orator*. Alsted starts out like Plato, dividing the soul into intellective, irascible, and concupiscible components—Plato's charioteer, white horse, and black horse.[62] The passage begins normally enough: the intellective faculty is the mind itself, to which Alsted attributes wisdom, prudence, and eloquence. But then the analysis takes a surprising turn. Plato's appetitive horse had been "crooked of frame, a massive jumble of a creature, with thick short neck, snub nose, black skin, and grey eyes; hot-blooded, consorting with wantonness and vainglory; shaggy of ear, deaf, and hard to control with whip and goad."[63] But for Alsted the concupiscible part of the soul contains the love of God and men, love of virtue, zeal for divine glory and the salvation of all men, and so forth. In the irascible part, which Plato associates with courage and a sense of personal honor, Alsted places hope and faith (fiducia), fear of God, fortitude, magnaminity, and (curiously) outspokenness.[64] In the process of Christianizing Plato's model of the soul, Alsted has to-

---

[62] *Phaedrus* 253–54; see also *Republic* 434d–441c.
[63] *Phaedrus* 253e.
[64] Alsted, *Orator*, pp. 208–209.

tally disregarded Plato's rationalism and mind/body dualism, although in some sense, Alsted's concupiscible faculty is not unrelated to the Platonic *eros*, the daimon in the middle space (metaxy) between gods and men. But this eros never appears in Plato's analyses of the parts or faculties of the soul; in these the model for appetite is physiological desire (food, sex), which he generally perceives as irrational and dangerous. If we might call Plato's model of the psyche, with its internal hierarchical subordinations, polytheistic, then Alsted's is Trinitarian—three coequal faculties subsisting in a single nature.

The evaluation of passionate discourse in Renaissance rhetoric follows from this assimilation of spiritual and affective experience. Movere is no longer thought of as deceptive and subrational obfuscation or dangerous enchantment. Rather, emotional persuasion aims at the transformation of moral and spiritual life by awakening a rightly ordered love, by redirecting the self from corporeal objects to spiritual ones. But it turns the heart toward spiritual reality by fulfilling, not subverting, man's need for the sensible and corporeal. It gives invisible truth a local habitation and a name through metaphor, symbol, prosopopoeia and all the figures that create drama, vividness, and force—primarily the figures of thought. The speaking pictures of poesy and the figures of rhetoric are parallel instruments for embodying moral and religious concepts and so making them able to move the heart and will. The criticism of passionate rhetoric as sophistic flattery and play fails because it ignores the Renaissance's unplatonic view of the seriousness of rhetoric, based on its unplatonic psychology of the emotions and their relation to knowledge and salvation.

As Stanley Fish observes, the aesthetic of conversion "is finally an anti-aesthetic . . . it is surely anti-art-for-art's-sake because it is concerned less with the making of better poems than with the making of better persons."[65] This comment describes the aesthetic found in Renaissance rhetoric, which everywhere juxtaposes the language of ornamental, gratifying self-display with passionate and redemptive discourse. The two are incompatible because insofar as language calls attention to itself as art, it under-

[65] Fish, *Self-Consuming Artifacts*, pp. 3–4.

cuts the possibility of emotional involvement, which depends on
at least the illusion of sincerity and spontaneity. *Arcadia* and *Eu-
phues* both illustrate this principle. The two Classical commonplaces are closely related: "if you wish me to weep, you must first
cry yourself," therefore "the highest art is to hide art."[66] Since sincerity is a necessary condition for passion, the evident playfulness
of conspicuous art defeats the psychagogic aims of serious rhetoric. The possibility of such serious rhetoric, in turn, rests primarily on the Augustinian interrelation of heart, mind, and will.
Augustine's psychology of the emotions established the potential
seriousness of rhetoric because it provided a justification of passion as part of the noetic quest and as the orientation of the self
with respect to God and the world. The direction of our love determines who we are. Insofar as language can alter this direction,
it converts and recreates.

Rhetoric and Philosophy

Historically, the challenge to the legitimacy of rhetoric has come
from the philosophers. This was well known in the Renaissance;
thus the immensely popular *Rhetorica* of Ramus's colleague,
Omer Talon, opens with the observation that Plato and Aristotle
thought rhetoric was a deceptive cosmetic that should be banished from all properly governed communities.[67] Philosophic
criticisms focused on passionate rhetoric, because this seemed to
subvert rational judgment, but also attacked rhetoric itself as a
mechanical skill based on probabilities and popular opinion and
therefore unable to penetrate beyond appearances and conven-
tion. Curiously, the philosophic criticism of rhetoric has often
been accepted by modern students of rhetorical theory. In this
Morris Croll has largely defined the problem for English scholarship. His equation of the plain style, "Atticism," and philosophy emptied traditional rhetoric of anything "pleasing to an intellect intent upon the discovery of reality."[68] The history of
Renaissance rhetoric for Croll thus narrated the triumph of the

[66] Horace, "Ars Poetica," l. 102; Aristotle, *Rhetoric* 3.2.1404b.
[67] Omer Talon, *Rhetorica e P. Rami . . . praelectionibus observata* (London, 1636).
[68] Croll, *"Attic" and Baroque*, p. 56.

philosophic essay style over humanistic formalism and the conservative, oral culture of the pre-Enlightenment. Primarily interested in the development of this plain style, he examined the grand style and sacred rhetoric only in passing, apparently considering these as atavistic relics of an earlier civilization.

The relationship between philosophy and rhetoric in the Renaissance, however, does not permit simple solutions, if only because the nature of that relation formulates itself differently in different kinds of texts. Philosophers give different answers than rhetoricians, Stoics than Peripatetics.[69] In addition, the debate between the two disciplines often takes the form of a series of non-sequiturs and straw men. In the well-known epistolary exchange begun by Pico della Mirandola and Ermolo Barbaro in 1485 and continued by Melanchthon seventy-three years later, Pico defines rhetoric as inherently meretricious and ornamental and criticizes it on those grounds. To which both Barbaro and Melanchthon naturally reply that the definition is false and the consequence therefore does not follow.[70] Similarly, among the philosophers, philosophy usually means a technical, esoteric subject, while the humanists prefer to define it as practical wisdom active in virtue.[71] Nor does the debate progress much beyond the Ciceronian topics already evident in Petrarch.[72] Through the seventeenth century, rhetoric is distinguished from philosophy as a practical and popular art, which endeavors to move the mind and heart and thus transform both individual and collective praxis. Philosophy (or logic) meanwhile maintains a learned and technical character,

[69] The Peripatetics were considerably more favorable toward rhetoric than the Stoics. In the Renaissance, humanist authors vacillated between these positions (cf. Seigel, *Rhetoric and Philosophy*, pp. 21–25, 52–54, 106; also Paul Oskar Kristeller, "Philosophy and Rhetoric from Antiquity to the Renaissance," in his *Renaissance Thought and its Sources*, ed. Michael Mooney [New York, 1979], p. 219).

[70] Quirinus Breen, *Christianity*, pp. 16–17, 32–33, 54–57.

[71] Melanchthon in Breen, *Christianity*, pp. 57–58, 65; Kristeller, *Renaissance Thought*, p. 243; Hanna H. Gray, "Renaissance Humanism: The Pursuit of Eloquence," *Renaissance Essays*, ed. Paul Oskar Kristeller and Philip P. Wiener (New York, 1968), pp. 199–216; Joachim Camerarius, *Elementa rhetoricae* (Basel, 1545), pp. 4–5.

[72] Seigel, *Rhetoric and Philosophy*, pp. 52–60.

less concerned with right action than speculative truth.[73] The distinction, it should be emphasized, has more to do with decorum than epistemology; that is, most rhetorics, especially the sacred, assume that orators and philosophers share the same basic dogmas and beliefs. But the philosopher explores intricate problems connected with these beliefs without regard for the capacities of an audience, while the orator adjusts his message to the requirements of his listeners.[74]

The claim, however, that both share the same fundamental truths differentiates the ancient quarrel of rhetoric and philosophy from its Renaissance counterpart. Plato, and even Cicero, presuppose that the wisdom of the philosophers differs in substance from the popular opinions that the orator must respect.[75] But Christian universalism and the humanists' conviction that antiquity had already discovered the truths of natural reason jointly mitigate the opposition between esoteric and exoteric belief. Since in addition Christianity subordinates knowledge to faith and love, it further weakened the Classical link between the philosophic quest and the *summum bonum*.[76] Once *gnosis* no longer leads to the fulfillment of human existence, it sinks from a divinizing power to a technical specialty.[77] At the same time, the Ref-

[73] Hemmingsen, *The Preacher*, p. 14; Hyperius, *The Practis*, pp. 1–2; Valiero, *De ecclesiastica rhetorica*, p. 95; Valades, *Rhetorica Christiana*, pp. 84, 239; de Granada, *Ecclesiasticae rhetoricae*, pp. 41–43; Carbo, *Divinus orator*, p. 187; Keckermann, *Rhetoricae* (1616), p. 42; *Systema*, pp. 1391–92, 1610; Sohnius, *Tractatus*, p. 160; Alsted, *Orator*, p. 148; Caussin, *De eloquentia*, p. 12.

[74] Keckermann, *Systema*, p. 1391; Ijsseling, *Rhetoric and Philosophy in Conflict*, p. 35; Breen, *Christianity*, pp. 42, 46–48.

[75] Seigel, *Rhetoric and Philosophy*, pp. 9–10, 19–25. Thus the Stoic psychology of Cicero's *Tusculan Disputations* seems inconsistent with his practice and advocacy of rhetoric.

[76] The Renaissance, however, displays a wide range of opinion concerning the value of philosophic inquiry. See Howard Schultz, *Milton and Forbidden Knowledge* (New York, 1955); Eugene F. Rice, *The Renaissance Idea of Wisdom* (Cambridge, Mass., 1958); Barbara J. Shapiro, *Probability and Certainty in Seventeenth-Century England: A Study of the Relationships between Natural Science, Religion, History, Law, and Literature* (Princeton, 1983).

[77] For the ancient view that philosophy alone fulfills man's longing for the divine, see Aristotle, *Metaphysics* 1.2.982b–983a; *Nicomachean Ethics* 10.7.1177b–1178a; Plato, *Symposium* 210–212; Eric Voegelin, "Reason: The Classic Experi-

ormation doctrine of *fides ex auditu* enhanced the importance of preaching. According to the mid-seventeenth century Protestant scholar, Johannis Ursinus, "the end [of preaching] . . . is to persuade: not, that is, only to arouse a probable opinion but rather divine faith . . . to the glory of God and their own salvation."[78] Insofar as saving faith is more valued than scientific certainty, the superiority of philosophy to rhetoric with respect either to their ends or substance seemed less evident than it had to Plato or Aristotle. Even at the close of the seventeenth century, Fénelon could still assert the substantial congruity of philosophy and rhetoric:

> A [Fénelon's spokesman]. But what would you say of a man who establishes truth in an exact, dry, naked way, who puts his arguments in good order or makes use of the method of geometers in his speeches, but who does not add anything living, anything figurative? Would he be an orator?
>
> B. No. He would merely be a philosopher.
>
> A. Then, in order to make an orator, we must choose a philosopher, that is, a man who knows how to establish the truth; and we must add to the exactitude of his arguments the beauty and vehemence of a living discourse if we would make an orator of him.[79]

For Fénelon, as for Cicero, oratory is wisdom speaking eloquently;[80] that is, speaking with a beauty and vehemence able to produce moral and spiritual change. Philosophy and rhetoric speak to different audiences and have different functions: if the former provides argumentative rigor, the latter makes this knowledge available to human life. Like most Renaissance rhetoricians, Fénelon is not particularly interested in exploring the matter much further.

---

ence," *Anamnesis*, ed. and trans. Gerhart Niemeyer (Notre Dame, Ind., 1978). The Christian position that faith, hope, and charity lead man to God and therefore that knowledge, however valuable, is not necessary for salvation can be found in Saint Thomas, *Summa Contra Gentiles* 3.39; for the late Middle Ages, see Steven Ozment, *The Age of Reform*, pp. 73–82.

[78] Ursinus, *Ecclesiastes*, p. 9.

[79] Fénelon, *Dialogues*, p. 89.

[80] Cicero, *Part orat* 79.

The distinction between philosophy and rhetoric is not identical to that between the plain and grand (or oratorical) style, even though both distinctions correspond closely to that between do-cere and movere. The surpassing eloquence of Plato remains a commonplace of both ancient and Renaissance rhetoric,[81] and some humanists even tried to argue for the rhetorical excellence of Aristotle.[82] The refusal to identify philosophy with the plain style received theoretical support from Hermogenes' influential description of grandeur (*megethos*). For Hermogenes, emotional power is not essential to the idea of grandeur, although inseparable from some of its subcategories, like vehemence and asperity. The first division of grandeur, solemnity (semnotes), character-izes philosophic discourse and, Renaissance rhetoricians added, theological. The *Timeaus*, Canticles, and *De Trinitate* are all sol-emn.[83] Solemnity treats matters concerning God, divine things (e.g., the immortality of the soul), and human heroism, using aphorism, *sententiae*, allegory, and mystic utterance.[84] It therefore resembles the Longinian sublime more closely than the Roman grand style. Hermogenic solemnity, it should be noted, is quite different from the Ciceronian concept of eloquent wisdom, pop-ular among the early humanists. The latter conceive of the rela-tion between philosophy and rhetoric primarily as one of res and verba; philosophy invents arguments, which eloquence then ar-ranges and adorns. Solemnity, on the other hand, refers as much to the substance of discourse as to its expression. Stylistically, in fact, it differs little from the idea of simplicity, just as Longinian sublimity manifests itself in the stark opening of Genesis. By em-phasizing the sublimity of thought rather than emotional power or stylistic richness, Hermogenes banished any necessary distinc-

[81] Strebaeus, *De verborum electione*, p. 147; Vossius, *Commentariorum*, 2: 102; Caussin, *De eloquentia*, pp. 41, 167.

[82] Seigel, *Philosophy and Rhetoric*, pp. 102–12; Breen, *Christianity*, pp. 32, 38, 54, 59; Strebaeus, *De verborum electione*, p. 147; Charles B. Schmitt, *Aristotle and the Renaissance* (Cambridge, Mass., 1983), pp. 70–76; Lullius, *De oratione*, pp. 433, 500.

[83] Hermogenes, *Opera*, pp. 243–46; Sturm, *De universa*, pp. 17, 572–74; Caus-sin, *De eloquentia*, pp. 133–35; Lullius, *De oratione*, p. 433; Erasmus, *Ecclesiastes*, 5: 844b; Trebizond, *Rhetoricorum*, pp. 532–36.

[84] Hermogenes, *Opera*, 243–47, 251.

tion between philosophical discourse and grandeur for the Renaissance. Throughout the period we thus find philosophy classed under all three genera. As in antiquity, humanistic philosophy of the sort found in Isocrates or in Cicero's dialogues usually belongs in the middle style, Plato in the grand style, and dialectic in the plain. This latter style then never exclusively possessed the connotations of intellectual depth and rigor associated with philosophy.

The attempt to link "philosophy" and the "plain" or "Attic" style in the Renaissance is further complicated by the fact that all three terms had several operative meanings stemming from their complex ancient origins. While the plain style is invariably yoked to teaching, it also remains associated with small, everyday subjects and the low, conversational idiom of comedy. Epistles, dialogues, and satire belong in the plain style not because they are more philosophic than other genres but because they reproduce a conversational idiom.[85] For Alsted, the grand style thus suits difficult, serious, and excellent subjects, while the plain style is restricted to jokes and paltry matters, although like everyone else, Alsted joins this ontological classification with the logically incongruous schema based on the officia, in which the plain style would be appropriate if one were attempting to teach, even about difficult and serious matters.[86] A few rhetorics explicitly recognize the range of meanings possible for terms like "plainness" or "simplicity." Flacius and Glassius, for instance, list various meanings of "plain" in their attempt to determine whether or in what sense plainness (simplicitas) characterizes the Bible. Glassius thus divides simplicitas into rusticity, lack of ornament, honesty, and clarity, and claims that only the latter two definitions apply to scriptural rhetoric.[87] According to this analysis, a work may possess simplicitas without belonging to the "plain style." No Renaissance rhetoric, however, formally admits the possibility of a

---

[85] Trebizond, *Rhetoricorum*, p. 580; Soarez, *De arte*, pp. 316–18; Sturm, *De universa*, p. 14; Vossius, *Commentariorum*, 2: 460–61; Lamy, *The Art of Speaking*, 2.33. Examples could be multiplied indefinitely; this is a commonplace of every Renaissance rhetoric that mentions the genera dicendi.

[86] Alsted, *Orator*, p. 64; *Encyclopedia*, p. 469.

[87] Glassius, *Philologia sacra* (1705), pp. 277–78; cf. Flacius, *Clavis*, 2: 463.

style at once plain (i.e., unornamented) and passionate except
some of the vernacular ars praedicandi. There what we have is not
any form of the Classical plain style but, as I have said, a traditional Christian fusion of aspects of the grand style with a deep
distrust of art. Even in these works, furthermore, "plain" often
means simply clear rather than dialectical.

Hence, although interrelated, the plain and philosophical styles
are not identical in the Renaissance any more than in the ancient
world. Similarly, "Attic," which Croll equates with "plain" and
"philosophic," in fact only partially intersects with these. When
contrasted to Asiatic prose, "Attic" does suggest a more succinct,
chaste, and restrained style, often connected with notions of
moral and intellectual probity.[88] But other meanings are at least
equally common. In particular, Renaissance rhetorics often follow Quintilian, for whom the Attic manner refers to the gaiety
and delicacy of the best Greek authors—as opposed to Latin massiveness (*robor*) (12.10.35–36). Thus Caussin speaks of "*Atticae
. . . elegantiae*" and Sturm of "*Attica illa suavitas.*"[89] For Erasmus,
"Attic" connotes brevity, wit, and grace, but not philosophical
acumen or depth. In the *Ciceronianus*, Bulephorus remarks, "Wit
was the peculiar gift of the Spartans and after them of the natives
of Attica. It was so exclusively theirs, that, when the pastoral
poem and comedy was most highly praised for its grace and wit,
the Romans did not even aspire to it."[90] In the same work, Erasmus also notes, "Thus those who aim at the Attic style become
dry instead of clever and charming"—implying that the latter
qualities are characteristic of true Atticism. Concerning Lazare de
Baif, he adds, "Although fitted for teaching, he preferred to be
witty as it seems, and a representative of the Attic school rather
than a Ciceronian."[91] Rather surprisingly, the same connection
between "Atticism," comedy, and graceful wit appears in the
writings of the neo-Stoic, Justus Lipsius. Speaking of Plautus and

[88] Lamy, *The Art of Speaking*, 2.19–20; Croll, *"Attic" and Baroque*, pp. 52–53,
60–61.
[89] Caussin, *De eloquentia*, p. 360; Sturm, *De imitatione oratoria libri tres* (Strassburg, 1574), p. 5.
[90] Erasmus, *Ciceronianus*, p. 36.
[91] Ibid., pp. 55, 101.

Terence, Lipsius writes, "from whom is the propriety of words better to be sought, from whom that Attic brilliance of phrasing, from whom is to be more often drawn first grace, then wit and civility, than from my writer of comedy?" Again, with reference to Plautus, he comments, "He is a writer . . . who offers urbanity, jests, wit, and that Attic grace which you seek for in vain in the rest of Latium."[92] In these passages, "Attic" describes a version of the plain style, but one characterized by polished wit and comic gaiety rather than intellectual depth.[93]

The fact that neither "Atticism" nor the plain style fit neatly into the dichotomy of philosophy and rhetoric suggests that this opposition was not central to Renaissance thought. At least in the rhetorics, the two disciplines seem interrelated rather than antithetical. Their relation appears in various forms, the best known among which is the humanists' ideal of eloquent wisdom, of wisdom made lucid and delightful, and thus available to the problems of human life. For Melanchthon, the orator is thus the true philosopher. In his 1558 reply to Pico he writes,

We indeed call that man an orator who teaches men accurately, clearly, and with a certain dignity concerning good and necessary things: whom you would call a philosopher I do not yet understand satisfactorily. As a matter of fact I call a philosopher one who when he has learned and knows things good and useful for mankind, takes a theory (*doctrina*) out of academic obscurity and makes it practically useful in public affairs, and instructs men about natural phenomena, or religions, or about government.[94]

This humanistic fusion of wisdom and eloquence belongs to the history of the plain style, as Melanchthon's emphasis on clarity and teaching indicates. For Melanchthon, the scholastics wrote without any style at all and therefore produced unintelligible jargon. What he then recommends is something close to the style of Bacon or Locke—a lucid, agreeable, and graceful simplicity.

[92] Quoted in Trimpi, *Ben Jonson*, pp. 66, 75.

[93] At least in Erasmus, "Attic" often simply means "without emotion." See *Ciceronianus*, p. 103; *On Copia of Words and Ideas*, trans. Donald B. King and H. David Rix (Milwaukee, 1963), p. 104; *Ecclesiastes*, 5: 857a.

[94] Breen, *Christianity*, pp. 57–58; see also Melanchthon's *Elementorum* 13: 418, 452, 454, 459, 481.

Such a fusion is the common ideal of almost all secular rhetorics during the Renaissance. Ramists, Erasmians, Ciceronians all claimed that the principal function of rhetoric was to render thought agreeable, lucid, and attractive. They have, therefore, very little to say about the grand style.[95]

The sacred rhetorics, however, also connect wisdom and eloquence but in a more original and radical fashion. They tend to reduce the Ciceronian officia to two—docere and movere—since delectare with its sophistic overtones has no place in Christian preaching. But they further indicate that docere and movere no longer correspond to two distinct styles; they exist simultaneously in sacred discourse, which thus differs from Classical precisely by refusing to compartmentalize noetic and affective experience.[96] It is not merely a question of clarifying and polishing thought but of joining intellectual precision and passionate force, a combination foreign to Roman rhetoric although less so to Greek, which classed Thucydides and Plato in the grand style. Flacius's chapter on biblical style opens by explaining this fusion of docere and movere in sacred discourse. He begins with the declaration that Holy Scripture primarily belongs in the grand style. The next paragraph then sets out the traditional division of teaching and moving:

These two things clearly seem totally distinct: to teach simply . . . and besides to move one's listeners . . . where the exact truth and explication of the subject is less regarded than how to move the listener however and wherever we desire.

As these two are wholly distinct . . . thus two wholly distinct *genera dicendi* serve these two enterprises. For a plain and low style is suitable for explication of things and scholastic instruction. . . . On the other hand a grand style better suits the self-display of the speaker, the pleasure of his

[95] Gabriel Harvey, *Ciceronianus*, ed. Harold Wilson, trans. Clarence Forbes, *University of Nebraska Studies, Studies in the Humanities* 4(1945): 73–75, 83–87. Fumaroli, *L'Age de l'éloquence*, pp. 87–89, 95.

[96] Keckermann, *Rhetoricae* (1614), p. 21; Lamy, *The Art of Speaking*, 2.51; Sohnius, *Tractatus*, p. 162; Brandolini, *De ratione scribendi*, p. 11; Carbo, *Divinus orator*, pp. 19–22, 45–48, 154, 241; Hyperius, *The Practise*, p. 6; Melanchthon, *De modo et arte*, p. 51; Glanville, *An Essay*, pp. 11, 53–54.

listeners, and emotional persuasion, especially for the unlearned crowd. Therefore it is used in forensic oratory (*concio*).

This is the Classical opposition between philosophic and oratorical discourse. But in the next paragraph, Flacius goes on to observe that this opposition does not apply to the Bible:

Moreover, Holy Scripture . . . consists of pure oratory (*concio*). For the books of the prophets are exclusively oratorical. Likewise the Evangelists and even the books of Moses are filled with these [oratorical speeches]. . . .
But there is a huge difference between sacred and profane oratory. For the latter often chooses to treat only a single proposition or idea and attempts to move and draw the crowd [to assent] to it by the power of language. But sacred orations are not exclusively occupied in moving the listener, as profane are, but also (or even primarily) in teaching—and teaching exactly and concerning the most weighty [and] difficult things. . . . Nevertheless they do not want to teach only in a theoretical fashion like mathematicians, but also to seize and move the heart. Nor do they only treat one subject but many simultaneously: for they teach and exhort and dissuade and accuse and terrify and again console their hearers and move, form, and reform their hearts until finally Christ is formed in them.[97]

Biblical eloquence, according to Flacius, alternates rapidly between passion and precision or combines them into a single style. Since the Bible mainly uses the grand style, in some sense this style must include *docere* as well as *movere*. It teaches passionately and moves without sacrificing intellectual depth.

This sense of the proximity of the noetic and affective persists throughout the sacred rhetorics. In part it rests on the Aristotelian position that emotion is not an irrational perturbation but the offspring of belief.[98] One feels fear, for example, because one believes that danger is imminent. Emotion is therefore bound up with argument; the orator moves by giving reasons. This Aristotelian view, which appears in many rhetorics,[99] underlies the

[97] Flacius, *Clavis*, 2: 459–60.
[98] Fortenbaugh, *Aristotle*, pp. 17, 83.
[99] Keckermann, *Systema*, p. 1610; Caussin, *De eloquentia*, p. 552; de Estella, *De modo concionandi*, p. 62; Carbo, *Divinus orator*, pp. 124–25; Glanville, *An Essay*, p. 55.

position, found in Agricola and in subsequent works, that the *loci* of dialectic and pathos are identical.[100] The same arguments used to prove that such-and-such is the case also arouse their listeners to love, hate, fear, etc. If you prove that God is good and merciful, I will love him. Obviously not all arguments arouse emotion since some subjects have no affective valence, being too abstract, trivial, or logically intricate. Nevertheless, in principle, passion flows from proof, and thus the discussion of *movere* often appears under invention rather than (or as well as) under *elocutio* and the characters of style.

A deeper ground for the interrelating of *docere* and *movere*, noesis and affect, lies again in the Renaissance revival of Augustinian thought.[101] For Augustine, love and knowledge are tightly interconnected, since the noetic quest is born out of love for its object, yet we can only love that which, in some sense, we already know. Rather than undermining rational judgment, love wings the mind's search for God and truth. As Augustine writes in the *Confessions*, "my weight is my love; wherever I am carried, it is my love that carries me there. By your gift we are set on fire and are carried upward; we are red hot and we go."[102]

Although Augustine himself never relates this psychology to rhetorical issues, his interpenetration of feeling, willing, and loving becomes tremendously influential for the rhetorics of the sixteenth century and following. The noetic quest begins in inchoate knowledge, in a dim and partially realized faith; that faith, in turn, stirs up love and a desire to grasp more fully the faintly glimpsed object. Impelled by desire, the person attempts to see and understand the beloved object, which achieved, creates the ardent love of full union. In his *De anima* Juan Luis Vives thus writes,

[100] Agricola, *De inventione*, pp. 199–200; Valades, *Rhetorica Christiana*, p. 84; de Granada, *Ecclesiasticae rhetoricae*, pp. 110–11; Alsted, *Orator*, p. 91; de Arriaga, *Rhetoris Christiani*, p. 9; Carbo, *Divinus orator*, p. 188.

[101] For Augustine in the Renaissance, see Bouwsma, "Two Faces"; Trinkaus, *The Scope*; Kristeller, "Augustine and the Early Renaissance," *Review of Religion* 8 (1944): 338–58.

[102] Saint Augustine, *The Confessions of Saint Augustine*, trans. Rex Warner (New York, 1963), 13.9, also 1.1; cf. Colish, *Mirror*, pp. 53, 77.

the object is known so that it may be loved but the knowledge need only be so much as is sufficient to elicit love. But where we are connected to the desired object we know it better and more intimately; and then we enjoy it. Our first knowledge leads us to believe the object is good; in the latter knowledge we feel (*experiri*) that it is so. . . . Thus love is the middle point between inchoate knowledge and the full knowledge of union, in which desire always disappears but not always love. This rather burns more fiercely, the more and greater goods are found in that union.[103]

A seventeenth-century English text, *A Treatise of the Passions* by Edward Reynolds, likewise states: "Love and Knowledge have mutuall sharpening and causalitie each on other: for as Knowledge doth generate Love, so Love doth nourish and exercise Knowledge. The reason whereof is that unseparable union which is in all things between the Truth and Good of them. . . . the more Appetite enjoyeth of [the Good], the deeper inquiry doth it make and the more compleat union doth it seek with [the Truth]."[104]

In Renaissance rhetorics these arguments belong to the defense of movere. In the *Ecclesiastes* Erasmus notes, "what Augustine, following Plato, said is true: nothing is loved unless known at least to some degree and again nothing is known unless loved in some respect. . . . In the *Hortensius* Cicero praised philosophy and aroused love for it before he taught it. And those who undertake to teach a subject first inflame their students, showing through amplification how noble it is . . . what great things it promises and how useful it will be."[105] The allusion to the *Hortensius* is significant because this was the book that first stirred Saint

[103] Vives, *De anima et vita* (Basel, 1538; repr. Turin, 1959), p. 178.

[104] Edward Reynolds, *A Treatise of the Passions and Faculties of the Soul of Man, With the Severall Dignities and Corruptions thereunto belonging* (London, 1650), pp. 103–104. On the interrelation of love and knowledge in Augustine and Aquinas, see Colish, *Mirror*, pp. 53, 185–87. In Aquinas and Hooker, this interrelation becomes the basis of religious faith, what Hooker calls the Certainty of Adherence. Although the intellect is unable to demonstrate the existence of God, the will falls in love with his goodness and so carries the mind to adhere to the Being it so dimly perceives (Colish, *Mirror*, pp. 185–87; Hooker, "Of the Certainty and Perpetuity of Faith in the Elect," *Works*, 3: 470–71). The relation between religious knowledge and rhetoric will be discussed more fully in Chapter Five.

[105] Erasmus, *Ecclesiastes*, 5: 952b.

Augustine to embrace philosophy. For Erasmus, it was not Cicero's philosophic arguments but his evident and eloquent praise that moved Augustine's love for a subject he barely knew. Eloquence is not philosophy but both are parts of the journey toward truth. The connection between love and knowledge appears again in Keckermann's *Systema rhetoricae*: "reason and will should be implicit in emotion, and emotions resolve into knowledge and understanding. . . . Will and emotion derive from reason and knowledge."[106] Here again emotion is bound up in the larger cognitive process. Our emotions spring from belief and lead us to further insight.

This sense of the inseparability of love and knowledge found support in the biblical anthropology of the Renaissance. Both Flacius's *Clavis Scripturae Sacrae* and Glassius's *Philologia sacra* point out that the Bible does not differentiate knowing and feeling as Classical philosophy did. Glassius comments, "[in Hebrew] to know or to think does not denote simply *gnosis* but also emotion and affect . . . or what is the same it signifies a living and efficacious knowledge. . . . Thus [in Hebrew] to know is the same as to love, to care for."[107] Flacius makes the same point: "the Hebrews attribute the whole psychic life of man to the heart and appear to place the rational soul completely in the heart . . . ascribing to the heart the power both of thought and choice, of wishing and doing. . . . On the other hand, the philosophers locate the rational soul . . . in the head or brain; leaving only emotion in the heart."[108] Both Classical and biblical anthropology coexist through the Renaissance, sometimes causing no small inconsistencies. The biblical however dominates what Bouwsma has called the Augustinian Renaissance, to which belongs most of the period's rhetorical theory and whose ideal was not Swift's stoical horses but a passionate and unitive knowledge. The rhetorics and psychologies written in this tradition treat emotion as part of man's cognitive as well as appetitive perfection. Rhetoric in particular belongs to the noetic quest; its emotional power does

---

[106] Keckermann, *Systema*, p. 1612.
[107] Glassius, *Philologia sacra* (1653), pp. 1053–54.
[108] Flacius, *Clavis*, 1: 178.

not subvert reason but animates it, drawing heart and mind toward union with the desired object. As Adam says in his conversation with Raphael, ". . . love thou say'st / Leads up to heav'n, is
both the way and guide" (*Paradise Lost*, 8.612–13).

Since Plato, rhetoric and philosophy have been at least potentially antagonistic. This well-known piece of history, however,
does not entail that these disciplines may be best understood in
terms of this tension.[109] At least during the Renaissance several
forces conspired to fade any sharp demarcation: the humanistic
ideal of eloquent wisdom, Aristotelian and especially Augustinian psychology, the relative lack of firm correspondences between stylistic qualities and a "grammar of assent," whereby de-
grees of certainty parallel those of simplicity. The very
complexity of Renaissance rhetoric discouraged any clear-cut bi-
furcations: "plain," "Attic," and "philosophy" all mean too many
things to conform to binary schemes. The conflict, such as it was,
between philosophy and rhetoric was further complicated by
Christianity. By subordinating knowledge to love and faith, it
weakened the claims of philosophy and relaxed the distinction
between knowing and feeling.[110] In addition, by positing a revelation accessible to all men, it allied the rhetorical *agon* with Truth
rather than political power struggles. Finally, because Augustinian voluntarism legitimated emotional appeal, Christianity had a

[109] Under the influence of critical theory, recent works on the relation between
rhetoric and philosophy have elevated the tension between them to the status of
conflicting metaphysical principles. Ijsseling's rather unreliable *Rhetoric and Philosophy in Conflict* is a chief offender here, although valuable for drawing together
rhetorical and contemporary critical issues. Historically, however, rhetoric and
philosophy have often operated in close conjunction (see the first chapter of von
Arnim's *Dio von Prusa* and Ernesto Grassi's *Rhetoric as Philosophy: The Humanist
Tradition* [University Park, Pa., 1980]). The modern discovery that philosophic
texts are permeated by rhetoric would not have surprised Renaissance thinkers,
nor would it have threatened the premises of their Christian semiotics, which acknowledged the inability of all language to name God adequately and literally (see
Colish, *Mirror*, on medieval sign theory and Voegelin, *Anamnesis*, on the Classical
conception of philosophy as the loving response to the attraction of the divine
ground, rather than as the discovery of "true" propositions).

[110] Valades thus states the standard preference for virtue over knowledge: "Me-
lior est profecto humilis rusticus, qui Deo servit, quam superbus Philosophus, qui
se neglecto, cursum coeli . . . considerat" (*Rhetorica Christiana*, p. 6).

crucial impact on conceptions of the grand style. For the ancient world, rhetorical passion had been justified by the pragmatics of social control; in the sacred rhetorics such passion belongs both to the noetic quest, with its dialectics of love and knowledge, and to the conversion of the will from appearances to spiritual and eternal goods.

CHAPTER FOUR

HELLENISM AND HEBRAISM: THE DEVELOPMENT
OF A NON-CICERONIAN
GRAND STYLE

IN ONE OF the most famous passages from the *Ciceronianus*, Erasmus ridicules the effort of Renaissance Ciceronians to classicize Christian discourse:

> Further, if the Ciceronian utters no word except from his dictionary, what will he do when the changes of time have brought new words, for he will not find those in the books of Cicero nor in his own word list? . . . Whither shall our painfully precise Ciceronian turn? Shall he use *Jupiter Optimus Maximus* for the *Father of our Lord*? For the *Son*, shall he say *Apollo* or *Aesculapius*? For the *Queen of Virgins*, shall he say *Diana*? For *heathen, public enemy*? For the *church* shall he say *sacred assembly* or the *state* or the *republic*?[1]

The story of the Ciceronian controversies has been told many times.[2] It was a crucial episode in the history of sacred rhetoric because it raised serious questions about the suitability of Classical rhetoric for Christian subjects. One may doubt whether there were many fanatic Ciceronians of the sort Erasmus derides, but from the fifteenth through the mid-sixteenth centuries many rhetorics advocated the exclusive imitation of Cicero. For sacred rhetoric, such Ciceronianism presents a particular problem. Not only was Cicero's vocabulary inadequate for Christian subjects, but his periodicity and concinnitas were alien to the unrhythmic parataxis of the Bible; his discussions of rhetoric do not mention religious oratory; his grand style is largely forensic. Neither

---

[1] Erasmus, *Ciceronianus*, pp. 66–67.

[2] On Renaissance Ciceronianism, see Croll, *"Attic" and Baroque*; Fumaroli, *L'Age de l'éloquence*, and "Rhetoric, Politics, and Society"; Izora Scott, *Controversies*; Thomas Greene, *Light in Troy* (New Haven, 1982); G. W. Pigman III, "Imitation and the Renaissance Sense of the Past: The Reception of Erasmus' *Ciceronianus*," *Journal of Medieval and Renaissance Studies* 9 (1979): 155–77.

Ciceronian practice nor theory allowed for a prose based on the Bible and Church Fathers, with their celebratory grandeur, their fusion of sublimity and ordinariness, their figurative density, or their unclassical syntax. The excesses of Ciceronian imitation Erasmus cites just highlight the absurdity of attempting to model sacred discourse on Roman rhetoric. After Erasmus, sacred rhetorics offer two main responses to this dilemma. The first derives from the Ramist simplification of rhetoric to a list of schemes and tropes, which could then be applied to any subject matter. We thus find several Ramist biblical rhetorics in seventeenth-century England—Barton's *The Art of Rhetorick*, Clarke's *Holy Oyle*, and Smith's *The Mysterie of Rhetorique Unvail'd*. Ramist formalism, however, simply avoided the central issues: the relation of sacred to Classical rhetoric and the nature of a distinctively Christian rhetorical theory. A deeper response to the problem of Ciceronian imitation appeared in the scholarly neo-Latin rhetorics that form the focus of this investigation. These turned to the hellenistic grand style of Longinus, Demetrius, Dionysius, and Hermogenes to provide an analysis of language better suited to Holy Scripture and Christian preaching. This chapter will explore their attempt to assimilate hellenistic theory to Christian practice.

Sacred Subject and Sacred Style

The primary contribution of hellenistic rhetoric was to provide Classical authority to the spiritualization of the grand style. The neoclassical instincts of both the Church Fathers and the early humanists conspired to exclude the Bible from the ranks of eloquence, its un-Ciceronian style and lower-class actors apparently incapable of grandeur.[3] Even Erasmus still preserves the idea that biblical style is rude and uncultivated, although concealing treasures of wisdom within.[4] Caussin thus begins his defense of sacred

---

[3] On the early church's view that the Bible lacked eloquence, see Norden, *Die antike Kunstprosa*, 2: 521–30; Saint Augustine, *Confessions* 3.5. See also Flacius, *Clavis*, 2: 459.

[4] Erasmus, *Ecclesiastes*, 5: 837f–838a; also "Sileni Alcibiades" from the *Adagia* (reprinted in *Erasmus on His Times: A Shortened Version of The Adages of Erasmus*, trans. Margaret Mann Phillips [Cambridge, 1967], p. 82).

eloquence with the speech of one Caecilius, who bitterly complains that Christianity has ruined prose style:

"Lofty minds are forced into sacred oratory as if into a corn-mill; here like noble steeds stripped of their breastplates and saddles they grow old at the grind stone and have barbarity instead of ornament. For what can this sacred eloquence be? About Christian doctrine, doubtless? What is more lowly (*humilius*) than that? . . . What pleasure is there in addressing plebian ears and yawning circles of females about some trite biblical histories in long and lifeless periods, or in explaining the rudiments of the Christian religion, or in condemning sins by some uncouth and rude gesticulation—trite matters and repeated so often as to make delicate stomachs sick?"[5]

Caecilius, whose favorite writers are Plautus, Pliny, and Tacitus, belongs to a later generation than the Ciceronians whom Erasmus mocks for their psuedo-Classicization of Christian themes, but both share a revulsion at the lowly situations and styles of Christianity. For religious humanists like Caussin, the only acceptable response to such criticism was not to justify the *sermo humilis* of Scripture but to demonstrate on Classical grounds that sacred themes and language were, in fact, supremely eloquent. To this end, the hellenistic rhetorics proved invaluable.

The single most important passage for legitimizing sacred grandeur is Hermogenes' statement that the subjects of solemnity are the true God, divine things (e.g., the order of the cosmos), the divine qualities present in man (e.g., the immortality of the soul), and human heroism.[6] As Hermogenes acknowledges, the first two topics are not generally appropriate in civic oratory; most of his examples come from the *Timeaus*. The possibility of a grand style not located in the forum or senate and the priority given to sacred subjects were eagerly appropriated by Renaissance rhetoricians. Hermogenes' hierarchy of solemn themes reappears under the grand style in Trebizond, Lullius, Sturm, Vicars, Keckermann, Vossius, and Caussin.[7] In the last three it appears in

[5] Caussin, *De eloquentia*, pp. 889–90.
[6] Hermogenes, *Opera*, pp. 243–46.
[7] Trebizond, *Rhetoricorum*, pp. 458, 532–33; Lullius, *De oratione*, p. 433; Sturm, *De universa*, p. 15; Vicars, *Manductio*, p. 59; Keckermann, *Systema*, p. 1670; Vos-

conjunction with Longinus's praise of Genesis, establishing a persistent connection between solemnity, sublimity, and sacred discourse. Moreover, the first topic of solemnity was explicitly understood in a Christian sense. Trebizond and Caussin consider solemnity characteristic of biblical and patristic language.[8] For Sturm, solemnity deals with God as Creator and Redeemer.[9] By the seventeenth century, Alsted can simply assert as beyond question that the grandeur of sacred subjects requires a commensurate grandeur of style.[10] In Hermogenes the Renaissance thus found at least a partial answer to Caecilius and his aspersion of sacred oratory.

Other aspects of hellenistic rhetoric also offered a theoretical grounding for the claim that Christian discourse belonged in the grand style. As we have seen, the Greeks, more than their Latin counterparts, emphasized the numinous qualities of grandeur, paying less attention to copia, periodicity, and concinnitas. Thus both solemnity and sublimity can exist without either verbal embellishment or forensic power. The *Timaeus* and Genesis unite grandeur of conception with the utmost simplicity of style. The shift from a verbal to a conceptual definition of the grand style allowed the Renaissance to enroll the manifestly unclassical, un-Ciceronian prose of the Bible and the Fathers in the highest ranks of eloquence and to counter the Ramist tendency to reduce eloquence to ornamentation.

Longinus occupies a prominent position in this redefinition. His influence can be seen in the late seventeenth-century *Art of Speaking* by Bernard Lamy, who gives a sophisticated analysis of the relation between word and concept in the sacred sublime.[11]

---

sius, *Commentariorum*, 2: 446; Caussin, *De eloquentia*, pp. 133–34. In the eighteenth century this classification reappears in poetics; see Samuel H. Monk, *The Sublime: A Study of Critical Theories in XVIII-Century England* (New York, 1935), p. 51, and David B. Morris, *The Religious Sublime: Christian Poetry and Critical Tradition in Eighteenth-Century England* (Lexington, Ky., 1972), p. 54.

[8] Trebizond, *Rhetoricorum*, pp. 532–33; Caussin, *De eloquentia*, p. 134.

[9] Sturm, *De universa*, p. 17.

[10] *Orator*, p. 155.

[11] Although *The Art of Speaking* was published a year after Boileau's edition of Longinus, Lamy, unlike Boileau, does not clearly distinguish the sublime from the grand style.

He begins with the conventional scientific demand for the close correspondence between res and verba. The pleasure we receive from speech, Lamy remarks, "proceeds only from the resemblance betwixt the Image form'd by the words in our mind, and the things whose Image they bear." What pleases us is truth or the conformity between words and things; therefore, Lamy adds, the sublime is simply "conformity in its perfection." So far, Lamy seems to be suggesting that an ideal language would consist of nothing but definitions and concrete nouns or other overtly denotative expressions; his notion of the sublime seems cut to the same measure as Thomas Sprat's antirhetorical original language, in which "men deliver'd so many *things*, almost in an equal number of *words*."[12] As an instance of such perfect correspondence, however, Lamy offers what appears to be a radically inappropriate passage: "*Longinus* in his Book of this Sublimity, has given us an example of a sublime expression taken out of the First Chapter of *Genesis*, where *Moses* speaking of the Creation, uses these words; And God said let there be light, and there was light." This is the true sublime, Lamy continues, because it "gives a strong *Idea* of the power of God over his Creatures." For sublimity arises from perspicuity and force, whereby "the mind of the Reader [is] led directly to the end of the design."[13] Myth and image become the most accurate expressions of the divine, not by virtue of any denotative correspondence, but by elevating the reader's mind to the superlinguistic idea. The mythic representations of Holy Scripture are not ornamentations of prose sense but are as precise intellectual tools as the language of religion can forge. Lamy's sublime deals with what is spiritual and invisible, and hence not amenable to the ordinary literal uses of language. To be precise, religious discourse must be psychagogic; it cannot name things directly, but only stir its audience toward the intuition of what is beyond language. In such a style, the polarity between linguistic exactness and emotional power taken for granted by critics of rhetorical discourse, both ancient and modern, dis-

---

[12] Cited in A. C. Howell, *"Res et Verba," Seventeenth Century Prose: Modern Essays in Criticism*, ed. Stanley Fish (New York, 1971), p. 195.
[13] Lamy, *The Art of Speaking*, 2.60–61.

appears. Language cannot talk about the supernatural, but it can function like an Augustinian sign and through figurative expressions point the hearer toward a reality beyond the words.[14]

Lamy's observations suggest the possibility of a distinctive religious prose style, one that refuses to fit into the traditional dichotomies of res and verba, philosophy and oratory, docere and movere. On the basis of its emotional power, such a style belongs to the genus grande, yet it lacks the practical, civic orientation of most Roman examples of the grand style, being more concerned to instill a "strong Idea" of the divine, to represent as fully as possible the supernatural reality behind the phenomenal world, than to effect persuasion. Thus, like solemnity, the sublime provided a basis for the Christian grand style as well as an escape from both a narrowly pragmatic and an excessively ornamental notion of grandeur.

The numinous qualities of the hellenistic grand style appear in Hermogenes and Demetrius as well as Longinus. In the Renaissance, the passages from the former two linking the grand style with allegory, mystical utterance, and the sacred terror of the Mystery initiations recur frequently, often illustrated by Christian examples. Trebizond thus mentions that Hermogenes' allegorical solemnity characterizes "the princes of theology."[15] For Sturm, such allegoresis conceals lofty matters under apparently slight and lowly images, such as Christ's "I am the good shepherd" or the erotic pastoral of Canticles.[16] Similarly, the mystic utterance of the initiation rites, which Hermogenes also locates under solemnity, reappears in Sturm examplified by Paul's "O altitudo."[17] Demetrius's passage on the relation between grandeur (megaloprepeia), allegory, and the Mysteries likewise becomes

[14] This harmonizes with the overall Augustinian character of The Art of Speaking. Lamy seems to hold the Augustinian position that learning is the bringing to consciousness of indwelling truths. He writes, "for my own part I value not the Art of Speaking, but as it contributes to the discovery of truths; as it forces it from the bottom of our thoughts where it lay conceal'd; as it disentangles it, and displays it to our eyes" (2.77).

[15] Trebizond, Rhetoricorum, p. 536.

[16] Sturm, De universa, pp. 572–74.

[17] Ibid., p. 572.

part of Renaissance depictions of the grand style. In his chapter, "De verbis magnifici," Vossius writes that allegory is impressive because "by its obscurity it resembles the darkness of night, which easily terrifies the fearful. Certainly the Athenians also held their mysteries in night and darkness in order to strike terror into the souls of the initiates."[18] The same passage appears in Caussin and in Keckermann, who remarks that "the ancients thus judged fear and terror to be indissolubly bound to religion."[19] For Keckermann, such solemnity pertains to "sublime matters and those which are hidden (*occultae*) and seem to contain mysteries." It is therefore mystical and hieratic (*sacris mos*), hinting at truths above the reach of ordinary comprehension.[20] All three rhetorics thus transmit the hellenistic feeling for the grandeur present in the awesome and terrible darkness of sacred mystery. When we come to discuss Caussin's description of majestic preaching, we will see this association of allegory, darkness, and numinosity adapted to a specifically Christian context. In Flacius too, allegory and obscurity reappear as prominent aspects of biblical grandeur.

Anti-Ciceronianism: Brevity and Harshness in the Grand Style

The Ciceronian controversies of the sixteenth century draw a variety of issues into their orbit: the question of imitation versus self-expression; the problem of historical change, especially the change from paganism to Christianity; the value of such Ciceronian characteristics as copia and formal beauty (concinnitas);[21] the relevance of an oral, public, popular rhetoric; and the relative importance of style versus subject. It has long been recognized

---

[18] Vossius, *Commentariorum*, 2: 451.

[19] Keckermann, *Systema*, p. 1672; Caussin, *De eloquentia*, p. 418.

[20] Keckermann, *Systema*, p. 1671*.

[21] It is not clear to what extent Renaissance writers perceived Cicero as a model for the grand style. Gabriel Harvey describes his prose in terms unmistakably reminiscent of the genus medium: *"mellitissima vox," "exquisita sermonis concinnitas," "suavitas," "incredibilis venustas," "elegans," "festiuitas"* (*Ciceronianus*, pp. 46–48). In general, anti-Ciceronianism does not seem to have been a protest against passionate rhetoric but against an excess concern for words and a flowery, copious sweetness.

that by emphasizing self-expression, brevity, writing, and res, anti-Ciceronianism played a large role in the creation of the seventeenth-century plain style. Anti-Ciceronians like Muret and Lipsius advocated a written terse epistolary style, both eclectic and individual, generally secular, and based on Silver Latin models (especially Seneca).[22] But anti-Ciceronianism also motivates the appropriation of hellenistic rhetoric to describe a sacred grand style. Both types of anti-Ciceronianism prefer brevity, aural harshness, asymmetry, and expressivity to Ciceronian fullness and formal, balanced harmonies. Both, interestingly, appeal to Silver Latin models. But the hellenistic-based sacred grand style remains an oral, popular mode, religious rather than secular, and emphasizing force and passion rather than epistolary simplicity and wit. Yet the common origin of the two movements appears in the fact that, as we shall see, Renaissance rhetorics make Lipsius and Seneca models for *both* the epistolary and the grand style.[23]

In Renaissance rhetorics, the shift away from a Ciceronian grand style appears very clearly in the definitions and models for that genus. In these texts, Greek rhetorical categories, like Demetrius's magnificent and forcible characters or the Longinian sublime, become the grand style. Flacius, for example, begins by claiming that the Bible uses the "grandis, sublimis, aut magniloquus" genus, and then proceeds to enumerate its attributes according to Hermogenes' Idea of Grandeur.[24] Similarly, Caussin, Keckermann, and Vossius all rely principally on hellenistic texts to describe the grand style. This conflation passes over from rhetoric into poetics. Tasso, for example, claims "it is clear that that Form which Demetrius called Magnificent, Hermogenes called

[22] See Croll, *"Attic" and Baroque*, and Fumaroli, *L'Age de l'éloquence*, on Lipsius, Muret, and the anti-Ciceronian plain style.

[23] The relation of Silver Latin to the genera dicendi has traditionally presented problems. For example, is Seneca an "Attic" plain stylist—as Croll classifies him and as he apparently wanted to be—or should his writings be classified under the sententious variant of Asianism (*Brutus* 325)? See also Fumaroli, *L'Age de l'éloquence*, pp. 96–100.

[24] Flacius, *Clavis*, 2: 459–60.

Grandeur, and Cicero called Sublime are one and the same."²⁵ Often Renaissance authors adapt and rearrange these Greek sources to fit the tripartite Roman pattern. Thus Vossius reduces Demetrius's four characters to the standard three by arguing that magnificence and force are both simply aspects of the grand style, not separate genera.²⁶

This syncretism entailed that each of the genera dicendi acquired considerable latitude. The *De oratione* (1558) of Antonio Lullius even criticizes Longinus's (presumed) attempt to confine the grand style to sublimity because this genus or Idea is not single but "multiplex."²⁷ In his chapter entitled "The Various Names of the Sublime Style among Latins and Greeks," Vossius provides a relatively exhaustive list of the Greek equivalents for the grand style:

Among the Greeks . . . this character is called *megaloprepes* because as in the homes of the rich all things are valuable, not common or ordinary. . . . Then it is called *hadros*. In addition it is also spoken of as *logos*, because it is mainly used by the learned, whom the Greeks call *logios*. . . . Furthermore, Aristotle names it *ogkos*, which does not signify bombast but amplitude of speech. For he uses this word in a positive way, as does Hermogenes; but it is taken in a bad sense by Socrates and Plato. In addition it is called *semnos*, which signifies full of dignity and solemnity. And likewise Hermogenes often calls it *axioma* because the greatness of speech ought not to be lacking in dignity. Finally, Dionysius Longinus . . . who has left a choice and golden little book on this character, calls it *hypsos*.²⁸

The multiplicity of connotations surrounding this syncretic grand style led to multiple criteria. Grandeur involves excellence of subject matter, emotional intensity, weightiness, height, fullness, and figurative richness. Because the Greek tradition placed much less emphasis on copia and periodicity than the Latin, these tend to fade as distinctive characteristics of the grand style. The

²⁵ Patterson, *Hermogenes*, p. 32. She also notes (p. 19) that Portus's 1570 commentary on Longinus equates the sublime with Hermogenic solemnity (semnotes).
²⁶ Vossius, *Commentariorum*, 2: 471.
²⁷ Lullius, *De oratione*, p. 432.
²⁸ Vossius, *Commentariorum*, 2: 433.

influence of Longinus, however, from the late sixteenth century on, meant that loftiness of soul and grandeur of conception rather than verbal heightening became primary attributes.[29] This stress on the inward, conceptual aspects of grandeur was further reinforced by the fact that Hermogenes as well as Longinus and Augustine allowed for an austerely simple and unornamented form of the grand style.[30]

Furthermore, the same rhetorics that give a hellenistic definition of the grand style often exemplify it with the standard non-Ciceronian Greek and Silver Latin models. According to Flacius, Caussin, Keckermann, and Vossius, the major anti-Ciceronian authors fall not within the plain but the grand style. Thucydides receives mention in Vossius's and Keckermann's discussion of this genus, and Flacius cites him over and over as the closest secular equivalent for the biblical grand style.[31] Caussin describes Tacitus as grand, splendid, and gravis; Sallust as harsh, gravis, sublime, and powerful.[32] Keckermann's chapter on the grand style praises Justus Lipsius, the father of Renaissance Stoicism and anti-Ciceronianism,[33] for his use of poetic words and his "great majesty of style."[34] Lipsius himself depicts his stylistic ideals in language unmistakably reminiscent of the grand style. One can see this by turning to a curious passage in which he is describing Seneca's style. One is struck by how little of what he praises belongs to the intimate, artless, plain style that Seneca himself advocated. Instead, Lipsius seems to be describing a Senecan form of the genus grande; it is brief and sweet, like the an-

[29] See Keckermann, *Systema*, p. 1670; Caussin, *De eloquentia*, pp. 133–34; Vossius, *Commentariorum*, 2: 447.

[30] Hermogenes thus writes, "The figures that produce solemnity are the same as those that produce purity, that is, simple direct statements and the like" (*Opera*, p. 250).

[31] Keckermann, *Systema*, p. 1671; Vossius, *Commentariorum*, 2: 441, 454; Flacius, *Clavis*, 2: 4, 461–63, 498, 500.

[32] Caussin, *De eloquentia*, pp. 105–107, 172.

[33] On Lipsius, see Croll's "Justus Lipsius and the Anti-Ciceronian Movement to the End of the 16th and the Beginning of the 17th Century," in *"Attic" and Baroque*; also Fumaroli, *L'Age de l'éloquence*, pp. 155–60.

[34] Keckermann, *Systema*, pp. 1671–72.

cient philosophic style, but also splendid, metaphoric, and passionate.

> In his terseness there is wonderful ἐνέργεια and effectiveness; in his
> brevity, clarity and splendor. One finds frequent, almost continuous, al-
> lusions, images, metaphors which both delight and teach, sending the
> mind in and out of the subject. There is care without affectation, beauty
> without meticulous neatness. . . . all suited for battle and the forum, not
> for enjoyment or performance (et pugnae atque arenae omnia, non de-
> lectationi aut scaenae parata). Even in this brief and taut manner of
> speaking there appears a certain rich abundance.[35]

A copious, figurative, and agonistic style must be placed within
the genus grande. If this is so, then we are faced with the interesting possibility that even the antagonism between Senecan and Ciceronian ideals resolves itself into a tension *within* the grand style.

That Silver Latin prose belongs to the top, not the bottom, of
the hierarchy of style is also indicated by the fact that Renaissance
critics of Seneca describe him not as flat or puny—faults of the
plain style—but as inflated and tumid—vices invariably associated with false grandeur.[36] Nor does Lipsius's commendation of
Senecan brevity militate against this, since brevity was often
associated with emotional power. If, then, for the Renaissance,
Seneca, Tacitus, and Thucydides represent a more concise and
pregnant form of the grand style, then we are left with a situation
similar to that sketched by R. F. Jones: on one side the Greek,
Ciceronian, Senecan, and Christian variants of a lofty and powerful prose, and on the other an unrhetorical plainness, at differ-

---

[35] Cited in Williamson, *The Senecan Amble*, p. 111.

[36] See also the description of Lipsius's style in Williamson (*The Senecan Amble*,
p. 122), where it is described as deficient in the principal characteristics of a plain
style—*perspicuitas, puritas*—and as almost excessive in ornament, beauty, and copia. Throughout antiquity and the Renaissance there exists a tendency to think of
Seneca as anything but a plain stylist. Both Norden (*Die antike Kunstprosa*, p. 307)
and Adolph (*The Rise of Modern Prose Style*, p. 137) note that in the first century
the Atticists regarded Cicero as natural and Attic, Seneca as artificial, brilliant, and
Asiatic. A similar judgment persists in the Renaissance. Genuine plain stylists like
Glanville, Montaigne, and Casaubon considered Seneca's writings "high and
tumid" (cf. Williamson, *The Seneca Amble*, pp. 187–88, 196; Adolph, *The Rise of
Modern Prose Style*, p. 86).

ent times connected with Puritans, scientists, and Anglican rationalists.[37]

The classification of non-Ciceronian prose in the grand style relates to hellenistic rhetoric because these Greek texts place brevity, harshness of sound, suggestiveness, and difficulty within the grand style or some aspects of it. Thucydides is, of course, representative of grandeur in both Demetrius and Dionysius of Halicarnassus. Renaissance rhetorics appropriated these features of the hellenistic grand style. The biblical and general rhetorics often reject the ideal of concinnitas, insisting rather that the grand style requires harsh sounds, asyndeta, ellipses, abrupt transitions, brief clauses, strange and dissonant images, and austere simplicity. Historians of prose style have long recognized these qualities as characteristic of late Renaissance or baroque literature,[38] but what has not been clearly enough seen is that they belong to the grand style through its Greek line of descent, that they are acknowledged aspects of the Renaissance grand style, and finally that they grow out of a deeply religious humanism.

This last point is particularly relevant because Croll linked these "anti-Ciceronian" features not only to the plain style but also to the "radical and rationalist" tendencies of the late Renaissance: libertine skepticism, *realpolitik*, Stoic detachment, and scientific positivism.[39] In fact, however, one of the earliest and best pieces of applied anti-Ciceronianism comes not from the pen of a Stoic but from that of an ardent and orthodox Lutheran—Flacius Illyricus. Flacius, whose sources throughout are the late hellenistic works of Demetrius and Hermogenes, is highly critical of the redundance and Asiatic prolixity of Cicero.[40] Instead, he compares Holy Scripture to the heroes of Roman "Atticism": Thucydides and Sallust.[41] He thus observes, "Cicero writes that

[37] See the articles by Jones collected in *The Seventeenth Century*.

[38] Croll, "The Baroque Style in Prose," in *"Attic" and Baroque*, pp. 207–33; Roy Daniells, "English Baroque and Deliberate Obscurity," *Journal of Aesthetics and Art Criticism* 5 (1948): 115–21; Rene Wellek, "The Concept of Baroque in Literary Scholarship," *Journal of Aesthetics and Art Criticism* 5 (1948): 89–92.

[39] Croll, *"Attic" and Baroque*, pp. 121–22.

[40] Flacius, *Clavis*, 2: 499.

[41] Ibid., 2: 4, 461–62, 494.

Thucydides was so full and crammed with matter (*res*) that the number of things was nearly equal to the number of words. . . . But Holy Scripture easily excells all other writers in this manner of speaking; in it often single words embrace one or even several thoughts (*sententiae*)."[42] Yet, as has been said, Flacius also affirms that the Bible belongs not to the plain but the grand style. His anti-Ciceronianism descends from Greek conceptions of grandeur, not Stoic plainness—a fact with repercussions for the development of sacred prose in the seventeenth century.

For Flacius, the Bible possesses a Thucydidean or laconic brevity, "for long members loose their force; that which encloses great strength in a small space is fiercer and more vehement."[43] The result is a dense, suggestive concision, at once powerful and mysterious.

Brevity is suited for *sententiae*, according to Demetrius; it is also suited for figurative sayings, for giving commands, for threats, mysteries, symbols, and allegory. It often speaks with a certain greater force than prolixity; now because [it is] like an spear hurled which strikes with a sudden impetus, while on the other hand prolixity looses intensity; now because it leaves many things to be suggested and hinted, and by this inflicts the hearer with anxiety. He suspects and fears things more weighty and sad than the matter often contains.[44]

Biblical language does not flow in an orderly, linear movement; rather, "individual ideas or passages are overloaded, pregnant, and darkened: thus the whole fabric of the discourse seems to swell as if impregnated with densely packed thoughts."[45] One consequence of such violent compression is obscurity. Sententiae, far-fetched metaphors, parentheses, figures of thought, types, and allegories intertwine without benefit of logical connectives.[46] Despite the fact that Flacius likes to cite what sound like positivistic formulas concerning brevity and the superiority of res to verba,[47] what he is describing is exactly the opposite of

[42] Ibid., 2: 498.
[43] Ibid., 2: 493.
[44] Ibid.
[45] Ibid., 2: 424.
[46] Ibid., 2: 3, 494–95.
[47] Croll, *"Attic" and Baroque*, p. 131.

"modern" or scientific prose. Scriptural brevity is prediscursive and metaphorical, not literal, and certainly not the urbane, lucid Classical plain style favored by Restoration rationalists.

Shared hellenistic influence also helps explain why Flacius's description of biblical *compositio* so closely resembles Croll's "Attic" or baroque prose. For Flacius, the Bible abandons the harmonious periodicity of Latin oratory in favor of the asyndetic, asymmetrical harshness characteristic of the Thucydidean grand style.[48] He remarks,

harsh *compositio* is found throughout even Holy Scripture; according to Demetrius learned writers are accustomed to use this on account of the grandeur of language as well as the austerity and weight of the subject matter itself.

The whole configuration of the discourse seems harsh to Latin ears. Neither the words nor the thoughts are joined or arrayed gently and harmoniously among themselves, as in many other writers; but they sometimes rush forward with a rough, surging, and eddying impetus. In this respect Thucydides and Sallust are not unlike Holy Scripture.[49]

Like Croll, Flacius notes both the tendency of such prose to link clauses by making each clause depend on the final word in the preceeding clause—a peculiarity Flacius terms "*lapsus styli*"—and its logical stasis, so that the final member of such loosely connected periods ends where the first had begun, creating "so to speak, a circle of thought (*circulus quidam sensuum*)."[50]

As so often in Renaissance rhetoric, the selection and use of Classical sources follow from religious demands. Flacius borrows from Hermogenes and Demetrius precisely what he needs to create an aesthetic appropriate for the Bible with its densely layered meanings, metaphoric language, and unclassical syntax. Biblical style in Flacius is symbolic and mythic; it seems brief because words and images function as complex signs in the Augustinian sense. Single images express the invisible inner activity of the psyche or move in depth to signify the analogical interrelation of visible and spiritual order. Therefore, Flacius compares the

[48] Flacius, *Clavis*, 2: 425, 461, 496.
[49] Ibid., 2: 4, 463.
[50] Ibid., 2: 433–34.

Bible both to a drama and a sacrament. It resembles a "comic play" insofar as it represents interior life through physical gestures and acts. Biblical language is also sacramental because its metaphors, types, and allegories are themselves "real words" which, in turn, signify other things.[51] Such sacramental discourse creates a dense brevity because it employs a single trope or image to point to multiple spiritual senses. Thus in the Bible "there is often a rich and felicitous brevity, in that a single text can exhibit a double meaning (*duplicatus sensus*). . . . Thus many psalms, although they concern David and other holy men who bore their own crosses, nevertheless principally refer to Christ."[52] Instead of expanding horizontally through a discursive sequence of words, biblical prose interweaves metaphor, type, allegory, and symbol to create a vertical movement from signifier to multiple levels of signification.

Aristotle wisely said, "the first step toward the knowledge of things is to find out what is not known." Wherefore, it will have been useful at the beginning to recount the reasons why the Bible is sometimes quite difficult. . . . The language is heavily figured and that in many ways. Much is [written] in similitudes, allegories, types, questions, vivid depictions, dramatizations, and similar figures. . . . Often [the Hebrews] put two or even three tropes in a single word. . . . Often they use far-fetched and difficult tropes. . . . They frequently summon various parentheses and reduplications, which unless they are carefully observed and considered, disturb the mind and memory of the reader, so that he looses the thread of the thought and meaning, and wanders alone as if in an unknown forest. . . .

The greatest difficulty and almost obscurity in this horn of sacred abundance (*illius sacri copiae-cornu*) arises from the fact that such vast and such diverse riches are forced within the strait confinements both of books and of discourse. . . .

Frequently metaphors, allusions, or similitudes are touched upon briefly, yet they embrace a vast abundance of things, which the Scriptures do not explicate; but they want the intelligent and industrious reader or hearer, having noted the thing mentioned and considered its various properties, . . . to note and find out [the meanings].[53]

[51] Ibid., 2: 480.
[52] Ibid., 2: 498.
[53] Ibid., 2: 2–3, 420, 501.

Fundamentally, then, Flacius's understanding of biblical language is Augustinian, but he uses hellenistic rhetoric to translate Augustine's theological treatment of biblical signs into stylistic categories.[54] The result, however, is an original and sophisticated theory of the Christian grand style.

Although Flacius's *Clavis* represents the fullest statement of an "anti-Ciceronian" grand style applied to problems of sacred discourse, the development of a grand style within the ranks of "anti-Ciceronianism" continues throughout the Renaissance. Juan Luis Vives's *De ratione dicendi* (1533), which cites Hermogenes, Demetrius, and Dionysius, as well as Trebizond,[55] begins with the traditional "Attic" criticisms of Ciceronian copia: "Often flesh and fat cover the sinews, so that they are weakened, and less apt to perform their functions; thus it happens in a speech, that the luxury of words and abundance of flesh, and a wandering, dissolute composition enfeeble the oration, which happened to Cicero, who while he dialated his subject with too many words, lost strength, like a river which expands too widely: therefore Calvus said he lacked sinews and Brutus that he was crippled and emasculate." One would expect some sort of plain style to be offered as the alternative to such bloated weakness, but instead Vives continues with the traditional contrast between the agonistic genus grande and sophistic *cultus* based on Demetrius's account of the forcible style: "For there is one kind of oration which fights, and another which skirmishes and represents rather the shadow of a fight. King Philip of Macedon called Demosthenes a soldier, Isocrates an athlete. Demosthenes struggles, Isocrates delights; whence the nation of the sophists remained loose and flowing, with pointed sententiae, sonorous words, more suitable for ceremony than battle."[56] Clearly Vives is not objecting to Cicero's neglect of dialectical plainness but his failure to achieve force and elevation. The contrast between battles and games or between Demosthenes and Isocrates always re-

[54] Saint Augustine, *On Christian Doctrine*, 2.1–23, 3.34–56.

[55] John O. Ward, "Renaissance Commentators on Ciceronian Rhetoric," *Renaissance Eloquence*, p. 167.

[56] Juan Luis Vives, *De ratione dicendi, Opera omnia*, 8 vols. (1782; repr. London, 1964), 2: 144–45.

fers to the opposition between the grand style and sophistic. The difference in the way Flacius and Vives interpret brevity and "Attic" compression, however, points to a distinctive feature of the Christian grand style. Vives, who deals only with secular oratory, omits the numinous or allegorical aspects of grandeur. Brevity for him means agonistic force, whereas Flacius connects the laconic style to sacramental and metaphoric utterance.

After Flacius, the hellenized grand style, with its association of grandeur with brevity and harshness, dominates the general rhetorics.[57] Vossius thus states, "and indeed Demetrius says that sweetness of composition is rarely allowed in magnificent discourse; and he proves this by the example of Thucydides, who strove after sublimity and therefore sedulously fled smooth composition and frequent transpositions of words, but loved harsh juxtaposition of vowels and consonants, like a traveler making a journey through rough and harsh places."[58] Vossius likewise quotes Demetrius to the effect that the grand style should possess a "succinct brevity of words . . . for when speech is cut short it often creates an impression greater than the thing itself."[59] Although Vossius modifies both comments with a warning against affectation, the effect is still to break any necessary connection between concinnitas, copia, and the grand style.

In Caussin, the conjunction of grandeur and an austere succinctness reappears in a religious context and therefore strengthened by a Christian revulsion at florid or luxuriant prolixity. Interestingly, Caussin is a militant Ciceronian in his discussion of secular prose, but rejects such Classicism in sacred works. The chapters on preaching are prefaced by a lengthy debate between one Logodaedalus and one Theophrastus on the permissibility of a sacred Ciceronianism. The latter, who represents the authorial

---

[57] While the sacred rhetorics also develop non-Ciceronian versions of the grand style (or passionate discourse), these texts rarely cite Classical sources except for the most familiar Latin ones. This seems to have been a question of generic decorum, since both Keckermann and Alsted each write a sacred as well as a general rhetoric but only cite hellenistic authorities in the latter.

[58] Vossius, *Commentariorum*, 2: 441. For the image of Thucydidean or hyper-Attic style as a rough journey, see Seneca, *Epistulae morales*, 114.15.

[59] Vossius, *Commentariorum*, 2: 452.

position, firmly disallows all embellishment, all excess care for diction, periodicity, or beauty. When Caussin then turns to explicate his ideal of Christian discourse, the first quality he mentions is *gravitas*. The gravis preacher is sublime and powerful. Yet he uses a style that is

close, harsh, austere, and condensed in sententiae. He wisely avoids sculpted sentiments, delightful and lascivious. . . . He cannot endure drawn out and slow conclusions nor speech tied to the laws of rhythm. . . . but if there are any weighty figures of thought for expressing the liberty of the speaker, for commanding, for castigating, for execrating, these he gladly seizes upon. . . .

He teaches acutely, fights fiercely, conquers powerfully, pursues magnanimously and commands and speaks all things as if from a tripod.[60]

This oracular, agonistic style has its roots in Caussin's hellenistic erudition. While such gravitas belongs to the same antisophistic tradition evident in Vives and throughout the Renaissance, Caussin connects it more specifically to the austere and compressed version of forensic power found in the hellenistic rhetorics. The gravis preacher resembles Longinus's picture of Demosthenes, whose leonine dignity ("*leonis maiestas*") draws wonder and passion even though "destitute of lighter ornaments, naked, and simple."[61] Caussin's Greek sources allow him to create a grand style free of the anxious refinement and second-hand ornament that had plagued earlier Renaissance attempts to construct a grand style along Ciceronian lines.[62] Such "anti-Ciceronianism" shifted the emphasis of rhetorical criticism from stylistic imitation to the "exalted mind . . . raised up by the contemplation of great things,"[63] although Caussin's thousand and ten pages still contain plentiful discussion of stylistic fine points. Even here, he tends to be nonprescriptive and less concerned with mere correctness than with the intellectual and spiritual failures debased

[60] Caussin, *De eloquentia*, pp. 965–66.
[61] Ibid., p. 972.
[62] On Renaissance Ciceronianism, see Baxandall, *Giotto*; Seigel, *Rhetoric and Philosophy*; Croll, *"Attic" and Baroque*; Scott, *Controversies*; Erasmus, *Ciceronianus*.
[63] Caussin, *De eloquentia*, p. 965.

speech reveals. His parodies of bad sermons and worse orations are wickedly incisive.

Several conclusions emerge from this examination of brevity, harshness, and related qualities in the Renaissance grand style. If "anti-Ciceronianism" was, as Croll suggests, a liberating influence, an escape from the reactionary formalism of humanist orthodoxy, it freed prose not only to express the rationalist inclinations of emerging modernism but also the spiritual intuitions of biblical Protestantism and the fierce energy of counter-Reformation devotion. If the individualism latent in "anti-Ciceronianism" breaks forth in Politian's assertion that he did not want to talk like Cicero but like himself, the religious impulse emerges soon after in Erasmus's scorn for the hyper-Classical frigidity of Ciceronian preachers who could not bear to use terms like "baptize" or "Holy Spirit."[64] In fact, Erasmus's attack on this squeamishness proved utterly successful. No subsequent Renaissance rhetoric even remotely suggests confining sacred discourse within Classical forms. Most of the ecclesiastical rhetorics freely ignore and transform Classical precepts to fit the actual requirements of the pulpit. The biblical and general rhetorics take another route; borrowing from hellenistic theory, they construct a grand style able to embrace the rich symbolic texture of the Bible and the austere power of patristic oratory. The result is a much more successful union of humanist and religious culture than seemed possible within the confines of Ciceronianism.

In addition, the existence of this hellenistic grand style from the mid-sixteenth century to the mid-seventeenth suggests a new schematization for the history of Renaissance prose. Croll and subsequent scholars identified the grand style with a balanced, schematic Ciceronianism, classifying all briefer, harsher, less symmetrical styles as variants of the genus humile. But, as we have seen, Renaissance rhetorics make no such classification; rather, influenced by hellenistic concepts, they have no difficulty in accepting a terse, rough, and unschematic grand style. This possibility upsets the accepted outline of Renaissance prose as the movement from a Ciceronian, oratorical grand style to an "Attic"

[64] Erasmus, *Ciceronianus*, pp. 50, 66–68.

plain style based on Silver Latin models. Indeed, if we accept Marc Fumaroli's suggestion that Ciceronian "Atticism," i.e., the imitation of Cicero's epistles and philosophical works, represents the main line of Renaissance Ciceronianism, running from Bembo to Muret and the classicism of the seventeenth century, we could almost invert Croll's categories and claim that Renaissance prose develops along two main lines: an urbane, elegant Ciceronian plain style and a dense, brief hellenistic grand style, the first being predominantly secular, the other embracing both sacred rhetoric and the secular manifestations of Croll's "ceremonious" and "grave" anti-Ciceronianism with its "curious sublimity."[65] From the late sixteenth century, then, we could say that the theory and practice of prose style move simultaneously in the direction of neoclassicism and the baroque. Although baroque prose covers a wide spectrum of styles, from Flacius's biblical grand style to the libertine *sermo* of Montaigne, it tends, as Croll himself noted, toward the grandeur and intensity of a Rubens, Bach, or Bernini, while neoclassicism cultivates the plain style genres of satire and epistle. In fact, however, the history of Renaissance prose is too complicated to fit comfortably into any binary ordering. Euphuism, scientific prose, the doctrine-and-use sermon, for example, do not belong to this paradigm at all because these are postclassical forms, emerging independently of the categories of ancient rhetorical theory. The only real purpose, perhaps, of such schematization is to dispel the notion that Renaissance prose develops in any obvious linear fashion from Ciceronianism to a rationalist, modern plain style.

Sweetness and Light: Epideictic Oratory and the Grand Style

While hellenistic theory pushed the Renaissance grand style in the direction of brevity and aural harshness, at the same time it contributed to quite a different transformation. In Roman rhetoric, epideixis and related qualities like pleasure, love, wonder, joy, splendor, and praise do not generally form part of the grand style

---

[65] Croll, *"Attic" and Baroque*, p. 194.

since they are not characteristic of forensic or political oratory. Instead, epideixis usually falls within the genus medium, sharing its association with sophistic and aestheticism.[66] In Christian rhetoric from Augustine on, epideictic oratory often receives the same condemnation meted out to all forms of ostentatious artistry.[67] But in the Renaissance, a combination of hellenistic and theological influences considerably alters this negative attitude. As O'Malley has shown, both rhetorical theory and humanistic practice between 1480 and 1520 appropriated epideixis to Christian purposes.[68] During this period and afterwards, the association of sacred oratory with epideictic tended to shift the latter toward the grand style.

Yet the authority of Cicero, added to the traditional Christian mistrust of epideixis, never wholly vanished, with the result that Renaissance discussions of epideictic and related qualities often show considerable ambivalence and occasional confusion. The definitions Erasmus offers for delectatio suggest these conflicting connotations of epideixis. According to him, the delightfulness (delectatio) of speech may signify just a certain loveliness and freshness characteristic of writers like Saint Bernard. But it also possesses two more restricted meanings. Happy subjects, such as the heavenly joy of the angels and blessed, require a more cheerful style. This sort of delectatio coincides with the subjects of Christian encomia—giving thanks and praise for the divine goodness revealed in all creatures and preeminently in the lives of saints and holy men.[69] But there is another species of delightfulness, a sort of sensual voluptas designed to titillate audiences with fables, jokes, and theatrical amusements.[70] Erasmus's latter two types of delectatio correspond to the divergent Renaissance views on epideictic: on the one hand, it is the style of the great festal sermons,

---

[66] Burgess, *Epideictic Literature*, pp. 93–95.

[67] Saint Augustine, *On Christian Doctrine*, 4.55; de Granada, *Ecclesiasticae rhetoricae*, p. 307; Carbo, *Divinus orator*, pp. 23, 251.

[68] O'Malley, *Praise and Blame*; see also O. B. Hardison, Jr., *The Enduring Monument: A Study of the Idea of Praise in Renaissance Literary Theory and Practice* (Chapel Hill, 1962) for a discussion of epideictic in Renaissance poetics.

[69] Erasmus, *Ecclesiastes*, 5: 859a.

[70] Ibid., 5: 859f–860e.

of hymns and psalms, of sacred praise and joy; on the other, it is a debased entertainment catering to the levity and sensuality of its listeners.

The origins of this first type of epideictic are both Greek and Christian. In hellenistic rhetoric, epideictic qualities exist within the grand style. This is most evident in Hermogenes, who assigns both solemnity and splendor, themselves both aspects of grandeur, to epideictic oratory.[71] The scope of epideictic in Hermogenes also extends far beyond praise and blame, including all noncivic discourse: poetry, history, and above all, the Platonic dialogues. The connection between solemnity and epideixis is particularly significant since the former also possesses distinctly religious overtones, facilitating the Renaissance association of the prophetic and mystical with a celebratory grandeur. Sturm thus links solemnity with the praise of God and with the festal sermons of the Cappadocian preachers.[72]

Greek influences also affect the meaning of "wonder" in the Renaissance. Greek and Roman rhetoric follows Aristotle in connecting wonder and pleasure,[73] but the Romans associate these qualities with sweetness and ornament,[74] the Greeks with grandeur and sublimity. Demetrius and Longinus thus use "wonder" to refer to the perception of a strange and unfamiliar grandeur, a usage based on the Aristotelian conjunction of "foreignness" with both solemnity and wonder.[75] Aristotle furthermore claims that wonder is pleasurable since it excites the desire to know, and all learning is pleasurable.[76] In the Renaissance, "wonder" almost always appears in the context of epideictic and delectatio, but it modifies this complex of ideas by reintroducing the Greek interrelation of wonder, grandeur, and cognition. As we noted previously, Rudolph Agricola is a seminal figure in this shift. Because

[71] Hermogenes, *Opera*, pp. 386–88.

[72] Sturm, *De universa*, pp. 17, 762.

[73] J. V. Cunningham, "Woe or Wonder: The Emotional Effect of Shakespearean Tragedy," *The Collected Essays of J. V. Cunningham* (Chicago, 1976), pp. 55–57, 62–68.

[74] Cicero, *Part orat* 22, 32, 58.

[75] Demetrius, 2.60, 2.70; Longinus, 35.5; Aristotle, *Rhetoric* 3.2.1404b.

[76] Aristotle, *Metaphysics*, 1.1.980a–1.2.983a.

delectatio is a movement (*permotio*) of the cognitive virtue, according to Agricola, it has two species. Some delight arises from sense perception, for example the perception of cheerful colors and gentle sounds. Thus at one extreme delectatio refers to pure aesthetic pleasure. But there are also pleasures of the intellect. Agricola writes: "[Since] the pursuit of truth and goodness is the proper activity [of the mind], it is delighted by everything that teaches, by all that is great, wonderful, unfamiliar, unexpected, unheard of; by the pursuit of hidden things, by knowledge of things past and placed at a distance (*res in longinquo posita*), by notable words and deeds of great men, and by virtue's gallant acts."[77] For Agricola, mental delectatio arises from the perception of the great, wondrous, and unfamiliar. The passage rests on the Aristotelian principle that those things which are "excellent and divine" are invariably "less accessible to knowledge" since they are remote from sense perception, the ordinary source of all our knowledge.[78] Agricola's "great, wonderful, and unfamiliar" are therefore not three distinct categories but closely interrelated; wonder is the psychological response to those things which are excellent yet strange, hidden, and at a distance. Agricola's delectatio thus contains the seeds for a union of joy, wonder, and elevation, along the lines of the Longinian sublime. In addition, by broadening the meaning of delectatio from aesthetic to intellectual delight, Agricola widened the potential scope of epideictic, linking it with the topics of the grand style and with the activity of the mind as well as the senses. In particular, delectatio seems inevitably related to sacred themes, these being both great and distant. Sacred rhetorics in the next two centuries exploit these implicit connections, creating a sacred epideixis of wonder, love, and contemplative joy.

The immense popularity of Agricola's *De inventione dialectica* gave his concept of delectatio wide currency. Keckermann particularly quotes almost the whole passage in his sections on delectatio and praise (laudatio). He adds, however, several important

---

[77] Agricola, *De inventione*, p. 395.
[78] Aristotle, *Parts of Animals*, 1.5.664b. This passage and its consequences for rhetorical theory will be more fully discussed in the next chapter.

details. First, he explicitly identifies delectatio as an emotion, thus reducing the officia oratoris to two—teaching and moving. Delight, love, thanksgiving, joy, and similar affects are grouped as "gentler emotions," as opposed to harsher emotions like hate and anger.[79] Laudatio or the epideictic oration likewise falls under the category of speeches expressing emotion.[80] This is not surprising, given the Renaissance tendency, noted in Chapter Three, to extend the meaning of emotion to include intellective as well as sensitive appetite. The result is, however, to move epideixis within the sphere of passionate discourse, which is virtually coextensive with the grand style.

Furthermore, Keckermann specifies the cognitive origin of delectatio more precisely than Agricola had done. It is not only the response to what is great and wondrous but the conjunction of this unfamiliar and remote excellence with perspicuity and clarity, since, as Keckermann notes, we delight neither in what is commonplace nor in what is unintelligible.[81] This position again goes back to Aristotle. His observation in the *Rhetoric* that oratory should combine the clarity of ordinary speech with words that are stately and give an unfamiliar air[82] rests on his basic epistemological premise of the inverse proportion between the most excellent objects, which are more knowable in themselves, and ordinary sensible things, which are better known by us.[83] The maximum balance between these poles of excellence and clarity creates, according to Keckermann, the sensation of delight. Therefore, the characteristic of delightful discourse is to be *illustris* or luminous—a word that for Keckermann connotes both an excellent unfamiliarity (he thus claims that things which are *illustria* are more noble than those which are *proxima* or near at hand) and a vivid clarity. Interestingly, illustris comes from Sturm's description of Hermogenic splendor, which Keckermann also bor-

---

[79] Keckermann, *Systema*, pp. 1614, 1645.
[80] Ibid., p. 1643.
[81] Ibid., p. 1614.
[82] Aristotle, *Rhetoric* 3.2.1404b.
[83] Aristotle, *Posterior Analytics*, 1.2.71b–72a. Wesley Trimpi, *Muses of One Mind: The Literary Analysis of Experience and its Continuity* (Princeton, 1983), pp. 83–240.

rows for his analysis of the grand style.[84] The term thus links his treatments of delight, epideictic, and splendor, associating all three with a luminous clarity that evokes love and wonder.

The hellenistic influence on the rehabilitation of epideictic cannot be separated from the theological. The Psalms, Canticles, Ephesians, Colossians, the Te Deum, and Gloria in excelsis are all, in Renaissance classifications, epideictic statements of praise, wonder, and love.[85] Because so much sacred literature belongs to this genus, it was necessary to develop a theory of epideixis freed from sophistic overtones of excessive cultus and ostentation. While hellenistic rhetoric assisted this development by suggesting the connection between epideixis, wonder, and greatness, a second source for the creation of a sacred epideixis lay within the theological tradition itself.

In Renaissance rhetorics, one immediately notes a shift in the meaning of words like "delight," "sweetness," and "pleasure," terms commonly associated with epideictic. In Roman rhetoric, as we have seen, they refer to the aesthetic (usually aural) response to lovely sounds and graceful ornament. The Renaissance replaces these meanings with ones drawn from Christian sources. Flacius thus defines delectare as to rest in God with trust and love;[86] Hemmingsen speaks of God's sweetness, Carbo of spiritual voluptas, Alsted of sacred joy and pleasure.[87] In accord with the Renaissance tendency to see spiritual experience in affective terms, not only delight and sweetness but a whole cluster of related concepts, especially joy, love, and wonder, are treated as sacred emotions proper to epideictic oratory. In fact, the emotions most characteristic of religious life overlap with these epideictic responses. Vossius thus claims that demonstrative oratory should awaken love, wonder, and emulation.[88] Carbo likewise connects

---

[84] Sturm, *De universa*, pp. 604–606; Keckermann, *Systema*, p. 1671.*

[85] Erasmus, *Ecclesiastes*, 5: 859a–e, 880e–81b; Melanchthon, *Elementorum* 13: 423, 449; Joannis Tesmarus, *Exercitationum rhetoricarum libri viii* (Amsterdam, 1657), p. 48.

[86] Flacius, *Clavis*, 1: 206.

[87] Hemmingsen, *The Preacher*, p. 58; Carbo, *Divinus orator*, p. 177; Alsted, *Theologia*, p. 9.

[88] Vossius, *Commentariorum*, 1: 387.

epideixis with praise, emulation, and wonder, Keckermann with joy, thankfulness, and hope, Caussin with love and wonder.[89] Renaissance rhetorics are committed to their Classical models and therefore, with the exception of Brandolini, refuse to spell out the implications of the similarity between epideictic and sacred emotion. Particularly in the ecclesiastical rhetorics not touched by hellenistic texts there remains the unfortunate tendency to identify preaching very closely with moral exhortation and rebuke.[90] But Renaissance rhetorics are also sufficiently eclectic and unsystematic that a second type of sacred grandeur, one more numinous than ethical, could spring up through the interstices of didacticism.

The connection found in Agricola and Keckermann between epideictic and what is wonderous, lofty, and strange appears in the sacred rhetorics. Only in these, the great and wonderful are specified as the mysteries of faith and the mighty acts of God. As early as Brandolini, epideictic involves not only the praise of God and the saints but also "leads men to wonder at and contemplate those things which cannot be understood by man but which we pursue with wonder and reverence," such as the hypostatic union or the Trinity.[91] Melanchthon observes that sacred epideixis arouses contemplative wonder.[92] In his chapters on epideictic oratory, Caussin similarly points out that religious encomia awaken wonder and "inflame their hearers with the love of God," a phrase suggesting the ardent power of the grand style.[93] Caussin continues his examination of sacred epideixis in his analysis of happiness (*laetitia*) and hope (*spes*): "Sacred orations also create happiness (*laetitiae affectus*) and [a happiness] indeed grand (*gravis*) and vehement, which they draw from the splendor, majesty, and loveliness of divine things. . . . The writings of the Fathers are filled with these emotions, especially where they survey the holy mys-

---

[89] Carbo, *Divinus orator*, pp. 136ff.; Keckermann, *Systema*, p. 1645; Caussin, *De eloquentia*, p. 581.

[90] O'Malley, "Sixteenth-Century Treatises," pp. 242–49.

[91] Brandolini, *De ratione scribendi*, pp. 94–95; see also O'Malley, *Praise and Blame*, p. 49.

[92] Melanchthon, *Elementorum* 13: 423.

[93] Caussin, *De eloquentia*, p. 581.

teries of our redemption or the benefits of the world to come."[94] These passages suggest not only the close link between sacred epideixis and the grand style—for words like "gravitas" and "maiestas" are invariably associated with that genus—but also the possibility of a magnificent, passionate oratory that is neither hortatory nor agonistic but contemplative and celebratory. Still less are such sermons equivalent to sophistic display pieces, for they deal with events at the heart of all Christian teaching and evoke emotional responses fundamental to Christian spirituality. They are therefore serious in a way that Classical epideictic, designed to set forth the speaker's skill and entertain his audience, never was.

If sacred epideixis is passionate, serious, and concerned with the most excellent subjects, its affinity to the grand style seems inescapable.[95] Yet Renaissance rhetorics persistently struggle with the proper place for such discourse in the system of the genera. The influence of Roman rhetoric naturally led to the identification of the grand style with vehemence and force. Furthermore, epideictic is primarily contemplative (although many rhetorics note that love and wonder encourage emulation), while the commonly accepted versions of the grand style associate its emotional power with moral praxis. The relation of epideixis to the grand style, then, becomes an important issue in Renaissance rhetorics, particularly those sensitive to the numinous, celebratory quality present in parts of Holy Scripture and the writings of the Fathers. We have already seen this problem in Saint Augustine, who defines the grand style in terms of harsh vehemence yet offers as a biblical example Saint Paul's passionate laudatio on the love of Christ.[96] Although the attempt to incorporate epideictic within the grand style during the Renaissance never produces the relatively stable categories such as followed from the eighteenth-

---

[94] Ibid., pp. 499–500.

[95] In the chapter entitled, "Quae sententiae grandem reddant orationem," Vossius writes: "Tertium locum obtenent sententiae Ethicae, ac Politicae: ut cum disseritur de virtute & felicitate eorum, qui secundum virtutem vivunt; aut cum exempla commemorantur, quibus homines ad virtutem excitentur" (*Commentariorum*, 2: 466).

[96] Saint Augustine, *On Christian Doctrine*, 4.43.

century distinction between beauty and sublimity, it marks an early step in the process of reinterpreting Classical terminology to create an aesthetic responsive to the spiritual and cultural demands of its civilization. The Renaissance's taste for a solemn yet exuberant magnificence, its meditative ardor and love of splendor, receive at least a partial recognition in these rhetorics and their endeavor to discriminate between power and elevation, massiveness and luminosity, weight and glory.

The difficulties involved in attributing epideictic qualities to the grand style manifest themselves in the contradictions and discontinuities of Strebaeus's *De verborum electione* and Carbo's *Divinus orator*. Strebaeus begins by positing a crucial distinction between sublimity and weight (gravitas). Sublime words "shine (*splendescere*) with dignity and fullness." The attributes and names of God(s) and heroes, the virtues, great natural phenomena, splendid metaphors, exotic places are all sublime. Sublimity indicates value; whatever is lofty and precious and extraordinary is sublime.[97] Thus its subjects parallel those of delectatio in Agricola and Keckermann. Weighty or gravis discourse, on the other hand, is characterized by words like "incest, crime, sin, embezzlement, sacrilege . . . parricide, madness, fury" and so forth—by terms related to a (somewhat declamatory) forensic vehemence. Here we have a clear-cut division between a "lofty splendor" and agonistic force. "*Gravitas* is a measure of weight, *sublimitas* of dignity. *Gravis* words have greater intensity and vehemence, sublime words greater magnificence and breadth."[98]

This distinction suggests that there exists not one but two forms of grandeur. Strebaeus, however, feels very uncomfortable about allowing this possibility. When he comes to analyze the genera dicendi, he keeps close to Ciceronian definitions. The middle style, which includes encomia, history, philosophy, odes, Juvenalian satire, and poems like *De rerum natura*, possesses a masculine sweetness and tranquil grandeur, but the terms "sublimitas" and "splendor" drop out.[99] The grand style is vehement,

---

[97] Strebaeus, *De verborum electione*, pp. 78–83.
[98] Ibid., pp. 90–91.
[99] Ibid., pp. 296–301.

harsh, and agonistic.[100] But then a problem emerges. How is one to categorize the sublime? "There are some things," Strebaeus notes,

spoken in a most weighty (*gravissime*) and full way, such as certain sayings of the philosophers, praises of the gods and illustrious men, [and] councils concerning the greatest matters. If someone treats these things in a lofty and sublime manner, I will scarcely disagree. This, however, will depart from the judgment of Cicero, who thought such matters— even if they possessed all the flowers of speech and splendid ornaments— should be placed in the middle style, because they are serene and tranquil and wish to compose minds rather than arouse them.[101]

Although Strebaeus will finally accept the Ciceronian position, it is not without much hesitation. Having made the distinction between sublimity and weight, he must admit that both seem to be species of grandeur, at least insofar as the genera signify the decorum between style and subject matter.[102] But with respect to forensic power, epideictic sublimity is clearly in some sense less or other than the grand style. Strebaeus does not provide a very satisfactory solution to the problem, but he is keenly aware of the issue.

Strebaeus, in fact, is a model of clarity compared to Carbo and his treatment of the same problem. Basically, Carbo employs three different systems of analyzing style: the Ciceronian *genera dicendi*, the Ideas of Hermogenes, and something he calls the *divine genus*. The Ciceronian genera present the most problems. He follows Cicero and Augustine in depicting the grand style as harsh and powerful, lashing out against sin and forcibly converting the impious.[103] But the first chapter of John's Gospel keeps intruding itself. The chapter entitled "On the Sublime or Grand Style," which begins by defining this style in terms of prophetic violence and ferocity, ends "John began in a grand manner when he said, 'In the beginning was the Word.' "[104]

---

[100] Ibid., pp. 302–303.
[101] Ibid., p. 311.
[102] Ibid., p. 268.
[103] Carbo, *Divinus orator*, pp. 345–49.
[104] Ibid., p. 349.

As long as he is using the genera dicendi, Carbo tends to "elevate" the middle style; it is the style of sacred epideictic, arousing love and joy.[105] At one point he compares Michaelangelo to the grand style, Raphael to the middle.[106] If Raphael represents the middle style, then clearly this genus has acquired a surprising dignity and loftiness. As in Strebaeus, Ciceronian influence excludes sweetness, no matter how lofty, from Carbo's depiction of grandeur. But this still does not solve the problem of John's Gospel and the relation of sublimity to gravitas—a distinction Carbo borrows from Strebaeus but does not exploit.[107]

When Carbo drops the Ciceronian genera the results are more satisfying. The "divine genus," which Carbo invents to describe the unique eloquence of the Bible, contains all three genera dicendi, but he emphasizes the fusion of majesty, sublimity, power, and splendor.[108] It thus inherits the traditional terminology of the grand style yet abandons the Ciceronian restriction to forensic vehemence. The eloquence of the Spirit is everywhere ardent and passionate, at times fiery and harsh, at times tender and loving.[109] It awakens both ethical and numinous desire, for the preacher empowered by the Spirit "wants to lead his listeners not only to morality but also to every spiritual perfection."[110] The shift from a Classical to a Christian concept of eloquence thus immediately replaces the distinction between forensic and epideictic with a broader concept of emotion that includes the prophets' zeal for righteousness, Johannine sublimity, and the majestic splendor of the Psalms. This divine genus or eloquence of the Spirit, like the Longinian sublime, is not a style in the ordinary sense but a quality present in various styles; it is the "ardor of *caritas*," giving language vividness, life, and power.[111] Biblical eloquence is there-

[105] Ibid., pp. 17–18, 350, 418. Carbo, however, also accepts the Augustinian position that insofar as the middle style serves only for delectatio, it is morally impermissible (ibid., p. 351).

[106] Ibid., p. 346.

[107] Ibid., p. 262.

[108] Ibid., pp. 19–22.

[109] Ibid., pp. 45, 237.

[110] Ibid., p. 238.

[111] Ibid., pp. 237–39.

fore not primarily a matter of surface ornament but of thought
and feeling, in the same way that the sublime is an "echo of a great
soul"—only Longinus's Stoic humanism has been changed into
Christian supernaturalism. The source of this divine genus is,
however, probably Hermogenes. The *Divinus orator* ends with a
lucid summary of the Ideas, and here again the Idea of Grandeur
includes epideictic splendor and solemnity, as well as asperity and
vehemence. Not only the opening of John but also the praise of
Wisdom in the Apocrypha and the Epistle to the Hebrews belong
under solemnity. Splendor is explicitly epideictic; it occurs when
"beautiful and precious things are praised in splendid language."[112] Carbo transplants the more flexible Hermogenic system into sacred rhetoric to provide a conception of divine eloquence that acknowledges the festal and numinous qualities of
religious discourse. The Idea of Grandeur is, to a large extent, the
eloquence of the Spirit.

In some of the general rhetorics, the relation of epideictic to the
grand style is given a clearer articulation. Especially in rhetorics
that rely heavily on hellenistic sources there appears a greater willingness to posit two distinct grand styles, one of force and gravitas, the other of splendor and sublimity. Here, as always, it must
be remembered that the Burkean association of the sublime with
dread and terror does not exist in the Renaissance, which regards
sublimity as elevation, a grandeur of subject and expression creating wonder, joy, and awe. It thus shares the celebratory qualities of sacred epideictic, although without the connotations of
rich ornament. Both, however, arouse "vertical," contemplative
emotions and both are associated with the terminology of light
(e.g., *illustris*, *splendidus*) and majesty, rather than vehemence or
weight. As I have suggested, the roots of the similarity between
the sublime and epideictic probably lie in Aristotle's interrelation
of pleasure, strangeness, wonder, and excellence, which passes
into Longinian sublimity as well as Renaissance interpretations of
delectatio and laudatio.

One can begin to see the distinction between two forms of the
grand style in the sixteenth-century works of Flacius and Valiero.

[112] Ibid., p. 424.

In comparing the styles of Saint Paul and Saint John, Flacius notes
that while Paul is weighty (gravis), austere, and harsh, yet possessing "much dignity, gravity, and even grandeur,"[113] John is no
less grand (grandis) than Paul, but sweeter and more gentle, rarely
using "Pauline gravity and austerity."[114] John speaks like a father
to his beloved sons, Paul like a magistrate or king. This contrast
between sweeter and more austere types of grandeur is not elab-
orated, yet it remains suggestive of the Renaissance's intuitive appreciation for a nonforensic elevation, just as Carbo's own difficulties with Saint John indicate his sense that sublimity cannot be
excluded from the grand style. Flacius is, of course, familiar with
Hermogenes and Demetrius. Valiero seems not to use any Greek
sources except Aristotle and therefore does not formulate the
problem in terms of two grand styles. Instead, he distinguishes
three officia: teaching, praising, and moving.[115] The Ciceronian
origins of this division are obvious, although Valiero, like Augustine, substitutes the epideictic laudare for the more general delectare. In addition, unlike Augustine, he drops the distinction
between the plain, middle, and grand styles. The style associated
with movere is "vehement and fiery."[116] Terms denoting grandeur and weight appear instead in his description of epideictic:
"When praising Christian virtues, such as faith, hope, charity,
virginity, martyrdom . . . you will speak properly if [the dis-
course] uses majesty, splendor, gravity of conception, and the
various lights of words which lend beauty and loveliness."[117] The
language should be both sweet and grand. Like many Renaissance rhetoricians, Valiero connects epideictic with vividness or
luminosity (illustratio).[118] This relation is striking because, as the
next chapter will indicate, the association of vividness and passion is one of the central principles of the Renaissance grand style.
The inquisitive reader may ask, why, if Renaissance writers
linked vividness with epideictic and vividness with passion, they

[113] Flacius, Clavis, 2: 508.
[114] Ibid., 2: 528.
[115] Valiero, De ecclesiastica rhetorica, p. 95.
[116] Ibid., pp. 95, 109.
[117] Ibid., p. 95.
[118] See O'Malley, Praise and Blame, pp. 63–67.

did not complete the syllogism and connect epideictic with passion. To which the only answer is that overly systematic minds should steer clear of Renaissance rhetoric. Movere sometimes means simply to move the emotions, sometimes—especially in the context of the Ciceronian genera—to move vehemently and harshly. Valiero thus uses movere almost synonymously with invective and reproof.[119] Even though movere in the broad sense applies to epideictic illustratio, its forensic connotations usually prevent an explicit conjunction of the two. Nevertheless, the interrelation of vividness, emotion, and epideictic *outside the genera dicendi* points to a wider understanding of emotion and the grand style than was possible within the confines of Ciceronian terminology. Although Valiero here uses movere in the forensic sense, it is clear that grandeur, traditionally tied to emotional power, now also exists in epideictic, that it too belongs to the grand style (a term Valiero rejects) insofar as magnificence, gravity, and splendor are themselves constituitive of that genus.

Flacius and Valiero transmit a glimpse of how epideictic might come to be part of the grand style. This possibility is most fully realized in the comprehensive general rhetorics of Sturm and Caussin, both of whom largely replaced Roman categories with Greek. Keckermann also belongs here, but since he simply repeats Sturm's analysis, his work does not require separate discussion.

Sturm's remarks are typically brief and cryptic. Several times in *De universa ratione elocutionis* he establishes a contrast between what we may call an aesthetic of light and an aesthetic of magnitude or weight, in Sturm's terms *illustratio* and *amplificatio*. To the aesthetics of light pertain both Hermogenic splendor and what Cicero calls evidentia or visual clarity. It is a measure both of luminosity and vividness. The aesthetics of magnitude concerns authority, power, and solemnity. It thus bears traces of forensic strength, or as Sturm notes, "the distinction between [illustratio] and amplification is this: amplification is directed against the errors of men, when they do not think a thing to be as great or necessary as it is. Vividness (evidentia) is directed not only toward

[119] Valiero, *De ecclesiastica rhetorica*, pp. 109–11.

showing the magnitude of things but also their splendor, dignity, and light."[120] But amplification is not exclusively forensic, since Sturm also relates it to Hermogenic solemnity, with its grave authority and dignity intimating immensity and depth beneath the veils of allegorical utterance and stark assertion.[121] Illustratio or vividness binds together the notions of epideictic celebration and a "splendid and luminous perspecuity."[122] It seems to derive in part from neo-Platonic aesthetics, with its emphasis on light, radiance, and brilliance,[123] in part also from rhetorical categories of vividness, which as previously noted frequently are connected with epideictic, probably because epideictic is traditionally associated with description rather than argument. Intense visual clarity energizes and "lights up" meaning; it confers value and is therefore itself a kind of praise or celebration.[124] Sturm deepens the concept of illustratio by dividing it into two species. The first creates pleasure, as in the vivid word painting of poetry. The second, however, contains emotional and persuasive power. As an example, Sturm offers the "Platonic hypotyposis" from the tenth book of the *Republic*, where Socrates depicts the rewards and punishments of an afterlife.[125] Here we again have the central premise of Renaissance rhetoric—the interrelation of vividness and power—but also the link between such visualization and the mythic image, the vivid rendering of the supernatural. This accords with Sturm's use of quasi-sacred terms like *luminosa* and *splendescens* to describe illustratio. It is not merely visual particularity but the embodying of the suprasensible in the language of symbol and myth. Sturm here is close to Lorenzo Valla, for whom also rhetorical vividness creates images of the invisible, strengthening faith and restructuring motivation through epideixis.[126]

---

[120] Sturm, *De universa*, p. 161.
[121] Ibid., pp. 569–74, 604–606.
[122] Ibid., pp. 159–60, 606.
[123] De Bruyne, *The Esthetics*, pp. 16–18, 55–59.
[124] Sturm, *De universa*, pp. 604–606; see also Tuve, *Elizabethan and Metaphysical*, pp. 29–32.
[125] Sturm, *De universa*, p. 172.
[126] Trinkaus, *In Our Image*, 1: 142–45.

Sturm's contrast between luminosity and magnitude suggests two forms of grandeur, one vivid and splendid, the other austere and weighty. But insofar as this distinction parallels Hermogenes' differentiation of splendor and solemnity, both are characteristics of epideictic, and for Sturm both are shot through with supernatural qualities, whether the solemn authority of Christ's words or the splendor of Platonic myth. Like Hermogenes, Sturm assigns splendor and solemnity to epideictic (laudatio), giving examples both from Plato and St. Gregory Nazianzus.[127] Epideictic exists at the center of Hermogenic grandeur, while forensic oratory requires vehemence and naturalness rather than solemnity or splendor.[128] Sturm, however, chooses to stress the distinction between solemnity and splendor, amplification and illustratio, rather than that between forensic and epideictic. As a result, grandeur loosens its connection with acerbity and force, while taking on vivid intensity, magnitude, and numinosity. Within this Hermogenic grand style, Sturm then establishes a distinction between a dark, mystic solemnity that points to depths of meaning hidden beneath pastoral allegory or gnomic asseveration and a luminous splendor revealing the light and glory of the invisible.

Because Sturm depends principally on Hermogenes, he can ignore the problematic relation between the Ciceronian grand style and epideixis. This polarity, however, is more natural for those brought up in the Latin-based Renaissance tradition, where the issue of how to classify nonforensic modes of elevation remained problematic. The tendency in many Renaissance rhetorics is implicitly to acknowledge two species of grandeur and to treat epideictic responses like love and wonder as emotions, yet at the same time to refrain from explicitly allowing an epideictic grand style. This is in part merely a question of terminology, although interesting as an example of the problems involved in harmonizing Greek, Roman, and Christian concepts. But the placement of epideictic gains urgency in the Renaissance due to the tension between two historically unrelated facts: on the one hand, the genus medium, traditionally the home of epideictic, possesses negative connotations of display and sophistry; on the other, epideictic emotions resemble Christian ones. If love, joy, and wonder lie at the heart of Christian spirituality, it seems incongruous to drop the language that expressed these emotions into the suspect middle style. If rhetoric is to reflect the structures of reality, then the shift from a civic to a theocentric humanism must redefine rhetorical concepts like grandeur, movere, sublimity, and the like. In fact, the correspondence between language and reality was built into the concept of decorum, with its provision that excellence of subject should determine "height" of style and intensity of emotional response. Most Renaissance rhetorics assimilated the psychological implications of Christianity and thus developed a distinctly sacred analysis of emotion. The attempt to translate this psychology into stylistic categories proved more difficult. Beneath the terminological quibbles, therefore, lies the fundamental issue of decorum and with it the possibility of sacred rhetoric.

Hellenistic theory helped provide a bridge between Classical rhetoric and sacred discourse by spiritualizing grandeur and allowing a "multiplex" interpretation of the grand style. Supported by this Greek tradition, Caussin's *De eloquentia* provides the clearest Renaissance articulation of a twofold Christian grand style. In the final book he lists several types of Christian prose, of which the first three derive from Hermogenes' Idea of Grandeur. The first two types, gravitas and maiestas, represent the central distinction, while the third, *vehementia*, is very close to gravitas. Caussin describes both gravitas and maiestas in terms of light, but gravitas burns with light as power, while maiestas shines with the light of splendor. The first is characterized by images of lightning, the second by those of starlight, of light sparkling in darkness.[129] As Caussin's images of lightning and violence suggest, gravitas descends from the Classical forensic grand style, particularly the Greek, since he emphasizes its austere force and compact severity. The examples Caussin offers—Athanasius against the Arians, Cyprian denouncing public bathing—likewise ally this style with the agonistic harshness of the forensic tradition. Vehementia is like gravitas only more torrential and vigorous;

[129] Caussin, *De eloquentia*, pp. 966, 969.

but both possess agonistic strength and moral fervor.[130] Maiestas is quite different. Instead of force, it displays splendor, grandeur, sublimity, and beauty. It is rich, delightful, and artistic, although free from redundancy and affectation. The splendor and sublimity of maiestas tie it to Renaissance depictions of epideixis, as does its subject matter. It does not deal with reproof of sin and error but with sacred mystery, arousing a contemplative wonder rather than fear and contrition. Thus it "sparkles in the lofty darkness of mysteries (*vibrat se in altam mysteriorum caligenem*) and treats the secrets of theology in a grander style."[131] Such majesty appears in Chrysostom, Gregory Nazianzus, and above all in Dionysius the Areopagite. The descriptions of Dionysian maiestas center on images of height, of sublimity in the Renaissance sense, with its connections to epideictic wonder and awe: "When [Dionysius] explores the Trinity, when he treats the divine Word and paints the majesty of sacred mysteries, he is now not like an eagle but an angel speaking from the whirlwind or like Elijah, who, carried in his fiery chariot, rises in his bold effort above the clouds and rains and winds and whatever is mortal."[132] For Caussin, as for later theorists of the sublime, elevation or sublimity is both a theological and stylistic concept,[133] yet he never associates it with the fearful and terrible manifestations of divine power and wrath, as subsequent critics were to do. Rather, he preserves the conjunction of sublimity, beauty, and cosmic order characteristic of the premodern sense of the infinite. The contemplation of mystic darkness evokes images of the starlit sky, of a tranquil sea, an eagle's flight, as well as prophetic rapture.[134] For this reason, sublimity remains close to epideictic, as Caussin's term "maiestas," with its connotations of royal dignity and ceremoniousness, suggests. Throughout the Renaissance, in fact, concepts associated with the apprehension of the divine or infinite, like loftiness,

---

[130] Ibid., 972–73.
[131] Ibid., pp. 968–69.
[132] Ibid., p. 969.
[133] Monk, *The Sublime*, pp. 31, 49–51, 72; M. H. Abrams, *Natural Supernaturalism: Tradition and Revolution in Romantic Literature* (New York, 1971), pp. 97–107.
[134] Caussin, *De eloquentia*, pp. 968–69.

wonder, and sublimity, appear in conjunction with the specifically epideictic vocabulary of delight, splendor, and praise.[135] The more terrible aspects of grandeur tend not to be linked with the divine per se but with the ethical realm of sin and punishment.

Caussin's contrast between gravitas and maiestas clearly parallels that between gravitas and sublimitas, force and elevation, found in Strebaeus and Carbo, but Caussin develops this pairing into two distinct styles or rather two aspects of grandeur, one close to Hermogenes' vehemence and acrimony, the other to his epideictic solemnity and splendor—although Caussin's hodgepodge of rhetorical theory, patristics, neo-Platonism, and scholasticism makes identifying specific sources impossible. That he is more indebted to Longinus than any other Renaissance rhetorician, however, may help explain his greater willingness to regard sheer elevation as a species of the grand style. From these diverse and eclectic sources, Caussin constructs two distinct versions of grandeur, which together articulate the dual ethical and meditative focus of Renaissance Christianity.

★

Hellenistic rhetoric provided a major influence on the Christian grand style in the Renaissance. It supplied an alternative to "Ciceronianism," whether we take that term to mean the cult of formal beauty and periodic fullness or the adherence to a forensic understanding of the grand style. Most modern scholarship on Renaissance rhetoric has assumed that the Ciceronian grand style was identical to its Renaissance counterpart and has therefore classified departures from Ciceronianism under the plain style. It should be evident at this point that this dichotomy is too simple to contain Renaissance concepts of style, that it overlooks the tendency apparent in the best and most important Renaissance

---

[135] In Boileau and subsequent writers, epideictic features continue to infiltrate the sublime. Boileau's association of sublimity with "the extraordinary, the surprising, and . . . the marvellous in discourse" (Monk, *The Sublime*, p. 31) points back to the notion of intellectual delectatio found in Agricola and Keckermann. Similarly, the persistent conjunction of sublimity with joy, wonder, and astonishment suggests the common origin of sublimity and epideictic (cf. ibid., pp. 40, 51, 75, 80).

rhetorics to reconstruct the grand style on a hellenistic and religious basis. This tendency altered and widened conceptions of the grand style, not only making room for Thucydides, Sallust, and Tacitus within its boundaries, but also for the Bible, Chrysostom, and Dionysius the Areopagite. Because Renaissance rhetorics draw from such a diverse collection of sources, different rhetorics borrowing from different ancient and modern texts, it is impossible to talk about *a* Renaissance grand style, but certain elements of hellenistic tradition had a decisive and widespread influence. In particular, the spiritualization of the grand style; the taste for brevity, difficulty, and harshness; and the elevation of epideictic all flow from hellenistic theory into the Renaissance grand style. In this transmission, however, the Renaissance reshapes hellenistic rhetoric into a distinctly Christian form. Flacius thus transforms Thucydidean brevity into a rhetorical version of polysemous signs. Brandolini and Caussin translate epideixis into contemplative wonder. Sturm uses Christ as the model for solemnity. While secular rhetorics often simply summarize Classical doctrine,[136] those dealing with sacred discourse had to adapt precept to the practice of a living oratory and to a body of texts radically different from a Classical oration. They therefore were forced to be more innovative and synthetic. The result is sometimes confusion, but at its best, in writers like Flacius, Keckermann, and Caussin, the effort to fuse hellenistic and sacred materials produced versions of the grand style capable of expressing the Renaissance's feeling for sublimity and power, for pregnant darkness and luminous clarity, for majestic ceremony and ethical rectitude.

[136] For example, Thorne, *Ducente Deo*; Butler, *Oratoriae*; Soarez, *De arte*; Thomas Farnaby, *Index rhetoricus, scholis & institutioni tenerioris aetatis accommodatus* (London, 1625).

CHAPTER FIVE

GOD, SELF, AND PSYCHE: THE
THEOLOGICAL BASES OF
THE GRAND STYLE

HELLENISTIC THEORY affects only a limited number of Renaissance rhetorics, although this number includes the most comprehensive and theoretical texts of the period. To find the common basis of almost all treatments of the Christian grand style, one must turn again to Renaissance discussions of emotion, for from antiquity on, emotional power is *the* definitive feature of the grand style. What we find by examining analyses of movere in Renaissance rhetorics is that the stylistic features of sacred grandeur grow out of the sources of emotion. Most rhetorics posit two principle sources: first, the conjunction of the excellent object with a sensuously vivid rendering and second, expressivity, or the passionate articulation of the speaker's own feelings. But these sources of emotion, in turn, draw on a complex of assumptions and premises derived from theology, psychology, and epistemology. What this means is that the precepts offered for the Christian grand style are neither technical "rules" borrowed from antiquity, as often the case in Renaissance poetics, nor empirically derived generalizations, but the deductive corollaries of broader cultural axioms, in the same way that modern critical theory derives in large measure from concepts originating in semiotics, anthropology, and psychology.

This willingness to interweave questions of style with psychology, theology, and epistemology runs counter to another better known strand of Renaissance rhetoric. The same decades (*c.* 1580–1620) that witnessed the flowering of the sacred and general rhetorics also saw the vogue of Ramism reach its climax. Ramism is distinctive because it stripped rhetoric of everything but elocution, understood as tropes and figures, and delivery. Invention, arrangement, the genera dicendi, amplification, and the emotions all disappear. For the first time, rhetoric became simply verbal

(193)

embellishment, divorced from any psychological, historical, or theoretical basis. It is not hard to conclude that the later seventeenth-century tendency to see rhetoric as "mere words," as verba isolated from res, descended (however unintentionally) from this Ramist simplification.[1] The tradition of the Christian grand style, however, moves in the opposite direction. It treats the specific characteristics of style (e.g., schemes and tropes) not as formal decorations of meaning but as the appropriate expression of the psyche in its attempt to apprehend and articulate transcendence. Because in Renaissance psychology that attempt hinges on emotion, imagination, and selfhood, questions of sacred discourse cannot be isolated from the structures of inner life nor from the theoretical nexus that conceptualizes the relation between these structures and the supernatural. Thus, unlike Ramism, sacred rhetorics refused to isolate words from things or to reduce rhetoric to a formalism. Indeed, the fact that sacred rhetoric preserved the tie between style and psyche finally caused its demise, for once Cartesian rationalism and scientific empiricism dissolved the Renaissance's religious psychology, the infrastructure of the Christian grand style was gone. But for rhetorics written under the influence of that psychology, the stylistic characteristics of sacred grandeur depend on the analysis of emotion, its sources in vividness and expressivity, and the relation of those sources to the mind's attempt to apprehend God.

Magnitudo and Praesentia

The first source of emotion, the vivid representation of the excellent object—what the Renaissance termed the union of *magnitudo* and *praesentia*—lies beneath the surface of Bacon's well-known declaration:

The duty and office of Rhetoric is to apply reason to imagination for the better moving of the will. . . . for the affections themselves carry ever an appetite to good, as reason doth. The difference is, that the affection beholdeth merely the present, reason beholdeth the future and sum of time.

[1] For Ramus and his influence, see Ong, *Ramus*; Miller, *The New England Mind*; and Tuve, *Elizabethan and Metaphysical*.

And therefore the present filling the imagination more, reason is commonly vanquished; but after the force of eloquence and persuasion hath made things future and remote appear as present, then upon the revolt of the imagination reason prevaileth.[2]

For Bacon, rhetoric makes the objects of reason, which are intrinsically excellent but also remote and difficult to grasp, imaginatively present, by making them sensuous and vivid. Or as Donne remarks in the course of a sermon, "Rhetorique will make absent and remote things present to your understanding."[3]

The contrast between the remote objects of reason and the immediate particulars of sense derives, as Wesley Trimpi has shown, from Aristotle's distinction between two types of knowability.[4] According to Aristotle, things can be knowable either to us or naturally and in themselves. While the concrete objects of sensation are most knowable to us, that which is clearest and most knowable in itself lies furthest from perception. According to the *Posterior Analytics*, "things are prior and more familiar in two ways; for it is not the same to be prior by nature and prior in relation to us, nor to be more familiar and more familiar to us. I call prior and more familiar in relation to us what is nearer to perception, prior and more familiar *simpliciter* what is further away. What is most universal is furthest away, and the particulars are nearest; and these are opposite to each other."[5] Since all our knowledge arises from sensation, cognition always involves a movement from that which is knowable or familiar to us toward the universal, better known in itself although harder to grasp. These two forms of knowability would then correspond to Bacon's contrast between the present and "things future and remote."

But it is not merely a question of knowability. For both Bacon and Aristotle, those things most distant from us are also more excellent than what we can perceive close at hand. The passage from

<hr/>

[2] *The Works of Francis Bacon*, 7 vols. (London, 1826), 1: 153–54.

[3] Donne, *Sermons*, 4: 87.

[4] Trimpi, *Muses*, pp. 87–129. The entire following section is deeply indebted to Trimpi's work on the ancient dilemma.

[5] Aristotle, *Posterior Analytics*, 1.2.71b–72a; see also *Metaphysics* 7.4.2–3.

The Parts of Animals mentioned in the previous chapter draws out
the implications of this antithesis:

Of substances constituted by nature some are ungenerated, imperisha-
ble, and eternal, while others are subject to generation and decay. The
former are excellent and divine, but less accessible to knowledge. The
evidence that might throw light on them, and on the problems which we
long to solve respecting them, is furnished but scantily by sensation;
whereas respecting perishable plants and animals we have abundant information, living as we do in their midst. . . . Both departments, however, have their special charm. The scanty conceptions to which we can
attain of celestial things give us, from their excellence, more pleasure
than all our knowledge of the world in which we live; just as a half-
glimpse of persons that we love is more delightful than an accurate view
of other things, whatever their number and dimensions. On the other
hand, in certitude and in completeness our knowledge of terrestrial
things has the advantage.[6]

Those objects which are less accessible to knowledge are more
valuable than what is near and therefore capable of being accurately known. There thus exists an inverse proportion between
the excellence of an object and our knowledge of it, an antithesis
which, following Trimpi, we may call "the ancient dilemma of
knowledge and representation." The problem then becomes how
to discover a method or way to bring that which is remote and yet
most worth knowing into some kind of relationship with what
we can more accurately grasp, to combine *magnitudo* and *praesentia*. Rhetoric, Bacon suggests, does just that by making the
distant and remote present to the imagination.

The religious overtones in the quotation from *On the Parts of
Animals* are not surprising if one remembers that for Aristotle the
stars were divine and therefore spatially as well as ontologically
distant. It was almost inevitable that Christian writers should
borrow this notion of an inverse proportion between the excellence of an object and its knowability, so that when the antithesis
reappears in Renaissance rhetoric, it has already been mediated
through a religious framework. In the *Summa contra gentiles*, Saint
Thomas writes,

⁶ Aristotle, *Parts of Animals*, 1.5.644b; see *De anima* 1.1.402a.

Therefore, however little be the knowledge of God to which the intellect is able to attain, this will be the intellect's last end, rather than a perfect knowledge of lower intelligibles.

Moreover, everything desires most of all its last end. Now the human intellect desires, loves and enjoys the knowledge of divine things, although it can grasp but little about them, more than the perfect knowledge that it has of the lowest things. Therefore man's last end is to understand God in some way.[7]

It is beyond the scope of this study to trace the ancient dilemma from Aristotle through the Renaissance, but we can get some idea of its function in theology by looking briefly at Donne and Hooker.

Hooker's account of the grounds of faith, which is largely based on Saint Thomas,[8] begins with the Aristotelian distinction between the two kinds of knowability: "*Certainty of Evidence* we call that, when the mind doth assent unto this or that, not because it is true in itself, but because the truth is clear, because it is manifest to us." The truths of logic and perception are certain because they are evident to us, but the far more valuable objects of faith lack this evidence. Hooker resolves the ancient dilemma by arguing for a second type of certainty, the certainty of adherence or what we might call love. The person who has once tasted God's "heavenly sweetness" hopes "against all reason of believing." Faith grasps its object by love, not evidence.[9] The merits of this very un-Aristotelian attempt to transcend the ancient dilemma do not concern us here. Its significance lies in the fact that Hooker not only accepts the terms of the dilemma as those relevant to the problem of Christian belief, but also assigns emotion a central role in the act of faith, a role very similar to that which the rhetorics attribute to *movere* in the art of persuasion.

The language of the ancient dilemma also suffuses Donne's treatment of the Incarnation and sacraments. Donne remains close to the rhetorical tradition with its concern to find a way to

[7] *Introduction to St. Thomas Aquinas*, ed. Anton C. Pegis (New York, 1945), p. 444.

[8] An excellent summary of Thomas's understanding of faith can be found in Colish, *Mirror*, pp. 186–87.

[9] Hooker, "Of the Certainty," *Works*, 3: 470–71.

make that which is remote seem near and present and therefore
knowable to us. The parallel between theology and rhetoric is
visible in Donne's own phraseology: as rhetoric makes "absent
and remote things present to your understanding," so preaching
and the sacraments bring Christ "nearer [to men] in visible and
sensible things."[10] The same spatial and visual imagery informs
Donne's description of the Incarnation: "the Object which we are
to see, *the knowledge of the glory of God*; and this Object being
brought within a convenient distance to be seen *in the face of Jesus
Christ.*"[11] Christ "could not have come nearer, then in taking this
nature upon him."[12] He is "the image of the invisible God, and so
more proportionall unto us, more apprehensible by us."[13] Because images and sacraments are perceptible, they are more
knowable to us. Yet they are also signs of the more excellent and
therefore less apprehensible object, thus conveying what is incorporeal and spiritual by means of visible representations that our
minds can grasp. Such images thus negotiate the poles of the ancient dilemma, establishing a connection between the excellent
object and that which we can more accurately know.[14]

As means for reconciling the terms of the ancient dilemma, the

---

[10] Donne, *Sermons*, 5: 144.

[11] Ibid., 4: 90–91.

[12] Ibid., 4: 125.

[13] Ibid., 2: 320.

[14] Luther sets out with impressive clarity the relation between the ancient dilemma, Protestant theology, and rhetorical theory: "Est autem summe necessa-
rium adhortari et urgere non solum alios, sed etiam nos ipsos propter illa visibilia
et instantia pericula et vexationes. Quia enim ista, quae contristant, praesentia
sunt, contra quae consolantur, sunt absentia, ideo opus est, dum durant praesentia, quae vexant, ut verbo excitemur ad perseverantiam et patientiam. Est enim
haec experientia coniungenda cum doctrina. Nam oculi nostri multo sunt obtu-
siores, quam ut possint ad invisibilia ista pertingere et finem praesentium afflic-
tionum videre. Hinc fit, ut natura semper circumspiciat de modo, quo liberari
possit, et dum eum non videt, sicut est absconditus et invisibilis, cruciatur. Opus
est igitur hortationibus, ut ista (liceat enim sic loqui) naturalis brevitas seu angus-
tia cordis nostri dilatetur, magnificetur, et prolongetur. Hoc potest is, qui videt
finem nostrarum tentationum, Eius verbum est audiendum, nostrum cor non est
audiendum, quod tantum sentit et videt principium tentationum, et doloris finem
non videt. Rhetoricatur igitur Spiritus sanctus iam, ut exhortatio fiat illustrior."
Quoted in Dockhorn, "Rhetorica movet," p. 28.

routes laid down by Hooker and Donne of love (or emotion in general) and sensuousness are fundamental to Renaissance rhetoric. These texts affirm that the emotions are moved by the conjunction of magnitudo and praesentia, by the union, that is, of the greatest object with the most vivid representation. Magnitudo and praesentia thus signify the polarities that must be brought into relation for the most excellent objects to penetrate our thought and feeling, for as the seventeenth-century psychologist, Edward Reynolds, notes, the emotions are moved only by the presence of their object.[15] The formula, magnitudo and praesentia, appears first in the Tridentine rhetorics and thereafter in the liberal Protestant tradition. Luis de Granada thus writes, "emotions are quickened (as philosophers say) both by the excellence of the objects (*magnitudo rerum*) and by placing them vividly before the eyes of the audience (*praesentia oculis subiecta*)."[16] The same idea, in almost the same words, appears in the Catholics, Valades and Carbo, and the Protestants, Alsted and Keckermann.[17] Keckermann writes, "the emotions are moved in two ways, by magnitudo and praesentia, or, to speak more clearly, by amplification and hypotyposis." This notion remains current through the late seventeenth century, where we find Bernard Lamy arguing that in order to make men love a truth that seems distant from their ordinary interests and pleasures, lucid argument will not suffice, for men naturally hate such truths. Instead, eloquence is necessary because "the Passions are the Springs of the Soul: It is they which cause it to act. . . . But the Passions are excited by the presence of their Object. . . . To kindle therefore these Passions in the Heart of a Man, we must present the Objects before him; and to this purpose, Figures do marvellously conduce."[18] For the most valuable things or truths to become objects of men's love, they must be brought "near" through the rhetorical techniques of vividness, often referred to as enargia or hypotyposis.

[15] Reynolds, *Treatise of the Passions*, p. 97.

[16] De Granada, *Ecclesiasticae rhetoricae*, p. 158.

[17] Valades, *Rhetorica Christiana*, p. 159; Keckermann, *Rhetoricae* (1614), pp. 18, 29; Alsted, *Theologia*, p. 20; Carbo, *Divinus orator*, p. 208.

[18] Lamy, *The Art of Speaking*, 1.139–40.

The emphasis on magnitudo and praesentia leads inevitably to a corresponding stress on the image or the use of concrete detail to suggest the supersensible. These images, either literal or metaphoric, enable the mind to move from the particulars of sense, which are more knowable to us, to the unseen truths of mind and spirit. As de Granada remarks,

[vividness] brings its object before the eyes, so that he who speaks seems not to speak but to paint, and he who hears not to hear but behold.

To this capacity pertains the type of similitude suited for elucidating obscure subjects: by which we reveal things hidden and dark through those which are better known, as if we drew them from darkness into light. For as Aristotle says, we naturally preceed from things which are known and perceived by the senses to those which are less known and grasped by the intellect.[19]

De Granada goes on to observe that sacred discourse relies on images for precisely this reason. Like Donne and Hooker, he adapts the Aristotelian formulation of the ancient dilemma to the problems of religious knowledge, for like Aristotle's universals, God is also incorporeal, remote, and excellent.

In the last quarter of the seventeenth century, when rationalism and empiricism combined to dismiss metaphoric discourse and the language of images, the nonconformist scholar, Robert Ferguson, forcibly restates the ancient dilemma and its implications for Christian rhetoric. The Bible uses metaphors, Ferguson writes, so that

Objects which lye remote from our Understandings (as all Spiritual Objects do) may, by being represented under some obvious and sensible Image, be the better attempered to our Minds to contemplate, and rendred the more facile to our Understandings to conceive. . . . The deep things of God do so far over-match our Reasons and Understandings, that in order to their being expressed to our Capacities, they are forced to be cloathed with as much external sensibility as may be; that so the disproportion between them and our faculties, being qualified and reduced, we may the better and more familiarly converse with them. . . . For as we

---

[19] De Granada, *Ecclesiasticae rhetoricae*, p. 332. See also E. H. Gombrich, "Icones Symbolicae," *Symbolic Images: Studies in the Art of the Renaissance* (Oxford, 1972), p. 153.

are more affected when the things of God are brought down to us, under sensible representations, so likewise the things themselves become more intelligible.[20]

As we shall see, Renaissance theories of sacred discourse grow out of this conception of the image allowing the mind to move from the seen to the unseen and the heart to embrace what is invisible under corporeal similitudes.

Keckermann's remarks on magnitudo and praesentia cited earlier suggest that these terms have their rhetorical equivalent in the concepts of amplification and hypotyposis, a remark echoed in several other rhetorics as well. Amplification shows the greatness or magnitude of its object, hypotyposis creates a vivid immediacy. These concepts are not unrelated, since the greatness of an object is often displayed by making it sensuously apprehensible, and therefore hypotyposis is often regarded as a species of amplification. Thus the preacher amplifies Christ's Passion by depicting the scene in all its agony and pathos. Nevertheless, they raise distinct issues insofar as hypotyposis concerns the role of images in cognition and emotion, while amplification deals with the question of true as opposed to popular evaluation. We will therefore treat these notions separately, although they are actually interrelated, just as magnitudo requires praesentia to be apprehensible, and praesentia needs magnitudo to be significant.

Image and Enargia

The discussions of vividness and imaging found in Renaissance rhetoric reflect concepts of the imagination that originate in antiquity and the Middle Ages. Despite their distrust of the imagination's creative or feigning capacity,[21] Renaissance thinkers inherit and preserve a view of the simple reproductive imagination that made it necessary for all feeling and cognition, including the knowledge of the supersensible. The crucial role of images in negotiating the ancient dilemma derives from this psychology of

[20] Ferguson, *The Interest of Reason*, pp. 320–23.
[21] William Rossky, "Imagination in the English Renaissance: Psychology and Poetic," *Studies in the Renaissance* 5(1958): 49–73.

the imagination. Since there exist several pertinent studies of the
pre-Romantic imagination, we need only review those aspects
that bear directly on rhetorical issues.[22]

For our purposes, the major figure in the development of a theory of the imagination is again Aristotle.[23] Indeed, into the seventeenth century, analyses of the imagination offer no more than
minor adjustments to Aristotelian theory.[24] The fundamental insight that subsequent psychologies derived from Aristotle was
that both cognition and appetite rely on the imagination. Even
speculative thought requires mental images or phantasms. Thus
in the opening of *On Memory* he states that "without an image
thinking is impossible. . . . So likewise when one thinks, although the object may not be quantitative, one envisages it as
quantitative, though he thinks of it in abstraction from quan-
tity."[25] Since the phantasms of imagination are themselves "pictures" of sensation, as well as the "matter" of thought, imagination links man's sensitive and rational natures, both by supplying
reason with its objects and by reflecting the abstractions of
thought in a visible shape. The imagination not only joins sensation and cognition but also plays a vital role in man's emotional
life. Although the phantasms of imagination do not themselves
arouse emotion any more than the picture of a lion engenders

[22] See Rossky, "Imagination"; Miller, *The New England Mind*, pp. 239–79;
Murray Wright Bundy, *The Theory of Imagination in Classical and Mediaeval
Thought, University of Illinois Studies in Language and Literature*, 12(1927); E. Ruth
Harvey, *The Inward Wits: Psychological Theory in the Middle Ages and the Renais-
sance*, Warburg Institute Surveys 6 (London, 1975); Baxter Hathaway, *The Age of
Criticism: The Late Renaissance in Italy* (Ithaca, 1962); John Scott Hunt, "Sir Philip
Sidney and the Psychology of Imagination" (Ph.D. diss., Stanford University,
1984), pp. 166–203.

[23] For Aristotle's theory of the imagination, see Bundy, *The Theory of Imagination*, pp. 68–74; Hunt, *Sidney*, pp. 166–99.

[24] Descartes's first and second *Meditations* are a direct attack on the Aristotelian
tradition of imagination. Descartes argues that the images of sensation do *not* provide clear and evident knowledge, that imagination is not necessary for all cognition. But up to the late seventeenth century, most psychological texts still adhere to the Aristotelian position. Walter Charleton's *Natural History of the Passions*
(London, 1674) thus argues that the chief seat of the rational soul is in the imagination because reason uses images in all her operations (pp. 61–63).

[25] Aristotle, *On Memory*, trans. J. I. Beare, *The Complete Works*, 450a.

fear, if these phantasms are judged to be real and either harmful
or beneficial they then produce aversion or desire. A person hears
a strange rustle alone at night, imagines an armed robber, believes
that robber to be real and dangerous, and panics. Even without
an immediate stimulus, the imagination can form pictures of desirable or hateful possibilities and respond emotionally to them.
We imagine the consequences of war and weep.[26] Indeed, all emotion is a response to such mental pictures. Thus, imagination is
also necessary for moral deliberation. We imagine the various
consequences of alternative choices and, having decided which
outcome seems most desirable, act accordingly. As Bacon noted
in the passage quoted at the beginning of this chapter, because
men can imagine the future, they can enlist desire in the service
of reason. Finally, for Aristotle memory too requires imagination
since what we remember are the phantasms either of things or
concepts. Like thought and feeling, memory operates through
images.

Aristotle's imagination is almost wholly visual. Although
there is no reason why we should not be said to "imagine" sounds
or tastes, Aristotle invariably thinks of imagination as picturing.
Psychic activity resembles ghostly postcards (the phantasms)
constantly flitting from the imagination to the reason, memory,
and appetite. We think and feel in images. This priority assigned
to the visual has obvious ramifications for discourse, as ancient
rhetorics were not slow to perceive. Language uses word-pic-
tures, whether metaphors, examples, descriptions, allegories, or
dramatizations, to make thought intelligible and affective. For
Quintilian, the orator thus quickens his own emotions and those
of his hearers by calling up vivid images: "From such impressions
arises that ἐνάργεια which Cicero calls illumination (illustratio)
and actuality (evidentia), which makes us seem not so much to
narrate as to exhibit the actual scene, while our emotions will be
no less actively stirred than if we were present at the actual occur-
rence."[27] In Longinus, too, images are a means of evoking sub-

[26] Bundy, *The Theory of Imagination*, p. 72.
[27] Quintilian 6.2.32; see also Scott Elledge, "The Background and Development in English Criticism of the Theories of Generality and Particularity,"
PMLA, 62(1947): 147–82.

lime passion; the speaker, "carried away by enthusiasm and passion," thinks he sees what he describes and places it before the eyes of his hearers, engendering in them a parallel response (15). Humanists like Melanchthon and Sidney emphasized the ability of images to render philosophic abstractions intelligible and therefore affective, since we can only desire that which we in some sense understand. Aristotle's theory of the imagination thus entailed that vivid imagery makes discourse more powerful and clear, an attitude responsible for the denigration of the aural *schemata verborum*, which only served for delight, as opposed to tropes and the figures of thought, most of which involved visualization.

In late antiquity these notions of the imagination and images are brought to bear on the problem of representing divine beings. Dio Chrysostom, writing in the first century A.D., defends Pheidias's portrayal of Zeus in human form by arguing that the sculptor has thus been able "to indicate that which is invisible and unportrayable by means of something portrayable and visible, using the function of a symbol."[28] In his *Life of Apollonius*, Philostratus justifies the same statue on the grounds that the imagination (*phantasia*) can create not only what it has seen but "equally what it has not seen; for it will conceive of its ideal with reference to the reality."[29] The imagination works by analogy, depicting the gods in human form because man alone of all visible creatures possesses the divine attribute of reason. The later Neo-Platonists, Proclus and Synesius, similarly argue for the power of imagination to represent what is incorporeal and spiritual. In myth and dream, the phantasy gives concrete shape to supersensible truth.[30]

Along with the basic outline of Aristotelian psychology, the Middle Ages inherited this association between the language of images and the representation of the divine. As Frances Yates has shown, medieval discussions of images often belong to the *ars memorandi* tradition; the faithful remember heaven and hell, the virtues and vices, by connecting these concepts with a graphic im-

---

[28] Dio Chrysostom, 59; cited in Trimpi, *Muses*, p. 158.
[29] Philostratus, *The Life of Apollonius of Tyana*, 2: 78–79.
[30] Bundy, *The Theory of Imagination*, pp. 143, 148–49.

age—a personification, allegorical figure, exemplary action, and so forth.[31] Following Aristotle, Aquinas argues that the mind cannot grasp intelligibles without the images or phantasms of corporeal things and, therefore, to remember spiritual truths, one must link them to concrete similitudes: "It is necessary . . . to invent similitudes and images because simple and spiritual intentions slip easily from the soul unless they are as it were linked to some corporeal similitudes, because human cognition is stronger in regard to the sensibilia."[32] The image negotiates the ancient dilemma, permitting the mind to rise from visible things to some knowledge of invisible ones. Even our knowledge of God (in this life) rests on sense and therefore on imagination: "the knowledge of God that can be gathered from the human mind does not transcend the genus of the knowledge gathered from sensible things."[33] Although spiritual objects possess no phantasm, they "are known to us by comparison with sensible bodies of which there are phantasms."[34] Significantly, Thomas applies this principle to his analysis of biblical metaphor. After noticing that the Holy Ghost does not speak like a scholastic theologian but like a poet, Thomas defends the propriety of such figurative language with the observation that "it is natural to man to attain to intellectual truths through sensible things, because all our knowledge originates from sense."[35] The problem of religious cognition and that of religious discourse both hang on the capacity of images to depict that which is knowable in itself in the sensible forms knowable by us.

Although Neo-Platonic theories of the imagination influenced poetics and the visual arts, most Renaissance psychology draws primarily on the Aristotelian tradition. Baxter Hathaway's study of the imagination in sixteenth-century Italian poetics justly warns against ignoring the diversity of Renaissance opinion on

[31] Frances A. Yates, *The Art of Memory* (Chicago, 1966), p. 60.
[32] *Summa Theologica* 2.2.49.1; cited in Yates, *The Art of Memory*, p. 74; see also Bundy, *The Theory of Imagination*, pp. 219–20.
[33] *Aquinas*, ed. Pegis, p. 463.
[34] Ibid., p. 397.
[35] Ibid., p. 16.

this topic,[36] yet such diversity seems to have existed within a relatively stable and reasonably Aristotelian framework. Bacon nicely sums up the prevalent view of the imagination in *The Advancement of Learning*: "It is true that the Imagination is an agent or *nuncius* in both provinces, both the judicial and the ministerial. For Sense sendeth over to Imagination before Reason hath judged: and Reason sendeth over to Imagination before the Decree can be acted; for Imagination ever precedeth Voluntary Motion: saving that this Janus of Imagination hath differing faces; for the face towards Reason hath the print of Truth, but the face towards Action hath the print of Good."[37] For Bacon as for Aristotle, imagination functions both in thought and appetition, transmitting the images of sense to the reason as the matter of thought and picturing the judgments of reason to the will and emotions in order to set them in motion toward praxis. In its initial function the imagination purports to exhibit the "truth" to reason, like a faithful mirror; in its second it holds up its phantasms to man's appetitive powers as good (or evil) and therefore to be pursued (or shunned), since while the true is the object of reason, the good is the object of appetite.[38] The same paradigm with slight modifications appears in Nicholas Coffeteau's *A Table of Humane Passions*, translated from the French in 1621. According to Coffeteau, the imagination "propounds" the phantasms stored in the memory

vnto the Appetite, under the apparance of things that are pleasing or troublesom, that is to say, under the forme of Good and Euill, and at the same instant the same formes enlightened with the Light of the vnderstanding, and purged from the sensible and singular conditions, which they retaine in the Imagination, and instead of that which they represented of particular things, representing them generall, they become capable to be imbraced by the vnderstanding; the which vnder the apparance of things which are profitable or hurtfull, that is to say, vnder the forme of Good and Euill, represents them vnto the Will. . . . And then as Queene of the powers of the soule she ordaines what they shall im-

---

[36] Hathaway, *The Age of Criticism*, p. 354.

[37] Cited in Karl Wallace, *Francis Bacon on Communication and Rhetoric* (Chapel Hill, 1943), p. 38.

[38] Aristotle, *Nicomachean Ethics* 1049a; *Aquinas*, ed. Pegis, p. 432.

brace, & what they shal fly as it pleseth her; whereunto the Sensitiue Appetite yeelding a prompt obedience to execute her command . . . quickneth all the powers and passions over which shee commands. . . .[39]

Ideally, the imagination should present its pictures to reason, which, after having passed judgment, sends them to the will, which, in turn, arouses appetite in accordance with reason. The imagination, like the emotions, is thus potentially rational, i.e., capable of being guided by reason. But, Coffeteau admits, the imagination also sends her phantasms straight down to the appetite before reason has a chance to evaluate them. That is to say, we react both instinctively and rationally to the same object, but reason often gets there a half-second too late.

Although the possibility that imagination would arouse desire before reason could judge the worthiness of the desired object created a good deal of anxiety concerning "lawless phansie," the close link between imagination and appetition was not always understood negatively. Edward Reynolds argues that the imagination acts directly upon both the understanding and the will—on the latter "to quicken, allure, and sharpen its desire towards some convenient object."[40] It does not, however, follow that desires aroused without consulting reason are therefore irrational. Reynolds demonstrates his point by reiterating the Renaissance commonplace that poetry and rhetoric created the first civil societies and the earliest apprehension of God: "[They] wrought upon the Will by the ministry rather of the Fancy, than of rigid Reason; not driving them thereunto by puntuall Arguments, but alluring them by the sweetnesse of Eloquence; not pressing the necessity of Morality, by naked inferences, but rather secretly instilling it into the Will, that it might at last finde it selfe reformed, and yet hardly perceive how it came to be so."[41] Or as Robert South defines it, persuasion is simply moving a person's emo-

[39] Nicholas Coffeteau, *A Table of Humane Passions, With their Causes and Effects*, trans. E. Grimeston (London, 1621), a5i^r^–a5ii^v^.

[40] Reynolds, *Treatise of the Passions*, p. 19. Reynolds uses will in the Augustinian sense, as including emotion.

[41] Ibid., pp. 20–21.

tions "according as objects suitable to those passions, shall be . . . set before his imagination, by the acts of speaking."[42]

One further point is worth noticing. In Aristotelian psychology, the imagination generally does not judge whether its phantasms are good or bad, pleasant or dangerous. That is, in Thomist terminology, the work of the estimative power, which culls the beneficial or harmful intentions from the phantasm and presents the evaluated image to the appetite.[43] Like Coffeteau and Reynolds, most Renaissance psychologies do away with this estimative power. The imagination itself elicits emotion by presenting its object as "an appearing or veritable good, or evil."[44] The connection between imagination and emotion in Renaissance psychology is thus direct, although reason may subsequently overrule the initial evaluation present in the imagination.[45]

---

[42] South, *Sermons*, 1: 261. In his *Philosophiae Christianae*, Libertus Fromondus offers a careful discussion, based largely on Medina, of how the higher appetite is transformed into emotion (the sensitive appetite) through the agency of imagination: "Medina existimat tribus modis voluntatem posse appetitum inferiorem movere. Primo, mediate & indirecte, applicando videlicet intellectum ad alicujus objecti convenientis, aut disconvenientis considerationem, ex qua judicium intellectivum, ac deinde mox phantasticum in imaginatione, sive cogitativa hominis excitetur; a quo demum judicio phantastio proxime appetitus inferior moveatur. Hic autem modus est quidem indirectus, sed maxime naturalis; quia est ex parte objecti, quod voluntas per operam intellectus, & deinde sensus interni, ponet ante oculos appetitus sensitivi, ut ab eo proxime & connaturaliter excitetur & moveatur. 'Sic cum homo timet poenas Inferni,' ait Medina, 'per voluntatem movet intellectum, & per intellectum, imaginationem ad formandum aliqua phantasmata poenarum ut ignis urentis, vermis rodentis &c. Et exinde sequitur passio timoris in appetitu sensitivo.' . . . Et licet intellectus rationibus quandoque spiritalibus passionem in appetitu sensitivo excitari suadeat; imaginatio tamen idola quaedam, tanquam altioris cogitationis rudimenta, formare potest, quibus argumenta intellectus, sensibili & familiari suo modo, appetitui sensitivo intimet ac insinuet" (pp. 935–36). Since in the Thomist tradition emotion is restricted to the desire for tangible goods, the possibility of spiritual emotion depends on the imagination's ability to offer a sensible picture of things in themselves incorporeal and so make them capable of arousing feeling.

[43] Etienne Gilson, *The Christian Philosophy of St. Thomas Aquinas*, trans. L. K. Shook, C.S.B. (New York, 1956), pp. 205–206.

[44] Senault, *The Use of Passions*, p. 17; Thomas Wright, *The Passions of the Minde*, pp. 8, 31; Bartholomew Keckermann, *Systema physicum*, 1: 1523, 1529.

[45] This follows from a tendency in Renaissance psychology to simplify medieval faculty psychology by reducing the number of internal senses from five (com-

Whether or not they believed in certain innate principles or moral axioms, those who wrote about the soul during the Renaissance accepted the Aristotelian postulates that all substantive knowledge derives from sense experience and that the mind cannot think without the images of sensation. Bacon and Coffeteau, as we have seen, simply presuppose that reason receives its information from sense via the imagination. The sixteenth-century scholastics, Francisco Suarez and Libertus Fromondus [Froidmont], argue at length that all cognition, even of the highest objects, relies on images.[46] These ideas in turn supported notions of vividness and the image in Renaissance rhetoric. Imagery creates both clarity and certitude—the first because, as Robert South says, "men naturally have only a weak confused knowledge of universals, but a clear and lively idea of particulars."[47] Fénelon interprets man's restriction to sense experience as a result of the Fall but draws the same conclusion: in our present state we can be reached through the language of images or not at all. "A simple story cannot move. It is necessary not only to acquaint the listeners with the facts, but to make the facts visible to them. . . . Since the time of the original sin, man has been entirely enmeshed in palpable things. . . . It is necessary to give a physical body to all the instructions which one wishes to inject into his soul."[48]

Images also create certitude because, in Aristotle's terms, concrete particulars are most knowable by us. So Brandolini states, "we assent most easily to what we perceive by sensation."[49] People disbelieve in God and spiritual truths because these things are invisible. By giving them a "local habitation and a name," the poet or preacher strengthens faith, making its objects intelligible

---

mon sense, imagination, phantasy, estimation, memory) to one. See Fromondus, *Philosophiae Christianae*, pp. 698–700; Francisco Suarez, s.j., *De anima, Opera omnia*, 23 vols. (Paris, 1856–1878), 3: 703–709. As Fromondus notes, this simplification, like so much in Renaissance psychology, derives from Augustine (p. 698).

[46] Suarez, *Opera*, 3: 738–40; Fromondus, *Philosophiae Christianae*, pp. 833–34; see also Nicholas Mosley, *Psychosophia, or natural and divine contemplations of the passions & faculties of the Soul of Man* (London, 1653), pp. 138–40; Keckermann, *Systema physicum*, 1: 1602.

[47] South, *Sermons*, 2: 78; cf. Lamy, *The Art of Speaking*, 1.90.

[48] Fénelon, *Dialogues*, pp. 93–94.

[49] Brandolini, *De ratione scribendi*, p. 53.

to us.[50] Flacius and Glassius describe this intense visual impression created by vivid description as producing "*intuitiva notitia*" or aesthetic intuition.[51] In late scholasticism, intuitiva notitia is the nondiscursive, immediate certainty created by sensory perception. When we see a cat in front of us we simply know it is there. The vivid hypotyposes of Scripture thus give the remote objects of faith a clarity and actuality that enable us to assent to their truth.

Not surprisingly, Renaissance rhetorics tend to emphasize the power of images for moving the will and emotions over their cognitive function. Almost every text insists upon the point familiar from Sidney's contrast between the philosopher and poet that abstractions are passionless. Our hearts respond to what is concrete and sensible, just as the phantasms of imagination awaken the sensible appetite.[52] In the seventeenth century this connection between vividness and passion, enargia and energia, fuses with the Longinian passages on the imagination. The fullest discussion of this theme appears in Vossius, who ties the idea of imaginative vividness to the grand style and also suggests its relation to the ancient dilemma. Following Longinus, Vossius associates sublimity with both lofty conceptions and the vivid representations of the phantasy, an association that suggests the representation of the most excellent objects is best achieved through the language of images.

Meanwhile, we can firmly conclude that it is required for the grand style both that we speak artistically and intelligently. . . . First of all, it is worthwhile to exhort you, as Longinus also does, to accustom your soul towards the conceiving of great things. The sublimity of speech arises from the greatness (*magnitudo*) of the soul: those whose soul always creeps on the ground and never rises to great things also will not create a

[50] See Valla's comments cited in Trinkaus, *In Our Image*, 1: 145.

[51] Flacius, *Clavis*, 2: 483; Glassius, *Philologia sacra* (1705), p. 287.

[52] Agricola, *De inventione*, p. 388; Flacius, *Clavis*, 2: 310; Keckermann, *Systema*, p. 1612, *Rhetoricae* (1614), p. 27; Caussin, *De eloquentia*, p. 467; de Arriaga, *Rhetoris Christiani*, p. 366; Lamy, *The Art of Speaking*, 1.141; Pangratius, *Methodus concionandi*, p. 23; Johann Hulsemannus, *Methodus concionandi, auctior edita* (Wittenberg, 1657), p. 208.

lofty (*grandis*) discourse. Wherefore, the orator, like the poet, should be felicitous in conceiving images. . . . For phantasy is that power, by which we consider absent things as if they were present (*praesentia*). . . . It brings it about that luminous metaphors and suitable lights of words and thoughts present themselves to us. . . . And it is thus clear why Longinus says that the end of phantasy is *enargia*; and why likewise he ascribes so much strength to the imagination, so that he says of the man who conceives all things relating to his subject by his phantasy, his speech will not only persuade his listener, but will make him his slave.[53]

In Vossius the imagination becomes a focal nexus, translating conceptual *magnitudo* into the sensible image; the imagination can consider absent things as if they were present, and it accomplishes this translation not by trying to represent the conceptions literally but through figure and metaphor.

During the Renaissance, images play an especially vital role in sacred rhetoric because of their capacity to make what is unseen accessible to both thought and feeling. Nor are these capacities unrelated. As we have seen, these rhetorics accept the Augustinian interrelation of love and knowledge; it is by love that man moves from an initial confused apprehension to the full knowledge of union. This is also what Hooker means when he claims that the love of God's goodness creates the certainty of adherence, a certainty firmer than all our empirical knowledge. Thus love in its own way bridges the poles of the ancient dilemma, since love, as Saint Thomas states, brings its object nearer (*propinquius*) to the lover.[54] But love is aroused by images, and therefore these help convey the mind and heart from the seen to the unseen. As the sacred rhetorics consistently repeat, *movere* is the primary goal of Christian discourse because we are oriented toward God by the quality of our love not the amount of our knowledge, and vividness conduces to this end.

In fact, the sacred rhetorics suggest several functions for images in religious discourse. These are nicely summed up in Henry Lukin's *An Introduction to the Holy Scripture* of 1669:

[53] Vossius, *Commentariorum*, 2: 447–48; see Longinus 15.9; Caussin, *De eloquentia*, pp. 141, 154.
[54] Aquinas, *ST* 1a.2ae.66, 6.

There is nothing more ordinary in Scripture then to represent *Spiritual* things by *natural*, that we may more clearly apprehend them: all our knowledge beginning at our *senses*. . . . the Scriptures shewing the *Analogy*, which is between *Natural* things and *Spiritual*; and how the *invisible things of God are clearly seen, and understood, from the things that are made* . . . they are thereby much illustrated, and made more intelligible. . . . we are likewise more lively affected with such things as are represented to our senses. . . . and this is also a great help to *Heavenly Meditation*, & a singular means to maintain in our thoughts a remembrance of Spiritual things.[55]

For Lukin then, such images serve a fourfold purpose: they make spiritual things more intelligible; they disclose an analogy between the realms of matter and spirit; they move the emotions; and they assist the memory. Each of these purposes deserves consideration, since each points to a different way in which rhetorical images, and therefore the Christian grand style, help create the knowledge and love of God.

Lukin's last function is the most obvious. The notion that images enable one to remember spiritual objects comes straight out of the medieval *ars memorandi*. As Yates notes, Thomas's remarks on the memory-image reappear in several Renaissance rhetorics to explain the value of images in discourse.[56] Erasmus thus argues that biblical allegory impresses spiritual truths more deeply in our souls and enables us to remember them.[57] Lullius likewise treats memory-images under *enargia*.[58] Even in the last quarter of the seventeenth century the same *topos* reappears in Ferguson's *The Interest of Reason in Religion*, which brings together so many themes pertaining to the Renaissance understanding of sacred vividness. Ferguson writes, "[for] the preserving the remembrance of spiritual Objects with the more facility, it becomes not only a matter of Relief and Advantage, but even sometimes of necessity to convey them to the Understandings of men, and commit them to their Memories, by having linkt and knit

---

[55] Lukin, *An Introduction*, p. 101.
[56] Yates, *The Art of Memory*, pp. 82–85.
[57] Erasmus, *Ecclesiastes*, 5: 1047cd.
[58] Lullius, *De oratione*, pp. 430–31.

them to Material Objects."[59] But as Yates also shows, by the Renaissance, the ars memorandi had become part of an esoteric "Platonism," which although sometimes connected with rhetoric, remained largely outside the more conservative and Aristotelian rhetorical tradition.[60]

Lukin also claims that images are necessary for sacred discourse because they reveal the analogy between matter and spirit. The principle of analogy, rooted in Platonic *mimesis*, is integral to the sacramental world view of the Middle Ages. Its relation to biblical language was articulated in Augustine's *De doctrina*, a text still regularly cited throughout Renaissance rhetorics. Broadly speaking, analogical images are either things signifying other things (e.g., Christ as pelican) or events foreshadowing future events (e.g., the sacrifice of Isaac as type of the Crucifixion). Typological relations, prophetic visions, apocalyptic images, and sacraments all function analogically. Significantly, in the Renaissance all these are categorized as rhetorical figures and often associated with enargia. This departs from medieval practice, in which rhetorical figures properly so-called belong to the literal level of exegesis, while types, visions, and other forms of analogy are aspects of the spiritual sense. The Renaissance tendency to lump these together has led to the suspicion that they were perceived *merely* as rhetorical figures. But in fact the opposite often appears to be the case. Analogy is rhetorical because rhetorical figures reflect the structures of existence. When Prideaux calls the contrast between Christ and Adam an antithesis, he does not mean that it is only a figurative expression but that rhetorical terminology can be mapped onto spiritual reality.[61] Perkins thus claims that the "mutuall, and as I may say, sacramentall relation" between external and internal things, "is the cause of so many figurative speeches and Metonymies which are used" in the Bible.[62] Likewise, Ferguson defends scriptural metaphor on the grounds

[59] Ferguson, *The Interest of Reason*, p. 364.

[60] But see Yates's remarks on the intermingling of the Hermogenic Ideas and the occult memory traditions (*The Art of Memory*, pp. 167–68, 238–39).

[61] Prideaux, *Sacred Eloquence*, pp. 20, 118–19. See also Keckermann, *Systema*, p. 1461.

[62] Cited in Lewalski, *Protestant Poetics*, p. 80.

that God "hath fram'd and contrived the Terrene World with a kind of subservient conformity to the World of Invisible things."[63] In the biblical rhetorics of Flacius and Glassius, vividness or evidentia is thus divided into two categories; there is a vividness of words but also of things. Types, visions, sacraments, prophetic acts all pertain to this "language of things (*realis sermo*)." They "place things as if before the eyes of the beholder. . . . And by such language not only is the soul moved but the things themselves are made clear and evident (*illustrari*)."[64] Insofar then as images function analogically, they reveal the actual relations between seen and unseen, past and future, shadow and fulfillment. They articulate the designs of Donne's "metaphorical God," who is not "a figurative, a metaphorical God in [his] word only, but in [his] works too."[65] Such images express the Christian concepts of history and the material world, through which God himself negotiates the ancient dilemma, making that which is remote present in sensible images.

Analogy, as Lukin indicates, belongs to the larger epistemic problem that things of the spirit can only be known via sense. Not surprisingly, therefore, Renaissance rhetorics advocate vividness because it lends intelligibility to spiritual objects.[66] According to Sohnius's *Tractatus de interpretatione ecclesiastica*, the preacher should "make an apt comparison of celestial things with earthly, of unknown with known, so that obscure matters and those remote from the ordinary apprehension of the people will not only be better understood by the mind but also more easily believed by the heart."[67] Such comparisons are essentially metaphoric. Thus under the heading "vivid metaphors," Glassius

[63] Ferguson, *The Interest of Reason*, p. 317. For the view that Ramism encouraged viewing tropes and figures as simply ornaments (in the modern sense) to the literal and therefore important meaning of the text, see Miller, *The New England Mind*, pp. 326–28.

[64] Glassius, *Philologia sacra* (1705), pp. 287–89; also Flacius, *Clavis*, 2: 480, 488.

[65] John Donne, *Devotions Upon Emergent Occasions* (Ann Arbor, 1959), pp. 124–25.

[66] Hathaway, *The Age of Criticism*, pp. 318–21.

[67] Sohnius, *Tractatus*, p. 153; cf. Lullius, *De oratione*, pp. 430–31; [Obadiah Walker], *Some Instructions concerning the Art of Oratory, Collected for the use of a Friend, a Young Student* (1659; Oxford, 1682), p. 25.

treats the anthropomorphic images of Scripture depicting God in human form. "By this," he notes, "[the Bible] confers a vividness (evidentia) and *autopsia* to those things which are by nature invisible."[68] This is not merely a matter of divine condescension. Such condescension is necessary because "the works and actions of God . . . are incomprehensible, nor would we be able to understand them, if the Bible did not use formulas for speaking about God which are near (*propinquae*) to human experience." But by carefully studying these images, guided by the Holy Spirit, "with a devout mind we ascend to God and . . . intuit that which is worthy of God and the sacred mysteries."[69] If such images are a condescension on God's part, for us they provide a means of ascent, the ladder by which we climb from what is knowable to us to that which is intrinsically knowable.

Implicit in Glassius's remark is a connection between the image and the emotions, for "ascend" suggests not only increased clarity of vision but also the growth of desire and sacred love. Since rhetoric is less concerned with cognition than passion, it naturally stresses the role of images in awakening desire. This is particularly true in the sacred rhetorics, where the formula magnitudo and praesentia always occurs in the context of movere: language must make the spiritual objects of faith visible and at hand in order to draw men's hearts to the love of absolute goodness.[70]

---

[68] Glassius, *Philologia sacra* (1705), pp. 290–91. Glassius glosses *autopsia* as *intuitiva notitia*, the same term that appears in Flacius, *Clavis*. "Intuitiva notitia" is a technical term from nominalist philosophy referring to the direct, infallible perception of contingent truths, e.g., I have intuitive knowledge of this yellow legal pad on which I am now writing. "Autopsia" is a Greek medical term for seeing with one's own eyes. Both terms, however, have overtones of supernatural intuition. In the neo-Platonic tradition, "autopsia" means spiritual vision, and "intuitio" or "intuitus" is also a common scholastic term for nondiscursive knowledge, such as that which God possesses. Both meanings seem to be implicit in the passages from Flacius and Glassius: sacred rhetoric creates an immediate awareness of spiritual and absent things, so that one seems to behold them directly, and therefore makes what is unknown and remote appear certain and present.

[69] Glassius, *Philologia sacra* (1653), p. 1116.

[70] Gombrich cites a 1626 encomium on the liberal arts by a professor of rhetoric, Christophoro Giarda, as claiming that personified abstractions (in this case of the arts) enable "the mind which has been banished from heaven into the dark cave of the body, its actions held in bondage by the senses, . . . [to] behold the beauty

Drawing from the sixth book of the *Institutes* where Quintilian suggests that in order for a speaker to move himself and his auditors he should vividly imagine his subject so that he almost sees the crime happening before his own eyes, Carbo remarks, "If anyone should behold [in his imagination] the terrible sight of the Last Judgment, the heavy tortures of hell, the high and inexplicable joy of eternal happiness, and like Stephen should see the heavens open, he certainly would easily stir up passion in himself and his listeners. . . . Plato said . . . the beauty of goodness and virtue is so great that if it were seen it would excite an amazing love of itself."[71] Because all appetition arises from the imagination of good or evil, the objects of love and desire must be in some sense present. "It is necessary," Reynolds states, "for the first working of Love, that the Object have some manner of Presence with the Affection."[72] The sacred rhetorics therefore instruct the preacher to paint vivid, circumstantial images of biblical events "so that the hearer as if placed outside himself seems to see for himself the affair placed in his midst. The Greeks call this hypotyposis, that is, the depiction of images, likewise *energeia* or vividness. . . . This . . . has a wonderful power in moving the emotions."[73] The relation between this imaginative scene painting and the Ignation *compositio loci* is obvious; both probably descend from the medieval practice of using images as aids to meditation.[74] As in the case of analogy, what has happened here seems to be a fusion of religious and rhetorical traditions. The devotional meditation on sacred history is rechristened as hypotyposis.

---

and form of the Virtues and Arts, divorced from all matter and yet adumbrated, if not perfectly expressed, in colours, and [the mind] is thus roused to an even more fervent love and desire for them" (*Symbolic Images*, p. 124).

[71] Carbo, *Divinus orator*, pp. 206–207, also 319ff.; cf. Bernard, *The Faithful Shepherd*, p. 32.

[72] Reynolds, *Treatise of the Passions*, p. 97.

[73] Keckermann, *Rhetoricae* (1614), p. 29; cf. Erasmus, *Ecclesiastes*, 984e–985f.

[74] V. A. Kolve, *Chaucer and the Imagery of Narrative: The First Five Canterbury Tales* (Stanford, 1984), p. 28; Fumaroli, *L'Age de l'éloquence*, pp. 108, 200; Marsha L. Dutton, "The Cistercian Source: Aelred, Bonaventure, and Ignatius," *Goad and Nail: Studies in Medieval Cistercian History X*, Cistercian Studies 84, ed. E. Rozanne Elder (Kalamazoo, 1985), pp. 151–78.

The correspondences between religious and rhetorical techniques arise from their common basis in the ancient dilemma. According to Reynolds, love and faith are closely related attempts to make that which is remote present: "Divine love hath the same kinde of vertue with Divine Faith; that as this is the being and subsisting of things to come, and distant in Time; so that is the Union and knitting of things absent, and distant in Place."[75] Whereas in the Classical tradition, the ancient dilemma is negotiated by *scientia* or discursive reasoning, in Christianity only faith working by love can traverse the distance between God and man. Saint Thomas thus writes, "by faith we know certain things about God which are so sublime that reason cannot reach them by means of demonstration. . . . Now in knowledge by faith, the will has the leading place."[76] This is also Hooker's point: in matters of faith, love outstrips evidence, supplying the deficiencies of argument. For Renaissance thinkers this means that the passionate images of rhetoric can carry the heart and will to God while reason flounders in its inevitable limitations. Again, this motif appears most clearly in Reynolds: "It often commeth to passe, that some plausible Fancie doth more prevaile with tender Wills, than a severe and sullen Argument. . . . And therefore in that great work of mens conversion unto God, he is said to allure them, and to speak comfortably unto them, to beseech, and to perswade them; to set forth Christ to the Soule, as altogether lovely as the fairest of ten thousand, as the desire of the Nations . . . that men might be inflamed to love the beauty of Holinesse."[77] The language of images brings us to love God, whereas no amount of argument can enable us to know him. The sacred rhetorics lay so much weight on imaginative vividness because it

[75] Reynolds, *Treatise of the Passions*, p. 96.

[76] *Aquinas*, ed. Pegis, p. 459. For Thomas, will here does not mean rational choice but intellective appetite, i.e., the desire for the good *qua* good. All love of incorporeal or spiritual objects is an act of will rather than affectus, since the latter is confined to the desire for corporeal things. Thomas, however, does not make it very clear whether this intellective appetite is subjectively experienced as emotion. In Hooker, on the other hand, it seems clear that the love arising from the taste of God's "heavenly sweetness" is experienced affectively.

[77] Reynolds, *Treatise of the Passions*, pp. 19–20.

creates both love and faith. In his section on hypotyposis, Flacius observes, "the Bible employs these pictures not only to move the stony heart of man more strongly . . . but also to strengthen [it] with greater certitude."[78] Rhetoric in this sense, then, is not below but beyond reason.

As Renaissance theology and psychology entailed the importance of images, so this focus on the image contains further stylistic implications. The characteristics of the Christian grand style evolve out of its theoretical premises, out of the intellectual framework of Renaissance culture. When the sacred rhetorics recommend vividness and hypotyposis, they are not calling for either a highly descriptive, quasi-Jamesian prose or sophistic ecphrasis. Instead, stress on the visual produces a stylistic ideal at once dramatic and metaphorical. The need to make the supernatural seem present or "evident" in order to make it emotionally effective gives rise to the demand for a dramatic treatment of scriptural events. As early as 1541, we find Erasmus praising the dramatic enargia of the Greek Fathers and the Bible. The preacher should recreate scriptural events in his imagination "and he himself will be moved and vehemently inflame others. 'Before whose eyes Christ was crucified,' says Paul. But the Galatians never saw Christ on the Cross, yet from Paul's vivid preaching He was represented to their souls as if they had seen what they only heard."[79] For de Granada, hypotyposis draws the listener "outside himself, as in a theater."[80] Keckermann writes that the preacher should comb the Bible for "the voices of contrite men pleading for forgiveness of sins, rendering thanks, suffering on the cross. . . . For this presents characters as in a theater and thus can move men's thoughts and feelings."[81] Alsted likewise notes that the hearer can be moved to pity by "the hypotyposis or image of Christ as if he stood before our eyes and begged for mercy."[82] In his discussion

[78] Flacius, *Clavis*, 2: 310.
[79] Erasmus, *Ecclesiastes*, 5: 983f.; cf. Melanchthon, *De ratione*, p. 77.
[80] De Granada, *Ecclesiasticae rhetoricae*, p. 132.
[81] Keckermann, *Rhetoricae* (1614), pp. 19–20. See also Glassius, *Philologia sacra* (1705), pp. 282–92; Lukin, *An Introduction*, pp. 39–40.
[82] Alsted, *Orator*, p. 234.

of evidentia, Flacius too emphasizes its dramatic component; for example, he notes that

dialogue places the object or act directly before us. . . . Thus frequently in the Evangelists and Prophets, the conversation of Christ and the Prophets, Apostles, and their adversaries is set forth as if now they were heard speaking to each other, as the colloquy of Christ with Nicodemus, with the Samaritan woman, with his mother at the Marriage at Cana, with the Canaanite. . . . It is characteristic of the Hebrew that speakers do not recount the conversations or discussions of others obliquely or in the third person, as Latin writers usually do, but directly, in first or second person. . . . Indeed, language becomes more intensely visual when the characters themselves are led onstage speaking.[83]

For both Flacius and Glassius, Holy Scripture resembles a "comic drama beheld by the theater of the universe."[84] As an example, Glassius analyzes the second Psalm: "*first*, like a prologue, the Psalmist summarizes the whole . . . then he brings in impious men speaking . . . *third* the Messiah . . . *then* God the Father . . . *finally* he again adds an ending, stepping forth like an epilogue, and concludes the whole action."[85] Despite the connection between images and the visual arts, rhetorical enargia is less like a painting than a play. Abstractions, inanimate objects, the dead all come alive; they become vivid through personification and similar figures like prosopographia (description of persons), somatopoeia (personifying abstractions), and idolopoeia (attributing speech to the dead).[86] The rhetorics recommend neither counting the streaks on a tulip nor the curls in Abraham's beard, but throwing everything into motion through dialogue, narration, and personification. Hence Flacius does not praise the Bible for describing what the ocean looks like, but for the vividness of " 'The sea saw and fled; the Jordan was driven back.' "[87]

Vividness is both dramatic and metaphorical. These two qualities are not wholly distinct, since the dramatic quality of a phrase

[83] Flacius, *Clavis*, 2: 486; cf. de Granada, *Ecclesiasticae rhetoricae*, p. 84.

[84] Flacius, *Clavis*, 2: 488; Glassius, *Philologia sacra* (1705), pp. 289–91.

[85] Glassius, *Philologia sacra* (1705), p. 289.

[86] Carbo, *Divinus orator*, pp. 320–21.

[87] Flacius, *Clavis*, 2: 484, quoting Psalm 114. I have used the King James translation for all biblical quotations.

like "the sea saw and fled" depends on metaphor, just as most forms of personification involve allegory. In the sacred rhetorics, enargia includes graphic description—for example, the narration of Christ's Passion—but also a broad array of tropes. Flacius and Glassius place metaphor, similitudes, visions, apocalyptic images, parables, metonomy, types, fables, and allegories under evidentia.[88] Both words and things are metaphoric; the vision of Babylon in Revelation is put "in place of" Rome, just as metaphor puts an improper word "in place of" a proper one. Metaphor thus shades off into analogy and type, and the vividness of sacred prose rests on and articulates the felt significance of the visible world. Flacius therefore compares the vividness of Scripture to that of the early Greek poets, especially Homer, with their sense of animate nature and indwelling spirit.[89] Such tropes are not decorative but, as de Granada remarks in his chapter on enargia, signs that enable the mind to move from that which is evident to an unseen reality.

Metaphor has both a cognitive and psychagogic value in sacred discourse. As we have seen, the connection between praesentia and emotion is basic to the Christian grand style. Insofar as tropes "give a sensible conception of the most abstracted thoughts," they create praesentia and can therefore spur the emotions to love truth.[90] The affective power of metaphor leads to a preference for concrete particularity over the sonorous generalities of Latin abstractions. Flacius remarks that the writer of Acts could have said that "the face of Stephen was glorious and magnificent, or full of dignity and gravity; instead more briefly and much more significantly Scripture says, 'then their eyes intent upon him, they saw his face as if the face of an angel.' "[91] Such grandeur does not consist of pompous Latinisms, like Shakespeare's "*honorificabilitudinitatibus*"[92] or eighteenth-century Miltonic imitations. Rather, it is metaphoric and therefore visually specific and particularized —although Tuve's point that the Renaissance valued these qual-

---

[88] Flacius, *Clavis*, 2: 483–89; Glassius, *Philologia sacra* (1705), pp. 287–92.
[89] Flacius, *Clavis*, 2: 463.
[90] Lamy, *The Art of Speaking*, 1.139–40, 2.37.
[91] Flacius, *Clavis*, 2: 475.
[92] *Love's Labors Lost*, 5.1.45.

ities not for themselves but for their affective power and significance should not be forgotten.

Renaissance writers also insist that metaphor does not simply
substitute improper for proper terms, but that sacred discourse is
inevitably metaphoric; there are no proper terms. This theme appears prominently both in the fifteenth-century humanists' battle
against scholasticism and in the late seventeenth century, in response to rationalist criticism. Coluccio Salutati thus argues that

> When, however, we wish to speak about God, since we do not know
> Him, lacking a concept, words also are lacking by which we could say
> something in the proper way concerning His indescribable majesty. . . .
> From this . . . it is clear that not only when we speak of God but also
> when we talk about incorporeal beings we speak of them improperly and
> according to the outer shell. . . . This mode of speaking is poetic. . . .
> From this you can easily see that all transfers of meaning or metaphors,
> figures, tropes, metaplasms and allegories, as well as tropology and
> parables, peculiarly pertain to this faculty. . . . Do you not see that di-
> vine literature and the entire Holy Scriptures consist entirely of this kind
> of speaking and nothing else?[93]

Lamy makes the same point in discussing the sublime: tropes
constitute the most accurate and significant way of speaking
about God.[94] In 1675 Ferguson uses this argument to disassociate
philosophy and religious discourse on epistemic grounds:

> I can very well allow that in Philosophy, where the Quality and Nature
> of things do not transcend and over-match words, the less Rhetorical or-
> naments, especially the fewer Metaphors . . . the better. But in Divinity,
> where no expressions come fully up to Mysteries of Faith, and where the
> things themselves are not capable of being declared in *Logical* and *Meta-*

---

[93] Cited in Trinkaus, *In Our Image*, 1: 62–63. See also his discussion of Valla on
the necessity of allegory and aenigma to approach spiritual realities (1: 143).

[94] Sir Thomas Browne thus writes, "I am now content to understand a mystery
without a rigid definition, in an easie and Platonick description. That allegorical
description of *Hermes* pleaseth mee beyond all the Metaphysicall definitions of Di-
vines; where I cannot satisfie my reason, I love to humour my fancy: I had as leive
you tell me that *anima est angelus hominis, est Corpus Dei*, as *Entelechia*" (*Religio
Medici, The Prose of Sir Thomas Browne*, ed. Norman J. Endicott [New York,
1967], 1.10).

physical Terms; Metaphors may not only be allowed, but are most accommotated to the assisting us in our conceptions of Gospel-mysteries.[95]

Ferguson accepts the rationalist and scientific criteria for discussing those things which we can accurately know, because language principally signifies the objects of sense experience: "As all words are instituted signs, so they were Originally invented to express natural Things and humane Thoughts by." But, he continues, "the utmost signification they can possibly bear, doth prove but scanty and narrow when they are applied to manifest things Spiritual and Heavenly."[96]

   Both the fifteenth-century humanists and Ferguson reflect the nominalist denial of a theological scientia (for Bacon, Hobbes, and the other major seventeenth-century English thinkers were all nominalists) and the consequent shrinkage of rational knowledge to empirical investigation.[97] To a greater or lesser degree, they accept the impossibility of a theological science, of a discursive negotiation between the two poles of knowability; in place of that discursive movement, they claim that through metaphorical adumbrations the heart and mind can attain the maximal awareness of God possible in this life. This view of metaphor still depends on a belief in analogy, that visible things bear traces of the invisible and exist in a real relation to them. If God were wholly unlike his creation, there could be no basis for metaphorical comparisons.[98] But the doctrine of analogy did not really die until Hume's critique in the late eighteenth century. The age of sacred rhetoric thus appropriately falls between the nominalist attack on the possiblity of a sacred science and Hume's dismantling of anal-

[95] Ferguson, *The Interest of Reason*, pp. 279–80.

[96] Ibid., p. 363.

[97] There are several relevant articles in *The Pursuit of Holiness in Late Medieval and Renaissance Religion*, ed. Charles Trinkaus with Heiko A. Oberman (Leiden, 1974). See especially, Oberman, "The Shape of Late Medieval Thought: The Birthpangs of the Modern Era," pp. 14, 25; William J. Courtenay, "Nominalism and Late Medieval Religion," pp. 45–46; Trinkaus, "The Religious Thought of the Italian Humanists and the Reformers: Anticipation or Autonomy?" pp. 344–45.

[98] See Colish's bibliography on the Thomist concept of analogy (*Mirror*, pp. 209–11).

ogy. Within this period, however, rhetoric could be justified not only as an instrument of mass persuasion, but as the discipline best able to traverse the distance between man and God in both its cognitive and affective aspects.

The Christian grand style, with its emphasis on drama, trope, and all forms of passionate vividness, develops out of a complex background of interrelated ideas: Aristotle's two forms of knowability, the role of images in cognition and appetite, the relation between love and faith, the principle of analogy. In one way or another, all these ideas bear upon the ancient dilemma and its consequences for religious epistemology. While many of the ideas contained in the sacred rhetorics derive from Aristotle, Aquinas, the ars memorandi, and so forth, it is not until the Renaissance that the problems associated with the ancient dilemma enter the rhetorical tradition. In the Renaissance they are the basis for both a rhetorical theology and a theological rhetoric. One could say that rhetoric became the characteristic of Renaissance humanism because it held the "solution" to the ancient dilemma, or at least the only "solution" available after the demise of the Thomist synthesis. The formula found throughout the sacred rhetorics—that passion results from the union of magnitudo and praesentia—indicates the nature of this solution; through vivid images the goodness of divine objects elicits love, and love provides what Hooker calls the certainty of adherence. Rhetorical images both awaken this love and enable the mind, which depends upon images for all thought, to move via analogy from the seen to the unseen.

True Greatness

In explaining the dictum that emotional power results from magnitudo and praesentia, Renaissance rhetorics, as previously noted, associate the latter with vividness, the former with amplification.[99] Amplification is itself one of the most important categories in Renaissance rhetoric. Basically it covers all the means

---

[99] Valades, *Rhetorica Christiana*, p. 161; de Granada, *Ecclesiasticae rhetoricae*, p. 158; Carbo, *Divinus orator*, p. 208; Keckermann, *Rhetoricae* (1614), p. 18; Alsted, *Theologia*, p. 20.

for endowing a subject with *magnitudo*, for making something seem exceptionally terrible, splendid, great, dangerous, desirable, and so on. Most tropes and figures, commonplaces, dialectical proofs, and rhetorical *colores* belong under amplification. One might amplify divine goodness by vivid examples, by arguments drawn from theological loci, by passionate exclamation, by enumerating the benefits of redemption, by depicting Christ's suffering. Amplification thus connects argument and passion in that it attempts to demonstrate that something is to be greatly loved or feared.[100] Because amplification is affective, it is also traditionally associated with the grand style, the style appropriate for subjects possessing *magnitudo*.[101] For the purposes of this study, the specific techniques of amplification are less important than its role in joining problems associated with the ancient dilemma to the Christian grand style.

To grasp this relation we must keep in mind that amplification in Classical rhetoric is frequently seen as a species of deception. It is another name for the sophistic boast that rhetoric can make small things appear great and great ones small.[102] The ancient distrust of oratory largely derives from ethical reservations concerning such distortion. In the sacred rhetorics of the Renaissance, however, amplification takes on a new meaning. Instead of making small things seem great and vice versa, it reveals the true greatness (*magnitudo*) of its subject, where true greatness now signifies the perspective of heaven—the value of something in God's eyes. Amplification draws men out of their ordinary ways of seeing to a spiritualized awareness of divine presence in all things. Erasmus thus comments on the difference between Classical and Christian concepts of amplification:

Through amplification, the forensic orator tries to make a thing seem bigger than it is; through diminution, smaller than it is. Each is a kind of wizardry and deception. For the preacher, it is enough if he make the

---

[100] De Granada, *Ecclesiasticae rhetoricae*, pp. 110–11.

[101] The opposite of amplification, meiosis or diminution, is correspondingly characteristic of the plain style genres of satire, burlesque, and invective.

[102] Plato, *Phaedrus* 267A; *Rhetorica ad Herennium* 2.30.47; Cicero, *Part orat* 15.52; Quintilian 8.4.1.

thing seem as great as it is, either greater or lesser than it appears to the multitude. For the people's judgement about things is rather upside-down; it chooses the worst instead of the best, embracing airy rather than substantial goods, and again neglecting true and loftiest goods for those worth least. For who is there who does not value more the goods of the body than those of the soul, temporal things more than eternal?[103]

The distinction between amplification as deception and Christian amplification, which displays the real magnitude of inward and spiritual goods, appears throughout Renaissance rhetoric.[104] In turn, the notion of Christian amplification rests on the ancient dilemma with its contrasts of near and remote, corporeal and spiritual, present and future. Erasmus presupposes an inverse relationship between true magnitude and that which ordinarily seems great to us. In the words of a seventeenth-century scholar, Nicholas Mosley, there is "a twofold Judgement in Man, one by Sense, which is External, and of things Material and Present; the other Internal by the Understanding of things Immaterial, Spiritual, and Future."[105] In the rhetorical tradition, it is the function of Christian amplification to present the world according to the judgment of the understanding, or as Carbo says, "one who amplifies does not lie but places before men's eyes things which are not seen and shows their true greatness by his manner of speaking."[106]

The question of true magnitude is thus implicitly a question of style, since, again in Carbo's words, "the whole power of eloquence rests in this—that language be commensurate with the excellence of its subject matter."[107] In a worldly sense, the persons and events of the Gospels and Christian history are not "excellent" but commonplace. As de Granada observes, in her martyrs, monks, and assorted *pauperi* the Church seems "vile and slavish to the eyes of carnal men," although "to erected minds it shines in

[103] Erasmus, *Ecclesiastes*, 5: 968f–969a.
[104] Hyperius, *The Practise*, p. 39; Valiero, *De ecclesiastica rhetorica*, pp. 20–21; Carbo, *Divinus orator*, pp. 187–88; Keckermann, *Systema*, p. 1429; Lamy, *The Art of Speaking*, 2.44; Melanchthon, *Elementorum* 13: 460.
[105] Mosley, *Contemplations*, p. 59.
[106] Carbo, *Divinus orator*, p. 188.
[107] Ibid., p. 336.

the splendor and worthiness of virtue."[108] The implications of this distinction between carnal and spiritual seeing for the Christian grand style are discussed in the fourteenth book of Caussin's *De eloquentia*, entitled "On the Majesty of Sacred Eloquence." The whole book attempts to refute the argument that the subject matter of Christian preaching is low (humilis) and hence unsuited for great oratory in the grand style. In this refutation, Caussin focuses on the transformation of seeing demanded by a Christian understanding of true greatness.

But, someone says, all these things are low; how much grandeur can they afford language? You are wrong, completely wrong. . . . You see Job approach, an exhibit in a great and illustrious procession moving along while God and the angels watch: but what Job? not the one called upon among his people, not grave with authority, not filled with abundance of riches, not crowded by numerous servants, not surrounded by surpassing glory, but Job nude and widowed, mocked. Job on the dunghill, ulcered, foul, diseased—you behold this Job, in whom, as in a bronze tower, the banner of heavenly triumph is placed. How great then think you was the grandeur of Christ?[109]

Caussin follows Augustine in severing the Ciceronian bond between the "levels" of style, the importance of the subject matter, and the officia oratoris.[110] Even the basest things, if pertaining to salvation, acquire the utmost magnitude. Christian preaching therefore admits an intermingling of the low and contemptible with the lofty and serious unknown to Classical oratory. But the resulting style cannot fairly be called the "genus humile"—Auerbach's term for the Christian prose of Augustine and the Church Fathers. In Caussin the accent falls not on the "lowliness of the sublime"[111] but on the sublimity of lowliness, and he defends the grandeur of Christian humility to show, as the book's title suggests, that sacred subjects may be treated with majestic eloquence. To use the grand style for such subjects insists on the priority of spiritual meaning; it is an act of faith and a paradig-

---

[108] De Granada, *Ecclesiasticae rhetoricae*, pp. 203–204.
[109] Caussin, *De eloquentia*, p. 898.
[110] *On Christian Doctrine*, 4.34–38.
[111] Auerbach, "Sermo humilis," in *Literary Language*, p. 43.

matic instance of the way the world looks to the spiritual eye. Like vividness or enargia, this sort of amplification belongs to the Christian grand style and the questions of representation and knowledge that arise out of the ancient dilemma.

For the Renaissance, as Klaus Dockhorn has observed, questions of faith and rhetoric are nearly allied.[112] Faith rests on the unseen, on a promise, whose truth seems contradicted by the empirical evidence.[113] That is, faith, like rhetoric, struggles in the tension between ordinary and spiritual perception, and this struggle to make the invisible and remote objects of faith luminous and actual relates these issues of seeing and believing to the ancient dilemma and the inverse proportion between praesentia and magnitudo. I would suggest that Renaissance rhetoric tries to negotiate this dilemma not by undermining discursive rationality but by the resources of rhetoric itself: hypotyposis, allegory, metaphor, icon, personification, apostrophe—all the devices for creating vivid immediacy, dramatic force, and emotional intensity. For the Renaissance, rhetoric seeks to make spiritual reality visible, or, according to Donne's succinct definition, "Rhetorique will make absent and remote things present to your understanding." Christian rhetoric, then, operates according to sacramental rather than dialectical modes. It incarnates the spiritual and elicits the affective/intuitive response that can spring from visible sign to invisible reality.

Si vis me flere

The Renaissance derives the characteristics of the Christian grand style from its understanding of movere, thus grounding stylistic precepts in the psychological and theological features of emotion. The union of magnitudo and praesentia is commonly cited as one primary source of emotional power. A second source of passion and thus a second criterion for the grand style is expressivity. Renaissance rhetorics repeatedly affirm that the speaker moves others by expressing his own emotions and that therefore he must

[112] Dockhorn, "Rhetorica movet," pp. 20–21, 27.
[113] The literary implications of this conception of faith are developed by Fish in *Self-Consuming Artifacts*, especially the chapter on *Pilgrim's Progress*.

be moved himself before attempting to stir up his auditors. Passionate discourse thus imitates the movement of thought and feeling, the contours of the speaker's inner life.[114] While the Renaissance never divorces expressivity from affective persuasion (one voices one's own emotions in order to move others), the emphasis on the former kept rhetoric from being merely an art of verbal manipulation. Instead, especially in the sacred rhetorics, discourse preserves a dialogic intimacy. Thus de Estella writes, "[words] must emerge from the soul, and you must feel within that which you would teach to others. For heart speaks to heart."[115]

The demand for expressivity, for a language that moves by articulating the speaker's own passion, appears not only in the major neo-Latin writers like Trebizond, Erasmus, de Granada, Keckermann, Caussin, and Alsted, but also in vernacular texts, by such men as Perkins, Baxter, Wilkins, Burnet, and Glanville, in which it is sometimes the only remaining traditional piece of rhetoric. In works influenced by hellenistic rhetoric, the stress on passionate expression often merges with the Hermogenic Idea of Truth (*aletheia*) and the Longinian concept of sublimity as an echo of a great soul.[116] In every case, Renaissance rhetorics yoke the power of discourse to the speaker's inner emotional life and suggest that that life is, in some sense, the proper object of imitation, that style should be a mirror of the heart. Erasmus says, "As the heart of man, so is his language (oratio). . . . Therefore to persuade, you must first love what you advocate: for a lover, his breast suggests the ardor of speech. . . . You must be ardent first and illuminate afterwards."[117] "You must be ardent," writes Caussin, "if you wish to set others on fire."[118] Lamy adds, "The

---

[114] On the relation between expressivity and syntax, see Croll, *"Attic" and Baroque*, pp. 67, 209–10. But unlike Renaissance rhetorics, Croll links expressivity with the plain style.

[115] De Estella, *De modo concionandi*, p. 8. See Auerbach, "Sermo humilis," on the intimacy of Christian discourse (p. 53).

[116] Caussin, *De eloquentia*, p. 154; Keckermann, *Systema*, p. 1670; Trebizond, *Rhetoricorum*, p. 579; Sturm, *De universa*, pp. 696, 725–28; Carbo, *Divinus orator*, p. 426.

[117] Erasmus, *Ecclesiastes*, 5: 773c, 790a.

[118] Caussin, *De eloquentia*, p. 462.

Writings of the Fathers are full of love and zeal for those truths that they teach. When the heart is on fire, the words that come from it must of necessity be ardent."[119] Although related to the dictum, popular from Isocrates through Jonson, that "*language most shewes a man*," the connection these rhetorics make between language and the *heart*—rather than, as in Jonson, the mind—shifts the focus of discourse from the imitation of moral character to that of passionate response. The sacred rhetorics in particular associate expressivity with passion and power, not with the revelation of character proper to the epistolary plain style.

The idea that one must be moved to move others plays a central role in Renaissance rhetoric as part of the wider contrast between what we may loosely call sophistic and oratory. The first excites applause for its embellished artistry, its rhythmic harmonies and splendid diction, while the latter is the natural and appropriate expression of deep feeling, in turn transforming and moving the audience rather than delighting them—a contrast we have already seen in discussing agonistic oratory. The emphasis on being moved reinforces this opposition by locating the source of passion within the speaker rather than in the artistic qualities of the speech. The speaker's ardor and its expression in the more passionate figures of thought replace the schemes and balances of sophistic prose as the foundation of effective oratory. De Granada remarks, "all the schools and precepts of rhetoric cannot assist the preacher in speaking as much as this ardor alone. This one emotion . . . teaches him to neglect whatever strokes the ears by the tinkling of words and sententious point more than instructing and healing the mind."[120] The vernacular rhetorics similarly argue that the power of preaching results from the speaker's own ardent devotion. As Baxter says, "the most reverend preacher that speaks as if he saw the face of God, doth more affect my heart, though with common words, than an unreverent man with the most exquisite preparations." In most of the vernacular rhetorics, the contrast between art and feeling is pushed to an antithesis.

[119] Lamy, *The Art of Speaking*, 2.52.
[120] De Granada, *Ecclesiasticae rhetoricae*, p. 29; cf. Carbo, *Divinus orator*, p. 476.

The most passionate style is also "most naked."[121] The neo-Latin rhetorics, on the other hand, remain faithful to the principle of decorum, attempting to discover a style appropriate to the expression of emotion and the *ardor caritatis*.

The conviction that passionate oratory results more from the speaker's own passion than any art can be found both in antiquity and the Renaissance. Cicero, Horace, and Quintilian affirm that the best way to move others is to be moved oneself and that powerful oratory differs sharply from schematic ornament. The sacred rhetorics of the Renaissance, however, in borrowing from their antique models, transform them. For the relationship between being moved and moving others, these alterations are crucial. They distinguish secular from sacred oratory and in so doing raise questions about the nature of the grand style, the relation between human effort and divine initiative, and the connection between language, self, and God.

The central Classical source for the relation between being moved and moving comes from the sixth book of Quintilian's *Institutes*. The context there is especially relevant, because, as we have seen, Quintilian explicitly treats pathos as a means for deceiving the judges: "The judge, when overcome by his emotions, abandons all attempt to enquire into the truth of the arguments, is swept along by the tide of passion, and yields himself unquestioning to the torrent."[122] Quintilian then continues, arguing that "the prime essential for stirring the emotions of others is, in my opinion, first to feel those emotions oneself." In order to "work up" the requisite emotions, the speaker should use his imagination to elicit vivid images.[123]

While Quintilian treats self-induced affect in the context of deception and the imagination, in the rhetorics of the Renaissance these connections relax. All the sacred rhetorics drop the association of pathos and deception, instead linking passionate oratory with salvation. Christian oratory redeems its hearers by moving

[121] Baxter, *Gildas Salvianus*, pp. 137–38.
[122] See Chapter One above for full quotation.
[123] Quintilian 6.2.5–7, 26–32.

the emotions. De Estella thus writes, "the particular end and scope of preaching the gospel . . . is the salvation of souls: this will take place if he moves, arouses, and inflames the broken and sorrowful. . . . But it is forbidden to move others unless you first move yourself."[124]

Even in the sacred rhetorics that retain Quintilian's connection between being moved to move others and imagination, the ability to feel is seen as a divine gift, the characteristic fruit of the indwelling Spirit.[125] The affective power of rhetoric also results from grace. God's synaptic power gives sacred discourse its regenerative and emotional force, transfusing spiritual efficacy into the dead letter. Caussin writes, "in moving the emotions, orators perplex the ears with the din and hammering of words and do not touch the soul at all, unless they have been supported by divine aid."[126] These rhetorics accept the paradox, already present in Augustine, that passionate oratory both is and is not a human art.[127] In the middle of his voluminous rhetoric, Erasmus observes that the Holy Spirit "bestows the fiery heart and burning tongue. . . . The Spirit itself speaks through [the preacher] and transfers its own gift into the listeners."[128] Similarly, de Estella begins by quoting Horace's "si vis me flere," but the next sentence reads "[the orator] will preach with the passion of this living voice and in the spirit of devotion, and God will suggest to him the richness of heavenly rhetoric, so that he shall soften the hearts of the obstinate."[129] The more conservative vernacular rhetorics, which displace art wholly with the Spirit, just dissolve one side of this paradox. Those we are considering, while perhaps less consistent, make sense from a theological viewpoint that habitually conjoined divine activity with man's voluntary agency.

[124] De Estella, *De modo concionandi*, p. 8.
[125] Erasmus, *Ecclesiastes*, 5: 773d; Hyperius, *The Practise*, p. 44; Caussin, *De eloquentia*, p. 462; de Estella, *De modo concionandi*, p. 61; de Granada, *Ecclesiasticae rhetoricae*, n.p.; Valades, *Rhetorica Christiana*, b3ᵛ.
[126] Caussin, *De eloquentia*, p. 462.
[127] Fish, *Self-Consuming Artifacts*, pp. 32–38; see also Alsted, *Theologia*, p. 8.
[128] Erasmus, *Ecclesiastes*, 5: 774e, 982b.
[129] De Estella, *De modo concionandi*, p. 61.

This theological viewpoint merits a brief discussion because it
raises a fundamental question about the nature of the self implicit
in the command to be moved oneself before moving others. As
Stanley Fish has observed concerning Augustine and Herbert, the
activities one would normally attribute to the self—speaking,
writing, moving—turn out to be, in some sense, the result of
God's activity; the self seems to have little of its own left to do. If
pushed to its extreme, this view leads to gnosticism or Averro-
ism, but neither Herbert nor Augustine ever blurs the absolute
distinction between self and God. The self is not consumed in the
crisscrossings of divine initiative. Both Aquinas and Luther are
explicit on this point. In the *Summa contra gentiles*, Aquinas argues
that the Holy Spirit makes us lovers of God and leads us to fulfill
his precepts; he then immediately adds: "For all that, one must
bear in mind that the sons of God are driven not as slaves, but as
free men. For . . . we do that freely which we do of our very
selves. But this is what we do of our will. . . . But the Holy Spirit
so inclines us to act that He makes us act voluntarily, in that He
makes us lovers of God."[130] Luther makes the same distinction between external compulsion and the necessity of immutability, so
that "when God works in us, the will is changed under the sweet
influence of the Spirit of God. It desires and acts not from compulsion, but responsively of its own desire and inclination."[131]
While Luther denies free will, he does not make God a pre-Carte-
sian ghost in the machine. God's inner activity on the heart and
will does not destroy the self but is the condition of its freedom
and creativity.

That the rhetorical dictum, one must be moved to move
others, occurs as a corollary to the notion that God bestows both
the ardor of the speaker and the power of his words suggests that
for Renaissance rhetorics expressivity does not mean expressing
one's individual personality with its distinctive desires and aver-
sions. The modern meaning of the self as an autonomous, unique

[130] Aquinas, *Summa contra gentiles, Book Four: Salvation*, trans. Charles J. O'Neil
(Notre Dame, Ind., 1975), 4.22.1–5.
[131] Martin Luther, *The Bondage of the Will, Discourse on Free Will*, ed. and trans.
Ernst Winter (New York, 1961), p. 111; see also Donne, *Sermons*, 1: 272.

individuality possessing a continuous internal awareness[132] is not
available in the Renaissance; even the term does not appear as a
substantive until the last quarter of the seventeenth century. Before that, one has to choose among "heart," "soul," "mind,"
"spirit," and "reason" as approximations for self. Rather, sacred
discourse expresses a selfhood created by the activity of the Spirit
within the heart, a selfhood both personal and yet generic. Luther's comments on the Psalms entail precisely such a notion of
inwardness. The Psalms both express "the very inmost sensations
and motions" of their authors, "the very hidden treasure of their
hearts' feelings," and "the feelings and experiences of all the faithful."[133] The possibility of an inwardness shared by "all the faithful" contained in Renaissance notions of expressivity implies a
selfhood formed in the interaction between a rather undifferen-
tiated or generic human nature and the indwelling Spirit. Donne
thus equates the "I" with "all mankinde": "*I*, that is, *This nature*,
is in that man that sins that sin; and *I*, that is, *This nature*, is in that
Christ, who is wounded by that sin."[134] The Renaissance saw the
self not as a reflexive internal awareness but as man's generic nature—the shattered *imago Dei*—existing in relation to various
"pulls" from a divine or demonic Beyond, pulls which exert an
almost magnetic attraction upon it. The orientation of this nature
with respect to these pulls constitutes the self. If it responds to
God's "pull," a certain kind of self emerges; if it responds to the
attraction exerted by the things of this world, a different self is
formed. Self therefore does not connote the awareness of oneself
as a unique individual but habitual volition; for the Renaissance,
as for Augustine, you are what you love. Thus, according to
Erasmus, the self (and language) emerges from the relationship
between the heart and its object: "Who has a worldly heart,
speaks worldly things; who has a carnal heart, speaks carnally;
who has the devil in his heart, speaks diabolically and infects

[132] Ann Ferry, *The "Inward" Language: Sonnets of Wyatt, Sidney, Shakespeare,
Donne* (Chicago, 1983), p. 46.
[133] Luther, *A Manual of the Book of Psalms*, trans. Henry Cole (London, 1837),
pp. 5–7. Cited in Lewalski, *Protestant Poetics*, pp. 42–43.
[134] Donne, *Sermons*, 2: 122.

others; who has the spirit of Christ in his heart, speaks things celestial, pious, holy, chaste, and worthy of God."[135] The self is an activity not a thing; Augustine terms this activity love: "they receive a name from what they love. By loving God, we become gods: therefore, by loving the world, we are called the world."[136] Love is the soul's weight and specific gravity, directing it toward either the divine or demonic pole of spiritual reality: "thus the body by its weight, so the soul is carried by its love, wherever it is carried."[137]

The notion of the self as a loving response to a divine drawing has its roots in Classical philosophy. In a series of articles, Eric Vogelin argues that Greek philosophy begins with the recognition of "man's existence in a state of unrest," of man as a questioner, aroused by wonder to seek "the ground of his existence." Voegelin writes: "In the Platonic-Aristotelian experience, the questioning unrest carries the assuaging answer within itself inasmuch as man is moved to his search of the ground by the divine ground of which he is in search. . . . Hence, philosophy in the classic sense is . . . a man's responsive pursuit of his questioning unrest to the divine source that has aroused it."[138] For Plato and Aristotle, the order of the soul becomes "the loving quest of truth in response to the divine drawing from the Beyond."[139] This experience of responding to an answering pull is repeatedly symbolized in the Platonic dialogues: in the Allegory of the Cave where the prisoner does not free himself but is "forced suddenly to stand up" and "dragged" by force into the sunlight; in the story of the puppets in the Laws, whose gold and iron strings are pulled by the gods; in Diotima's myth of Eros as a daimon in the space between (metaxy) earth and heaven.

[135] Erasmus, Ecclesiastes, 773cd.
[136] Cited in Anders Nygren, Agape and Eros: The History of the Christian Idea of Love, 2 vols., trans. Philip Watson (London, 1939), 2: 266.
[137] Saint Augustine, The City of God, 11.28; see also Confessions, 13.9.
[138] Eric Voegelin, Anamnesis, ed. and trans. Gerhart Niemeyer (Notre Dame, Ind., 1978), pp. 92–96.
[139] Eric Voegelin, "Wisdom and the Magic of the Extreme: A Meditation," unpublished monograph, p. 23.

Christian theology preserves and modifies the Classical analysis of the self as human eros in response to divine agape, yet also pulled by the iron cords of sin and Satan. The poles of divine and demonic attraction are experienced as Beyond but also as within; Christ or Satan dwells in the heart. The Christian self emerges in its loving response to God's drawing, a response itself created by God's presence within the heart. In an early sermon, Donne writes:

[God] cals us as Birds do their young, as he would gather us as a Hen doth her Chickins. . . . shall our carnal affections draw us, though they do not force us, and shall not Grace do the same office too? . . . *Draw me, and I will run after thee,* saies the Spouse . . . . He came to save by calling us, as an eloquent and a perswasive man draws his Auditory, but yet imprints no necessity upon the faculty of the will. . . . I drew them saies God there; But how, and with what? *With cords of man* saies he, and with bands of love. . . . God saves us by a calling, and he saves us by drawing; but he cals them that hearken to him, and he draws them that follow upon his drawing.[140]

The self emerges in these movements of attraction and response, drawing and hearkening. It is not the divine ground that it seeks, but what it is, it is only by virtue of the indwelling Beyond by whom and toward whom it moves.

The expressivity of sacred rhetoric is therefore not the articulation of an introspective self-consciousness but the mimesis of this double movement of seeking and being sought. It is the expression of a love created by the Spirit and oriented towards it. In Carbo's words, "the Spirit is a power given to the preacher by God through which his words have the strength (energia), weight, and force to move the hearts of his hearers. . . . Or it is an ardor born of charity, from which arises the desire of divine glory and of saving souls, placed by the Holy Spirit in the hearts of preachers, which gives life to the dead word . . . inflames the heart of the speaker, and moves the breasts of his listeners."[141] To express one's own feelings is to express one's response to the in-

---

[140] Donne, *Sermons,* I: 312–14.
[141] Carbo, *Divinus orator,* p. 45.

ner presence of the Spirit. Carbo continues, "whoever has been touched by this divine Spirit, what he himself first will feel, what he will taste, that he shall set powerfully before others; he will persuade them and, like the good cock, arouse both himself and others to well-doing."[142] Almost all sacred rhetorics insist that the preacher possess an experiential knowledge of God. According to Melanchthon, "taught by the Holy Spirit, [the preacher] must experience the power [of Sacred Scripture] in the various circumstances of his life."[143] A century later, Wilkins similarly concludes that preaching must proceed "from the heart, and an experimentall acquaintance with those truths which we deliver. . . . This is to speak in the *evidence and demonstration of the spirit and of power*,"[144]

It is clear from these remarks that the presence of the Spirit manifests itself as power and as passion, rather than, let us say, understanding or *ataraxia*. The Spirit, de Granada writes, arouses the emotions (*affectus*) to desire spiritual things (*res spirituales*).[145] Similarly, Caussin argues that the ability to excite intense and vehement emotion is a gift of God.[146] The Holy Spirit, in Luther's words, is a rhetorician (*rhetoricatur igitur Spiritus sanctus*).[147] Erasmus explains how the heart's response to God's drawing impassions and spiritualizes language, making it the image of the loving heart and therefore able to move others: "With the heart one believes to justification, which promises salvation through faith in Christ; and because it speaks spiritual things, it speaks to the heart. No one, however, is able to speak to the heart of the people, unless he speaks from the heart." Christian discourse moves by dramatizing the speaker's passionate response to a divine Beyond, but this response itself is a gift, for the Holy Spirit is "the

---

[142] Ibid., p. 48.

[143] Melanchthon, *De officiis*, p. 8.

[144] Wilkins, *Ecclesiastes*, p. 106. See also Glanville, *An Essay*, p. 54; Baxter, *Gildas Salvianus*, p. 138; Carbo, *Divinus orator*, pp. 45–46; Flacius, *Clavis*, 2: 16.

[145] De Granada, *Ecclesiasticae rhetoricae*, p. 161.

[146] Caussin, *De eloquentia*, p. 462; cf. Carbo, *Divinus orator*, pp. 45–47.

[147] Cited in Dockhorn, "Rhetorica movet," p. 28.

creator and renewer of hearts."[148] Because the same Spirit dwells in all the faithful, the preacher's articulation of his emotions is both an act of self-expression and a witness to the communal inwardness formed by the action of grace upon nature. Because such inwardness is experienced as affect, the language of self-expression—which is also the language of the Spirit—is passionate and moving. As Donne unhesitatingly compares oratory and grace, so Carbo links rhetorical *movere* and the language of the Spirit; in speaking, he notes, "the Spirit is called energia and power (*efficacitas*)."[149] The link between this passionate discourse and the grand style is obvious. It remains to be seen whether any more explicit stylistic features derive from these Renaissance doctrines of expressivity and the language of the Spirit.

The Spirit must endow the preacher with the ardor of charity, de Granada observes, because "this emotion (affectus) . . . exclaims (exclamat), confutes (arguit), implores (obsecrat), rebukes (increpat), terrifies (terret), astonishes (stupet), expresses wonder (admiratur), and transforms itself into all emotions and figures of speech: it awakens the dead (defunctos excitat), addresses the absent (absentes alloquitur), [and] implores God's aid (Dei opem implorat)."[150] The characteristics de Granada here attributes to the language of the Spirit bear a striking resemblance to the figures listed in the sacred rhetorics as designed to express and move the emotions and as especially suited for sacred discourse. Although the lists vary somewhat from rhetoric to rhetoric, ten or so figures—all figures of thought—appear in almost every case; these are interrogatio, exclamatio, admiratio, apostrophe, adiuratio, prosopopoeia, sermocinatio, obsecratio, imprecatio, optatio.[151] The table below suggests the intersection between de Granada's language of the Spirit and these figures of thought.

[148] Erasmus, *Ecclesiastes*, 5: 774e, 835d.

[149] Carbo, *Divinus orator*, p. 240; cf. de Granada, *Ecclesiasticae rhetoricae*, p. 27.

[150] De Granada, *Ecclesiasticae rhetoricae*, p. 29. Carbo repeats this passage with minor changes (*Divinus orator*, p. 47).

[151] Keckermann, *Rhetoricae* (1614), p. 39; Hemmingsen, *The Preacher*, p. 55; Carbo, *Divinus orator*, pp. 297ff.; Bernard, *The Faithful Shepherd*, p. 299; Alsted,

interrogatio	
exclamatio	exclamat
admiratio	admiratur, stupet
apostrophe	absentes alloquitur
adiuratio	
prosopopoeia	defunctos excitat
sermocinatio	
obsecratio	obsecrat
imprecatio	increpat
optatio	Dei opem implorat

The passage from de Granada indicates that he realized this connection between the language of the Spirit and the rhetorical figures of thought. The ardor of charity manifests itself in such figures. A similar conjunction appears in Ursinus's *Ecclesiastes*, which lists the figures of thought immediately following the precept that the preacher must himself experience the emotions he desires to transmit.[152] Additional evidence for the parallel between the sanctified passion and the figures of rhetoric appears in Valiero's description of the sacred grand style: "He, however, who intends to move souls . . . to reflect on their own salvation . . . must influence his hearers in various and wonderful ways: by threatenings, exhortations, pleading (obsecrans), scolding, accusing, rebukes (obiurgans) . . . he must assume the persona of one who . . . threatens, terrifies. . . . [He must] wonder, call witnesses . . . hope, pray, plead, promise, implore . . . exclaim . . . address his listeners . . . ."[153] As in de Granada, we notice the presence of exclamatio, admiratio, prosopopoeia, obsecratio, imprecatio, optatio, and apostrophe.

The overlap between the figures of thought and the expressivity resulting from the inward drawing of the Spirit should not be surprising. Throughout the Renaissance, the figures of thought are valued not only for their ability to arouse emotion but for their expressive capacities. They "express the commotions and

Theologia, p. 20; de Arriaga, *Rhetoris Christiani*, p. 103; de Granada, *Ecclesiasticae rhetoricae*, pp. 168–74.

[152] Ursinus, *Ecclesiastes*, pp. 33–34.

[153] Valiero, *De ecclesiastica rhetorica*, pp. 95–96.

violent agitations of the Mind, in our passions . . . [for] the Passions have a peculiar Language, and are expressed only by what we call Figures."[154] In the sacred rhetorics, the figures of thought articulate the soul's ardent response to God's presence. According to Keckermann, apostrophe spontaneously turns to address Christ; admiratio voices the speaker's wonder at the immense love of God toward mankind.[155] In de Granada, the conjunction of exclamatio and apostrophe is used when "the mind, moved by the greatness of some thing, turns its speech to mute and inanimate creatures. . . . such a figure bursts out from the greatness of desire. . . . The immense ardor of longing expresses itself in this figure." The examples he offers depict Isaiah's yearning anticipation of Christ, as " 'Sing, O ye heavens; for the Lord hath done it: shout, ye lower parts of the earth: break forth into singing, ye mountains, O forest, and every tree therein: for the Lord hath redeemed Jacob, and glorified himself in Israel.' "[156]

These examples clarify the nature of expressivity in Renaissance rhetoric. If such language, in Trebizond's words, "strips bare the mind's passions," it does so dramatically rather than reflexively. That is, expressivity does not mean talking *about* one's own desires and experiences but revealing this inwardness through the affective valences figures bestow upon language. The influence of the Psalms on sacred poetry during the Renaissance encouraged a reflexive, introspective presentation of spiritual life. The traditions of sacred oratory, however, led to the more indirect expressivity of figurative language—and also of voice and gesture, since the sacred rhetorics rarely ignore the affective potential of oral delivery. The numerous attempts to transfer the rhetorical figures of thought to music are based on this understanding of expressivity as a matter of evocative signs (notes, verbal figures) rather than reflexive statement.[157] Figures like exclamatio and prosopopoeia, although scarcely language such as men

---

[154] Lamy, *The Art of Speaking*, 1.34, 92.
[155] Keckermann, *Rhetoricae* (1616), pp. 115–16.
[156] De Granada, *Ecclesiasticae rhetoricae*, p. 168. The biblical quotation is from Isaiah 44: 23.
[157] Brian Vickers, "Figures of Rhetoric / Figures of Music?" pp. 1–44. On the expressivity of sound and cadence, see Lamy, *The Art of Speaking*, 1.206–200.

do use in a state of excitement, nevertheless signify emotion in much the same way that certain arrangements of tones can convey joy or grief.

As the emphasis on vividness in Renaissance rhetoric unites questions of style to a broad theological and psychological background, so the demand for expressivity connects notions of self and Spirit with rhetorical precept. The fusion of the Classical dictum that the orator must himself be moved to move others with the Christian doctrine of the indwelling Spirit led to an identification of the language of the Spirit with expressivity and passionate discourse. Such a language expressed the soul's ardent hearkening to the drawing of the Spirit in an interaction that did not destroy the will but renewed and invigorated it. The more liberal sacred rhetorics extend this analysis a step further, describing this expressivity in terms of the figures of thought, characteristic in both ancient and Renaissance rhetoric of passionate oratory and the grand style. These texts thus yoke the rhetorical figures to the complexly intertwined activities of self and Spirit in a way that neither obliterates the self into the passive medium of an *afflatus* nor narrows expressivity into a display of personality.

CONCLUSION

T HE CENTRAL tradition of the grand style originates in the passionate agonistic oratory mentioned in Book III of Aristotle's *Rhetoric* and exemplified in the achievement of Demosthenes. This central tradition defines grandeur in opposition to the polish and schematic balance of Isocratic prose—the original grand style. In the fourth century, however, it was not yet clear that Aristotle's agonistic oratory, and not Isocratic epideixis, would become the central tradition. Although the relevant texts have been lost, the gradual shift from an Isocratic to a Demosthenean definition of the grand style must have taken place between the fourth and first centuries B.C. After Aristotle, the next surviving rhetorical texts date from late Republican Rome and by then the grand style has been firmly identified with vehement affective oratory on matters of greatest public concern. But even in the hellenic period, the definition of the grand style is complicated by additional connotations, especially those stemming from the Theophrastean conjunction of power and beauty and from the association of the grand style with the qualities of epic and tragedy. The former, which, generally speaking, dominates the Roman tradition, adds rhythm and periodicity to the skiagraphic roughness of Aristotelian deliberative oratory. The latter, more characteristic of later Greek rhetoric, broadens the scope of the grand style to include solemnity and heroic loftiness as well as agonistic strength.

From Aristotle on, passion remains the defining quality of the grand style. Between the first and fourth centuries A.D. this emphasis on emotional power increases at the expense of the Theophrastic union of power with artistic richness. In Longinus and Augustine, affective strength becomes the only necessary criterion for grandeur or sublimity; while the artistic resources of rhythm and figure often support the passion of the grand style, it can exist without them. By late antiquity, loftiness of conception and intensity of emotion thus overshadow the rhythmic-ornate components of grandeur. In addition, during the same period,

Roman and Greek conceptions of the grand style separate. The Roman genus grande remains the agonistic civic prose of the practical orator, combining forensic vehemence with the oral rhythms and periodic fullness of the Theophrastian ideal. The hellenistic grand style, on the contrary, tends to be written, brief, and austere. It loosens the bond between the grand style and civic oratory, instead associating elevation with the more "vertical" and sacral emotions of wonder, terror, and sublimity. Thus, by the end of the Classical era, the grand style exhibits a considerable range of meaning, allowing dense brevity as well as periodic fullness, forensic vehemence as well as numinous awe, Thucydidean darkness as well as Ciceronian copia. Yet all these variants share the triple decorum of Classical rhetoric: the belief that language should sustain an emotional effect in proportion to the greatness of the subject matter—and therefore that the most serious and important subjects should be treated in passionate and elevated style.

The Classical grand style defines itself not in opposition to a philosophical plain style but rather to sophistic (or Isocratic) cultus and passionless refinement. In antiquity, philosophy and rhetoric were not polarized because, despite Plato's strictures, philosophical style was often rhetorical and the rhetorical tradition refused to recognize an eloquence not based on wisdom. According to ancient rhetorics, the real danger to the ideal of grandeur came from the sophists, declaimers, and the various umbratilis teachers, who set up schools of fine speaking—often fine speaking divorced both from real learning and real life—and threatened to supplant the passion and practical strength of the grand style with an artificial and ostentatious elegance. The response to this threat insisted upon the seriousness and agonistic commitment of passionate oratory; but it nevertheless avoided confronting the epistemological status of passion. Classical thought is intellectualist and tends to view passion as deceptive and subrational. Ancient rhetorics defend emotional appeals as necessary to sway the populace or judges, but this pragmatic defense does not refute the suspicion that passionate oratory usually subverts truth.

An internally coherent view of the grand style does not emerge until Saint Augustine subverts the assumptions of Classical intellectualism. Augustine redefines emotion as the experiential component of volition or love. Therefore, emotion is not hostile to reason, but passionate volition and reason together carry man to his highest end. Spiritual life is always passionate; love of God, pity for the suffering, contrition, supernatural desire, hatred of evil, all flow from a rightly directed will. True goodness for Augustine is thus not "apathetic" but embraces intense affectivity, and insofar as the grand style can move the emotions to love what is worthy of love, it becomes an instrument of salvation. Although Augustine does not quite recognize the implications of his psychology for his own description of the grand style, subsequent Christian rhetorics increasingly stress the passion of sacred discourse on the Augustinian grounds that Christian spirituality is ardently emotional.

In the Middle Ages, sacred rhetorics follow Augustine in their treatment of passion, stressing the affective qualities of all Christian preaching. But while Augustine had attempted to hold together the notion of eloquence as a human art and as a gift of grace, the medieval artes praedicandi emphasize the latter exclusively. Concern for language and style drops away because the passion of sacred discourse springs from the divinely given ardor of the preacher. This theological position produces what can only be called a passionate plain style—a combination unknown to antiquity, which invariably associated passion and grandeur. The passionate plain style does not derive from the Classical genus tenue, which was always either conversational or dialectical, but from a theological revision of the grand style. The Classical plain style, however, mutates into scholastic plainness, resulting in a sharp distinction between philosophy and rhetoric—a distinction again not present in antiquity, at least not in such an acute form. The Renaissance not only inherits the traditions of Classical rhetoric but also the medieval passionate plain style and the tendency to bifurcate philosophy and rhetoric. The first of these medieval legacies deeply influences vernacular sacred rhetorics in the English Renaissance, the latter important aspects of secular rhetoric.

One of the most striking features of Renaissance rhetoric is the split between the secular and sacred traditions. Secular rhetoric moves in the direction of either a scientific or an introspective plain style; sacred rhetoric creates the Christian grand style. In England, the vernacular sacred rhetorics tend to carry on the medieval passionate plain style under Protestant auspices, but England also made extensive use of the continental neo-Latin texts. In general, Renaissance Latin culture was international. The following remarks, therefore, apply to the European Renaissance as a whole, although the tension between the vernacular and neo-Latin traditions seems to have been unique to England, and investigation of the rhetorical traditions in other countries would no doubt bring to light further local variants.

The Christian grand style comes to fruition between 1560 and 1620 in the Tridentine, liberal Protestant, and general rhetorics, but its main features surface in a more scattered fashion in the sacred rhetorics of the previous century. In the mid-fifteenth century, George of Trebizond begins the association between the hellenistic grand style and Christian discourse. Toward the end of the century, Brandolini and Agricola redefine epideictic (delectatio) in a way that brings it closer to sacred grandeur. Agricola identifies an intellectual delectatio produced by contemplation of the heroic, lofty, and unusual—a delight not far from the Longinian sublime. Brandolini explicitly defines delight as an emotion and further claims that feelings of veneration, wonder, and love, which he associates with epideixis, characterize Christian preaching; they are man's response to the mysteries of faith. For both men, delight and epideixis are linked to the most serious and important subjects, whereas Roman rhetoric had connected them to the flowery, schematic oratory of the sophists. The most significant development begins in the early sixteenth century with the renewal of Augustinian rhetoric and an emphasis on its psychological bases. In Erasmus and Melanchthon, one thus finds the treatment of emotion as inseparable from spiritual existence and an affirmation of the interdependence of love and knowledge. But while Melanchthon's sacred rhetorics adhere to the medieval passionate plain style in their distrust of conscious art, Erasmus renews the ancient triple decorum of style, subject, and effect and, like Augustine, attempts to harmonize the functions of grace and rhetoric. The passion created by the Holy Spirit manifests itself in passionate *language*, and language becomes passionate not

only because it expresses inward emotion, but through its vividness, drama, and figures of thought.

The hellenistic grand style, the new appreciation for epideixis,
Augustinian psychology, the notion of passionate expressivity as
resulting from the inner action of the Spirit, and the emphasis on
the visual, dramatic, and figurative as the verbal equivalents of
emotion remain the central features of the Christian grand style
throughout the Renaissance. Sacred rhetorics after 1560 bring
these qualities together, explicating and developing certain aspects, but not essentially changing them. Between 1560 and 1620,
the grand style evolves in three directions: toward a greater use of
hellenistic rhetoric, a more explicit and detailed treatment of
emotion, and a more developed theoretical basis.

Both the general and the biblical rhetorics describe sacred discourse in terms borrowed from the hellenistic grand style. The
religious sense of grandeur present in Longinus, Demetrius, and
Hermogenes facilitated the yoking of Christian discourse and the
grand style while shifting the connotations of grandeur from the
forensic to the sublime and solemn. Hellenistic rhetoric also provided an alternative to Ciceronianism. The hellenistic grand style
and its Renaissance counterparts are not periodic or copious, but
possess a pregnant, dense terseness and harsh, asymmetrical intensity. Their grandeur flows from thought and emotion, not
from the harmonious ordering of syntax and rhythm. While hellenistic influence pushed the sacred grand style toward a terse
agonistic fierceness—Caussin's gravitas—it simultaneously encouraged an epideictic version of elevation—Caussin's maiestas.
The Longinian sublime and Hermogenes' splendor pointed to a
celebratory grandeur arousing love, wonder, and joy—a conception of grandeur earlier sketched in Brandolini and Agricola. Hellenistic influence thus both spiritualized the grand style and en-
larged its definition to encompass both fierce brevity and
epideictic passion.

The major sacred rhetorics from the late sixteenth to the early
seventeenth century also expand the consideration of affective
psychology already present in Erasmus and Melanchthon. For
the first time since Aristotle, rhetorics begin to include separate
sections on emotion, defining its nature and classifying the var-

ious types. These sections—except for Vossius's, which follows Aristotle closely—reflect Augustinian theory, explicitly distinguishing between the pity and fear of Classical rhetoric and Christian affective spirituality with its love, hope, penitence, and gratitude. Even more perhaps than Augustine, the sacred rhetorics interpret the struggle between sin and grace in affective terms: sin results not from ignorance but from wrongly directed love; God's inner presence is experienced as ardent charity; conversion is the redirection of emotion. As a result, Christian discourse is increasingly identified with the grand style, with the passionate rhetoric that can move the will and emotions. Likewise, the almost universal preference for vividness, the figures of thought, and expressivity derives from the fact that these are considered sources of emotion.

The growth of a theoretical outlook manifests itself in these discussions of emotion, which are not just recipes for evoking this or that response but studies of the theological and psychological implications of affective discourse. The orientation toward theory rather than precept evolves through the central decades around 1600 into the end of the century. Ferguson and Lamy, even more than Caussin and Flacius, stress the grounds and implications of sacred rhetoric. This shift reflects the growing theoretical sophistication of seventeenth-century thought, as well as the fact that by the middle of the century the premises of the Christian grand style were being seriously questioned by an emergent rationalism and empiricism, forcing a deeper consideration of the assumptions sustaining sacred rhetoric. Although theorizing in the rhetorics written between 1560 and 1620 tends to be sporadic and incomplete from a modern perspective, they nevertheless begin to take up questions implicit in the enterprise of fusing Christianity and rhetoric: the interplay between rhetoric and history, the necessarily metaphorical nature of supernatural signifiers, the rhetorical implications of the ancient dilemma, the relation between grace and art. Not until Ferguson does one have a text devoted to the exploration of these issues, but Ferguson's ideas are all present in earlier rhetorics, although in less systematic form. But this new theoretical orientation entailed that the sacred rhetorics, far more than most of their secular counterparts, were alert to the interrelations of language and reality, to the stylistic implications of theological and philosophical beliefs.

In the second half of the seventeenth century the traditions of the Christian grand style gradually faded, supplanted not by the vernacular rhetorics of the passionate plain style—for this was actually only a variant of the grand style and often amounted to the same thing in practice—but by the rise of rationalism and empiricism and their new understanding of language and emotion. In fact, protorationalist and empiricist tendencies had been present in the secular rhetorics throughout the Renaissance, but their effect on sacred texts had been slight before about 1650. Thus the Ramist tendency to divorce words from things by confining rhetoric to ornament gained strength from the scientific preoccupation with physical objects isolated from culturo-linguistic contexts. For Bacon and his successors, words possessed a natural inclination to distort reality by imposing an interpretive grid between the mind and the external world of things. Rhetoric seemed particularly suspect because it muddied objectivity with emotion; Locke thus argues, "If we would speak of things as they are, we must allow that all the art of rhetoric, besides order and clearness; all the artificial and figurative application of words eloquence hath invented, are for nothing else but to insinuate wrong ideas, move the passions, and thereby mislead the judgement; and so indeed are prefect [sic] cheats."[1] Rationalism reinforced the Lockean preference for order and clearness by denying the Aristotelian premise that all thought depends on imagination. Descartes' clear and distinct ideas are *not* images but abstractions severed from all connection with sensible phantasms. But if images block the mind's apprehension of reality, instead of being essential for it, then the ground of the Christian grand style disappears, its vividness no longer necessary to negotiate the ancient dilemma. Along with these epistemic changes, a new conception of personhood challenged the assumptions of the sacred rhetorics. In part this involved a revival of Stoicism with its distrust of

[1] John Locke, *Essay Concerning Human Understanding* 3.10.34. Quoted in K. G. Hamilton, *The Two Harmonies: Poetry and Prose in the Seventeenth Century* (Oxford, 1963), p. 33.

the emotions, in part a nominalist conception of the self as an individual personality constituted by reflexive awareness rather than by love. Stoicism and self-conscious individuality both found expression in the plain style epistle and essay, not in passionate and communal preaching. Finally, the shift from communal to private reflects the gradual switch from orality to the silent, spatial, and abstract world of print. Print culture emphasized the diagrammatic and analytic functions of language over the dialogic and affective, thus pushing traditional rhetoric into obsolescence.

The premises of the Christian grand style were incompatible with these changes in epistemology, psychology, and textuality. The Christian grand style is fundamentally oral in giving priority to the passionate, sensuous, and dramatic aspects of language. It rests on an Augustinian view of the emotions as modalities of love and therefore both part of the noetic quest leading to union with the beloved object and inseparable from spiritual life. Our emotions—our loves—unite us to God, and because passionate rhetoric awakens hope, repentance, joy, charity, and so forth, it is not, in Locke's words, a cheat but an instrument of truth and goodness. Similarly, the sacred rhetorics accept the Augustinian notion of self as love, as man's response to God's drawing. Christian selfhood is not primarily self-awareness but a communal inwardness created by the inner activity of the Spirit on a more or less generic human nature. Such activity articulates itself in the passionate figures of thought (and therefore in the grand style), connecting them with expressivity rather than ornament. Like the Augustinian view of the emotions and the self, the epistemology implicit in these rhetorics also supports the grand style. The Christianized Aristotelianism of Renaissance psychology views the interconnected functions of imagination and emotion as necessary for making the excellent object apprehensible and desirable. It follows that the drama, vividness, and metaphorical richness of sacred discourse become means for bridging the ancient dilemma. Again, trope and figure are not decorative but necessary to create the love and knowledge of supernatural reality. The belief that physical things are analogical signs of spiritual also deepens the demand for vividness: images have both a psy-

chogogic function and an ontological ground. They both carry
the mind and heart to God and manifest Him to the senses—the
only source of all human knowledge. Thus, the Christian grand
style refuses on multiple grounds to divorce words from things.
Sacred discourse becomes a mirror of inwardness, expressing the
passions of the heart; its images and tropes are analogical representations of transcendence; it makes possible the loving apprehension of a distant and invisible reality.

Although the developments in secular culture just mentioned
begin to affect the sacred rhetorics after the middle of the seventeenth century, the split between secular and sacred rhetoric is
visible considerably earlier. In general, secular rhetoric belongs to
the tradition of the plain style: the "Attic" Ciceronianism of
Bembo and Muretus, Ramism, neo-Stoic cultivation of the epistolary style, Anglican rationalism, the linguistic program of the
Royal Society. Sacred rhetoric, on the contrary, creates the Christian grand style or that medieval hybrid, the passionate plain
style. This extraordinary bifurcation of the rhetorical tradition
reflects a fundamental division in European civilization. By the
sixteenth century, the secular Renaissance is moving in the direction of autonomous reason and scientific objectivity; the religious
Renaissance, however, vigorously reaffirms dogmatic faith, affective inwardness, and sacramentalism. The early modern period is also the Age of Orthodoxy. Thus, speaking of the Reformation and Renaissance, Ernst Troeltsch writes: "they appear
very clearly as the schism of European culture into its main components, the separation of the Christian-supernatural-ascetic element from the antique, inner-worldly human element.[2] Nor
need one confine Troeltsch's remarks to the contrast between the
Protestant Reformation and the Renaissance alone. Yet the Age of
Orthodoxy is not merely a continuation of the Middle Ages.
Etienne Gilson located the break in the nominalist critique of
scholasticism, which denied that reason could demonstrate the

[2] Ernst Troeltsch, "Renaissance and Reformation," trans. Lewis Spitz, in *The Reformation: Basic Interpretations*, ed. Lewis Spitz (Lexington, Mass., 1972), p. 40. See also Paul Tillich, *A History of Christian Thought from Its Judaic and Hellenistic Origins to Existentialism*, ed. Carl E. Braaten (New York, 1967) both on Nomi-nalism and the Age of Orthodoxy.

truths of Christianity and thus destroyed the Thomist synthesis of reason and faith. More recent scholars are inclined to discredit the alleged radical implications of nominalist theology, yet the break remains, whether nominalists, humanists, Lutherans, or Papists were ultimately responsible.[3] While modern science and modern philosophy are emerging out of secular culture, religious thought in the Age of Orthodoxy, with the exception of Pascal, remains conservative and static. Ordinary histories of Christianity have a good deal of difficulty with the period between 1550 and 1650 precisely because nothing interesting seems to be happening, just the multiplication of opposing creeds. Nevertheless, the same period witnesses the flowering of an aesthetic and affective spirituality. It is the age of the great Anglican preachers and devotional poets, of Christian triumphalism in architecture and painting, of the early baroque sacred cantatas. Like Barbara Lewalski's Protestant poetics, sacred rhetoric emerges out of this reorientation of religious culture from scholastic scientia to affective devotion. As reason loses its transcendent and intuitive capacities, the potential of emotion widens and it becomes the primary arena of religious life, absorbing both the volitional and intuitive powers formerly assigned to the rational soul.[4] The Christian grand style occupies a pivotal role in the religious culture of the Renaissance because it articulates this passionate spirituality and creates a "method" that could bring man and God into a relationship based on love rather than knowledge.

★

Students of rhetoric often feel a bit defensive about their chosen field. The usual justification of rhetorical studies is that they provide a means for interpreting literature, but the nature of that assistance lies open to misunderstanding. "Rhetorical analysis" often evokes notions of interpretation by tropes and schemes: counting the number of hyberbata in Shakespeare's plays or some

---

[3] Etienne Gilson, *History of Christian Philosophy in the Middle Ages* (New York, 1955), pp. 454–98. See Obermann and Courtney in *The Pursuit of Holiness* for modern interpretations of Nominalism. The debate is clearly summarized in the opening of Steven Ozment's *The Age of Reform*.

[4] Blaise Pascal, *Pensées*, trans. A. J. Krailsheimer (London, 1966), 110.

such thing. Yet traditional rhetoric is weakest in its analysis of specific works. Identifying tropes and figures offers only limited information concerning the function of verbal structures in a specific context. The fact, for instance, that the first quatrain in the opening sonnet of *Astrophil and Stella* and the first chapter in the Gospel of John both use gradatio does not take one very far, although this may be an extreme example. The predicament of rhetoric is not unique; Renaissance poetics also seem singularly uninformative with respect to particular poems. The close reading of individual texts that we have come to expect from criticism remains alien to Renaissance habits of interpretation. On the other hand, both rhetoric and poetics deal much better with large-scale issues, like the purpose of literature, its relation to moral and spiritual life, its connection with other disciplines and ways of knowing. Rhetoric and poetics in the Renaissance are like a book about mammals. It is not much use if one wants to know something about a particular collie. For that, one is better off watching the development and habits of the dog itself. But sometimes one desires to learn about mammals, their relation to other phyla, their evolution, characteristics, and subspecies. In that case a book about mammals would be indispensable. The great merit of the early rhetorical scholarship of Croll and Jones lies in their realization that rhetoric provided a clue to the larger cultural ramifications of style rather than a terminology for analyzing individual authors.

The relationship between "historical background" and literature, to use another "far-fet" simile, is like that between the ingredients for a cake—eggs, butter, flour, sugar—and the finished cake. If one did not know anything about baking, it would be hard to predict by looking at the ingredients what sort of foodstuff would emerge from their combination and equally hard from looking at the cake to decide what the ingredients had been. Historical scholarship resembles a guessing game of the latter kind. We have the literature—the cake, in this case—and try to figure out what it is made of: perhaps Jesuit meditations with a dash of heliocentrism and some emblem books. Rhetorical theory, to continue this image, offers a recipe, a way of connecting theological, ethical, psychological, and other cultural material with literary artifacts. It does not take much scholarship to see that vividness, drama, and passion are principal features of sacred literature in the Renaissance as well as characteristics of the Christian grand style of the rhetorics. But rhetorical theory also interprets these qualities, grounding them in problems of religious epistemology; the interconnection between thought, feeling, and imagination; the decorum of biblical style; and so forth. It deals with the implications of stylistic choice.

The primary value of rhetorical studies, as of all historical scholarship, is the elimination of unnecessary error, especially the errors of a priori theorizing. The general ignorance of Renaissance rhetoric has meant that this field is littered with mistakes: Fish's confusion between rhetoric and dialectic, Croll's misidentification of the non-Ciceronian grand style as a rationalist and libertine genus tenue; the pervasive assumption, now reinforced by Derridean theory, that because Plato opposed rhetoric and philosophy they must be eternal and inevitable antagonists. The only way to dispel these Idols of the Theater is, as Bacon knew, empirical investigation, the study of what Renaissance thinkers actually said about discourse.

In eliminating error, rhetorical studies also proffer a positive interpretation of Renaissance literature. They suggest, for example, that the pervasive Renaissance tendency to "emotionalize" sacred literature, visible in the shift from the *Fowre Hymns*, let us say, to the devotional poems of Donne, Herbert, and Crashaw, rests on the revival of Augustinian psychology with its affective view of spiritual experience. They likewise provide an explanation for the development of a non-Ciceronian sacred prose—a very curious phenomenon if anti-Ciceronianism represents a rationalist reaction against humanist orthodoxy. If, however, this prose derives from the intertwined models of biblical and hellenistic grandeur found in a work like Flacius's *Clavis*, it becomes more comprehensible. A major achievement of both Renaissance rhetoric and prose was the creation of a sacred grand style—the style of Donne, Andrewes, Browne's *Urn Burial*, Taylor's *Holy Dying*, Isaac Barrow's Passion sermon, Joseph Hall's meditations, and a host of lesser known writers, like John Cosin, Samuel Ward, and Mark Frank. This style, with its passion, vividness, drama, expressive figures of thought, and density of meaning, cannot be understood as a variant of neo-Stoic or libertine prose, even though both are responses to the decline of positive theology with its attempt to create a discursive, "scientific" negotiation between things evident to us and the excellent objects of faith. Because sacred prose cannot easily be squeezed into conventional descriptions of what is often referred to as "the rise of modern prose style," descriptions generally based on secular paradigms, scholarship has tended to neglect it. It seems anomalous and devoid of a theoretical basis that could guide interpretation. The sacred rhetorics, however, open the possibility of a new history of English Renaissance prose that recognizes a distinctive Christian aesthetic as the basis for meditation, treatise, and sermon. This aesthetic does not demand denotative precision, introspective analysis, or neo-Classic urbanity but endeavors to make language traverse the ancient dilemma by lifting the emotions and imagination to the supersensible, to express and evoke the reality of divine presence through a communal and passionate inwardness, and to create a style proportioned to both the magnitude of its subject and the affectivity of spiritual life. The most characteristic features of Renaissance sacred prose (with the exception of an ineradicable taste for sound-play) derive from this endeavor: Andrewes's brevity and drama, Donne's expressivity, the use of vivid detail and paradox in Browne, Taylor's sensuous imagery, the prevalence of prosopopoeia, apostrophe, dramatization, typology, metaphor, interrogatio, and hypotyposis throughout these works. One result of this study, therefore, is to suggest a revised theoretical context for sacred prose in the English Renaissance, one which would enable a clearer understanding both of individual authors and broad patterns in the history of Renaissance prose style.

The sacred rhetorics appear to belong to the history of critical theory as well as to that of Renaissance literature. Certain broad similarities between these rhetorics and later poetics seem clear: the emphases on expressivity, passion, the sublime, and visual particularity. The question is whether there exists any evidence to link the neo-Latin texts with the vernacular poetics of the eighteenth and nineteenth centuries. We have reason to believe that the

CONCLUSION

254

rhetorical tradition remained part of the university curriculum into the late seventeenth century. What we therefore need to find is a critic schooled during the Restoration who shows signs of having been influenced by the sacred rhetorics and whose work was studied by the Romantic poets. Such a critic offers himself in the person of John Dennis. Dennis was a Cambridge man in the 1670s and, despite his severe drubbing at the hands of Pope, a favorite author for Wordsworth and Coleridge. Moreover, Dennis's advocacy of sacred poetry displays strong traces of the ideas prominent in the sacred rhetorics.

We can see this by looking briefly at Dennis's two major treatises on poetry: "The Advancement and Reformation of Modern Poetry" (1701) and "The Grounds of Criticism in Poetry" (1704). Dennis argues at length that the distinctive characteristic of poetry is not imitation but passion. "The Nature of Poetry consists in Passion; and that of the Greater Poetry in great Passion."[5] By "Greater Poetry" Dennis means the traditional grand style genres of tragedy, epic, and the greater ode. Dennis is aware that this definition allies poetry with Renaissance conceptions of sacred grandeur as primarily affective. Passion makes "the Greatness and Beauty of Poetry, as well as it does of Eloquence."[6] The enthusiastic passion of poetry, Dennis continues, requires a religious subject; for this reason, he prefers Milton and the Greek dramatists above the predominantly secular poetry of the Restoration. As in the rhetorics, the connections between sacred subject, grandeur, and passion rest on decorum, hellenistic theory, and Augustinian psychology. While in the poetic traditions of the Renaissance, decorum usually means the adequation of language to character type—king, servant, *senex*, *alazon*—Dennis reverts to the rhetorical concept of decorum as the interrelation of subject, language, and affect. By expressing "great Passions," the poet treats "a Subject with Dignity equal to its Greatness."[7] Likewise "the Ideas which [religious] Subjects afford" should be "express'd

[5] John Dennis, *The Critical Works of John Dennis*, ed. Edward Niles Hooker, 2 vols. (Baltimore, 1943), 1: 332.

[6] Ibid., 1: 211.

[7] Ibid., 1: 229.

with Passion equal to their Greatness."[8] To reinforce his claim
that sacred themes are the most appropriate subjects of passionate
grandeur, Dennis turns to the same authorities found in the rhetorics—Longinus and Hermogenes. Dennis's attachment to Longinus is well known, but the citations for Hermogenes are
perhaps more interesting. Like the rhetorics, Dennis cites
Hermogenic solemnity as evidence for his assertion that "the
strongest Enthusiastick Passions in Poetry are only justly and reasonably to be rais'd by religious Ideas." In addition, solemnity ties
together sacred passion and the grand style; its subjects—God,
great natural phenomena, and the divine virtues in man—lend
"Elevation and Gravity to a Discourse."[9]

By far the most important element in Dennis's defense of sacred passion is the Augustinian psychology that pervades the rhetorical tradition. Christianity is superior to both ancient philosophy and modern Deism because while it shares their recognition
of a struggle between man's rational and appetitive natures, it
does not try to subdue this conflict by strangling passion but by
redirecting and intensifying it. "The Christian Religion," he
writes,

exalts our Reason, by exalting the Passions. . . . it gains its End, which
is the Happiness of its Believers, in so plain, so sure, and so short a Way,
that the Way to Happiness, and the End, is but one and the same Thing,
and differs only in Degree. *Set your Affections on Things above, and not on
Things below*, says the Apostle. . . . And as the Reason rouzes and excites
the Passions, the Passions, as it were, in a fiery Vehicle, transport the
Reason above Mortality, which mounting, soars to the Heaven of Heavens, upon the Wings of those very Affections, that before repress'd the
noble Efforts that it made to ascend the Skies.[10]

This psychology both releases the passions from the imputation
of subrationality and justifies the claim that passionate discourse
is the natural and appropriate language of religion. God converts

[8] Ibid., 1: 370.
[9] Ibid., 1: 340–41.
[10] Ibid., 1: 260–61.

the soul by its passions and therefore "the Design of the True Religion and Poetry are the same."[11]

Although there are obvious differences between homiletic and poetic style, even Dennis's comments on the language of sacred grandeur show the influence of the sacred rhetorics. This is particularly evident in his demand for animated and vivid imagery. As in the rhetorics, enargia creates energia; the poet makes the absent object seem present to eye and ear and thus creates in his readers an emotional response identical to that produced by the object itself.[12] This association of vividness and passion connects poetic imagery to the ancient dilemma. "Reveal'd Religion, whether true or pretended, speaks to the Senses, brings the Wonders of another World more home to us, and so makes the Passions which it raises the greater."[13] Because deistic theology tends to operate in abstractions, it cannot arouse emotion and so cannot make the supernatural present and effective. Sacred discourse requires images to make that which is remote seem "more home to us."

It would be beyond the scope of a conclusion to trace how Dennis's notion of sacred poetry infiltrates later poetics or to analyze additional parallels between Renaissance rhetorics and subsequent criticism. Such a task would not, I think, reveal that sacred rhetoric is the hidden source of Romanticism; too many other factors influenced the development of poetic theory in the eighteenth and nineteenth centuries to render that a plausible thesis.[14] Sacred rhetoric has significance as part of the *history* of critical theory rather than as a major unacknowledged source for later writers. It represents the bridge between ancient theories of discourse and early modern criticism and in this respect is more important than a good deal of Renaissance poetics with their neo-Aristote-

---

[11] Ibid., 1: 251, 337.

[12] Ibid., 1: 218, 269, 362–63.

[13] Ibid., 1: 363–64.

[14] Walter Jackson Bate, *From Classic to Romantic: Premises of Taste in Eighteenth-Century England* (Cambridge, Mass., 1946), pp. 24, 43, 91; Meyer H. Abrams, *The Mirror and the Lamp: Romantic Theory and the Critical Tradition* (Oxford, 1953), pp. 70–99; Steven Shankman, *Pope's "Illiad": Homer in the Age of Passion*, Princeton Essays in Literature (Princeton, 1983), pp. xiii–xviii, 19–32.

lian emphasis on rules and imitation. These rhetorics embody an early attempt to adapt Classical theory to the postscholastic world, to create an aesthetic based on the new primacy of emotional experience as the means by which the soul orients itself toward a transcendent Beyond.

APPENDIX

THE SEVEN IDEAS OF HERMOGENES

SAPHENIA	*clarity*
MEGETHOS	*grandeur*
—SEMNOTES	*–solemnity*
—TRACHYTES	*–asperity*
—SPHODROTES	*–vehemence*
—LAMPROTES	*–splendor*
—AKME	*–vigor*
—PERIBOLE	*–abundance, amplification*
KALLOS	*beauty*
GORGOTES	*speed*
ETHOS	*character*
—APHELEIA	*–simplicity*
—GLYKYTES	*–sweetness*
—DRIMYTES	*–subtlety*
—EPIEIKEIA	*–modesty*
ALETHEIA	*verity, truth, sincerity*
—BARYTES	*–ironic weightiness*
DEINOTES	*gravity, decorum*

Renaissance rhetorics translated these terms in various ways and often omitted some of the less important. The following chart gives Hermogenes' terms and their equivalents in Vossius and Carbo.

HERMOGENES	VOSSIUS	CARBO
saphenia	perspicuitas	perspicuitas
megethos	magnitudo	magnitudo
—semnotes	–gravitas	–dignitas
—trachytes	–asperitas	–asperitas
—sphodrotes	–vehementia	–acrimonia
—lamprotes	–splendor	–splendor
—akme	–vigor	–vigor
—peribole	–oratio cumulata	–circumductio
kallos	pulchritudo	pulchritudo
gorgotes	concitata	celeritas
ethos	oratio morata	affecta oratio
—apheleia	–simplicitas	–simplicitas
—glykytes	–suavitas	–suavitas
—drimytes	–acrimonia	–acumen
—epieikeia	–modestia	–aequitas
aletheia	–veritas	veritas
—barytes	–gravitas	
deinotes	dicendi vis	decorum

GLOSSARY OF RHETORICAL TERMS

Adjuratio.   Appealing to one's hearers in God's name (more generally, a swearing to something by something), as in 2 Tim. 4:1–2: "I charge thee therefore before God . . . Preach the word."

Admiratio.   Exclamation of wonder and amazement.

Agon.   Battle, struggle. In rhetorical theory, agon connotes a sense of urgency, power, and purpose.

Apostrophe.   Direct address to person or thing, either present or absent.

Ars praedicandi.   Usual term for medieval arts of preaching.

Concinnitas.   Beauty and grace of style produced by smooth, flowing connection of words and clauses.

Concio (also *contio*).   In Classical Latin, a discourse held before a popular assembly but, beginning with Erasmus, the usual term for a sermon.

Copia.   Abundance or the art of saying the same thing in different ways. In the Renaissance this can either be a positive term (i.e., fecundity) or a negative one (i.e., prolixity).

Ecphrasis.   A descriptive set piece on a place, thing, person. This kind of static description was popular among writers of the Second Sophistic.

Efficacia.   Power, forcefulness. In Renaissance rhetoric it is synonymous with vis, energia, and deinotes.

Elocutio.   One of the five parts of an oration (the others being invention, distribution [organization], memory, and delivery). Elocutio deals with language and style—tropes and figures, the genera dicendi, the Theophrastean virtues (clarity, purity, appropriateness, and ornamentation). I have avoided translating this word since in modern English "elocution" suggests delivery rather than lexical properties.

Emphasis.   Suggestiveness, implying more than is stated.

Evidentia.   Vividness. In Renaissance rhetoric it is synonymous with illustratio and enargia.

Exclamatio.   Exclamation expressing emotion.

Figure of thought (figura sententiae).   A striking or powerful or unusual mode of expression, where the effect does not result from the sound or order of the words but from the "shape" of the idea. This is admittedly a difficult distinction, but easier to see from examples. "How long, O Cataline, will you abuse our patience" is a figure of thought (apostrophe, interrogatio) because you could change the words and their order and still preserve the figure (e.g., O Cataline, for how much longer will you abuse our patience?). Figures of sound (schemata verborum) depend on the sound and order of the words themselves, as in "not loathsome but lazy, not bad but bored" (alliteration, anaphora, isocolon, paramoion). If you changed "lazy" to "indolent" or switched the order of the words, the scheme would be lost. Rightly or wrongly, ancient and Renaissance rhetoric tends to associate figures of thought with power and passion, schemes of sound with ornament and artificiality.

Genera causarum.   Types of speeches, usually deliberative (political), forensic/judicial (legal), and demonstrative/epideictic (concerned with praise and blame, also all ceremonial oratory; may even include history, philosophy, and poetry). Melanchthon adds a fourth genus causarum, the genus didaskalikon or teaching oration.

Genera dicendi.   In Cicero refers to the three main styles of oratory: the plain style (genus tenue, genus humile), the middle style (genus medium, genus floridum), and the grand style (genus grave, genus grande). More broadly, genera dicendi can just mean kinds of style, not in the sense of individual stylistic traits but of broad stylistic categories, like Demetrius's four characters or Hermogenes' seven Ideas.

Hypotyposis.   All forms of vividness.

Icon.   Vivid imagery.

Imprecatio.   Curse, invoking of evil.

Interrogatio.   Questioning the audience or an imagined auditor.

Obsecratio.   Pleading, beseeching.

Officia oratoris.   In Cicero, the ends of oratory which are associated with the genera dicendi: the plain style for teaching (docere), the middle style for delighting (delectare), and the grand style for moving the emotions (movere).

Optatio.   The speaker's expression of his own longing and desire.

Prosopographia.   Description of (imaginary) persons or beings.

Prosopopoeia.   Attributing life to dead or imaginary or absent persons; attributing human qualities and speech to animals or inanimate objects.

Psychagogia.   Literally, enchanting the soul. It refers to all the non-rational persuasive or affective powers of language, especially emotional force of sound, figure, and trope.

Sermocinatio.   Imaginary dialogue (a form of prosopopoeia).

Umbratilis.   Shady. It generally refers to the protected seclusion of both the philosophic schools and the halls of declamation, in contrast to the sun and heat of the forum, the locus of agonistic oratory.

BIBLIOGRAPHY

Primary Sources*

Ad. C. Herennium: de ratione dicendi (Rhetorica ad Herennium). Trans. Harry Caplan. Loeb Classical Library. Cambridge, Mass., 1954.

AGRICOLA, Rudolph. *De inventione dialectica libri tres* [1480?]. Cologne, 1523 [*sic*]; repr. ed. Frankfurt, 1967.

ALSTED, Johann-Heinrich. *Encyclopedia.* Herborn, 1630.

—— *Orator, sex libris informatus* [1612]. 3d ed. Herborn, 1616.

—— *Rhetorica, quator libris proponens universam ornare dicendi modum* [1616]. 2d ed. N.p., 1626.

—— *Theologia prophetica, exhibens rhetoricam et politiam ecclesiasticam. acc. theologia acroamatica.* Hanover, 1622.

AQUINAS, Thomas. *Introduction to Saint Thomas Aquinas.* Ed. Anton C. Pegis. New York, 1945.

—— *Summa contra gentiles, Book Four: Salvation.* Trans. Charles J. O'Neil. Notre Dame, Ind., 1975.

ARDERNE, James. *Directions Concerning the Matter and Stile of Sermons.* London, 1671.

ARISTOPHANES. *The Frogs.* Trans. Benjamin Rogers. Loeb Classical Library. Cambridge, Mass., 1924.

ARISTOTLE. *The "Art" of Rhetoric.* Trans. John Henry Freese. Loeb Classical Library. Cambridge, Mass., 1975.

—— *The Complete Works of Aristotle: The Revised Oxford Translation.* 2 vols. Ed. Jonathan Barnes. Bollingen Series 71:2. Princeton, 1984.

ARRIAGA, Pablo Jose de, S.J. *Rhetoris Christiani partes septem.* Lyons, 1619.

AUGUSTINE, Aurelius. *The City of God.* Ed. David Knowles O.S.B. Trans. Henry Bettenson. London, 1967.

—— *The Confessions of St. Augustine.* Trans. Rex Warner. New York, 1963.

—— *On Christian Doctrine.* Trans. D. W. Robertson. Indianapolis, 1958.

BACON, Francis. *A Selection of His Works.* Ed. Sidney Warhaft. New York, 1965.

—— *The Works of Francis Bacon.* 7 vols. London, 1826.

---

* Where relevant, the date of the first edition is given in brackets following the title.

(265)

BARTON, John. *The Art of Rhetorick, Concisely and Compleatly Handled, Exemplified Out of Holy Writ.* London, 1634.

BAXTER, Richard. *Gildas Salvianus: or the Reformed Pastor* [1656]. Ed. John T. Wilkinson. London, 1939.

BENSON, Thomas, Joseph MILLER, and Michael PROSSER, eds. *Readings in Medieval Rhetoric.* Bloomington, 1973.

BERNARD, Richard. *The Faithful Shepherd.* Rev. ed. London, 1621.

BORROMEO, Frederico. *De sacris nostrorum temporum oratoribus libri quinque.* Milan, 1632.

BRANDOLINI, Lippo (Aurelio). *De ratione scribendi libri tres* [1549]. London, 1573.

BROWNE, Thomas. *The Prose of Sir Thomas Browne.* Ed. Norman J. Endicott. New York, 1967.

BURNET, Gilbert. *A Discourse of the Pastoral Care.* London, 1692.

BUTLER, Charles. *Oratoriae libri duo.* Oxford, 1629.

—— *Rhetoricae libri duo.* Oxford, 1597.

CAMERARIUS, Joachim. *Elementa rhetoricae* [1540]. Basel, 1545.

CARBO, Ludovicus. *Divinus orator, vel de rhetorica divina libri septem.* Venice, 1595.

CAUSSIN, Nicholas. *De eloquentia sacra et humana, libri XVI* [1617?]. 3d ed. Paris, 1630.

CHAPPELL, William. *The Preacher, or the Art and Method of Preaching.* London, 1656.

CHARLETON, Walter. *Natural History of the Passions.* London, 1674.

CHEMNITZ, Christian. *Brevis instructio futuri ministri ecclesiae in Academia Jenensi antehac publice praelecta.* 2d ed. Jena, 1660.

CICERO, Marcus Tullius. *De finibus.* Trans. H. Rackham. Loeb Classical Library. London, 1914.

—— *De inventione.* Trans. H. M. Hubbell. Loeb Classical Library. Cambridge, Mass., 1949.

—— *De officiis.* Trans. Walter Miller. Loeb Classical Library. London, 1913.

—— *De optimo genere oratorum.* Trans. H. M. Hubbell. Loeb Classical Library. Cambridge, Mass., 1960.

—— *De oratore.* 2 vols. Trans. E. W. Sutton and H. Rackham. Loeb Classical Library. Cambridge, Mass., 1942.

—— *De partitione oratoria.* Trans. H. Rackham. Loeb Classical Library. Cambridge, Mass., 1942.

—— *Orator, Brutus,* rev. ed. Trans. H. M. Hubbell and G. L. Hendrickson. Loeb Classical Library. Cambridge, Mass., 1971.

—— *Pro Archia*. Trans. N. H. Watts. Loeb Classical Library. Cambridge, Mass., 1923.

CLARKE, John. *Holy Oyle for the Lampes of the Sanctuarie: or Scripture-phrases Alphabetically Disposed*. London, 1630.

COFFETEAU, Nicholas. *A Table of Humane Passions, With their Causes and Effects*. Trans. E. Grimeston. London, 1621.

DEMETRIUS. *On Style*. Trans. W. Rhys Roberts. Loeb Classical Library. Cambridge, Mass., 1927.

DENNIS, John. *The Critical Works of John Dennis*. 2 vols. Ed. Edward Niles Hooker. Baltimore, 1943.

[DIETRICH, Viet]. *Ratio brevis sacrarum concionum tractandarum*. Ulm, 1535. Rpr. in *De arte concionandi ut breves, ita doctae et piae*. London, 1570.

DIOGENES LAERTIUS. *Lives of the Eminent Philosophers*. 2 vols. Trans. R. D. Hicks. Loeb Classical Library. Cambridge, Mass., 1959.

DIONYSIUS OF HALICARNASSUS. *The Critical Essays I*. Trans. Stephen Usher. Loeb Classical Library. Cambridge, Mass., 1974.

—— *On Literary Composition*. Trans. W. Rhys Roberts. London, 1910.

DONNE, John. *Devotions Upon Emergent Occasions*. Ann Arbor, 1959.

—— *The Sermons of John Donne*. 10 vols. Ed. Evelyn M. Simpson and George R. Potter. Berkeley, 1953–1962.

DUGARD, William. *Rhetorices elementa*. London, 1648. Repr. Menston, England, 1972.

ERASMUS, Desiderius. *Ciceronianus; or A Dialogue on the Best Style of Speaking* [1517]. Trans. Izora Scott. New York, 1908. Repr. New York, 1972.

—— *Ecclesiastes sive concionator evangelicus* [1535] in vol. 5 of *Opera omnia emendatiora et auctiora*. Ed. J. LeClerc. 10 vols. Leiden, 1703–1706. Repr. London, 1962.

—— *Erasmus on His Times: A Shortened Version of the Adages of Erasmus*. Trans. Margaret Mann Phillips. Cambridge, 1967.

—— *On Copia of Words and Ideas*. Trans. Donald B. King and H. David Rix. Milwaukee, 1963.

ERNESTI, Johann. *Lexicon technologiae graecorum rhetoricae*. Leipzig, 1795.

—— *Lexicon technologiae latinorum rhetoricae*. Leipzig, 1797.

ESTELLA, Diego de. *De modo concionandi liber et explanatio in psalm. CXXXVI. Super flumina Babylonis* [1576]. Repr. in *Ecclesiasticae rhetoricae*. Verona, 1732.

—— *Modo de predicar y Modus concionandi*. 2 vols. Ed. Pió Sagüés Azcona. Madrid, 1951.

FARNABY, Thomas. *Index rhetoricus scholis et institutioni tenerioris aetatis accomodatus, Editio altera emendatior & locupletior.* London, 1625.

FÉNELON, François. *Fénelon's Dialogues on Eloquence* [1717]. Trans. Wilbur Samuel Howell. Princeton, 1951.

FENNER, William. *A Treatise of the Affections; or The Souls Pulse.* London, 1650.

FERGUSON, Robert. *The Interest of Reason in Religion; with the Import & Use of Scripture Metaphors.* London, 1675.

FLACIUS ILLYRICUS, Matthias. *Clavis Scripturae Sacrae, seu de sermone sacrarum literarum, in duas partes divisae* [1562]. Leipzig, 1695.

FRANCIS DE SALES. *On the Preacher and Preaching* [1637]. Trans. John K. Ryan. Chicago, 1964.

FROMONDUS [FROIDMONT], Libertus. *Philosophiae Christianae de anima libri quator.* Louvain, 1649.

GLANVILLE, Joseph. *An Essay Concerning Preaching: Written for the Direction of a Young Divine and Useful also for the People, in order to Profitable Hearing.* London, 1678.

GLASSIUS, Salomon. *Philologia sacra liber quintus, qua rhetorica sacra comprensa.* Frankfurt, 1653.

—— *Philologia sacra qua totius SS. Veteris et Novi Testamenti Scripturae tum stylus et literatura, tum sensus et genuinae interpretationis ratio et doctrina libris quinque expenditur ac traditur* [1623]. Leipzig, 1705.

GRANADA, Luis de. *Ecclesiasticae rhetoricae, sive, de ratione concionandi, libri sex, denuo editi, ac diligenter emendati* [1576?]. Cologne, 1582.

—— *Ecclesiasticae rhetoricae.* . . . Repr. in *Ecclesiasticae rhetoricae.* Verona, 1732.

HARVEY, Gabriel. *Ciceronianus* [1577]. Ed. Harold Wilson. Trans. Clarence Forbes. University of Nebraska Studies. Studies in the Humanities 4 (1975): 1–146.

HEMMINGSEN, Niel. *The Preacher or Method of Preaching.* Trans. John Horsfall. London, 1574.

HEPINUS, Joannis. *De sacris concionibus compendiaria formula.* Basel, 1540. Repr. in *De arte concionandi formulae ut breves, ita doctae et piae.* London, 1570.

HERBERT, George. *The Country Parson, The Temple.* Ed. John N. Wall, Jr. Classics of Western Spirituality. New York, 1981.

HERMOGENES. *Opera omnia.* Ed. Hugo Rabe. Leipzig, 1913.

HIERON, Samuel. "The Dignitie of Preaching." London, 1615.

—— "The Preacher's Plea." *All the Sermons of Samuel Hieron.* London, 1614.

HOOKER, Richard. *The Works of Mr. Richard Hooker.* 7th ed. 3 vols. Ed. John Keeble. Oxford, 1888. Repr. New York, 1970.

HULSEMANNUS, Johann. *Methodus concionandi, auctior edita.* Wittenberg, 1657.

HUMBERT OF ROMANS, O.P. *Treatise on Preaching.* Trans. the Dominican Students, Province of St. Joseph. Ed. Walter M. Conlon, O.P. Westminster, Md., 1951.

HYDE, Thomas. *Catalogus impressorum librorum bibliothecae Bodleianae in Academia Oxoniensi.* Oxford, 1674.

HYPERIUS, Andreas. *The Practis of Preaching.* Trans. John Ludham. London, 1577.

ISOCRATES. *Isocrates.* 4 vols. Trans. George Norlin. Loeb Classical Library. Cambridge, Mass., 1962.

JAMES, Thomas. *Catalogus universalis librorum in bibliotheca Bodleiana.* Oxford, 1620.

KECKERMANN, Bartholomew. *Rhetoricae ecclesiasticae, sive artis formandi et habendi conciones sacras* [1600]. In *Opera omnia quae extant.* 2 vols. Geneva, 1614.

—— *Rhetoricae ecclesiasticae, sive artis formandi et habendi conciones sacras, libri duo.* Hanover, 1616.

—— *Systema physicum septem libris adornatum.* In *Opera omnia quae extant.* 2 vols. Geneva, 1614.

—— *Systema rhetoricae in quo artis praecepta plene et methodice traduntur* [1606]. In *Opera omnia quae extant.* 2 vols. Geneva, 1614.

[LAMY, Bernard]. *The Art of Speaking: Written in French by Messieurs du Port Royal: In Pursuance of a former Treatise, Intuitled "The Art of Thinking"* [1675]. London, 1676.

LONGINUS. *On the Sublime.* Trans. W. Hamilton Fyfe. Loeb Classical Library. Cambridge, Mass., 1927.

—— *On the Sublime.* Ed. Donald A. Russell. Oxford, 1964.

LUKIN, Henry. *An Introduction to the Holy Scripture, Containing the several Tropes, Figures, Properties of Speech used therein; with other Observations necessary for the right Understanding thereof.* Preface by John Owen. London, 1669.

LULLIUS [LULLE], Antonio. *De oratione libri vii, quibus non modo Hermogenes ipse totus, verum etiam quisquid fere a reliquis Graecis ac Latinis de arte dicendi traditum est, suis locis aptissime explicatur.* Basel, 1558.

MELANCHTHON, Philip. *De modo et arte concionandi* [1537–1539]. In *Supplementa Melanchthoniana* 5.2. Ed. Paul Drews and Ferdinand Cohrs. Leipzig, 1929. Repr. Frankfurt, 1968.

MELANCHTHON, Philip. "De officiis concionatoris" [1529]. In *Supplementa Melanchthoniana* 5.2. Ed. Paul Drews and Ferdinand Cohrs. Leipzig, 1929. Repr. Frankfurt, 1968.

—— "De ratione concionandi" [1552]. In *Supplementa Melanchthoniana* 5.2. Ed. Paul Drews and Ferdinand Cohrs. Leipzig, 1929. Repr. Frankfurt, 1968.

—— *Elementorum rhetorices libri duo* [1519]. In volume 13 of *Opera quae supersunt omnia*. 28 vols. Ed. Carolus Gottlieb Bretschneider. Brunswick and Halle, 1834–1860.

—— *Liber de anima* [1540]. In volume 13 of *Opera quae supersunt omnia*. 28 vols. Ed. Carolus Gottlieb Bretschneider. Brunswick and Halle, 1834–1860.

—— *Loci communes theologici.* Ed. Wilhelm Pauck. Trans. Lowell J. Satre. In *Melanchthon and Bucer*. The Library of Christian Classics 19. Philadelphia, 1969.

—— *Quomodo concionator novitius concionem suam informare debeat* [1531–1536]. In *Supplementa Melanchthoniana* 5.2. Ed. Paul Drews and Ferdinand Cohrs. Leipzig, 1929. Repr. Frankfurt, 1968.

MILTON, John. *A Treatise on Christian Doctrine*. 2 vols. Trans. Charles R. Sumner. Boston, 1825.

MOSLEY, Nicholas. *Psychosophia, or natural and divine contemplations of the passions & faculties of the Soul of Man*. London, 1653.

MURPHY, James J. *Three Medieval Rhetorical Arts*. Berkeley, 1971.

NASHE, Thomas. *Christ's Teares over Ierusalem* [1593]. Repr. in vol. 2 of *The Works of Thomas Nashe*. 5 vols. Ed. Ronald McKerrow. London, 1904–1910.

NAZIANZEN, Gregory. *Select Orations of Saint Gregory Nazianzen*. Trans. Charles Browne and James E. Swallow. A Select Library of Nicene and Post-Nicene Fathers of the Christian Church. Vol. 2, second series. Grand Rapids, Mich., 1978.

Officium concionatoris [1567]. Cambridge, 1655.

PANGRATIUS, M. Andrea. *Methodus concionandi* [1571]. Wittenburg, 1594.

PASCAL, Blaise. *Pensées*. Trans. A. J. Krailsheimer. London, 1966.

PERKINS, William. *The Workes of that Famous and Worthie Minister of Christ, in the University of Cambridge, M. William Perkins*. 3 vols. Cambridge, 1609.

PHILODEMUS. *The Rhetorica of Philodemus*. Ed. and trans. H. M. Hubbell. *Transactions of the Connecticut Academy of Arts and Sciences* 23 (1920).

PHILOSTRATUS. *The Life of Apollonius of Tyana*. 2 vols. Trans. F. C. Conybeare. Loeb Classical Library. London, 1912.

PLATO. *The Collected Dialogues*. Ed. Edith Hamilton and Huntington Cairns. Bollingen Series 71. Princeton, 1961.

PRIDEAUX, John. *Sacred Eloquence: Or, the Art of Rhetorick, As it is layd down in Scripture* [1657]. London, 1659.

QUINTILIAN. *Institutio Oratoria*. 4 vols. Trans. H. E. Butler. Loeb Classical Library. Cambridge, Mass., 1920.

RAPIN, Rene. *Reflections on Eloquence in General; and particularly on that of the Barr and Pulpit*. Repr. in Vol. 2 of *The Whole Critical Works of Monsieur Rapin*. 2 vols. London, 1706.

REUCHLIN, Joannis. *Liber congestorum de arte praedicandi* [1504]. Repr. in *De arte concionandi formulae ut breves, ita doctae et piae*. London, 1570.

REYNOLDS, Edward. *A Treatise of the Passions and Faculties of the Soul of Man, With the Severall Dignities and Corruptions thereunto belonging*. London, 1650.

SENAULT, Jean Francois. *The Use of Passions*. Trans. Henry, Earle of Monmouth. London, 1671.

SENECA. *Ad Lucilium epistulae morales*. 2 vols. Trans. Richard Gummere. Loeb Classical Library. Cambridge, Mass., 1953.

SENECA THE ELDER. *Declamations*. 2 vols. Trans. M. Winterbottom. Loeb Classical Library. Cambridge, Mass., 1974.

SIDNEY, Sir Philip. *An Apologie for Poetrie. Elizabethan Critical Essays*. 2 vols. Ed. G. Gregory Smith. London, 1904.

SMITH, John. *The Mysterie of Rhetorique Unvail'd*. London, 1657.

SOAREZ, Cyprianus. *De arte rhetorica, libri tres, ex Aristotle, Cicerone, et Quinctiliano praecipue deprompti* [1557]. Verona, 1589.

SOHNIUS, Georgius. *Tractatus de interpretatione ecclesiastica*. Bound with Bartholomew Keckermann, *Rhetoricae ecclesiasticae, sive artis formandi et habendi conciones sacras, libri duo*. Hanover, 1616.

SOUTH, Robert. *Sermons Preached upon Several Occasions*. 4 vols. Philadelphia, 1845.

STREBAEUS, Iacobus Lodoicus. *De verborum electione et collocatione oratoria, ad D. Ioannem Venatorem Cardinalem libri duo* [1538]. Basel, 1539.

STURM, Joannis. *De imitatione oratoria libri tres, cum scholis eiusdem authoris, antea nunquam in lucem editi*. Strassburg, 1574.

——— *De universa ratione elocutionis rhetoricae, libri IV* [1575]. Strassburg, 1576.

SUAREZ, Francisco, S.J. *Opera omnia*. 23 vols. Paris, 1856–1878.

SUTCLIFFE, Matthew. *De recta studij theologici ratione, liber unus*. London, 1602.

272   BIBLIOGRAPHY

TACITUS. *Dialogus de oratoribus.* Ed. Charles Edwin Bennett. New Rochelle, N.Y., 1983.

TALON, Omer. *Rhetorica e P. Rami . . . praelectionibus observata* [1548]. London, 1636.

TERTULLIAN. *De anima.* Ed. J. H. Waszink. Amsterdam, 1947.

TESMARUS, Joannis. *Exercitationum rhetoricarum libri viii* [1621]. Amsterdam, 1657.

THORNE, William. *Ducente deo. Willelmi Thorni Tullius seu Rhetor in tria stromata divisus.* Oxford, 1592.

TRAPEZUNTIUS, George (George of Trebizond). *Georgii Trapezuntii rhetoricorum libri V* [*c.* 1470]. Paris, 1538.

URSINUS, Johann-Henricus. *Ecclesiastes, sive de sacris concionibus libri tres.* Frankfurt, 1659.

VALADES, Didacus. *Rhetorica Christiana ad concionandi, et orandi usum accommodata* [1574]. Perugia, 1579.

VALIERO, Agostino. *De ecclesiastica rhetorica libri tres* [1575]. Repr. in *Ecclesiasticae rhetoricae.* Verona, 1732.

VICARS, Thomas. *Cheiragogia, Manductio ad artem rhetoricam ante paucos annos in privatum quorundam Scholarium usum concinnata* [1619]. London, 1628.

VIVES, Juan Luis. *De anima et vita.* Basel, 1538. Repr. Turin, 1959.

—— *De ratione dicendi* [1533]. In volume 2 of *Joannis Ludovici Vivis Valentini opera omnia.* 8 vols. Valencia, 1782–1790. Repr. London, 1964.

VOSSIUS, Gerardus. *Gerardi Joannis Vossi commentariorum rhetoricorum, sive oratorium institutionum libri sex* [1606]. Leiden, 1643. Repr. Kronberg, 1974.

—— *Rhetorices contractae, sive partitionum oratoriarum libri quinque.* Oxford, 1631.

[WALKER, Obadiah]. *Some Instructions concerning the Art of Oratory, Collected for the use of a Friend, a Young Student* [1659]. Oxford, 1682.

WARD, Samuel. *A Collection of Such Sermons and Treatises as Have Been Written and Published by Samuel Ward.* London, 1636.

WILKINS, John. *Ecclesiastes; or a Discourse concerning the gift of preaching.* London, 1646.

WRIGHT, Thomas. *The Passions of the Minde in Generall. In Six Bookes.* London, 1630.

Secondary Sources

ABBOTT, Don Paul. "The Renaissance." *The Present State of Scholarship in Historical and Contemporary Rhetoric.* Ed. Winifred B. Horner. Columbia, Mo., pp. 74–100.

ABRAMS, Meyer H. *The Mirror and the Lamp: Romantic Theory and the Critical Tradition.* Oxford, 1953.

—— *Natural Supernaturalism: Tradition and Revolution in Romantic Literature.* New York, 1971.

ADOLPH, Robert. *The Rise of Modern Prose Style.* Cambridge, Mass., 1968.

ARNIM, Hans von. *Leben und Werke des Dio von Prusa.* Berlin, 1898.

AUERBACH, Erich. *Literary Language and Its Public in Late Latin Antiquity and in the Middle Ages.* Trans. Ralph Manheim. Bollingen Series 74. New York, 1965.

BALDWIN, T. W. *William Shakespeare's Small Latine & Lesse Greeke.* 2 vols. Urbana, 1944.

BARFIELD, Owen. *Saving the Appearances: A Study in Idolatry.* New York, n.d.

BATE, Walter Jackson. *From Classic to Romantic: Premises of Taste in Eighteenth-Century England.* Cambridge, Mass., 1946.

BAXANDALL, Michael. *Giotto and the Orators: Humanist Observers of Painting in Italy and the Discovery of Pictorial Composition.* Oxford, 1971.

BAYLEY, Peter. *French Pulpit Oratory, 1598–1650.* Cambridge, 1980.

BONNER, Stanley F. "Dionysius of Halicarnassus and the Peripatetic Mean of Style." *Classical Philology* 33 (1938): 257–66.

—— *The Literary Treatises of Dionysius of Halicarnassus: A Study in the Development of Critical Method.* Cambridge, 1939.

BOUWSMA, William. "The Two Faces of Humanism. Stoicism and Augustinianism in Renaissance Thought." *Itinerarium Italicum: The Profile of the Italian Renaissance in the Mirror of Its European Transformations.* Ed. Heiko A. Oberman with Thomas Brady, Jr., 3–60. Leiden, 1975.

BOZELL, Ruth. "English Preachers of the Seventeenth Century on the Art of Preaching." Ph.D. diss., Cornell University, 1939.

BREEN, Quirinus. *Christianity and Humanism: Studies in the History of Ideas.* Ed. Nelson Peter Ross. Grand Rapids, Mich., 1968.

BROWN, Peter. *Augustine of Hippo: A Biography.* Berkeley, 1967.

BRUYNE, Edgar de. *The Aesthetics of the Middle Ages.* Trans. Eileen B. Hennessy. New York, 1969.

BUNDY, Murray W. " 'Invention' and 'Imagination' in the Renaissance." *JEGP* 29 (1930): 535–45.

—— *The Theory of Imagination in Classical and Mediaeval Thought.* University of Illinois Studies in Language and Literature 12 (1927): 183–472.

BURGESS, Theodore. *Epideictic Literature.* Chicago, 1902.

CAPLAN, Harry. *Of Eloquence: Studies in Ancient and Medieval Rhetoric.* Ed. Anne King and Helen North. Ithaca, 1970.

CAPLAN, Harry, and Henry H. KING, "Latin Tractates on Preaching: A Book-list." *Harvard Theological Review* 42 (1949): 185–206.

—— "Pulpit Eloquence: A List of Doctrinal and Historical Studies in English." *Speech Monographs* 22 (1955): 1–52.

CHASE, J. Richard. "The Classical Conception of Epideictic." *Quarterly Journal of Speech* 47 (1961): 293–300.

COGAN, Marc. "Rudolphus Agricola and the Semantic Revolutions of the History of Invention." *Rhetorica* 2 (1984): 163–94.

COHEN, Murray. *Sensible Words: Linguistic Practice in England, 1640–1785.* Baltimore, 1977.

COLISH, Marcia. *The Mirror of Language: A Study in the Medieval Theory of Knowledge.* New Haven, 1968.

CONNORS, Joseph, S.V.D. "Homiletic Theory in the Late Sixteenth Century." *The American Ecclesiastical Review* 138 (1958): 316–32.

COSTELLO, William, S.J. *The Scholastic Curriculum at Early Seventeenth-Century Cambridge.* Cambridge, Mass., 1958.

COURTENAY, William J. "Nominalism and Late Medieval Religion." *The Pursuit of Holiness in Late Medieval and Renaissance Religion.* Ed. Charles Trinkaus with Heiko A. Oberman, 26–59. Leiden, 1974.

CREWE, Jonathan V. *Unredeemed Rhetoric: Thomas Nashe and the Scandal of Authorship.* Baltimore, 1982.

CROLL, Morris. *"Attic" and Baroque Prose Style: Essays by Morris Croll.* Ed. J. Max Patrick and R. O. Evans with John M. Wallace. Princeton, 1966.

CUNNINGHAM, J. V. *The Collected Essays of J. V. Cunningham.* Chicago, 1976.

CURTIS, Mark H. "Library Catalogues and Tudor Oxford and Cambridge." *Studies in the Renaissance* 5 (1958): 111–20.

CURTIUS, Ernst Robert. *European Literature and the Latin Middle Ages.* Trans. Willard R. Trask. Bollingen Series 36. Princeton, 1973.

DANIELLS, Roy. "English Baroque and Deliberate Obscurity." *Journal of Aesthetics and Art Criticism* 5 (1948): 115–21.

DAVIE, Donald. "The Rhetoric of Emotion." *The Poet in the Imaginary Museum: Essays of Two Decades,* 242–48. Manchester, 1977.

DOCKHORN, Klaus. "Rhetorica movet: Protestantischer Humanismus und karolingische Renaissance." *Rhetorik; Beitrage zu ihrer Geschichte in Deutschland vom 16.–20. Jahrhundert.* Ed. Helmut Schanze, 17–42. Frankfurt, 1974.

DUTTON, Marsha L. "The Cistercian Source: Aelred, Bonaventure, and Ignatius." *Goad and Nail: Studies in Medieval Cistercian History X.* Ed. Rozanne Elder, 151–78. Cistercian Studies 84. Kalamazoo, 1985.

EHNINGER, Douglas. "Bernard Lamy's *L'art de Parler*: A Critical Analysis." *Quarterly Journal of Speech* 32 (1946): 429–34.

ELDER, Rozanne. "William of St. Thierry: Rational and Affective Spirituality." *The Spirituality of Western Christendom*, 85–105. Kalamazoo, 1976.

ELLEDGE, Scott. "The Background and Development of English Criticism of the Theories of Generality and Particularity." *PMLA* 62 (1947): 147–82.

FERRY, Anne. *The "Inward" Language: Sonnets of Wyatt, Sidney, Shakespeare, Donne.* Chicago, 1983.

FISH, Stanley E. *Self-Consuming Artifacts: The Experience of Seventeenth-Century Literature.* Berkeley, 1972.

FLETCHER, Harris. *The Intellectual Development of John Milton.* 2 vols. Urbana, 1956–1961.

FORTENBAUGH, W. W. *Aristotle on Emotion.* New York, 1975.

FRYE, Northrop. *Anatomy of Criticism.* Princeton, 1957.

FUMAROLI, Marc. *L'Age de l'éloquence: Rhétorique et "res literaria" de la Renaissance au seuil de l'époque classique.* Geneva, 1980.

—— "Rhetoric, Politics, and Society: From Italian Ciceronianism to French Classicism." *Renaissance Eloquence: Studies in the Theory and Practice of Renaissance Rhetoric.* Ed. James J. Murphy, 253–73. Berkeley, 1983.

GARDINER, H. M., Ruth METCALF, and John BEEBE-CENTER. *Feeling and Emotion: A History of Theories.* New York, 1937.

GERBAL, François. *Bernard Lamy (1640–1715): Etude biographique et bibliographique.* Le Mouvement des Idees au XVIIᵉ Siècle. Paris, 1964.

GILSON, Etienne. *The Christian Philosophy of St. Thomas Aquinas.* Trans. L. K. Shook, C.S.B. New York, 1956.

—— *History of Christian Philosophy in the Middle Ages.* New York, 1955.

GOMBRICH, E. H. *Symbolic Images: Studies in the Art of the Renaissance II.* Oxford, 1972.

GRASSI, Ernesto. *Rhetoric as Philosophy: The Humanist Tradition.* University Park, Pa., 1980.

GRAY, Hanna H. "Renaissance Humanism: The Pursuit of Eloquence." *Renaissance Essays.* Ed. Paul Oskar Kristeller and Philip P. Wiener, 199–216. New York, 1968.

GREENE, Thomas. *Light in Troy.* New Haven, 1982.

GRUBE, G.M.A. *A Greek Critic: Demetrius on Style.* Toronto, 1961.

HALLER, William. *The Rise of Puritanism or, the Way to the New Jerusalem as Set Forth in Pulpit and Press from Thomas Cartwright to John Lilburne and John Milton, 1570–1643.* New York, 1937.

HAMILTON, K. G. *The Two Harmonies: Poetry and Prose in the Seventeenth Century.* Oxford, 1963.

HARDISON, O. B. *The Enduring Monument: A Study of the Idea of Praise in Renaissance Literary Theory and Practice.* Chapel Hill, 1962.

HARVEY, E. Ruth. *The Inward Wits: Psychological Theory in the Middle Ages and the Renaissance.* Warburg Institute Surveys VI. London, 1975.

HATHAWAY, Baxter. *The Age of Criticism: The Late Renaissance in Italy.* Ithaca, 1962.

HELMS, Lorraine. "Popular and Scholastic Styles: The London Playhouses 1599–1609." Ph.D. diss., Stanford University, 1986.

HENDRICKSON, G. L. "The Origin and Meaning of the Ancient Characters of Style." *AJP* 26 (1905): 249–90.

—— "The Peripatetic Mean of Style and the Three Stylistic Characters." *AJP* 25 (1904): 125–46.

HOWELL, A. C. "*Res et Verba*: Words and Things." *Seventeenth Century Prose: Modern Essays in Criticism.* Ed. Stanley Fish, 187–99. New York, 1971.

HOWELL, Wilbur Samuel. *Logic and Rhetoric in England, 1500–1700.* Princeton, 1956.

HUNT, John Scott. "Sir Philip Sidney and the Psychology of the Imagination." Ph.D. diss., Stanford University, 1984.

IJSSELING, Samuel. *Rhetoric and Philosophy in Conflict: An Historical Survey.* Trans. Paul Dunphy. The Hague, 1976.

JENNINGS, Margaret, C.S.J. "The *Ars componendi sermones* of Ranulph Hidgen," *Medieval Eloquence: Studies in the Theory and Practice of Medieval Rhetoric.* Ed. J. J. Murphy, 112–26. Berkeley, 1978.

JONES, Richard Foster. "The Attack on Pulpit Eloquence in the Restoration: An Episode in the Development of the Neo-Classical Standard for Prose." *The Seventeenth Century: Studies in the History of English Thought and Literature from Bacon to Pope,* 111–42. Stanford, 1951.

—— "The Moral Sense of Simplicity." *Studies in Honor of Fredrick W. Shipley.* Washington University Studies, N.S. 14 (1942): 265–88.

—— "Science and English Prose Style in the Third Quarter of the Seventeenth Century." *The Seventeenth Century: Studies in the History of English Thought and Literature from Bacon to Pope,* 75–110. Stanford, 1951.

—— "Science and Language in England of the Mid-Seventeenth Century." *The Seventeenth Century: Studies in the History of English Thought and Literature from Bacon to Pope,* 143–60. Stanford, 1951.

KENNEDY, George. *The Art of Persuasion in Greece.* Princeton, 1963.

—— *The Art of Rhetoric in the Roman World, 300 B.C.–A.D. 300.* Princeton, 1972.

—— *Classical Rhetoric and its Christian and Secular Tradition from Ancient to Modern Times.* Chapel Hill, 1980.

—— "Theophrastus and Stylistic Distinctions." *Harvard Studies in Classical Philology* 62 (1957): 93–104.

KNOTT, John R., Jr. *The Sword of the Spirit: Puritan Responses to the Bible.* Chicago, 1980.

KOLVE, V. A. *Chaucer and the Imagery of Narrative: The First Five Canterbury Tales.* Stanford, 1984.

KRISTELLER, Paul Oskar. "Augustine and the Early Renaissance." *Review of Religion* 8 (1944): 338–58.

—— *Renaissance Thought and its Sources.* Ed. Michael Mooney. New York, 1979.

KUSTAS, George L. "The Function and Evolution of Byzantine Rhetoric." *Viator* 1 (1970): 55–73.

—— *Studies in Byzantine Rhetoric.* Analecta Vladtadon 17. Thessalonica, 1973.

LANHAM, Richard A. *The Motives of Eloquence: Literary Rhetoric in the Renaissance.* New Haven, 1976.

LEEMAN, A. D. *Orationis Ratio: The Stylistic Theories and Practice of the Roman Orators, Historians, and Philosophers.* 2 vols. Amsterdam, 1963.

LEVI, Anthony, S.J. *French Moralists: The Theory of the Passions: 1585 to 1649.* Oxford, 1964.

LEWALSKI, Barbara Kiefer. *Protestant Poetics and the Seventeenth-Century Religious Lyric.* Princeton, 1979.

MANNIS, Alastair J. *Medieval Theory of Authorship: Scholastic Literary Attitudes in the Later Middle Ages.* London, 1984.

MARROU, Henri. *Saint Augustin et la fin de la culture antique.* Paris, 1938.

MATTIS, Norman. "Robert South." *Quarterly Journal of Speech* 15 (1929): 537–60.

McKEON, Richard. "Rhetoric in the Middle Ages." *Speculum* 17 (1942): 1–33.

McMANAMON, John M., S.J. "Innovation in Early Humanist Rhetoric: The Oratory of Pier Paolo Vergerio the Elder." *Rinascimento* 22 (1982): 3–32.

—— "Renaissance Preaching; Theory and Practice: A Holy Thursday Sermon of Aurelio Brandolini." *Viator* 10 (1980): 355–73.

MILLER, Perry. *The New England Mind: The Seventeenth Century.* New York, 1939. Repr. Boston, 1965.

MILNE, Marjorie Josephine. "A Study in Alcidamas and his Relation to Contemporary Sophistic." Ph.D. diss., Bryn Mawr College, 1924.

MOHRMANN, Gerald. "Oratorical Delivery and Other Problems in Current Scholarship on English Renaissance Rhetoric." *Renaissance Eloquence: Studies in the Theory and Practice of Renaissance Rhetoric.* Ed. James J. Murphy, 56–83. Berkeley, 1983.

MONFASANI, John. "The Byzantine Rhetorical Tradition and the Renaissance." *Renaissance Eloquence: Studies in the Theory and Practice of Renaissance Rhetoric.* Ed. James J. Murphy, 174–87. Berkeley, 1983.

—— *George of Trebizond: A Biography and a Study of His Rhetoric and Logic.* Leiden, 1976.

MONK, Samuel H. *The Sublime: A Study of Critical Theories in XVIII-Century England.* New York, 1935.

MORRIS, David B. *The Religious Sublime: Christian Poetry and Critical Tradition in Eighteenth-Century England.* Lexington, Ky., 1972.

MURPHY, James J. *Renaissance Rhetoric: A Short-Title Catalogue.* Garland Reference Library of the Humanities 237. New York, 1981.

—— *Rhetoric in the Middle Ages: A History of Rhetorical Theory from Saint Augustine to the Renaissance.* Berkeley, 1974.

—— ed. *Medieval Eloquence: Studies in the Theory and Practice of Medieval Rhetoric.* Berkeley, 1978.

NORDEN, Eduard. *Die antike Kunstprosa vom VI. Jahrhundert v. Chr. bis in die Zeit der Renaisssance.* 2 vols. Leipzig, 1898.

NYGREN, Anders. *Agape and Eros: The History of the Christian Idea of Love,* 2 vols., trans. Philip Watson. London, 1939.

OBERMAN, Heiko A. "The Shape of Late Medieval Thought: The Birthpangs of the Modern Era." *The Pursuit of Holiness in Late Medieval and Renaissance Religion.* Ed. Charles Trinkaus with Heiko A. Oberman, 3–25. Leiden, 1974.

O'MALLEY, John, S.J. "Content and Rhetorical Forms in Sixteenth-Century Treatises on Preaching." *Renaissance Eloquence: Studies in the Theory and Practice of Renaissance Rhetoric.* Ed. James J. Murphy, 238–52. Berkeley, 1983.

—— "Erasmus and the History of Sacred Rhetoric: The *Ecclesiastes* of 1535." *Erasmus of Rotterdam Society Yearbook* 5 (1985): 1–29.

—— *Praise and Blame in Renaissance Rome: Rhetoric, Doctrine, and Reform in the Sacred Orators of the Papal Court, c. 1450–1521.* Duke Monographs in Medieval and Renaissance Studies 3. Durham, 1979.

ONG, Walter J., S.J. *Orality and Literacy: The Technologizing of the Word.* London, 1982.

—— *Ramus, Method, and the Decay of Dialogue: From the Art of Discourse to the Art of Reason.* Cambridge, Mass., 1958.

—— "Tudor Writings on Rhetoric." *Studies in the Renaissance* 15 (1968): 39–69.

ONIANS, John. *Art and Thought in the Hellenistic Age: The Greek World View, 350–50 B.C.* London, 1979.

OZMENT, Steven. *The Age of Reform, 1250–1550: An Intellectual and Religious History of Late Medieval and Reformation Europe.* New Haven, 1980.

PARKANDER, Dorothy. "Rhetorical Theory and Practice: The Sermons of the English Puritans from 1570–1644." Ph.D. diss., University of Chicago, 1962.

PATTERSON, Annabel. *Hermogenes and the Renaissance: Seven Ideas of Style.* Princeton, 1970.

PIGMAN, G. W., III. "Imitation and the Renaissance Sense of the Past: The Reception of Erasmus' *Ciceronianus.*" *Journal of Medieval and Renaissance Studies* 9 (1979): 155–77.

PLETT, Heinrich Franz. *Der affecktrhetorische Wirkungsbegriff in der rhetorisch-poetischen Theorie der Englischen Renaissance.* Bonn, 1970.

QUADLBAUER, Franz. *Die antike Theorie der genera dicendi im Lateinischen Mittelalter.* Vienna, 1962.

—— "Die genera dicendi bis Plinius d.J." *Wiener Studien* 71 (1958): 55–111.

REBHOLZ, Ronald A. *The Life of Fulke Greville, First Lord Brooke.* Oxford, 1971.

RICE, Eugene F. *The Renaissance Idea of Wisdom.* Cambridge, Mass., 1958.

ROMILLY, Jacqueline de. *Magic and Rhetoric in Ancient Greece.* Cambridge, Mass., 1975.

ROSSKY, William. "Imagination in the English Renaissance: Psychology and Poetic." *Studies in the Renaissance* 5 (1958): 49–73.

SANDFORD, William. "English Rhetoric Reverts to Classicism, 1600–1650." *Quarterly Journal of Speech* 15 (1929): 503–24.

SCAGLIONE, Aldo. *The Classical Theory of Composition from its Origins to the Present: A Historical Survey.* Chapel Hill, 1972.

SCHMITT, Charles B. *Aristotle and the Renaissance.* Cambridge, Mass., 1983.

SCHNELL, Uwe. *Die homiletische Theorie Philipp Melanchthons.* Arbeiten zur Geschichte und Theologie des Luthertums 20. Berlin, 1968.

SCHULTZ, Howard. *Milton and Forbidden Knowledge.* New York, 1955.

SCOTT, Izora. *Controversies Over the Imitation of Cicero as a Model for Style and Some Phases of their Influence on the Schools of the Renaissance.* Columbia University Contributions to Education 35. New York, 1910.

SEIGEL, Jerrold E. *Rhetoric and Philosophy in Renaissance Humanism: The Union of Eloquence and Wisdom, Petrarch to Valla.* Princeton, 1968.

SHANKMAN, Steven. *Pope's "Illiad": Homer in the Age of Passion.* Princeton, 1983.

SHAPIRO, Barbara J. *John Wilkins, 1614–1672: An Intellectual Biography.* Berkeley, 1969.

—— *Probability and Certainty in Seventeenth-Century England: A Study of the Relationships between Natural Science, Religion, History, Law, and Literature.* Princeton, 1983.

SHUGER, Debora K. "The Christian Grand Style in Renaissance Rhetoric." *Viator* 16 (1985): 337–65.

—— "The Grand Style and the *genera dicendi* in Ancient Rhetoric." *Traditio* 40 (1984): 1–42.

—— "Morris Croll, Flacius Illyricus, and the Origin of Anti-Ciceronianism." *Rhetorica* 3 (1985): 269–84.

SOLMSEN, Friedrich. "The Aristotelian Tradition in Ancient Rhetoric." *AJP* 62 (1941): 35–50, 169–90.

—— "Greek Ideas about Leisure." *Wingspread Lectures in the Humanities* 1 (1966): 25–38.

STEADMAN, John M. *The Hill and the Labyrinth: Discourse and Certitude in Milton and His Near Contemporaries.* Berkeley, 1984.

STREIER, Richard. *Love Known: Theology and Experience in George Herbert's Poetry.* Chicago, 1983.

STREUVER, Nancy. *The Language of History in the Renaissance: Rhetoric and Historical Consciousness in Florentine Humanism.* Princeton, 1970.

TILLICH, Paul. *A History of Christian Thought from Its Judaic and Hellenistic Origins to Existentialism.* Ed. Carl E. Braaten. New York, 1967.

TRIMPI, Wesley. *Ben Johnson's Poems: A Study of the Plain Style.* Stanford, 1962.

—— "Horace's 'Ut Pictura Poesis': The Argument for Stylistic Decorum." *Traditio* 34 (1978): 29–73.

—— *Muses of One Mind: The Literary Analysis of Experience and its Continuity.* Princeton, 1983.

TRINKAUS, Charles. *In Our Image and Likeness: Humanity and Divinity in Italian Humanist Thought.* 2 vols. Chicago, 1970.

—— *The Poet as Philosopher: Petrarch and the Formation of Renaissance Consciousness.* New Haven, 1979.

—— "The Religious Thought of the Italian Humanists, and the Reformers: Anticipation or Autonomy?" *The Pursuit of Holiness in Late Medieval and Renaissance Religion*. Ed. Charles Trinkaus with Heiko A. Oberman, 339–66. Leiden, 1974.

—— *The Scope of Renaissance Humanism*. Ann Arbor, 1983.

TROELTSCH, Ernst. "Renaissance and Reformation." *The Reformation: Basic Interpretations*. 2d ed. Ed. and trans. Lewis W. Spitz, 25–43. Lexington, Mass., 1972.

TUVE, Rosemund. *Elizabethan and Metaphysical Imagery: Renaissance Poetic and Twentieth-Century Critics*. Chicago, 1947.

VAN HOOK, LaRue. "Alcidamas Versus Isocrates; The Spoken Word Versus the Written Word." *Classical Weekly* 12 (1919): 89–94.

VICKERS, Brian. *Classical Rhetoric in English Poetry*. London, 1970.

—— "Figures of Rhetoric/Figures of Music?" *Rhetorica* 2 (1984): 1–44.

—— "Rhetorical and Anti-Rhetorical Tropes: On Writing the History of *elocutio*." *Comparative Criticism: A Yearbook* 3 (1981): 105–32.

—— "Territorial Disputes: Philosophy Versus Rhetoric." *Rhetoric Revalued: Papers from the International Society for the History of Rhetoric*. Ed. Brian Vickers. Medieval and Renaissance Texts and Studies. Binghamton, N.Y., 1982.

VOEGELIN, Eric. *Anamnesis*. Trans. Gerhart Niemeyer. Notre Dame, Ind., 1978.

WALLACE, Dewey D., Jr. *Puritans and Predestination: Grace in English Protestant Theology, 1525–1695*. Chapel Hill, 1982.

WALLACE, Karl R. *Francis Bacon on Communication and Rhetoric*. Chapel Hill, 1943.

WARD, John O. "Renaissance Commentators on Ciceronian Rhetoric." *Renaissance Eloquence: Studies in the Theory and Practice of Renaissance Rhetoric*. Ed. James J. Murphy, 126–73. Berkeley, 1983.

WATSON, Foster. *The English Grammar Schools to 1660: Their Curriculum and Practice*. Cambridge, 1908.

WELLEK, Rene. "The Concept of Baroque in Literary Scholarship." *The Journal of Aesthetics and Art Criticism* 5 (1948): 77–97.

WHITE, Eugene E. "Master Holdsworth and 'A Knowledge Very Useful and Necessary.' " *Quarterly Journal of Speech* 53 (1967): 1–16.

WILLIAMSON, George. *The Senecan Amble: Prose Form from Bacon to Collier*. Chicago, 1951.

YATES, Frances A. *The Art of Memory*. Chicago, 1966.

INDEX

Abbot, George, 113

Abelard, 35

*Ad C. Herennium: de ratione dicendi
(Rhetorica ad Herennium)*, 24n, 26–
28, 37n, 224n

Adolph, Robert, 100

Aeschylus, 18–20

agon, agonistic, 11, 15, 17, 21–22, 28,
37, 50, 85, 88, 126, 129, 152, 169–
71, 180–82, 189, 229, 241–42, 245

Agricola, Rudolph, 61–62, 66, 84, 90,
99, 112–15, 127, 149, 175–77, 179,
181, 210n, 244–45

Alain de Lille, 49n, 52n

Alcidamas, 16

Alsted, Johann-Heinrich, 80–81, 89,
97, 105–106, 113, 115–17, 228; *Encyclopedia*, 86–87, 127n, 144; *Orator*,
86, 120, 130n, 137–38, 141n, 144,
149n, 157, 218; *Theologia*, 90, 123n,
178, 199, 237

amplification, 32, 48, 54, 62, 66, 76–
78, 91, 186–88, 193, 199, 201, 223–
27

analogy, 105, 168, 204, 212–16, 220–
23, 248–49

ancient dilemma, 194–201, 205, 210–
11, 214, 217, 222–27, 246–48, 253,
256

Andrewes, Lancelot, 252

Anglican, 3, 13, 98–100, 104, 165,
249–50

anti-Ciceronianism, 72, 75, 161–73,
252

Apsinus, 80

Aquinas, Thomas, 35, 66, 72, 79, 87,
122n, 132–35, 142n, 196–97, 205,
208, 211–12, 217, 223, 232, 250

Aquinas-tract, 52n

Arderne, James, 103, 123n, 127n

Aristophanes, 18–20, 26

Aristotle, 4, 15, 20, 28, 35, 43, 66, 72,
77n, 80, 87, 91, 99, 132–37, 139,
142–43, 148, 162, 168, 184–85, 197,
200, 203–209, 213, 223, 234, 247–
48; *De anima*, 196n; *Metaphysics*,
141n, 175, 195; *Nicomachean Ethics*,
141n, 206; *On Memory*, 202–205;
Parts of Animals, 176, 196; *Poetics*,
17–18, 25–27; *Posterior Analytics*,
177, 195; *Rhetoric*, 15–18, 21, 23n,
24, 26–27, 38, 45, 86, 120, 175–77,
241, 245–46

Arriaga, Pablo Jose de, 77, 78n, 79n,
149n, 210n, 238n

ars memorandi, 204, 213, 223

Athenasius, 88, 189

Atticism, 3–4, 8, 31–32, 139, 144–46,
152, 165, 169–73

Auerbach, Erich, 5, 74, 226

Augustine, 3, 5, 8–10, 13, 22n, 30–33,
37, 41–51, 54, 62, 71, 108–109, 115,
122n, 150–51, 155n, 159, 163, 167,
169, 174, 180, 182, 185, 211, 213,
226, 231–34, 241, 243–44; psychology of, 8, 46–48, 57, 63, 66–67, 72,
84, 90, 100, 107, 119, 132–39, 149,
152, 242–48, 252, 254–56

B

Bacon, Francis, 74, 81, 146, 194–96,
203, 206, 209, 247, 252

Bacon, Roger, 52n

Baldwin, T. W., 112

Bancroft, Richard, 113

Barbaro, Ermolao, 140

baroque, 41, 165, 173

Barrow, Isaac, 252

Barton, John, 96, 155

Baxter, Richard, 3, 89, 94, 228–30,
236n

Library of Congress Cataloging-in-Publication Data

SHUGER, DEBORA K., 1953–
SACRED RHETORIC.
BIBLIOGRAPHY: P.
INCLUDES INDEX.
I. ENGLISH LANGUAGE—EARLY MODERN,
1500–1700—STYLE. 2. RHETORIC—1500–1800. 3. CHRISTIAN
LITERATURE, ENGLISH—HISTORY AND CRITICISM.
4. RENAISSANCE—ENGLAND. I. TITLE.
PE877.S58 1988 810'.9'003 87–25755
ISBN 0–691–06736–8 (ALK. PAPER)